The Struggle for Syria

A Study of Post-War Arab Politics
1945 – 1958

PATRICK SEALE

Issued under the auspices of the
Royal Institute of International Affairs
OXFORD UNIVERSITY PRESS
LONDON   NEW YORK   TORONTO
1965

Oxford University Press, Amen House, London E.C.4

GLASGOW NEW YORK TORONTO MELBOURNE WELLINGTON
BOMBAY CALCUTTA MADRAS KARACHI LAHORE DACCA
CAPE TOWN SALISBURY NAIROBI IBADAN ACCRA
KUALA LUMPUR HONG KONG

*Printed in Great Britain
by Hazell Watson & Viney Ltd.,
Aylesbury, Bucks*

1. General Sir Edward Spears in Damascus, 1945

2. The Old *Serail*, Damascus

For my
mother and father

Preface

THIS book deals with a recent and highly controversial period of Arab history: the dozen years or so after the Second World War when Arabs first achieved something approaching real independence and were able to exercise an independent foreign policy. The roots of much that is happening in the Middle East today were then put down.

To Arab readers I would like most earnestly to say that I have tried to be fair and objective although I may not always have succeeded. This is not a book for or against any particular Arab leader, party, state, or doctrine. I wanted to explain and illumine the background to some contemporary problems, not to add fuel to present-day feuds. I would be glad if Syrians, in particular, would accept the work, with all its flaws, as a tribute to a country to which I am greatly attached.

I am deeply grateful to the Warden and Fellows of St Antony's College, Oxford, for granting me a scholarship to write this book. My main debt is to Mr Albert Hourani, director of the Middle East Centre at St Antony's, for his teaching, guidance, and affectionate encouragement at every stage. To Miss Elizabeth Monroe I owe the enormous stimulus of a friendship nearly ten years old. Mr Hourani, Miss Monroe, and Professor Bernard Lewis read and criticized the typescript, detecting many errors. I am also very grateful to Mr Peter Calvocoressi and to friends at the American University of Beirut, Hanna Batatu, Joseph Malone, Yusuf Ibish, David Gordon, and Khaldun al-Husri, for many valuable suggestions. I owe a special debt to the staff of the Chatham House Press Library, to Miss Jill Sangster for typing the manuscript, to Miss Hermia Oliver of the editorial department of Chatham House for her elegant scalpel work in preparing the book for the press and to Mr C. H. Inge for compiling the index.

July 1964   P.S.

Contents

Plates

The portrait of M. Michel 'Aflaq is by courtesy of *al-Nahar*, Beirut. All the other photographs are by Mr Georges Derzi of Damascus whose window display of portraits has long provided a guide to the changing political climate of the city.

Abbreviations

Arab Lib. Movt:	Arab Liberation Movement.
BBC:	BBC, Summary of World Broadcasts, 2nd series, Pt IV: The Middle East.
Cahiers:	*Cahiers de l'Orient contemporain.*
Con. bloc:	Constitutional bloc.
Dem. bloc:	Democratic bloc.
Is. Soc. Front:	Islamic Socialist Front.
MEJ:	*Middle East Journal.*
NP:	National Party.
PP:	People's Party.
RIIA, *Survey*:	Royal Institute of International Affairs, *Survey of International Affairs* (annual).
Rep. Front:	Republican Front.

He [Husayn] and his sons agreed that Ali, the eldest, should succeed their father as King of the Hejaz; that Abdullah, the second, should be King of Iraq and that Faisal, the third, should become King of Syria . . . At the end of the fighting in 1918 Faisal found himself in Damascus and proclaimed himself King of Syria a few months later, thereby carrying out his part of the family programme. The father became King of the Hejaz with the Amir Ali as his Heir Apparent, and because the future of Iraq was still uncertain, the Amir Abdullah became his father's Minister for Foreign Affairs in the hope that his kingdom would come into being in the mean-while. The plan, however, soon broke down, because Faisal could not come to terms with the French, who had ambitions in Syria, and he was ejected from his new kingdom by a French army in July 1920. Instead of going home to the Hejaz a defeated man, Faisal shrewdly went to the Peace Conference at Paris, from which he emerged after various manoeuvres as the candidate for the throne of Iraq who had the backing of His Majesty's Government. He succeeded in winning the support of the Iraqis and was crowned King at Baghdad in October, 1921.

When Faisal became the chosen candidate for the throne of Iraq the Amir Abdullah was, not unnaturally, furious, but there was not much that he could do about it as he was out of the picture internationally and failed to establish any degree of contact with the Iraqi politicians who alone could have given him the means of achieving his ambition.

While all this was going on, a mandate over Palestine, a geographical term which included Transjordan also, was granted to Great Britain in July, 1920.

'Abdallah, seeing that he could not become King of Iraq, recruited a private army and announced his intention of marching on Syria to expel the French. On his way north in January 1921 he entered British mandated territory east of the Jordan where he set up a central administration in Amman, taking over the whole country in March 1921.

It was not until the following July that His Majesty's Government decided to follow its usual policy of accepting a *fait accompli* and announced that they were prepared to recognize the Amir Abdullah's rule over that part of the mandated territory which lay east of the river Jordan, provided (*a*) he recognised the validity of the mandate in question and (*b*) renounced his avowed intention of attempting to conquer Syria. Being well content with the way matters had fallen out, the Amir accepted both conditions without argument . . . In due course, the remarkable discovery was made that the clauses of the mandate relating to the establishment of a National Home for the Jews had never been intended to apply to the mandated territory east of the river.

In later years, when Jordan proved the staunchness of its friendship during the bad years of the Second World War, politicians in Great Britain took credit for the way in which they dealt with the country's future during its earliest days.[2]

The point to note is that the Hashimite failure to carry out their family plan resulted in two powerful currents of thwarted ambition. First, Faysal could not readily forget his old capital, Damascus, from which he had been ejected with little ceremony by the French. The determination to return and liberate Syria consumed his heirs and became a main plank in the pan-Arab programme. The Iraqi historian Majid Khadduri has suggested that on moving from Damascus to Baghdad, Faysal carried with him the centre of pan-Arabism so that Iraq became from 1921 to 1941 the most promising country to lead the Arabs in attaining their national aspirations.[3] In any event, Hashimite claims to Syria based on Faysal's twenty-month rule in Damascus from 1918 to 1920 provided a good part of the justification for the plan of Fertile Crescent unity advanced by the Iraqi statesman Nuri al-Sa'id during the Second World War.

The second current of dissatisfaction was inspired by 'Abdallah, Husayn's second son. He could not easily forgive his younger brother Faysal for accepting the throne of Iraq for which he had himself been destined. He too sought consolation in Syria: Faysal's lost Syrian kingdom should, he claimed, be his, particularly as Faysal's heirs had succeeded to the throne of Iraq. This was the origin of 'Abdallah's long campaign for a 'Greater Syria': the reunification under his crown of the four territories of Syria, Lebanon, Transjordan, and Palestine.

THE 1941 TURNING-POINT

There is a sense in which both Nuri al-Sa'id's Fertile Crescent project and 'Abdallah's Greater Syria were doomed before they were fully formulated, towards the close of the Second World War. They were stillborn because the Hashimite family had by then lost its influence on the Arab nationalist movement. If a date can be set for the divorce between Hashimites and nationalists, it was probably 1941, following the restoration by British arms of Hashimite rule in Iraq on the ruins of Rashid 'Ali al-Gaylani's brief revolt.

[2] Ibid. pp. 27–28.
[3] Majid Khadduri, 'The Scheme of Fertile Crescent Unity: A study in Inter-Arab Relations', in R. N. Frye, ed., *The Near East and the Great Powers* (1951), p. 137.

Pan-Arab aspirations at this time were to liberate Syria from the French, to liquidate the Jewish National Home in Palestine, and to unite the Fertile Crescent under an independent Arab regime. But on all three counts they ran up against the higher interests of Britain and France. Western hegemony over the Levant came, therefore, to be the primary target for pan-Arab attack. It followed that nationalist Arab leaders would seek to use the war as a lever to promote their cause and that their more active members—such as the Mufti of Jerusalem, 'Ali Maher in Egypt, and Rashid 'Ali al-Gaylani in Iraq—should court Axis support. Britain, engaged in a struggle for survival, called these movements wavering and disloyal; but if the more extreme pan-Arabs failed to appreciate the wider issues at stake in the war, it was primarily because they had their gaze fixed on more immediate local objectives.

Rashid 'Ali, the author of the *putsch* in Iraq on 1 April 1941, was first and foremost an Arab nationalist. He had no sinister Nazi predilections and was not playing a part in a German master plan for seizing the Eastern Mediterranean. He was driven to revolt by his failure to extract concessions from the British for the Palestine Arabs.[4] His movement interests us here primarily because the manner in which it was put down fatally damaged future working relations between Hashimites and Arab nationalists in both Iraq and Syria. I have suggested that the career of Faysal I could not easily be distinguished from the course of the Arab nationalist movement: for most of his life he embodied Arab aspirations. His son Ghazi, who succeeded him on his death in 1933, shared something of his aura and attracted by his ardour and extravagance a youthful following; but he was never a convincing candidate for Arab leadership. When he, in turn, was killed in a car accident in 1939 his own son Faysal was an infant, so that his cousin, Prince 'Abd ul-Ilah, son of the Amir 'Ali, was appointed Regent, remaining the effective ruler of Iraq until his death at the hands of the army in July 1958. (He lost the title of Regent but not the reality of power on the accession of Faysal II on 1 May 1953.) From 1939 to 1958 'Abd ul-Ilah was the Hashimite with whom the nationalists had to deal. To the last, his gaze remained fixed on his grandfather's kingdom of Hijaz, lost to Ibn Sa'ud, and on his uncle Faysal's lost kingdom of Syria, an interest which was heightened by the termination of his own regency in 1953. His ambition was to revive the throne of Damascus for himself.

[4] See G. E. Kirk, *The Middle East in the War* (1953), pp. 77 and 78 n.1.

Almost from the start he found himself in opposition to more extreme nationalist opinion. When Italy entered the war, the Iraq Government refused to break off relations with her in spite of representations from the British Embassy. Rashid 'Ali al-Gaylani, who had replaced Nuri al-Sa'id as Prime Minister on 31 March 1940, did, however, make a semi-official offer to the British to declare war on Italy if Britain agreed, in return, to accelerate the fulfilment of the Palestine White Paper of 1939 by immediately setting that country on the way to independence.[5] But when the British Government refused, the result was to damage the standing of all moderates who chose to co-operate with Britain and defer pressing pan-Arab claims. To extreme nationalists, the loyalties of the Regent and Nuri were thus seen to be given to Britain rather than the Arab cause.

Rashid 'Ali's coup on 1 April and the opening of Iraqi hostilities against British forces a month later aroused great excitement in nationalist circles where the outbreak was thought to be the beginning of the great conflagration which would liberate Syria from the French and Palestine from the British. In Damascus Shukri al-Quwatli, hero of the younger nationalists, headed a Syrian committee to raise funds for Rashid 'Ali, while a young political agitator called Akram al-Hawrani from Hama in central Syria gathered a few junior officers around him and dashed to his aid.[6] Thus were laid the early foundations for Hawrani's many friendships in the Syrian army which were later to be of much consequence. In Damascus itself, the nascent Ba'th Party found in the stirring events in Iraq an occasion to demonstrate its devotion to the wider Arab cause. It formed student committees in support of Rashid 'Ali and launched a 'Victory in Iraq' movement. 'It was an opportunity to bring home to our young followers the significance of our Party's basic doctrine of Arab unity', the party founder Michel 'Aflaq later explained.[7] It was not to be expected that these men, who were to gain great influence in post-war Syria, would ever come to terms with the Regent, Nuri al-Sa'id, and their British friends. Their basic attitudes of hostility were to remain unshaken. Iraqi nationalists themselves who had dreamed most ardently of Fertile Crescent union came to prefer to see Syria in-

---

[5] Ibid. pp. 63–64 for a detailed account of these events.
[6] When Rashid 'Ali's revolt collapsed, the handful of Syrian supporters crossed back into Syria and were locked up briefly in a French barracks at Deir ez-Zor. Among the internees were Hawrani, 'Afif al-Bizri, later to become Syrian Chief of Staff, and Jamal al-Atasi, a founder member of the Ba'th party. (Dr Jamal al-Atasi to the author.)
[7] Michel 'Aflaq to the author, Beirut, 3 Jan. 1961.

dependent rather than linked with an Iraq ruled by Nuri and bound by treaty to Great Britain.

On the night of Rashid 'Ali's *putsch*, the Regent escaped in disguise from his palace and next day flew to Basra where he tried in vain to organize a resistance movement. He then left for Palestine and the security of his uncle 'Abdallah's fief in Transjordan, whence he returned in triumph to Iraq three weeks later behind British and Arab Legion guns. Rashid 'Ali was overthrown, but the Hashimites lost the confidence of nationalist opinion—a breach which could not easily be healed once a number of senior officers implicated in the revolt had been hanged.

FERTILE CRESCENT AND GREATER SYRIA

Nuri al-Sa'id's Fertile Crescent plan and Amir 'Abdallah's Greater Syria were given their first formal expression during the Second World War. Of the two, Nuri's plan was the more ambitious. It was his achievement to give substance, in the form of an official document, to the nebulous aspirations for a union of Arab states in the Fertile Crescent which had been in the air for years. The fall of France early in the war encouraged him to think that Britain must now support the Arabs in realizing their national goals. He put this view to the British Minister of State for the Middle East, Richard Casey, whom he met in Cairo early in 1942; Casey asked for the proposals in writing. The result was the famous 'Note on the Arab cause with particular reference to Palestine, and suggestions for a permanent settlement' which was presented to the Minister and confidentially circulated in interested quarters.[8]

Nuri al-Sa'id proposed a two-stage plan: first, the union in one state of Syria, Lebanon, Palestine, and Transjordan, whose form of government, 'whether monarchical or republican, whether unitary or federal', should be decided by the people themselves, with semi-autonomy under international guarantee for the Jewish minority in Palestine and safeguards for Christians in Lebanon. Secondly, once this 'Greater Syria' had been formed, it should immediately join Iraq in an Arab League to which other Arab states could later adhere at will. At the head of the League would be a permanent Council, nominated by the member states, and presided over by one of their rulers 'chosen in a manner acceptable to the states concerned'. The

---

[8] Nuri al-Sa'id, *Istiqlal al-'Arab wa wahdatahum* (Baghdad, Govt Press, 1943). See also J. C. Hurewitz, *Diplomacy in the Near and Middle East* (1956), ii. 236–7.

Council would be responsible for defence, foreign affairs, currency, communications, customs, and the protection of minorities. Nuri's vision, then, was of an expanded Syria bound to Iraq in a Fertile Crescent association which other Arab states might eventually join.

It is doubtful whether 'Abdallah ever looked beyond the first stage of this programme. His view of Arab unity was the reunification under his leadership of the four territories of 'Greater Syria'. The problem of the Palestine Jews should be solved by granting them administrative autonomy; if the unity of all four regions could not be immediately realized, a start should be made by uniting Syria and Transjordan, with provisions for the later adherence of Palestine and Lebanon to form a union on the model of the United States of America or the Swiss Confederation. As may be seen, the heart of 'Abdallah's proposals—and their only practical feature—was the immediate merger of Transjordan and Syria. This was the plan which he put forward, with minor variants, in speeches, official memoranda, and private communications to Syrian politicians and in instructions to his representatives at the grand confrontation on Arab unity to which Egypt's Prime Minister, Mustafa al-Nahhas, invited the Arab states in 1943 and which resulted in the Arab League Charter of 1945.[9]

'Abdallah got little encouragement from the British Government to which he first advanced his proposals. Raised after the fall of France, the question was broached again when Mr Oliver Lyttelton, Minister of State in the Middle East, visited Amman in 1941 and on a number of subsequent occasions. 'Abdallah's first concern in the war years was to ensure that the British Government would not invoke its treaty rights in Transjordan to prevent him from discussing the matter with the Syrian and other Arab Governments. The British Government's attitude throughout appears to have been that the attempted execution of the 'Greater Syria' plans must await the return of stable conditions after the war; nothing but confusion would result from raising such a controversial constitutional issue at a time of general uncertainty; nothing should be done which might further bedevil relations with the French in Syria, where material

[9] See Transjordan, *al-Kitab al-urduni al-abyad: al-watha'iq al-qawmiyya fi'l-wahdat al-Suriya al-tabi'iya* (The Jordan White Book: National Documents on the Unification of Natural Syria) (Amman, 1947). See also Abdullah ibn al-Hussein, *The Memoirs of King Abdullah of Transjordan*, ed. P. P. Graves (1950), pp. 254–7, 261–9.

weakness caused them to be all the more vigilant in defence of their 'historic rights'. 'Abdallah did, however, secure British agreement for the view that there could be no harm in the project being studied, pending a suitable occasion for it to be put into execution.

On 28 March 1946 'Abdallah secured his full independence from Great Britain and felt free to promote more actively his long-cherished expansionist ambitions: on the opening of parliament on 11 November 'Greater Syria' was formally proclaimed a principle of Transjordan's foreign policy. He let pass no occasion to press his case: 'There is neither great nor little Syria', he told the Egyptian newspaper *al-Ahram*,[10] 'there is only a single country bounded to the west by the sea, to the north by Turkey, to the east by Iraq and to the south by the Hejaz—which constitutes Syria.'

My father [he declared in March 1947 to the Lebanese newspaper *Kul Shai*] fought neither for the independence of Lebanon, nor for that of Syria, nor for that of Transjordan; he fought and died for the Arab countries as a whole. . . . My policy is clear: I want a state which includes Syria, Transjordan, Palestine, and Lebanon; yes, Lebanon. . . .

It was natural that he should simultaneously attack Egypt and the Arab League which obstructed his hopes, as will be seen in the next chapter: 'Everyone knows', he cried, 'that the Arab League was no more than a game organized by Nahhas Pasha for his own ends. . . .'[11]

In August 1947 he sought to bring matters to a head by calling a meeting in Amman of 'regional Syrian governments' to discuss his union plans. It need only be said that these declarations and *démarches* met with unrelieved hostility from Cairo, Riyad, Beirut, and Damascus. Each capital reaffirmed its attachment to the League Charter with its built-in guarantee of the independence of member states, and expressed surprise at 'Abdallah's persistence. President Quwatli of Syria publicly denounced Greater Syria on his re-election in 1947, while the Syrian chamber newly emerged from the July 1947 elections met in special session to 'protest unanimously against the project which conceals personal ambitions, Zionist designs, as well as ties which threaten Syria's independence, sovereignty and her republican regime. . . .' 'Abdallah never won the initiative in Syria. His rare supporters were to be found among some veteran politicians who had known Faysal I and had remained faithful to the family, as

---

[10] *al-Ahram* (Cairo), 31 Aug. 1946.   [11] *L'Orient* (Beirut), 28 Mar. 1947.

well as in the traditionally pro-Hashimite Jabal Druze in southern Syria on the Transjordan frontier.[12]

'Abdallah was no more successful in his relations with his Hashimite neighbour, Iraq. Throughout 1945 and 1946 he discussed at length the possibility of a union between Iraq and Transjordan with his nephew 'Abd ul-Ilah, Regent of Iraq. He made a number of proposals, notably that he should accede for life to the joint thrones of Iraq and Transjordan, the succession passing at his death to the young King Faysal and not to his own heirs. Another plan was that 'Abd ul-Ilah should become king of Transjordan and Palestine and 'Abdallah king of Iraq for life, the succession once again passing to Faysal. Both plans were stillborn. They met with the usual outcry from Syria and Lebanon, who saw in them a first step towards a Greater Syria; from Saudi Arabia and Egypt, opposed as ever to any extension of Hashimite power; from Arab nationalists everywhere, suspicious of 'Abdallah's ties with Britain, and from Iraqi politicians who did not relish the prospect of 'Abdallah interfering in their domestic affairs. Britain also did not encourage a union of Transjordan and Iraq, wishing perhaps to keep her stronghold in Transjordan free from tubulent Iraqi influence. At all events, splitting the Hashimites contributed to their ineffectiveness in Syria; the Syrians inquired with some pertinence why Amman and Baghdad did not first unite before coming to bother them.

'Abdallah had to be content with a watery treaty of alliance and brotherhood signed with Iraq on 15 April 1947 which came into effect on 10 June. He had, in fact, aroused such fierce opposition that he seemed more of a liability than an asset to the Hashimite cause. His close relations with Great Britain and his alleged complaisance towards the Zionists made him suspect to nationalist opinion. Moreover, his cause was not served by the general belief that he was driven by personal ambition alone to seek the Syrian throne.

The keen interest of Iraq and Transjordan in Syria never developed into a political union of the Fertile Crescent. Some of the early causes of this failure have been briefly outlined, among them the divorce between Hashimites and nationalists as well as the emergence in 1945 of a rival pattern of inter-Arab relations in the Egyptian-dominated Arab League. There were, in addition, other obstacles

---

[12] The Druze notable Hasan al-Atrash told the author (Beirut, 21 Oct. 1960) that in 1947 he had invited King 'Abdallah to enter the Jabal and take over. Glubb Pasha had referred the matter to London but received a discouraging reply.

of great importance such as the persistence of French influence in Syria in which Britain acquiesced, and the opposition of Saudi Arabia. Moreover the twenty-five-year struggle against French rule had bred in Syrian nationalists an attachment to republican institutions and to their capital city of Damascus which distinguished Syria from the neighbouring kingdoms centred on Baghdad and Amman. The impact of all these developments on Hashimite hopes in Syria did not become clear for a number of years. 'Abdallah's concern with Syria continued unabated until his murder in 1951, while Iraqi interventions remained, as will be seen, a permanent feature of Syrian politics up to the union with Egypt in 1958.

3
Egypt and Arab Unity

EGYPT was a late convert to the cause of Arab unity; it was not until the last years of the 1930s and early 1940s that pan-Arab ideas came to have an important influence on her political thinking and orientation. In the first decades of this century she marched out of step with the Arab national movement in Asia which, emerging after 1908 in reaction against Turkish nationalism, grew with British support in 1916 into a rebel movement against Turkish rule.

These developments left Egypt unaffected. This was partly because she had already long since wrested all but formal independence from the Ottoman Empire, but also because the strict natural boundaries of the Nile Valley and a long history of centralized government had caused her to develop a distinct, self-contained national identity. After 1882 she was, moreover, wholly engrossed with the British occupation. But in spite of the British presence, the Ottoman Sultan remained the titular suzerain of Egypt until the outbreak of the First World War. Thus while Arab nationalists in the Hijaz, Syria, and Iraq plotted in the early years of the century to destroy the Ottoman Empire and liberate themselves from it, Egyptian nationalists tended in contrast to see in its preservation and in their own tenuous link with Constantinople the main safeguards against Britain's formal annexation of their country. But the declaration of the Protectorate in 1914 put an end to such thinking. From then until the middle 1930s the British occupation remained the sole major preoccupation of Egyptian politics, further contributing to her isolation from currents of opinion in the Arab world.

Islam was one of the vehicles which carried Egypt into closer relations with her sister Arab states when, after the conclusion of the 1936 treaty with Britain, she felt free to pursue a more independent foreign policy. Rapprochement with the Arabs was then only one of a number of alternative courses open to her.

There were those who looked upon Egypt as nothing less than a mature European nation whose future lay westwards rather than eastwards. There were those who would have had her look to the south, not only to the Sudan but to a grand federation of Nile states including Abyssinia, Eritrea and Uganda—a school of thought much stimulated by the Italian defeat in 1941. Some wanted Egypt to become the link between East and West, others advocated her leadership of the Orient against colonisers and materialists. Most important were the Panislamists, ranging from fully-fledged supporters of an Egyptian Caliphate to more cautious believers in Moslem solidarity.[1]

What could not be denied was that Egypt enjoyed a definite feeling of national identity, but that this was cast within an Islamic cultural framework which, in spite of the inroads made by western ideas, was still the dominant influence on her national life. Indeed, Islam had provided at the turn of the century, through a school of reformers inspired by Muhammad 'Abdu, the first systematic attempt to answer the question of how Muslim Egypt could modernize herself without destroying the moral basis of her society.[2]

People of all classes saw Egypt's role in the world as an Islamic role—this was what separated them from some and bound them to others. Islam was in their bones and was at the centre of their resistance to the West. Carried into foreign policy this sentiment implied solidarity with all other oppressed Muslims. When the French bombed Damascus in 1925 or Italy put down the Cyrenaican rebellion in 1930, Egyptian protests were made in defence of Islam— and not yet in the name of Arab nationalism.[3]

Palestine was the decisive factor which swung Egyptian politicians in favour of a pan-Arab policy. Zionist colonization, British policy, and the repeated Arab eruptions between 1936 and 1939 made a sharp impact on Egyptian opinion, contributing to the growth and power of Muslim political organizations and providing them with their main propaganda themes. But while it was Muslim rather than Arab fellow feeling which was outraged, such was the strength of the emotions aroused that Egyptian party leaders came to see that a policy of support for oppressed Arabs would pay dividends at home.

Of the three main groups which mobilized opinion—and in par-

[1] J. W. D. Gray, 'Abdin against the Wafd', *Middle East Forum*, Feb. 1962, p. 17. I am also indebted to Mr Gray for unpublished material on this period of Egyptian history.
[2] See A. H. Hourani in Preface to J. M. Ahmed, *Intellectual Origins of Egyptian Nationalism* (1960), p. ix.
[3] See Marcel Colombe, *L'Évolution de l'Égypte, 1924–1950* (1951), p. 169.

ticular student opinion—in favour of the Palestine cause, the Muslim Brethren were the most proletarian and vital. Their founder, Hasan al-Banna, preached a return to the puritanism of early Islam and demanded action to save Muslim Palestine from materialist Zionism. He revived Islam as a political force to be reckoned with and brought the youth of Egypt back to their religion. At the time of his assassination in 1949 he had built up his movement into perhaps the most powerful pressure group in the Arab Near East with a membership of over half a million.[4] The Association of Muslim Young Men (YMMA) was a more bourgeois and less missionary body but equally convinced that concerted Arab action was the means to save Islam from Zionism and the corruption of the West. The Young Egypt party, although Fascist in its social thinking, also campaigned for an alliance with the Arabs and thus served, with its two more influential rivals, to channel Egyptian sentiments of Muslim solidarity into the narrower area of Arab self-consciousness. Both the Young Egypt party and the Muslim Brothers were unashamed in their advocacy of revolutionary change at home.

Yet by the beginning of the Second World War these Islamic groups had done little more than give an eastward orientation to Egyptian policy. On the official side, there was as yet little which could be described as a coherent view of Egypt's place in the Arab world. Egyptian party leaders had made speeches about Palestine; they had brought the issue up at the League of Nations; teachers and engineers had been sent to the Arab countries and trade missions opened there; Egypt had agitated in favour of the Syrian nationalists, then entering the final phase of their struggle against French Mandatory rule. But the idea of some sort of political association with the Arabs did not mature until the early war years. Few Egyptians could distinguish between Muslim and Arab fellow feeling; indeed, the systematic confusion of the two is perhaps more characteristic of Egypt than of any other Arab country. Cairo was then, as it is now, the first intellectual city of the Arab world, a refuge for Arab exiles and a focus of interest for Arab opinion everywhere. But this interest was essentially one-sided: Egypt had not yet made any sort of conscious choice in favour of Arab unity. She had at most a family feeling for other Arabs but little interest in closer political ties with them. The rare Egyptians who understood the Arab cause in national

[4] For further details see J. Heyworth-Dunne, *Religious and Political Trends in Modern Egypt* (1950), and Ishak Musa Husaini, *The Moslem Brethren* (1956).

rather than religious terms were principally those who had travelled outside the Nile Valley or who had, in Egypt itself, come into contact with exiled or visiting Arab nationalist leaders.

The Arab outbreak in Palestine in 1936 may well have seen the genesis of 'Ali Maher's ideas—perhaps the first Egyptian premier to conceive of making Egypt the champion of the Arab world.[5] From the death of King Fu'ad in April 1936, he gradually became the 'strong man' of Egypt, alternating as Chief of the Royal Cabinet and Premier until he had to withdraw from the Government in June 1940. He and 'Abd al-Rahman al-'Azzam, later to become the first Secretary-General of the Arab League, were in the late 1930s attempting to work out an Egyptian policy on Palestine, and they both attended the London Palestine Conference of 1939 where it first became evident that Egyptian leadership of the Arabs was acceptable both to Britain and to the Arabs themselves.

But political leaders were not the real initiators of Egypt's Arab policy: they responded to pressures which had become too powerful to ignore. The origins of the trend may be traced to intellectuals and religious movements which popularized ideas that the politicians were later persuaded, or forced, to espouse. It was those who busied themselves with culture who first realized that part at least of the West's oppression lay in its domination of technical language and education and who stressed therefore the need to modernize and invigorate the Arabic language. Similarly, it was those concerned with religion who felt most acutely the predicament of their neighbours, largely of the same creed, who were faced with imperialist pressures of a subtler, Zionist, sort. If these were at the start minority movements, forces in Egypt made their cause a popular one: student unrest, graduate unemployment, poverty and disease were all deemed curable if Islam were given the reins of government and the infidel— the foreigner—dispossessed. Faced with the large-scale agitation that followed this fusion of intellectual zeal, religious fervour, and revolutionary potential, the politicians did what was obvious for survival—they adopted it. The idea of Arab unity was thus eventually taken up—via the agitation over Palestine and domestic social unrest—by the Wafd early in the war and by Faruq himself in 1943.

The war gave a decisive boost to this incipient pro-Arab orientation of Egyptian policy. In particular it helped to secularize Egyptian thinking on the question by directing opinion away from the nebulous

[5] Heyworth-Dunne, p. 23.

aspirations for pan-Islamic union towards the more practical course of closer ties with the Eastern Arab world. This change happened largely because the war muzzled the extremist Islamic groups which had played so prominent a role in the 1930s in mobilizing Egyptian opinion in defence of oppressed fellow Muslims. The Young Egypt party was suppressed because of its Fascist tendencies; the Muslim Brethren suspended their political activities; their founder, Hasan al-Banna, was jailed and emerged chastened; the Association of Muslim Young Men lost much of its effectiveness with the death of its President, 'Abd al-Hamid Sa'id. Advocacy of the Arab cause passed to more moderate men favouring a gradualist approach beginning with cultural co-operation with Egypt's sister Arab states. The same line was taken by party leaders who realized both that a pro-Arab policy would be popular at home and that Egypt's national interest lay in association with, and even leadership of, the movement towards regional unity which appeared to be gathering pace in Arab Asia. Anthony Eden's statements in 1941 and 1943 pledging British support for Arab unity were a public recognition of this trend by the reigning Great Power in the area, which Egypt could not ignore. No doubt the encouragement of independent regional groupings given by the Atlantic Charter and at Dumbarton Oaks contributed to this way of thinking.

Cairo was also the centre from which the Allied war effort in the Middle East was principally conducted. A wartime organization was set up—the Middle East Supply Centre—which some thought might serve later as a nucleus for inter-Arab co-operation. This was, in effect, a central directorate for economic affairs, managed first by Britain alone and later by Britain and the United States, responsible from 1941 onwards to the British Minister of State in Cairo. In association with local governments, it controlled shipping and supplies and had a decisive say in agricultural and industrial production throughout the area. Thus Cairo became the most accessible and internationally important Arab capital during the Second World War. It was only a short step from there to envisage it as the capital of a united post-war Arab world.

The ground was therefore well prepared for Egypt's entry as a leading member into the family of Arab states. But when pan-Arabism became Egypt's official policy in the early 1940s, it did so less out of deep-seated conviction than because of personal enmity between King Faruq and Mustafa al-Nahhas, the leader of the great national movement of the Wafd. Both the Palace and the Wafd accepted this new orientation which events seemed to be forcing upon Egypt, but immediately put it to work in their domestic struggle for power. The feud between them had early roots in Nahhas's shabby treatment of the young Faruq in 1936–7, in the fulsome praise showered by the press on the Wafd leader, and in the party's repeated claim to be the sole representative of the nation—a claim which carried an implicit threat to the authority of the Palace. The quarrel reached a climax in February 1942 when, in a celebrated incident, the British surrounded the Abdin Palace with tanks and forced Nahhas—a Prime Minister with whom they could co-operate —on a reluctant Faruq.

Wholehearted espousal of the pan-Arab cause and a bid for the title of 'Leader of the Arabs' seemed then to Nahhas a means of bolstering his position in the face of Faruq's hostility. He thus set in train the series of conversations on Arab unity which took place between July and November 1943 with the leaders of Iraq, Transjordan, Saudi Arabia, Syria, Lebanon, and Yemen, and which resulted in the Alexandria Protocol of October 1944 and eventually in the Arab League Charter of March 1945.[6] But on the morrow of the signature of the Protocol Nahhas was peremptorily dismissed by Faruq who proceeded by means of speeches, journeys abroad, and an inspired press campaign to replace him as the acknowledged champion of Egypt and Arab unity.

It was clear that both the Palace and the Wafd had embraced the cause of pan-Arabism and sought its leadership primarily to inflate their own reputations. 'We noted with surprise and concern the struggle between Faruq and Nahhas', a member of the Syrian delegation to the talks said later.[7]

We realized that their chief concern in promoting the League was not for the Arabs but for their own position inside Egypt. But we closed our eyes to what we had seen. We were happy that Egypt—for whatever motive—was beginning to consider itself a part of the Arab world.

But granted these personal rivalries, popular indignation in Egypt, as in other Arab states, at the fate of the Palestine Arabs remained the main pressure on the negotiators. One result of the Alexandria

[6] For the minutes of these negotiations see *al-Hayat* (Beirut), 31 Mar.–14 Apr. 1960; French trans. in *Orient*, no. 14, 1960, pp. 177–216.
[7] Dr Najib al-Armanazi—a distinguished Syrian public servant and former ambassador, who in 1943 was secretary-general at the Presidency of the Republic— to the author, Damascus, 9 July 1961.

Protocol was to make the problem of Palestine once and for all the responsibility of the whole Arab world, and thus incorporate into more formal and permanent form the precedent set by the London Conference on Palestine of 1939.[8] The independence of most of the Protocol's signatories was at this time still partial and precarious. Many of them had foreign troops stationed on their territory. In Syria and Lebanon, in particular, France was reluctant to give up her Mandatory rights without securing a new treaty guaranteeing her a 'special position' there. An important objective of the negotiators was in fact to preclude the possibility of any such treaty being concluded with France, and it was primarily with this in view that the Protocol envisaged a common Arab orientation towards the outside world. It was, in turn, this aspect which more than any other aroused French suspicions that the whole notion of the Arab League was a British 'trick' to get the French out of the Levant.

Britain had, it is true, guaranteed Syrian and Lebanese independence in 1941, and in 1945 had given decisive support to the Syrian nationalist leaders in their final tussle with the French. But in declaring her sympathy for Arab unity—as in Eden's famous Mansion House speech in May 1941—Britain did no more than swim with the tide and attempt to conciliate Arab opinion at a critical moment in the war. She did not create the movement for Arab unity but merely tried, as the strongest Power in the area, to direct it into channels not incompatible with her interests. She did not devise the Arab League, but the form it finally took owed something to her influence. It may be said, in particular, that it was largely due to British pressure that the leaders of Syria and Iraq were induced to grant Egypt the leadership of the organization.[9] This was the price for including her in it. As a result, both the Iraqi Premier, Nuri al-Saʻid, and the Syrian Premier, Saʻdallah al-Jabiri, played up to Nahhas's vanity and personal ambition and decided to take a chance on the strength of Egypt's Arab sentiment, about which there was at the time considerable doubt.[10]

[8] For further details on this and the following paragraphs see Cecil A. Hourani, 'The Arab League in Perspective', *MEJ*, i (Apr. 1947), pp. 125 ff.
[9] Nuri al-Saʻid admitted as much to Musa al-ʻAlami, the Palestine representative at the talks (Musa al-ʻAlami to the author, Beirut, 19 Sept. 1960).
[10] An Iraqi official related to the author how Nuri, awaiting a return visit from Nahhas at the Iraqi embassy in Cairo after one of the sessions, had carefully drilled a reception committee on how to welcome the Egyptian statesman. Nuri himself would be at the foot of the stairs, ready to greet Nahhas as he alighted from his car with the words: 'Welcome, Leader of the leaders of the Arabs!' Nahhas would then be passed up the stairs to the chargé d'affaires whom Nuri had schooled in

Britain wanted Egypt included in a regional Arab organization on the ground, it may be assumed, that the whole area could thereby be more easily controlled. In the event, conferring the leadership on Egypt served only to build her up into a rival to British power in the area, so that in the last decade of British supremacy in the Middle East—1945–54—Egyptian recalcitrance was a major irritant. Far from being an instrument for British control, the League became a vehicle for Egyptian influence.

But perhaps the main consequence of its creation was to deal a death-blow to schemes for union restricted to Arab Asia. Both King 'Abdallah's Greater Syria plan and Nuri al-Sa'id's Fertile Crescent union—which were examined in the last chapter—were doomed once the League formula was adopted of an association of sovereign states grouped around the Egyptian 'elder sister'. The careful and specific safeguards of the sovereignty of member states written into the League Charter precluded any attempt by Iraq or Transjordan to merge with Syria or seek to change her form of government from a republic to a monarchy. Nuri got a bad press in Egypt in 1944: there was oblique talk of Iraq's 'territorial aspirations' not only with reference to the Fertile Crescent project but also to Iraq's alleged desire for an outlet to the Mediterranean. Indeed, once Egypt opted for membership of the Arab family she quickly saw that her national interest lay in containing the Hashimites, in preventing the emergence in the Eastern Arab world of a power strong enough to challenge her, in preserving the *status quo* of small sovereign nation-states subordinate to herself. To retain her primacy, she needed in particular to prevent Syria from falling under the influence of either Baghdad or Amman. Since the Middle Ages rulers of the Nile have opposed the establishment of a strong Government in Baghdad or Damascus which might threaten their security or outweigh their influence in the Eastern Mediterranean. To list these principles is perhaps to give them somewhat greater precision than they had in men's minds at the time. But they became, as will be seen, the constants of Egypt's Arab policy which 'Abd al-Nasir inherited when he in turn came to consider Egypt's role in the Arab world.

another high-sounding phrase, while at the door of the embassy itself, yet another member of the staff would be ready with a florid welcome carefully prepared by Nuri. 'Nahhas will surely think we are laughing at him', someone objected to the Pasha. But Nuri was right. The car arrived, flag flying. Nahhas was hailed as planned and was passed, beaming and gratified, from hand to hand. 'Flatter an Egyptian and you fuddle his brain', Nuri was wont to say.

4

The Overthrow of the Veteran Nationalists

THE story of the first years of Syrian independence is not one of great statesmen or powerful political ideas but of lesser men who, called upon to deal with a situation in flux, spent themselves in the task of retaining power. With few well-tried institutions or recognized political traditions to guide them, they were more often engrossed in the trivia of personal rivalry than in statesmanlike acts in their newly-won independence.

On 30 March 1949 the army Chief of Staff, Colonel Husni al-Za'im, seized power in Damascus. Supported by a handful of nationalist officers and radical politicians he overthrew the existing regime, to the general satisfaction of the public, thus introducing the young army to politics and the country to a troubled decade before the union with Egypt. But before relating the details of the coup and the motives of its perpetrators, the regime which Za'im overthrew will be described.

THE NATIONAL BLOC

The National Bloc, or *Kutla al-Wataniya*, was a group of veteran nationalists who had waged the struggle for Syrian independence against France between the wars;[1] but by 1945 it had lost all cohesion. It touched the peak of its influence in the 1930s when its leaders, men of talent and character drawn from all parts of Syria, agreed to sink their differences and unite to face the French. The climax of their efforts was the negotiation of a treaty with the Blum Administration in 1936, followed by the formation of a triumphant all-Bloc Government in Damascus under Jamil Mardam Bey, including such leading figures of the movement as the Aleppo leader Sa'dallah

---

[1] For the history of Syria between the wars see A. H. Hourani, *Syria and Lebanon* (1946) and S. H. Longrigg, *Syria and Lebanon under French Mandate* (1958).

al-Jabiri and the Damascus notable Shukri al-Quwatli, whose nationalist record dated back to the First World War. The veteran Hashim al-Atasi, who had been King Faysal's Prime Minister in Damascus in 1920, became President of the Republic and the Protestant lawyer Faris al-Khuri President of the Chamber. Some of these men had suffered imprisonment at the hands of the Turks; all had been imprisoned or exiled by the French.

But the French parliament, after interminable delays, failed to ratify the treaty; the authority and popularity of the Bloc were in consequence fatally undermined and it is probable that only the threat of an impending world war prevented a breakdown of public order and a national uprising. On the eve of war, the Bloc had already been crippled by its first experience of government: not only had its treaty negotiations with France ended with the collapse of nationalist hopes, but it had failed to prevent the loss of the Alexandretta sanjaq to Turkey in 1939; its authority at home was undermined by the large numbers of French officials and advisers to whom a genuinely independent Syria was still an anomaly, while the streets were made hideous by the brawls, mass demonstrations, and stone-throwing of rival para-military youth movements.

Syria and Lebanon were formally recognized as independent in 1941, but the essential prerogatives of sovereignty—full legislative and administrative powers and control over the armed forces—had to be wrested inch by inch from the French over the next four years. In particular, the Syrian and Lebanese Governments demanded the immediate and unconditional transfer of the *Troupes spéciales du Levant*—a force some thousands strong raised locally by the French—a step which, by allowing the creation of national armies, would alone have made self-government effective. But the French persisted in making the transfer dependent on the conclusion of a treaty binding Syria to themselves, a dispute which was violently terminated by open hostilities in May 1945 between French troops and Syrian civilians, stiffened by deserters from the *Troupes* and the *gendarmerie*. The nationalist leaders counted on British intervention to separate the combatants; they may well have received assurances in this sense from the British representative, General Spears. It seems very probable that the Syrians were anxious to bring matters with the French to a head while the British were still there. They were haunted by the memory of 1919 when the British withdrew leaving the French to dispose of them as they pleased. At all events, the

British intervention in line with Syrian expectations ended the disturbances and was followed a year later, in April 1946, by the withdrawal of all foreign troops from Syrian territory.

But so long as relations with France continued to dominate the Syrian political scene and her troops continued to occupy the country, the National Bloc, for all its disabilities, remained the only candidate for office. It traded on its claims to a monopoly of nationalism and was duly returned to power at the July 1943 elections. Shukri al-Quwatli was elected President of the Republic, while his old associate Sa'dallah al-Jabiri formed a Government in which the nationalist old guard was strongly represented.

Quwatli's chance to lead the Bloc had followed the unexpected murder, on 7 July 1940, of Dr 'Abd al-Rahman Shahbandar, a man of vision and character, who had been one of the Bloc's severest critics. For a time suspicion for his death rested on the leaders of the Bloc, three of whom—Jamil Mardam, Lutfi al-Haffar, and Sa'dallah al-Jabiri—fled to Iraq,[2] leaving Quwatli virtually alone in the field. He emerged as the accepted leader of the national movement in the troubled months between the fall of France and the Allied occupation of Syria in June 1941, backing his demands for the formation of a National Government by strike action throughout the country. It was not surprising that he should at this time make contact with the Italian Armistice Commission and with the numerous German visitors to Syria who undermined French prestige and openly encouraged pan-Arab ambitions. In both Damascus and Baghdad extreme nationalists felt they had more to gain from an Axis victory. But when the Allies invaded Syria, Quwatli found it expedient to leave for Saudi Arabia, returning only in the spring of 1942 after King Ibn Sa'ud had used good offices on his behalf with the Free French in Damascus.

Quwatli's friendship with the Sa'udi royal house was to have a determining influence on his career and on Syria's foreign alignments. His family had for many years served as commercial agents for the Sa'udis in Damascus, a connexion which was consolidated by mutual political support. Quwatli proved useful to Ibn Sa'ud from the early 1920s, sending him as aides a number of talented Syrians such as Yusuf Yasin, who later became the king's principal adviser on foreign affairs. Quwatli was far from being the ablest man in the National Bloc but he was tenacious and dependable. After his election

---

[2] They returned to Syria in 1941 when officially exculpated.

to the Presidency in 1943, his nationalist record, stentorian tones, and sash of office formed a glorious front behind which his wilier colleagues could pursue their intrigues and share out the spoils. They used to recall how at school in Istanbul before the First World War he was called the 'Camel', a slow-witted beast but nasty when roused. But his nationalist sentiment was beyond reproach and his complaisance towards the peccadillos of his colleagues could be relied upon.

The French sociologist Jacques Berque has shown that the first co-ordinated nationalist thrust in an Arab country tended to produce a broad heterogeneous grouping such as the Syrian National Bloc, the Egyptian Wafd, the Moroccan Istiqlal, or the Tunisian Neo-Destour. Men of vastly different backgrounds and ambitions bound themselves together in pursuit of the sole aim of independence. But the first successes, resulting either from negotiation with the foreign occupying Power or revolt against it, usually split the group. Personal and ideological dissensions arose and more subtle distinctions supplanted the original militant nationalism.[3]

Opposition to the ruling faction within the Bloc had been growing since France's failure to ratify the 1936 treaty. By 1939 the national movement showed signs of splitting into two factions, of which one seemed rather more sensitive to social and economic questions and spoke of broadening the base of the struggle against the French. But these differences should not be exaggerated: both the ruling veterans and the dissidents were prosperous conservatives, resisting change rather than promoting it. They were divided on personal lines rather than on matters of policy. The origins of the split lay in Aleppo city politics where two rising men, Rushdi al-Kikhia and Nazim al-Qudsi, broke away from the entourage of the national leader Sa'dallah al-Jabiri. Deeper divergences of policy were later to underline these personal disputes but neither faction in the Bloc understood party organization in the modern sense of the word; both took it to mean at most a political alliance of notables or men of influence, each contributing his own network of friends and patronage.

With Quwatli at the Presidency, three prominent veterans—Sa'dallah al-Jabiri, Jamil Mardam, and Faris al-Khuri—alternated as Prime Minister between August 1943 and 1947, but these Governments laboured against great odds. The French, as has been noted, were reluctant to abandon the last vestiges of power without

[3] Jacques Berque, 'L'Univers politique des Arabes', *Encyclopédie française*, xi (1957).

extracting from the Syrian Government a treaty to secure their cultural and other interests, while the Bloc dared not appeal to the people whose full confidence it no longer enjoyed. It was in consequence weak and hesitant. Tarnished in the eyes of the public, it could not even count on that popular enthusiasm which might have been reserved for the new era of national independence. It was welcomed only by those who hoped to derive some profit from its tenure of office. It suffered a further blow with the death, on 20 June 1947, of Sa'dallah al-Jabiri, the bravest and straightest of the Bloc leaders and perhaps the one man whose reputation and authority had survived the trials of the preceding years. Sa'dallah's death weakened the Bloc but strengthened Quwatli's position: Sa'dallah had persistently opposed Quwatli's wish to amend the constitution in such a way as to allow himself to stand for re-election as President for a second five-year term. The July 1947 elections which followed closely on Sa'dallah's death brought into the open the fragmentation of the Bloc and the forces ranged against it.

THE NATIONAL PARTY

In the spring of 1947, a few months before the elections, the ruling wing of the Bloc coalesced into a National Party, *al-Hizb al-Watani*, with Damascus as its stronghold where men like Quwatli, Jamil Mardam, Faris al-Khuri, Lutfi al-Haffar, and Sabri al-'Asali each had a personal following. In the main, however, the party reflected Damascus city politics at their most parochial. It produced no detailed programme, exercised little discipline over its members, and could boast of no clear hierarchical structure of command. Its electoral strength did not even depend on the personal qualities of its leaders, although some of them were very able men, but rather on the aura of their nationalist record, powerfully sustained by their family roots and affiliations in the various quarters of the city. To this day, family connexions are more important than character in Damascus. Ties created by living in the same street, belonging to the same sect, or the link of some distant but tirelessly proclaimed marriage relationship were infinitely stronger than those of allegiance to a common political cause.

Notions of electioneering were at the time virtually restricted to securing the backing of the 'strong men' or *abadayat*[4] in the various *ahya'* or quarters of the city, which housed a vast lower middle class

[4] From Turkish *kabadayi*—a swashbuckler, bully, or boss (lit. 'coarse uncle').

of tradesmen, merchants, and craftsmen, divided into various religious, racial, and functional groups. The *abadayat* were local bosses, defending the weak against the strong, taking bribes from the rich and administering a sort of rough and ready justice in the network of streets over which they ruled. Rival candidates at elections bade for their support and, under the Mandate, the French themselves had sometimes bought their services and a temporary respite from disorder. But over the years, particularly in the 1950s, their position was undermined by the exodus from the old quarters to the new residential areas of the city and by the increasing hold which modern ideologically-based parties came to have over the young. This hold in turn was associated with the growth of political clubs where young men spent their evenings and with the emancipatory and educational role of political cafés like the old *Brazil* in Damascus, where men of different backgrounds met to talk and read newspapers.

THE PEOPLE'S PARTY

At the time of the 1947 elections, the dissident wing of the Bloc, united in its opposition to Quwatli, had not yet developed that minimum degree of internal cohesion which would have turned it into a political party. It consisted of a number of loosely disciplined parliamentary groups—such as the Constitutional Parliamentary Group and the People's Parliamentary Group—led primarily by such Aleppo leaders as Rushdi al-Kikhia, Nazim al-Qudsi, and Mustafa Barmada. These men enjoyed a reputation for greater personal integrity than their National Party rivals; they had for the most part resigned from the Bloc in 1939 and had not therefore enjoyed the fruits of office. But in August 1948 this opposition likewise coalesced to form the *Hizb al-Sha'b*, or People's Party,[5] mainly representing business interests in Aleppo and the north, and winning the support of the great landed family of the Atasis, whose fief was Homs and who were equally opposed to the rule of Quwatli and the Damascus politicians.

To Aleppo merchants and bankers, Mosul and Baghdad sometimes seemed as close as Damascus. Aleppo had for generations sat astride the great trade route from Europe and Anatolia to Mesopotamia, Iran, and India. It had prospered within the unity of the Ottoman Empire and had suffered more than Damascus from the arbitrariness of the 1920–3 frontiers: the new Syria was too small a

[5] *Le Jour* (Beirut), 17 Aug. 1948.

hinterland for it, and it dreamed of other and wider geographical possibilities.[6] The newly formed People's Party was not a Hashimite or a monarchical party; it was as attached as its Damascus rival to Syria's republican institutions; but it was essentially an Aleppo party and, as such, lent its political weight to the abolition of the Syrian-Iraqi frontier and the destruction of that *blocus infernal*[7] of trade barriers and political boundaries within which Syria suffocated. On 23 November 1948, four months after its formation, the party came out into the open with a memorandum to President Quwatli calling for an Arab federation—in effect a union with Iraq—as alone capable of countering the Israeli menace. At the time of the 1947 elections, before the party's pro-Iraqi tendencies became plain, it also enjoyed the support of the Ba'th, a rising pan-Arab movement which was steadily improving its claim to control the student body.

The Ba'th leader, Michel 'Aflaq, gives this analysis of the situation at the time:[8]

In 1947–8 the People's Party was still little more than a parliamentary group opposed to Quwatli. It seemed honest and was attached to constitutional and democratic procedures. Its reactionary face was not then apparent and the Ba'th joined forces with it in opposing the Government.

But the Ba'th had itself begun to show its revolutionary face. It attacked the feudal and bourgeois class in power, accusing it of half-measures, of compromise with the French, of failing to see through to the end the struggle for independence. It taught the public that the explanation of the Government's hesitation was to be found in its class interests and class mentality.

To understand the bankruptcy of the Bloc one must appreciate that the men of whom it was composed had no overall view; their ambition was restricted to securing their own political survival and a limited degree of independence for the country. They lagged a long way behind public opinion, particularly the young, who had for several years been subject to Ba'th and Communist ideas. The Ba'th gave the public wider ambitions, on both the social and national plane.

The Bloc was not concerned with Arab unity or with the independence of other Arab states. It seemed content with Syrian independence, limited and unreal as its conception of this was. Quwatli even considered signing a treaty with France in 1945, an aim which had been laudable ten years earlier but which bordered on treachery after the war.

[6] See Pierre Rondot, 'Tendances particularistes et tendances unitaires en Syrie', *Orient*, no. 5, 1958, p. 135.
[7] Rabbath, p. 288.
[8] Michel 'Aflaq to the author, Beirut, 7 Jan. 1961.

Syrian youth was beginning to demand full and real independence as the starting point for reform in every sector of national life. It also sought independence at home as a springboard from which to launch a movement to free and unite other Arab states. But these ambitions were remote from the views of the governing classes. The Ba'th spoke a language which the rulers found incomprehensible but which the people understood. The men in power accused the Ba'th of idealism and utopianism—they could find no worse charge.

THE 1947 ELECTIONS

At the July elections the Ba'th and the People's Party in embryo formed a common front to campaign for electoral reform and for a number of mildly progressive measures.

We tried [Nazim al-Qudsi later explained] to win over the electorate to our programme. We spoke of the need for more roads, for piped water in the villages and so on. The National Party, in contrast, preferred to dwell on its past successes. It seemed unaware of the changes in the social structure of the country and sought to monopolize the privilege of having fought the French.[9]

The elections marked the success of the opposition's campaign for direct suffrage and single-stage elections, for which they were rewarded by winning 33 new seats. This result carried total opposition representation in the Chamber to 53 against 24 National Party deputies, and a large amorphous group of 'Independents' with no party or ideological affiliation numbering over 50, who were to remain a feature of Syrian parliamentary life, holding the balance between rival blocs and serving as the hunting ground for political opportunists, until the disappearance of the Syrian parliament in 1958. They were landowners, businessmen, tribal and minority leaders, heads of the largest and most powerful families, bearing witness by their number in all Syrian elections to the continued strength of local and traditional forms of loyalty and to the weakness of party organization.[10] In Aleppo all the main opposition leaders were returned: Rushdi al-Kikhia, Nazim al-Qudsi, Mustafa Barmada, Wahbi al-Hariri, and Ahmad al-Rifa'i. In Damascus most of the National Party stalwarts—Jamil Mardam, Faris al-Khuri, Sabri al-'Asali, Lutfi al-Haffar, etc.—failed to secure the necessary 40 per

[9] Nazim al-Qudsi to the author, Aleppo, 3 Nov. 1960.
[10] Ralph Crow, 'A Study of Political Forces in Syria based on a survey of the 1954 elections', May 1955 (unpublished: by courtesy of the author).

cent of the votes in the first round. They were returned, however, in the second round, when a simple majority was sufficient, with a suspiciously inflated poll, giving rise to allegations of government interference through the Ministry of Interior.[11] The new Chamber elected Faris al-Khuri as its President or Speaker at its first session on 27 September 1947. The following day Jamil Mardam submitted the resignation of his cabinet but was called upon to form another.

But the sober vocabulary of politics—terms such as 'deputy' and 'opposition', 'President of the Chamber' and 'Foreign Affairs Commission'—failed to cloak the lamentable confusion reigning in the Syrian parliament. 'I look around me', writes Habib Kahaleh in his *Memoirs of a Deputy*,[12] 'and see only a bundle of contradictions. . . .' Men whom nothing united, sharing no principles, bound by no party organization, elected to parliament by some mysterious travesty of free and unhampered elections; some were illiterate, others distinguished men of letters; some spoke only Kurdish or Armenian, others only Turkish; some wore a *tarbush*, others a *kafiyeh;* townsmen and beduin. It was all play-acting.

In November 1947 President Quwatli induced the Government to table a bill amending Article 68 of the constitution, thereby permitting his re-election for a second five-year term on 18 April.[13] Profiteers rejoiced and scrambled for their share of the loot; the old team was back in power for another stretch; there was much talk of trafficking in import licences and in the agencies for imported goods. Quwatli himself, too trusting of his associates or too weak to bring them to order, sat on top of an edifice of nepotism and mismanagement eroded at the base by price inflation, by crop failures due to drought, and by rumblings of discontent from the emerging labour unions. Tired politicians, their energies spent in the abrasive argument with the French; untried institutions; the whole creaking network of family patronage and administrative venality; a young ill-trained and ill-equipped army were all soon to suffer the trauma of the Palestine War. But Quwatli's constitutional amendment to perpetuate his regime blocked a movement of reform when this was

[11] It was also alleged (possibly in jest) that Sabri al-'Asali and Lutfi al-Haffar allowed their names to be announced in the poorer quarters as *Shaikh* Sabri and *Hajj* Lutfi, religious titles calculated to draw the Muslim vote.
[12] *Dhikriyat na'ib*, pp. 43 f.,193, published by *al-Mudhik al-Mubqi*, a celebrated satirical newspaper which Kahaleh edited.
[13] Muhammad Kurd 'Ali, *al-Mudhakkarat* (1948), ii. 530; Wajih al-Haffar, *al-Dustur wa'l-hukm* (1948), pp. 123-30.

still possible, and contributed to the collapse of Syria's parliamentary system fourteen months later.

THE PALESTINE WAR

The Syrian army's weakness was disclosed within ten days of the Arab League's intervention in Palestine in May 1948. The Defence Minister, Ahmad al-Sharabati, resigned on 24 May and the Premier, Jamil Mardam, himself took over the portfolio of Defence. The early reverses had demonstrated that a change in command was required. The Chief of Staff, 'Abdallah 'Atfi, was retired and replaced by the Director of Public Security, Colonel Husni al-Za'im. Arab politicians had made grandiloquent speeches misleading the public into expecting an early victory, but the war revealed a total lack of preparedness. No unified Arab command existed; staff work and communications were poor; arms, ammunition, and medical services were defective or in short supply; perhaps the main fault was that the strength of the enemy had been underestimated. For the young Syrian officers the experience was a turning-point. They came to believe, with some justice, that their political leaders had been criminally negligent: greater inter-Arab solidarity could have been achieved; more arms could have been bought abroad or secured from the French before their departure in 1946. Syrian troops went into battle in 1948 with barely a few hundred rounds of ammunition apiece. Charges were made of corruption and profiteering, notably in the case of Captain Fu'ad Mardam who, sent on an arms-purchasing mission to Italy, had through negligence or fraud allowed the arms to be intercepted by Israel.[14] Victims of this mismanagement, the young officers, came to see themselves as the sole champions of the country's welfare, on guard not only against the enemy on the frontier but also against the incapacity if not the treachery of the political clique at home.

All Mardam's efforts could not stem the rising wave of discontent. The Ba'th leader Michel 'Aflaq was arrested in September 1948 for circulating tracts denouncing the failure of the Government and demanding the dissolution of the Chamber. In November Mardam was deserted by three ministers from his own party—Sabri al-'Asali, Lutfi al-Haffar, and Mikhail Ilyan—while the newly formed People's Party moved squarely into opposition and announced that it would

[14] The scandal was alluded to in a well-known poem by 'Umar Abu Rishah, a Syrian poet and diplomatist.

s.s.—4

only take part in a coalition Government if those responsible for the Palestine débâcle were brought to trial. To mark the first anniversary of the 1947 United Nations vote on the partition of Palestine, the Ba'th brought the students out on strike. The *suks* were closed; demonstrators petitioned the Government demanding an immediate resumption of hostilities in Palestine, the rejection of all alliances with foreign Powers, and the cancellation of a recent decree increasing the price of bread. The Chamber itself was in an uproar: the former Defence Minister, Ahmad al-Sharabati, came to blows with another deputy while the Premier could be heard shouting his resignation. Outside, police reinforced by *gendarmerie* used tear gas to disperse the crowds which threatened to take the Chamber by assault.

The strikes spread to the main towns and degenerated into riots. Police fired on the mobs killing four people in Damascus. A state of emergency was declared over the whole country, the army moving into the capital with armoured vehicles to impose a 6 p.m. to 6 a.m. curfew and to prohibit gatherings of more than three persons. This was its first taste of power. The officers, fresh from the humiliating reverses at the front, were given a front-seat view of the crumbling political positions at home.

After Jamil Mardam's resignation on 1 December 1948, President Quwatli cast around desperately for a successor. The People's Party leaders, Kikhia and Qudsi, refused to try their hand at cabinet making. Appeal was then made to the venerable ex-President Hashim al-Atasi, who wearily travelled down to the capital from his native Homs only to return three days later after failing to form a National Government. Another independent but less distinguished figure, the Druze notable Amir 'Adil Arslan, also tried and failed. Quwatli then sent an urgent summons to Khalid al-'Azm, a millionaire financier then serving as Minister in Paris whose ancestors had been governors of Damascus in the eighteenth century.

KHALID AL-'AZM'S MINISTRY

'Azm was one of the ablest men in Syrian public life. His background, wealth, and natural inclination had given him opportunities for travel and he had outgrown and probably come to despise the parochial city politics in which most Syrian leaders were immersed. He was a man of fastidious and educated tastes, with a sounder understanding of the workings of international politics and finance than many of his colleagues. But measured by a nationalist yardstick he cut a poorer figure. His father had been one of those notables who had thought of themselves as Turkish rather than Arab and had therefore defended the *status quo* of the Empire against the Arab nationalists. 'Azm himself had never joined the National Bloc or shared in its struggle against the French. Worse still, when at a low point in French fortunes in April 1941, the Vichy High Commissioner General Dentz had failed to come to terms with the nationalists, Khalid al-'Azm had formed a 'neutral' cabinet to put an end to the disorders. His cabinet survived the brief Allied campaign in Syria, the expulsion of Vichy, and the Free French occupation, but was asked to make way in September 1941 for a ministry under which independence could be proclaimed. He served in subsequent wartime Governments but always in semi-technical ministries such as Finance or Supply. His career later provided one of the major enigmas of Syrian politics: rich and cultured, the representative of big business and the product of an expensive western education, he was to ally himself with Communism in 1957 and frighten the world into believing that Syria was in danger of falling under Soviet domination.

But this could not have been foreseen when he hurried home from Paris in 1948 to put an end to a crisis which had left Syria without a Government for over a fortnight. He formed a ministry of non-parliamentarians on 16 December, and ten days later faced a rebellious Chamber. Two problems which in retrospect seem overshadowed by the Palestine conflict deeply preoccupied the Government at the time: first, the need to conclude a monetary convention with France, which was denounced by the opposition as a 'prelude to the revival of French influence in Syria;' second, the question of granting transit facilities to the Mediterranean for an American pipeline from Saudi Arabia. The Trans-Arabian Pipeline Company (Tapline) had in 1947 started building a pipe to link up the Aramco oilfields with Sidon on the Lebanese coast. Work due for completion in 1950, was interrupted by the Palestine War and by the difficulty of negotiating agreements for the passage of the line through the four Arab states, Saudi Arabia, Jordan, Lebanon, and Syria, where it was represented by the Government's opponents as the vanguard of American colonialism.

Khalid al-'Azm's plans to support the shaky Syrian pound and replenish the treasury by negotiating agreements with both France and the United States came under bitter attack—inside the Chamber from the People's Party and the Muslim Brothers, outside from the

Ba'th and their student phalanxes. He was not, however, to be deterred and on 7 February 1949 a Franco-Syrian agreement was signed in Damascus[15] settling all outstanding financial problems posed by the termination of the Mandate. It was followed on 16 February by an agreement with Tapline.[16] Both documents had, however, to be ratified by parliament. Before this could be done Colonel Husni al-Za'im had overthrown Quwatli's regime and seized power.

Khalid al-'Azm explains the position as follows:[17]

It was clear to me that the Chamber wished to ratify neither the currency agreement with France nor the Tapline convention which aroused special hostility. Some deputies were afraid United States interference in Syria would follow. Other, less honourable, members hoped perhaps that by making a show of opposition they would be offered bribes for their votes; others still were subject to the pressures and inducement of interests suspicious of the West and resentful at western support for Israel.

The United States believed, rightly or wrongly, that there was little chance of securing parliamentary ratification. They may therefore have looked with sympathy on anyone who promised to remove this obstacle. The facts speak for themselves: shortly after Husni al-Za'im came to power he ratified both conventions.[18]

---

[15] Text in *L'Orient* (Beirut), 20 Feb. 1949.
[16] Text ibid. 18 Feb. 1949.
[17] Khalid al-'Azm to the author, Damascus, 8 Nov. 1960.
[18] The monetary agreement with France was ratified on 21 April and the convention with Tapline on 16 May. 'Azm's suggestion is that the U.S. encouraged Za'im to carry out his coup, a view the author has not been able to confirm. Reliable American sources report that U.S. and British intelligence knew of the impending coup but did nothing to promote it. The possibility of French backing for Za'im cannot be dismissed so confidently. The French certainly gave him strong support after he took over. According to Gen. Shawkat Shuqayr, a Druze officer of Lebanese origin whom Za'im recruited as head of his *Cabinet militaire,* later to become Syrian Chief of Staff, Za'im's ratification of the two agreements should be taken to reflect his conscious need to win friends *after* his coup, rather than American or French backing *before* it.

5

The First Coup d'État

To the generation of nationalist youth which grew to manhood in the last years of the Second World War, the Syrian army, after the departure of the French in April, 1946, seemed the symbol of independence and the greatest of all national institutions. Secondary schoolboys flocked to enrol at the Homs military college, which became a nursery for nationalist, politically-minded officers. The 1946–7 class was of special importance as it was the first generation of 'patriot officers'—the men who had the task of transforming the *Troupes spéciales* into a national army and who, almost immediately, had a political role thrust upon them. Their two-year course was interrupted by the Palestine War and they passed hurriedly out of the Academy to join their ill-equipped, ill-trained troops in the Jordan Valley.

Older officers in the Syrian army tended to be men from large and influential families whom the French had enlisted into the *Troupes spéciales* in order to secure the allegiance of the minority communities from which they were primarily drawn. But after 1946 the great majority of cadets at the Homs military college came from the lower middle class, moulded no doubt in their schooldays by one or other of the doctrinaire youth movements which had sprung up in the 1930s and 1940s. The Muslim landed families, being predominantly of nationalist sentiment, despised the army as a profession: to join it between the wars was to serve the French. Homs to them was a place for the lazy, the rebellious, the academically backward, or the socially undistinguished. Few young men of good family would consider entering the college unless they had failed at school or been expelled. The conservative 'right' in Syria neglected the army as a source of political power, with disastrous consequences, as it was the army, an eager and indoctrinated instrument, which later destroyed the power of the landed families and urban merchants, with the result that a veteran Syrian politician of the 1940s would find little to recognize or approve of in the political scene fifteen years later.

AKRAM AL-HAWRANI AND THE ARMY

The Hama leader Akram al-Hawrani was one of the first to recognize how powerful a weapon a politically-conscious officer corps could be, and what fertile ground the cadets at the Homs military college provided for his ideas. As has been seen, his first contacts in the army were made when he gathered a group of young officers around him and hurried off in high hopes to join Rashid 'Ali's revolt in Iraq in 1941. When Hawrani first emerged in Hama politics in the late 1930s effective political and economic power lay squarely in the hands of the great landed families. In 1939 Hawrani took over a youth movement which a cousin of his had founded two or three years earlier. The movement had no particular ideology; it was merely a youthful revolt against the Mandate and the established order. Hawrani stiffened it by affiliating it secretly to one of the most effective anti-Mandate movements of the time—a paramilitary, rigidly hierarchical formation known as the Parti Populaire Syrien, or PPS, which from its Beirut base had, by the outbreak of war, extended tentacles to many neighbouring Arab countries. It is doubtful whether Hawrani, a man of action rather than a thinker, ever fully embraced the cult of discipline and mystical pan-Syrianism preached by the PPS leader Antun Sa'ada. He was in revolt against the French and found in the PPS a convenient vehicle for his natural pugnacity. The PPS, like Hawrani's local movement, was typical of the many semi-uniformed youth formations which sprung up in the Middle East in the mid-1930s and 1940s, modelled on fascist prototypes, marshalling their supporters in street parades and sports rallies, and preaching the virtues of service and sacrifice. Mobilized in this fashion, schoolchildren, university students, and militant youth generally were gradually to become formidable extra-parliamentary pressure groups, rivalled only by the army as repositories of political power.

In 1944, when relations with the French were becoming tense, Hawrani joined groups of young officers in guerrilla attacks against French garrisons in the Hama area. So effective were these attempts at 'local liberation' that the Syrian Government telegraphed instructing him to avoid destroying military installations since these would no doubt revert to Syria when the French departed. In the spring of 1945 Hawrani and two officers, the brothers Salah and Adib al-Shishakli, also PPS men, took over the Hama citadel, expelling the French garrison. Quixotically they prepared to march on Damascus, where hostilities had broken out between the French and a Syrian rabble army of civilians and *gendarmerie*. But these plans were foiled by British intervention. In that same month, May 1945, Hawrani founded his Arab Socialist Party as a front for his secret PPS affiliations,[1] but before long he began to drift away from the PPS with their narrow view of Syrian nationalism towards the more popular Arab nationalist and socialist doctrines of the nascent Ba'th Party. By the end of the war Hawrani had distinguished himself as one of the most promising popular leaders in northern Syria.

In the immediate post-war period Hawrani extended his influence in the army by making contact with officer cadets at Homs through a number of intermediaries, notably a history instructor, Nakhle Kallas, one of whose brothers, Khalil Kallas, was to become the first Ba'th Minister of Economics in 1955, while another, Bahij Kallas, was an officer in close alliance with Hawrani. These friendships were consolidated and greatly extended during the Palestine War. With Adib al-Shishakli, later dictator of Syria, Hawrani was one of the first to lead bands of irregulars across the Palestine frontier in January 1948, in attacks against Jewish settlements.[2] Much of his later power was to spring from these bonds with prominent young nationalist officers to whom he appeared as guide, political tactician, mob leader, and ideological source.

A second wing of Hawrani's support was the peasant following he built up in the villages around his home town of Hama, a stronghold of landed 'feudalism'. In the great plain between Damascus and Aleppo, the two small towns of Homs and Hama are centres of thickly populated rural areas where much of the good land before the 1958 land reform was taken up by large estates. Share-croppers were worse off here than in other parts of the country and small ownership was almost unknown. Late in the 1950s conditions of extreme poverty could be seen in the villages on landowners' estates in the

[1] Ghassan Tweini, owner-editor of the Beirut daily, *al-Nahar* and a former PPS leader, to the author, 4 July 1961. In May 1945 Tweini was sent by the PPS headquarters in Beirut to make contact in Hama with Hawrani and the local cadres.
[2] Both Hawrani and Shishakli were operating under the general command of Fawzi al-Qawaqji, a Muslim from Lebanese Tripoli who had served in the Ottoman army in the First World War and had then had a varied career as intelligence officer under French command in Syria, military adviser to Ibn Sa'ud, officer in the Iraqi army and 'generalissimo' of the Palestine Arab guerrillas in the 1936 rebellion. Qawaqji had also fought in the abortive Iraqi *putsch* against Britain in 1941. Escaping to Germany, he was detained by the Russians, later finding sanctuary in France before returning to the Middle East in 1947. (See G. E. Kirk, *The Middle East 1945–50* (1954), p. 253.)

region. The old landowning families had installed canals, pumps, and tractors, but 'they are still *rentiers* in mind and income, who live on the labour of their share-croppers, advancing seed or lending money to the cultivator in return for three-quarters of the gross produce. Their mentality is that of the *grand seigneur*.'[3]

Before the war distinctions between peasantry and notables were sharp, but before Hawrani emerged on the scene there was nothing that could properly be called class conflict. Hawrani hated the 'Azms, Barazis, and Kaylanis who ruled Hama and overshadowed his childhood. These families lived on vast *latifundia*, policed by armed retainers. They rode fine horses, owned numerous villages and great herds of cattle. Their sons were to be seen in Beirut cabarets. The whole apparatus of the state, the *gendarmerie*, and local government officials were pressed into their service. They had everything to excite the envy of the dispossessed and the hostility of the politically conscious. Hawrani's own father had been a landlord who had stood unsuccessfully as a candidate for the Ottoman parliament. But the family's wealth had been dissipated by an uncle and Hawrani surrounded himself with a group of bitterly resentful young men. Perhaps he never saw, as did the young Trotsky in Russia in the 1880s, a group of labourers 'coming from the fields, in the twilight, with uncertain steps and with their hands stretched out in front of them—they had all been struck by night-blindness from undernourishment.'[4] But he saw enough of the landlord-sharecropper relationship to wish to break the monopoly of property and power held by a handful of families. He wanted to set fire to their houses and drive them off the land. From the late 1940s he incited the peasants to violence. He encouraged them to burn their crops and refuse to work. As a prominent landowner put it, 'if he could have drunk our blood and eaten our flesh he would have done so'.[5]

When Hawrani first started his political career, organized political power was in the hands of the National Bloc which was returned in the 1943 elections—the first to be held after the formal proclamation of Syrian independence in 1941. Hawrani campaigned with the Bloc—there was no alternative for an ambitious young man—and was elected as the representative of the younger Hama generation. Shortly after his arrival in Damascus as a parliamentary novice in

[3] Doreen Warriner, *Land Reform and Development in the Middle East* (1957), p. 96.
[4] Isaac Deutscher, *The Prophet Armed* (1954), p. 10.
[5] Husni al-Barazi, landowner and former Premier, to the author, Beirut, 21 Oct. 1960.

1943, he met two young schoolmasters, inseparable since their Paris student days in the 1930s, who had recently launched among young people a left-wing Arab nationalist movement called the *Hizb al-Ba'th al-Arabi*, or Arab Resurrection party. They were Michel 'Aflaq, a Christian, and Salah al-Din Bitar, a Muslim. Hawrani did not at that time develop any official connexion with this group, but he raised questions in the Chamber on its behalf and was a frequent visitor at party headquarters. Their ties became still closer in the dramatic circumstances of the armed rebellion against the French in May 1945, in which the Ba'th leaders played an active role, calling on nationalist officers to desert from the French-led *Troupes spéciales*.

Hawrani's alliance with 'Aflaq and Bitar was later to produce one of the most dynamic forces in Syrian politics. But their revolutionary socialism sprang from vastly different roots. The Ba'th leaders were intellectuals, eager to apply at home the Marxist ideas they had learned at the Sorbonne. Hawrani's belligerency was rooted in personal resentment, not abstract theory; it had a sharp edge of rancour from which 'Aflaq and Bitar were free. But even a man like 'Aflaq, if less sanguinary than Hawrani, was not the meek and self-effacing poet and theorist that he at times appeared to be; in the tradition of the Damascus burgher, all docile amiability towards his Turkish overlord, he too, was seething with revolutionary ideas.

THE COOKING-FAT SCANDAL

In the search for a scapegoat after the Palestine catastrophe, the army blamed the politicians and some politicians the High Command. The appointment of Colonel Husni al-Za'im as Chief of Staff in the first month of the war checked for a moment the flood of mutual recrimination but did not end it. Soon the army was restive again as it daily became clearer that the Government had made no provision for the war: front-line troops had been given defective and insufficient arms and equipment; the lamentable failure of Captain Fu'ad Mardam's arms-purchasing mission was still very much in people's minds; allowances had been trimmed; food deliveries to the front were uncertain; at the same time the army's fighting qualities were under insulting attack in the Chamber from Faysal al-'Asali, a deputy from the town of Zabadani, who led a small but noisy right-wing faction called the Socialist Co-operative Party. This secondary personage would scarcely deserve a mention were it not that his strictures against the army degenerated into a bitter personal quarrel between Za'im and himself. Never had the army been so insulted by a member of parliament. Many sources quote 'Asali's attacks as a factor which triggered the crisis and drove Za'im to revolution.[6]

Early in 1949 there occurred another bizarre incident to which, more directly even than Faysal al-'Asali's attacks, the timing of Za'im's coup may be attributed. When he took over command of the army in May 1948, Za'im naturally reshuffled a number of senior appointments. A notable newcomer as chief supply officer was Colonel Antoine Bustani, whom Za'im had known at school. Some months later, shortly after Khalid al-'Azm became Premier in December, President Shukri al-Quwatli and his new Prime Minister set off on a tour of front-line positions and supply points. The story has it that the two politicians noticed a pungent smell coming from a field kitchen. On making inquiries they were told that it came from burning cooking fat. Quwatli demanded that a new tin be opened and an egg cooked before him. The fat once more gave off a nauseating smell: the President tasted it and pronounced it of inferior quality. Samples were sent for testing and revealed that the fat was made from bone waste. To appreciate the shocking nature of this finding it must be observed that fat made from sour milk and known in Arabic as *samnah* is the unshakable basis of all Arabic cooking. No self-respecting Arab will cook in anything else, no Arabic food tastes right without it, and great health-giving qualities are imputed to it.[7] That the heroes at the front should be defrauded of this essential ingredient was a hideous crime. Quwatli immediately ordered the arrest of Colonel Bustani on a charge of profiteering at the army's expense. But Za'im, instead of complying with the order, installed Bustani in an attic at the Defence Ministry, inspired, it would appear, either by loyalty to his old friend or by a desire to ensure that Bustani would be in no position to talk and perhaps implicate others in the affair.

[6] Gen. Shawkat Shuqayr to the author, 18 Dec. 1960. See also a first-hand account by Lt. Col. Bahij Kallas in *Alif Ba'* (Damascus), 27 June 1949: 'The coup was contemplated on the day Faysal al-'Asali ... attacked the army in parliament. The army commander gathered the senior officers around him at his Qunaytra headquarters and talked to them of the seriousness of the situation. . . .' 'Asali was one of the first men to be arrested after the coup. His luxuriant head of hair, of which he was inordinately proud, was shaved clean on Za'im's orders. See also Communiqué no. 9 issued by Za'im after the coup (*al-Nasr*, 31 Mar. 1949): 'The motive for the movement undertaken by the army is the repeated assaults on and the disgrace brought to the army both inside and outside the Chamber of Deputies; and the ill-treatment of the army. . . .'

[7] As any housewife will confirm, *samnah asliyah samnah hadidiyah*: genuine samnah is iron samnah.

The officers, meanwhile, far from rallying to Quwatli, were indignant at the summary treatment of one of their number, seeing in the incident further criminal meddling by incompetent and corrupt politicians in military matters. It was intolerable that army officers should be made out to be thieves. Street urchins held their noses when officers passed on the pavements as if to say what evil-smelling *samnah*. The issue grew into a trial of strength between the army and the politicians. Quwatli learned that Bustani was skulking in the Defence Ministry and demanded his transfer to Mezze prison outside Damascus. But in pressing the charges the President over-looked Za'im's close relationship with Bustani and misjudged the mood of the officers. Defeated in Palestine, ridiculed in parliament, faced with the disorder of civilian politics, this was the last straw.

Za'im himself may have been implicated in the *samnah* scandal. An emissary,[8] sent by him to visit Bustani in prison, reports the latter as saying: 'Tell Za'im that if there is an inquiry I shall be obliged to tell all'. On this view Za'im carried out his coup d'état not to save the country but to save himself. His earlier career had not been blameless. When in June 1941 Imperial and Free French forces advanced into Syria to put an end to German infiltration, the withdrawing Vichy authorities entrusted Za'im, then an officer in the *Troupes spéciales*, with a mission to organize guerrilla operations against the invaders. A sum of about 300,000 Syrian pounds was put at his disposal. But as the Vichy cause seemed hopeless and the situation confused, Za'im preferred to abscond with the money. At the end of the brief campaign, Vichy exposed Za'im's defection to its Free French opponents (and compatriots) in a radio appeal. He was arrested, brought to trial, and sentenced in 1942 to ten years' hard labour. Quwatli released him at the end of the war when he was reinstated in the newly-formed Syrian national army.

Za'im was a heavy, thickly-built man with broad cheeks, a fierce eye and the florid face of a Latin American dictator. Born in Aleppo at the turn of the century into a relatively prosperous business family of Kurdish origin, he retained until the end of his life the boisterous, jocular manner of that city. He started his career in the Ottoman

[8] Ferzat al-Mamluk, an 'Independent' deputy in the Syrian Chamber, to whom the author owes many of the details of the '*samnah* scandal'. The importance of the incident was, however, confirmed by Shawkat Shuqayr, by Edmond Homsi, a prominent banker and former minister, and by Khalid al-'Azm himself, who added that Quwatli had probably been tipped off about the inferior cooking fat and had staged the scene in the field kitchen: 'C'était de la mise en scène'.

army, was captured by the British in the First World War, before joining the *Troupes spéciales* during the Mandate, a force which formed an integral part of the French army of the Levant.

Men who knew Za'im agree that he was an adventurer with few ideals; that he was emotionally somewhat unstable and easily inflamed; that he was brave to the point of foolhardiness but that he had few gifts as a strategist. His military record in Palestine had not been dishonourable. His ambition, which later flowered extravagantly, found a ready instrument in the core of nationalist officers in the Syrian army who, after the Palestine campaign, came to take a high-minded view of their role as guardians of the country's welfare and among whom Akram al-Hawrani's influence was already dominant.

THE PUTSCH

Hawrani did not himself plan the coup but two of his warmest army supporters, Bahij Kallas and Adib al-Shishakli, became Za'im's most intimate fellow conspirators, with Hawrani joining in on the very first days of the new regime. Kallas was Za'im's second in command while Shishakli led the infantry and armoured units which were to carry out the coup. He marshalled his force at Qatana within twenty miles of the city, receiving orders to march on the capital at 2.30 a.m. on 30 March.[9]

There then took place a scene which was often to be repeated: one detachment of troops arrested the President in hospital where he was receiving treatment for a gastric ulcer and heart complaint; another the Prime Minister; a third secured the radio station; a fourth took over police headquarters; a fifth the headquarters of the *gendarmerie;* a sixth the central telephone exchange. Other units, each with its assigned objective, filtered through the sleeping city picking off the chief of police, the commandant of the *gendarmerie,* and a number of ministers and deputies, including Faysal al-'Asali, whose attacks in the Chamber the army chiefs had found so distasteful.[10] Radio and telephone communications with the outside world were interrupted and the frontiers closed. Later that morning Colonel Antoine Bustani was released from prison and reinstated as army supply chief. The merchants who had supplied the inferior

---

[9] Fadlallah Abu Mansur, *'Asir Dimashq* (1959), p. 47.
[10] Ahmad 'Isa al-Fil, *Suriya al-jadida f'il inqilabayn al-awwal wa'l-thani* (1949), p. 33.

cooking fat were arrested and held responsible. The London *Times* reported that the revolution was 'bloodless, complete and successful'. The populace waking to the news greeted it with an explosion of joy, demonstrating yet again that it is a perennial civilian illusion to put one's trust in senior officers.

The old regime passed unregretted. It was made up of men whose political experience had been gained in resisting, obstructing, and tilting at the Mandate. They were not traitors as their successors were sometimes to call them, but they had had little opportunity of learning the craft of state-building. They were a group of politicians with few roots among the people, who had been denied a training in government by the policies of the Mandatory, and who since independence had shared power between them in traditional style, with little understanding of what a popularly-based, representative government really meant. No one was more surprised than Quwatli at the coup. It is said, although the story remains unconfirmed, that Za'im gave orders for the deposed President and Premier to tour the city concealed in an armoured vehicle to see for themselves the people dancing in the streets.

Za'im's successful *putsch* was the first intervention of the army in politics in the Middle East: it set a fashion which was to be widely followed. It demonstrated not so much the reforming zeal of the army—we have seen that Za'im's own motives were questionable— but the fragility of a western constitutional formula stretched like a new skin over the fissures of a traditional society. The Palestine experience showed up the incompetence of the old regime and sharpened the army's disaffection. But the movement which carried Za'im to the presidential palace was powered by the rise of radical pressure groups and political agitators on the left who undertook the political education of the young, in the army as outside it, giving them a new view of politics and wider ambitions for the Arabs in general.

6

Rival Bids for Syria

On acceding to power, Za'im's first discovery was that Syria's internal stresses and strains, which he had momentarily harnessed, could not be contained within her frontiers but were at once exported to her neighbours. Za'im's coup must, therefore, be seen in a wider inter-Arab context: Egypt, Saudi Arabia, Iraq, Jordan, and Lebanon were immediately vitally concerned and the question on everyone's lips was: Who is backing Za'im? Which way will he turn?

The first three hectic weeks of the new regime in April 1949 well illustrate the view that Syria, in moments of crisis and uncertain government, is a shuttlecock lobbed back and forth between rival neighbours. Within hours of the announcement of the coup, anxious envoys from the surrounding states poured into Damascus on exploratory missions. As has been noted, Egypt won the battle of the Arab League in 1945, setting her face against any mergers in Arab Asia and imposing on the Arab states a pattern of relations in which the dominant role was reserved for her. The League formula gave Egypt the leadership and doomed King 'Abdallah's Greater Syria and Nuri's Fertile Crescent which were, in effect, schemes for the unification of Arab Asia—excluding Egypt and the Arabian Peninsula. But the League had been discredited by the failure of its intervention in Palestine; the fiction of Arab solidarity had never been more apparent; defeat had bred in Egypt a mood of isolationism; in those Asian Arab countries most directly threatened by Israeli power, the common danger acted as a spur to unity, a sentiment which Musa al-'Alami, the former Palestinian leader, memorably expressed in his dissection of the Arab debacle, 'Ibrat Filastin (The Lesson of Palestine, 1949). There were, therefore, in the late 1940s good reasons for believing that the chances of an Iraqi-Syrian union were not entirely hopeless.

In Syria itself, the People's Party had been formed primarily to represent the interests of Aleppo and the north which, as has been suggested, saw in Iraq their natural outlet and in union with that country the best guarantee of their security and future prosperity. Just as the People's Party leaned towards Iraq, so Quwatli and the National Party became dependants of Egypt and Saudi Arabia. To King Ibn Sa'ud the prospect of his old Hashimite enemies ruling Syria, Jordan, and Iraq, dominating the land bridge between the Mediterranean and the Persian Gulf and sealing off the Arabian Peninsula from the rest of the world was a nightmare. When, therefore, the People's Party and a number of 'Independents' started to make contact with Iraq in the 1940s, Ibn Sa'ud intervened to check this trend. The year immediately before Za'im's *putsch* in 1949 saw the emergence of Iraq and Saudi Arabia as rival backers of Syrian political factions: both countries began to pour bribe-money into Syria. For the next decade the whole weight of Saudi resources was directed at driving a wedge between Iraq and Syria.[1] As Quwatli's close connexions with Saudi Arabia were common knowledge, it was Za'im's first instinct on deposing him to turn to Iraq for support.

ZA'IM'S ADVANCES TO IRAQ

As a soldier, Za'im had a special reason for enlisting Baghdad's aid: armistice talks with Israel were imminent. They had been due to start in the last week of March 1949 but had been postponed to early April because of the coup. Za'im believed that the announcement of a Syro-Iraqi military agreement would strengthen his hand in these negotiations. He therefore gave a cordial welcome to the two Iraqi envoys who arrived in Damascus before the new regime was a day old: Jamil Baban, the newly-appointed Iraqi Minister in Lebanon, and Awni al-Khalidi, an Iraqi representative at the truce talks with Israel. Baban carried a letter from the Premier, Nuri al-Sa'id, to Faris al-Khuri, the President of the Syrian Chamber and an old friend of Iraq who, in the new and frightening conditions created by the *putsch*, seemed an island of familiar territory.

On 1 April Baban reported to Baghdad that he had seen the new master of Damascus and had conveyed to him Iraq's readiness to lend him such assistance as he might need.[2] He had asked Za'im

---

[1] Fluctuations on the Damascus gold market announced the arrival of aircraft from Saudi Arabia.
[2] The main source for the following account of Iraqi diplomatic activity in the first three weeks of April 1949 is an Iraq official report marked 'very confidential' and entitled *Majra al-hawadith al-muta'tiya . . . bi'l-hukuma al-'Iraqiya* (1949).

whether he intended establishing a republican or monarchical regime—a question of overriding importance to the Regent in Baghdad—but the reply had been non-commital. On foreign policy, Za'im had said that he had told the British and American ministers that he was ready to reach agreements with them and benefit from Marshall aid. Baban then saw the aged lawyer and elder statesman Faris al-Khuri, who had taken to his bed in a fit of nerves; he assured him of Iraq's support should he form a government and 'save the situation'. But Faris protested that he was too old and the outlook too uncertain. To Awni al-Khalidi, the second Iraqi envoy, Faris Bey confessed that the coup in his view was the greatest disaster to fall upon Syria since the repression of the young Turks. After half a century of honourable public life he could not now co-operate with an illegal government. The Syrian colonel, he said, had no plan save to sweep away the old politicians and draft a new constitution. But he advised Iraq not to oppose Za'im by force. Baban also met the People's Party leader but, as he reported to his Foreign Ministry, 'he is so afraid that I could get no opinion out of him'. (This is perhaps the first hint of that timidity which was to blight the later career of the People's Party and of its leaders, Rushdi al-Kikhia and Nazim al-Qudsi.)

From the start Za'im appears to have been seized with doubts as to the 'legality' of his action. With a view to forming a government, he contacted Faris al-Khuri and Amir 'Adil Arslan immediately after the *putsch*. But it was felt that he must first secure President Quwatli's resignation, so Faris Bey was sent to visit the deposed President in the military hospital where he was being detained. Quwatli, however, obstinately refused to give way ('so long as there is blood in my veins'), and rejoined by urging Faris to call the Chamber into special session and declare the coup illegal. But troops had surrounded the parliament building and denied members entry. Seventy-six deputies (out of a Chamber of 136) then held an all-night session at the Foreign Ministry on 31 March and decided to back Za'im. But he considered this support inadequate and, tiring of constitutional quibbles, dissolved the Chamber by decree on 1 April. Amir 'Adil Arslan was retained as his chief political aide, while Akram al-Hawrani, the political head of the young nationalist officers, assumed the vague functions of 'legal adviser' to the regime with offices in the Ministry of Defence. He had been present at Za'im's temporary headquarters in the Police Directorate from the first hour of the coup and is believed to have drafted the early communiqués of the revolutionary movement.

On 3 April the Iraqi Minister in Damascus reported to Baghdad that Amir 'Adil Arslan had told him it was the desire of 'educated opinion' in Syria to unite with Iraq on a basis of internal autonomy for each territory—but excluding Transjordan. The Iraq Government cautiously welcomed this invitation, replying that it was a project requiring careful study which could only be brought about by legal means. This accorded with a cable which the Iraqi Foreign Minister sent to its Cairo Embassy on 3 April saying that Iraq was adopting a 'wait-and-see' attitude towards Damascus and instructing her envoy further to sound out Egyptian opinion and to warn 'irresponsible persons' in the Arab League secretariat against interference. This was a clear reference to 'Azzam Pasha, the League's secretary-general. The Iraqi envoy saw the Egyptian Prime Minister and reported back that the Premier wished to assure Nuri that the League secretariat would not be allowed to become 'a Government above Governments' and that the secretary-general would not go to Damascus.

The Egyptian press, stunned by the overthrow of Egypt's ally Quwatli, did not comment on the coup until 2 April, but it then warmly welcomed Za'im's assurances that he would jealously defend Syria's independence. King Faruq sent two envoys to Za'im with verbal messages and joined King Ibn Sa'ud in an appeal on behalf of Quwatli. Ibn Sa'ud also felt it necessary to warn King 'Abdallah, who had greeted the news of the coup somewhat too eagerly, that he would consider any aggression against Syria as an attack on himself. To still the fears of the Egyptian and Saudi sovereigns, Za'im dispatched two of his aides, including his brother-in-law Nazih Fonso, to Riyad on 12 April and Cairo on 13 April with his respects and assurances.

On 9 April Baghdad cabled its Cairo embassy to inquire urgently into the truth of the reports that Egypt intended to recognize the new Damascus regime. The embassy replied on 10 April that the Egyptian Premier had promised to inform other Governments should he decide to recognize Za'im, and suggested a meeting of Arab states to examine the situation in Damascus. Baghdad replied that it would welcome any responsible Egyptian for talks in the Iraqi capital, but the Egyptian Premier begged to be excused, expressing the hope that the two Governments would, nevertheless, remain in contact. While these exchanges were taking place, Za'im continued to probe Iraqi intentions: armistice talks with Israel were due to open on 12 April and he felt in need of support. On 9 April the Iraqi embassy in Damascus reported that Zaʻim wished to conclude a military defence pact immediately, offering to send negotiators to Baghdad for this purpose.

THE NEGOTIATIONS

The Iraq Government decided to send its own team to Damascus and three days later, on 12 April, Colonel ʻAbd al-Mutallib Amin arrived in the Syrian capital and cabled Zaʻim's proposal to his Government that same day. Zaʻim, he reported, wanted the broadcast of a joint statement announcing the conclusion of a Syro-Iraqi pact. Amin had objected that such a declaration would be of little value if unsupported by troops; he explained the need for bases and lines of communication for Iraqi forces in Syria. Zaʻim had then asked for a statement of the maximum help Iraq could give him, with special reference to artillery, armour, anti-tank weapons, and aircraft. Amin asked his Government for detailed instructions so that he could face the Syrians with firm proposals. He stressed the importance of a quick decision in view of the opportunity for an agreement presented by the armistice talks with Israel. A further meeting was held the next day at which the Syrians outlined their detailed requirements and agreed to give Iraqi forces whatever facilities they might need on Syrian soil.

But while these exchanges were in progress, the Iraqi representative in Jeddah reported to Baghdad on 12 April the arrival of envoys from Zaʻim to Ibn Saʻud. The latter, he told his Government, would consider the conclusion of a Syro-Iraqi military or economic agreement as a hostile act directed against Saudi Arabia. He believed this was also the feeling of the Egyptian Government. Sobered by these reports, Baghdad cabled its Damascus embassy to inquire what Zaʻim's attitude would, in fact, be if Egypt and Saudi Arabia opposed the granting of Iraqi aid to Syria. On 13 April Zaʻim sent a mission to Baghdad to lay the draft of a military agreement before the Iraq Government. It provided for common defence against attack from any quarter; immediate co-operation in the event of attack by Israel; a joint command in time of war headed by an officer from the country first attacked; a joint planning staff in peacetime, and so on. In a personal letter to Nuri, Zaʻim called for a quick agreement in the interests of the whole Arab nation.

So far Syria had made all the running. Fertile Crescent unity had long been a slogan in Iraq, but when action was called for the Government seemed overtaken by a sort of paralysis. It was bound by its treaty with Britain; it did not wish to arouse the hostility of Egypt and Saudi Arabia; Nuri did not like Za'im's brusque, unconstitutional procedures; he resented his violent disturbance of the Middle East scene; he probably felt he was too dangerous a man to treat with. All these reservations were made explicit in Nuri's reply to the Syrian proposals which he gave at a meeting with the Syrian envoys on 14 April. He began with an account of the historical connexions between Iraq and Syria and of the assistance Iraq had given Syria since the First World War. He recalled that in 1946 he had discussed with the late Syrian Premier, Sa'dallah al-Jabiri, the possibility of close Iraqi-Syrian co-operation, but that the subject had been dropped because Sa'dallah had not wished to displease Egypt or Ibn Sa'ud. Why, Nuri now inquired suspiciously, had Za'im sent a mission to Cairo and Riyad? He could not consider entering into an agreement with Syria until constitutional government had been restored there. In the meantime there would be no harm in looking into the minutes of his meeting with Sa'dallah which the Syrians would find in their Foreign Ministry archives. As for a military pact, this presupposed a coherent foreign policy. But Syria, until the very recent past, had had no independent foreign policy and had not defined her position with regard to East and West. Perhaps she was trying to come to terms with both or to oppose both. 'As for us', Nuri declared, 'we have a clear foreign policy and we are linked by treaty to Britain. If we wanted to enter into any military pact, we should have to inform the British Government.'[3]

The Syrian envoy, Farid Zayn al-Din, replied reassuringly that it was his Government's view that both countries should adopt the same foreign policy. But Nuri was not to be rushed. The conclusion of any military pact would have to await the clarification of the situation in Syria. In the meantime he was ready to pledge that the Iraqi army would come to Syria's aid in the event of a Zionist attack—without the need for a prior military agreement or indeed for a specific Syrian request. Nuri made it quite clear that Iraq either could not or would not enter into any formal agreement with Za'im, nor would he agree to the joint public statement which Za'im wanted in order to strengthen his position *vis-à-vis* the Israelis at the armis-

tice talks. On that same day, 14 April, Za'im's envoys to Egypt and Saudi Arabia returned to Damascus to report in clear terms that the two kings looked to him to defend Syria's independence against Hashimite encroachment. 'You have taken over from Quwatli a wholly independent Syria', he was cautioned in the Egyptian press; 'watch over that independence'.

FRENCH OBSTRUCTION

In the very first days of the new regime France entered the fray to throw her weight against the Hashimite connexion. Her opposition was to carry great weight, not only on account of the resources she could muster but also because Britain continued after the war to acknowledge her predominance and respect her wishes in Syria. In spite, however, of repeated British assurances of disinterestedness, French policy remained deeply suspicious of Britain and hostile to Arab nationalism. Any Syrian association with a neighbouring Arab state would have meant a move out of a French into a British sphere of influence. France, therefore, opposed Arab unity in general and a union between Syria and Jordan or Iraq in particular. And Britain, in deference to French susceptibilities, could not actively encourage the unionist ambitions of either King 'Abdallah or the Iraqi Regent. No more could she risk incurring the hostility of Arab nationalists by openly opposing all plans of union. She sat on the fence and suffered her ambiguous policy to be misinterpreted on all sides: French suspicions of British motives were not dispelled; the Syrian public believed the Fertile Crescent and Greater Syria plans were no more than a cloak for British imperialism and rejected them accordingly, while those Arab leaders who understood the balance Britain was attempting to strike accused her of bowing to French ambitions and keeping alive the spirit of the Mandate.

On the morrow of the Allied invasion of Syria and Lebanon in the summer of 1941, Britain had been careful to acknowledge the primacy of France's position over that of any other European Power. In the exchange of letters between Mr Oliver Lyttelton, the Minister of State in the Middle East, and General de Gaulle on 15 August 1941—known as the de Gaulle–Lyttelton agreement—Mr Lyttelton wrote:

I am happy to repeat to you the assurance that Great Britain has no interest in Syria or the Lebanon, except to win the war. We have no desire to encroach in any way upon the position of France. Both Free France and

Great Britain are pledged to the independence of Syria and the Lebanon. When this essential step has been taken, and without prejudice to it, we freely admit that France should have the predominant position in Syria and the Lebanon over any other European Power. It is in this spirit that we have always acted.[4]

Mr Churchill repeated these guarantees even more emphatically in the House of Commons on 9 September 1941:

> We have no ambitions in Syria. We do not seek to replace or supplant France, or substitute British for French interests in any part of Syria. We are only in Syria in order to win the war. . . . We recognize that among all the nations of Europe the position of France in Syria is one of special privilege, and that in so far as any European countries have influence in Syria, that of France will be pre-eminent.[5]

But these declarations by the British Government were often disbelieved by the French authorities on the spot who, in spite of General Catroux's proclamation of independence on 8 June 1941, attempted in the last years of the war to reassert their full control over Syria and Lebanon in the face of a politically more progressive British policy towards the Arabs in general. All French fears seemed confirmed when Britain intervened in Syria in May 1945 to separate French and Syrian combatants, thereby ending French military authority there for ever. Nevertheless, the Anglo-French agreement on military evacuation signed on 13 December made a renewed reference to separate spheres of influence: 'Each Government affirms its intention', the agreement states, 'of doing nothing to supplant the interests or responsibilities of the other in the Middle East. . . .'[6] Whether or not Britain gave a further (and yet unpublished) undertaking to recognize France's special interests in independent Syria, she appears to have remained bound after the war not to lend active support to either Baghdad or Amman in a bid to unite with Syria. Indeed, the British Government felt obliged more than once to issue formal denials that it favoured the Greater Syria project, as for instance the statement in the House of Commons by the Minister of State on 14 July 1947, that the Government's attitude on the subject was one of strict neutrality.[7] Anxiety for a treaty with Egypt and the desire not to offend Ibn Sa'ud must have played their part in inclining British officials in this direction.

[4] See Hourani, *Syria and Lebanon*, pp. 244–5.
[5] H. C. Deb., vol. 374, col. 76 (cited ibid. pp. 245–6).
[6] Hurewitz, ii. 258.   [7] Kirk, *Middle East in the War*, p. 34.

France had also been concerned at the extent to which the idea of Arab unity had gained currency in Syria. At the preliminary inter-Arab conversations in Cairo in 1943–4 resulting in the Alexandria Protocol, Syria alone had stood for complete Arab union. France knew that Quwatli was opposed to the Fertile Crescent and Greater Syria schemes but she was unsure of his steadiness, since he had had close contacts with Iraq during the long period of conflict with the Mandatory: he could not in any sense be counted a friend of France. Za'im, on the other hand, had been trained by the French and had served half a lifetime with French forces. In an interview with the Beirut newspaper al-Hayat[8] after Za'im's overthrow, Amir 'Adil Arslan threw further light on the Colonel's relations with the French. They continued, he said, to think of Syria and Lebanon as falling within their sphere of influence—with the tacit agreement of Britain and the United States. Moreover French influence remained strong in some military circles in Syria among those men who had been brought up by the French; Za'im himself remained attached to the French connexion in spite of his wartime imprisonment and spoke French in preference to Arabic. The Syrian army had originally been equipped with French arms and he could not look elsewhere for spares and renewals. According to Arslan, France attempted to improve her relations with Syria in the last days of Quwatli's regime but made still greater efforts when Za'im came to power.[9] The French ambassador called on him daily and France spared no efforts to induce other countries to recognize his regime. Many of the men who had lent their support to the French authorities under the Mandate emerged once more and, Arslan maintained, Za'im even entered into secret treaty negotiations with Paris.

THE TURNING-POINT

By the end of the second week of April 1949 Za'im had received such assurances of support from France and had been so much impressed by Saudi and Egyptian arguments that his interest in an agreement with Iraq had slumped. When, therefore, on 16 April Nuri al-Sa'id decided to journey to Damascus himself, at the head of a high-level Iraqi team which included the Ministers of Defence and Foreign Affairs and the Chief of Staff, he found Za'im somewhat

---

[8] al-Hayat (Beirut), 20 Aug. 1949.
[9] On 21 March France lifted her Palestine truce embargo on sales of arms to Syria and Lebanon.

less assiduous and eager than he had expected. That same morning Za'im formed his first cabinet with himself as Vice-Premier and Foreign Minister. At the full-dress meeting of the Syrian and Iraqi delegations (with Nuri in general's uniform with revolver belt) Nuri's tone tended to be patronizing. The interests of sister Syria were never far from his thoughts. He wished to assure Za'im that in the event of a Zionist attack he could count on Iraqi help. But, he soon added, if Za'im's aims were wider in scope than the receipt of military aid, Iraq wished to know in which direction this would lead them. The treaty of alliance with Britain, although it would expire in a few years, was still binding. If Za'im wanted a common defence pact, Britain would have to be consulted.[10]

Nuri then broached his favourite speculative theme. The world was changing fast; they were approaching a time when it might be possible to conclude not just a bilateral agreement between two countries but a defence pact embracing most, if not all, the countries of the Near East. Such a pact would provide the very guarantees Za'im was seeking. He reviewed once more the history of Iraqi-Syrian relations, referred to his 1946 talks with Sa'dallah al-Jabiri, and concluded by saying that if Iraq were to take the initiative to bring about closer ties her intentions might be misunderstood. Iraq was waiting for sister Syria to consider the time ripe to put forward proposals for examination. Iraq would look into every suggestion made. Common defence against the Jews need no longer preoccupy them but it would be best to defer all other questions to a later occasion.

Za'im's reply to this wary and prudent speech was crisp and brief. He was quite ignorant of Nuri's proposals to Sa'adallah but if they were in the Foreign Ministry files he would take a look at them. The Jews had, in the meantime, stopped their attacks on Syrian positions and 'we fear them no longer'. 'I will not hide from you', he added, 'that we have received arms . . . and will receive more, so that any Jewish attack will cost them dear.' He mentioned the need for an air force; the importance of building a railway from Homs to Deir ez-Zor for strategic purposes; the possibility of getting Turkey to join in the defence of the whole area, and the need for co-operation against Communism. He did not press the question of a defence pact.

A member of the Iraqi delegation which accompanied Nuri to Damascus relates that, as they filed into the conference chamber,

---

[10] Iraq, *Majra al-hawadith.*

Nuri grasped Za'im by the wrist and led him into an adjoining room. When the two men reappeared Za'im looked pale and angry. It was generally believed that Nuri had used threatening language. To him Za'im was a dangerous adventurer who had thrown open the door to revolution in the Middle East. It was not surprising that he returned empty-handed to Baghdad on 17 April. The following day 'Azzam Pasha, the Arab League secretary-general and Iraq's *bête noire*, flew to Damascus to complete the weaning of Za'im away from the Hashimites—in spite of earlier Egyptian assurances to Iraq that he would not be allowed to interfere.

The real turning-point in the tug of war between Iraq and Egypt came three days later, on 21 April, when Za'im made his secret visit to King Faruq at his Inshas estate, arriving in time for a gay informal breakfast. The king was as lavish and open-handed as Nuri had been darkly circumspect. By lunchtime, after several hours of talks, Za'im was completely won over, declaring that he adored everything Egyptian. Arm in arm, the king and the colonel toured the royal plantations before an Egyptian Spitfire escort started Za'im on his return flight. That evening Damascus radio interrupted its programmes to announce the visit. Egyptian opinion was jubilant: it was clear that Syria was safely back in the Arab League fold under Egyptian control. Barely had Za'im set foot in Damascus than, still tingling from his contact with royalty, he telegraphed his profound gratitude for 'the interest which Your Majesty deigned to show in the future of Syria'. He returned from Egypt a changed man, his Foreign Minister, Amir 'Adil Arslan, later declared,[11] believing that the world lay within his grasp. Within a few days of the visit, Egypt, Saudi Arabia, and Lebanon had recognized Za'im's regime, Quwatli was released from prison (somewhat hurt at the speed with which Egypt had come to terms with Za'im) and rejoined his family before going into exile; Iraq and Jordan were discomfited and the Jordanian Premier, Tawfiq Abu'l-Huda, journeyed to Baghdad to take council with Nuri. But they had lost a decisive round and blamed each other for it.

Za'im, meanwhile, was becoming more forthright.

My journey to Cairo [he declared on 26 April] was an unpleasant surprise to Jordan. The Lords of Baghdad and Amman believed that I was about to offer them the crown of Syria on a silver platter, but they were disappointed. The Syrian Republic wants neither Greater Syria nor

---

[11] *al-Hayat* (Beirut), 22 Aug. 1949.

Fertile Crescent. We will pit our forces against these two projects of foreign inspiration. To counter the military measures taken by the Amman Government,[12] we have concentrated our forces at the frontier and have decided that all persons entering into contact with the Government of Jordan or travelling to that country will be charged before a military court for the crime of high treason and will be sentenced to death. We have decided to call up new drafts of 20,000 men. We are awaiting the immediate arrival of large quantities of arms, ammunition, and equipment of all kinds. Our army will soon be second only to that of Turkey in the Middle East. Our air force will surpass the Israeli and Turkish air forces combined. We will tolerate no threat or pressure, whether it come from Iraq, Jordan, or any other country. . . . As for Jordan, which is and remains a Syrian province, she will sooner or later rejoin the mother country and become the 10th *muhafaza* of the Syrian Republic. It must not be thought that certain foreign powers support the projects of Greater Syria or Fertile Crescent: we have assurances that Great Britain is for the *status quo* and that France and the United States would never accept a change in the situation.[13]

The same day Za'im closed the frontier with Jordan for twenty-four hours in protest against 'Abdallah's 'aggressiveness', while Amir 'Adil Arslan quotes him as saying 'I shall hang anyone who mentions Iraq in this country'.

One myth which the Iraqi-Syrian exchanges explode—but which is widely believed to this day in the Middle East—is that Nuri, and his British allies, toiled sleeplessly for union with Syria. The record shows that, confronted with a situation where prompt action might have produced a merger, Nuri dragged his feet, and Britain did nothing to encourage him. French pretensions were no doubt another major obstacle. Ibn Sa'ud checked his Hashimite rival when he could, while Egypt—under Faruq, as later under 'Abd al-Nasir,— intervened decisively when the Arab League formula guaranteeing her leading role in Arab affairs was threatened.

---

[12] Amir 'Adil Arslan said later (although to a pro-Iraqi newspaper) that the only source for Za'im's 'dangerous accusations' of Iraqi and Jordanian troop concentrations was his own fertile imagination (ibid. 22 Aug. 1949).
[13] *Journal d'Égypte* (Cairo), 27 Apr. 1949.

7

Zaʻim's Rule

ZAʻIM'S rule lasted a brief four and a half months of 1949, but he left a permanent mark on Syria and provided a model for future military dictators. He reinforced and re-equipped the army and restored its morale, bringing the police and *gendarmerie* under its control: it could no longer escape its political role. The civil service was pruned and officials were made to choose within ten days between private business interests and the public service; the statutes and curricula of Damascus university were brought up to date; twelve bakers convicted of selling poor-quality bread were flogged in front of their shops; numerous public-works projects were planned and agreements ratified for the passage of oil pipelines through Syria; literate women were, for the first time, given the vote; the use of such titles as Bey and Pasha was banned; the process of breaking up the fossilized *awqaf* or religious endowments and of substituting modern civil, criminal, and commercial codes for the Muslim *shariʻa* law was taken an important stage farther; new provincial governors were appointed with both civil and military authority.

These men were sent to their posts in army planes, welcomed with parades and escorted about their duties by squads of military police on motor-cycles. In all these changes the public took pride, as evidence of a decisive new start in national life. . . .[1]

Zaʻim shocked Damascus society out of its stuffy puritanism. He let it be known that he disapproved of traditional Arab clothing and headgear, and the streets blossomed with a curious collection of aged European hats; women appeared more freely in public and danced to American tunes in night-clubs which, in Syria at this time, as is sometimes the case in iron curtain countries, gave a clue to the tone of public life and to the nature of the regime.

But as a political tactician he was less successful; power went to his head. Concerned from the start with the illegitimacy of his regime,

[1] Alford Carleton, 'The Syrian Coups d'Etat of 1949', *MEJ*, iv (1950), p. 5.

his desire was to become President and stand as an equal beside the kings and Heads of State with whom he now had to deal. This ambition and his ardent temperament led him successively to alienate his major supporters. He was subject, Amir 'Adil Arslan explained, to attacks when he would lose all logic.[2] To his craving for the Presidency was attributed his dissolution of political parties in May 1949, and his eagerness to conclude an armistice with Israel which would allow him to withdraw the army from the front to strengthen his position at home; the same reasoning was thought to lie behind his accusations that Jordan and Iraq were threatening Syria's frontiers. Gradually he moved into the rarified air of untrammelled personal authority and broke with the handful of activist officers with whom he had planned and carried out his *putsch*.

As soon as his hostility towards Iraq became plain, the People's Party which had welcomed his accession moved into opposition. Faydi al-Atasi, a People's Party member of the cabinet which Za'im had formed on 16 April, resigned three days later. The Ba'th, in turn, protested at the restriction of the press and at the growing army of police informers. In a memorandum to Za'im dated 24 May 1949, the Ba'th warned him against falling into the error of previous regimes by taking sides in inter-Arab disputes and requested a meeting to state their views on constitutional questions and workers' rights. Za'im replied by jailing Michel 'Aflaq as well as the People's Party leaders, Rushdi al-Kikhia, Nazim al-Qudsi, and Faydi al-Atasi. With the approach of the presidential elections and referendum set for 25 June, Iraq and Jordan renewed their press and radio assaults on Za'im, and Nuri sent Muzahim al-Pachachi, a former Iraqi Premier, to Egypt in a vain attempt to 'dissipate misunderstandings' and to induce the Egyptians not to recognize the Syrian poll. These manoeuvres only sent Za'im flying once more into the arms of Faruq and Ibn Sa'ud: on 16 June he announced that he counted for support on a Cairo–Damascus–Riyad triangle. 'King Faruq and myself', Ibn Sa'ud declared, 'will not remain with arms folded in the face of attacks on Syria.'[3]

Za'im was the only presidential candidate and was duly elected by an overwhelming majority.[4] On the same day, 25 June, he gave up the

---

[2] *al-Hayat* (Beirut), 23 Aug. 1949.
[3] *Journal d'Égypte* (Cairo), 19 June 1949.
[4] Number of eligible voters: 816,321; number of votes cast: 730,731; number of votes for Za'im: 726,116 (*al-Nasr* (Damascus), 27 June 1949). The ballot introduced a literacy test in that voters had to write the name of the President.

premiership and called on Muhsin al-Barazi to form a government. Barazi was a French-educated lawyer who before the coup had been Quwatli's faithful prompter, speech-writer, confidant, and senior aide at the Presidency. It was later rumoured that he had at the same time been treacherously in contact with Za'im. The two men had worked together in the disturbed months which preceded the Palestine War, Barazi as Minister of the Interior and Za'im as Director of Public Security. Like Za'im, Barazi was of Kurdish origin, and their enemies maintained that he was driven to betray Quwatli by dreams of using Za'im to set up an independent Kurdish state. But these fantasies, if they were ever entertained, were evidently quickly dispelled by the realities of office.

Barazi framed the four questions put to the electorate on the ballot paper at the referendum[5] and defended the constitutional validity of the procedure. His critics called him the 'Mufti of the Republic' because, under Za'im as under Quwatli, his role was to provide the legal whitewash.[6] His name was also linked with some of the less reputable dealings whereby, in the last extravagant weeks of the regime, state funds were said to have been diverted to Za'im's private account. A natural consequence of Za'im's predilection for Barazi was to alienate Hawrani—the sworn enemy of the Barazi family in Hama.

On his election, Za'im made his international alignments clear. If the League could not be strengthened to stand up to Israel, 'I would then envisage an alliance with Egypt, Saudi Arabia, and Lebanon', he told a visiting correspondent.[7]

[5] a. Do you agree to the direct election by the people, and by secret ballot, of the President of the Republic from among all Syrians enjoying their civil rights and at least forty years of age when presenting their candidacy; that his election be declared by the Council of Ministers, and that the period of office be fixed by the constitution?
 b. Do you agree to vesting power in the President to prepare the new constitution on the basis of a legislative decree adopted by the Council of Ministers within a period not exceeding four months subsequent to his election, provided that the new constitution be ratified by the people in a referendum or by parliament?
 c. Do you agree that the President of the Republic be empowered, pending the preparation and ratification of the constitution, to issue legislative decrees, including those of a constitutional character, which are adopted by the Council of Ministers?
 d. Do you agree that the prerogative granted to the President specified in question (c) will have retroactive effect on all legislative decrees issued since 30 March 1949?
[6] Amir 'Adil Arslan in *al-Hayat* (Beirut), 24 Aug. 1949.
[7] Richard Didier of the *Gazette de Lausanne*, 1 July 1949.

From the very first day my relations with King Faruq have been more than excellent. ... As for Iraq, I am and shall remain categorically opposed to the establishment of a Greater Syria. Nuri Pasha thought to frighten me with troop concentrations on the Syrian border. He has been compelled to withdraw them. If he should again wish to intimidate me ... he must know that the Iraqi people and army have their heart with Syria and not with him.

France, he declared, was a friendly Power and he foresaw a new era of understanding between Paris and Damascus. He hoped the United States would help Syria with her reconstruction. As for Britain, she must adopt a frank attitude towards Syria: 'We cannot hide from her that we will in no event accept the creation of a Greater Syria and that we shall fight everything that is hatched in the Middle East under the aegis of the Fertile Crescent.' He distinguished between the Soviet Union and the local Communist Party, warning the latter that he would give it no quarter.

But the coherence of this programme was rapidly undermined by the vagaries of the man. A decree issued on the eve of the referendum specified that the Head of State, if a military man, would assume the rank of Marshal. When he donned his glorious uniform and grasped his new \$3,000 baton,[8] Za'im's good sense appears to have deserted him. He was seen strutting in front of mirrors in his residence and was overheard telling his wife: 'One day you shall be queen.' The Premier was sent to Egypt to confer on Faruq, at his summer court at Alexandria, Syria's highest decoration, a jewel created for the occasion by Paris craftsmen, while the head of his *cabinet militaire* was ordered to draw up plans for a private bodyguard of Yugoslav Muslims swearing allegiance only to himself.[9]

To seize power, Za'im had harnessed the resentment of a group of nationalist officers, convincing them that only a military Government could carry on the war against the Jews. 'Palestine' had been the magic slogan with which he had won the dissident army to his cause. The eagerness with which he then sought to conclude an armistice came as a shock to his entourage. Formal talks with Israel began on 12 April and, according to Amir 'Adil Arslan, would have ended in an agreement that same month had not Fawzi Selu, the chief Syrian negotiator, held out for better terms than those Za'im was

---

[8] A large-sized rolling-pin in gold and green velvet which may be examined at the military museum, Damascus.
[9] Gen. Shawkat Shuqayr to the author, Beirut, 18 Dec. 1960.

ready to settle for.[10] Syrian forces had occupied three small areas on the Palestine side of the frontier in a region awarded to Israel by the General Assembly's resolution of November 1947. The most important of these areas, which Syria insisted on retaining, lay on both banks of the Jordan below Lake Hula. To break the deadlock, the Acting Mediator proposed that this area, together with some adjacent land controlled by Israel, should become a demilitarized zone, supervised by a Mixed Armistice Commission under a United Nations chairman. This solution was finally embodied in the armistice agreement signed on 20 July 1949. Persistently throughout the negotiations Za'im manoeuvred secretly for a high-level meeting with an Israeli leader, a suggestion which horrified his aides, to whom it seemed like a formal recognition of Israel. According to Arslan, Za'im proposed to meet Ben-Gurion himself, but the Israelis replied by suggesting a meeting at Foreign Minister level.[11] The armistice was, however, signed without recourse to any such expedient.

One by one Za'im severed his links with the forces which had brought him to power. His alliance with the French was too blatant and the French ambassador too frequent a visitor at the presidential palace for a country so recently freed from French rule. Muslim opinion, mobilized by the Syrian branch of the Muslim Brotherhood which was increasingly influential in the late 1940s, denounced his reforms as secular and foreign-inspired. For garrison duties in the main towns he appeared to rely unduly on Circassian and Kurdish units, relegating the purely Arab troops to the Palestine front. His own Kurdish ancestry was now remembered, enabling Arab newspapers outside Syria to berate in the name of Arabism and Islam the 'Kurdo-military republic' set up in Syria and to predict for it a fate such as befell Hitler in Europe.[12] Za'im's rapprochement with Turkey was not universally approved by a public still indignant at the loss of Alexandretta to Turkey ten years earlier. Nor did the young officers welcome the arrival on 20 July of a Turkish military mission, led by a former Chief of the General Staff, whom Za'im had invited to reorganize the Syrian army.

Za'im's rule awakened opinion to the dangers of military dictatorship, but the army in his time became too powerful and too committed to a political role ever again to fall wholly under civilian control. Nevertheless he swept away much dead wood from Syrian public

----

[10] *al-Hayat* (Beirut), 18 Aug. 1949.   [11] Ibid., 19 Aug. 1949.
[12] *al-Nahda* (Amman), 27 June 1949.

life; he spoke a language of reform and made promises which, even
if unrealized, tended to change the nature of the support on which
any future regime had eventually to depend. He admired Atatürk,
but was too indisciplined, impulsive and *naïf* a politician to build on
the original momentum which carried him to power. In a very few
weeks he made many enemies: Quwatli and his friends whom he had
displaced; Akram al-Hawrani and his officer friends; the Ba'th and
its student following; the People's Party and its bourgeois membership; all those friendly to the Hashimites or to Britain, or bought with
Iraqi gold, or distrusting the rise of French and Egyptian influence,
or resentful of Za'im's monopoly of power and the spoils of office,
now wished his downfall.

Za'im had good intentions but poor equipment or, as Bismarck
said of the Italians—a good appetite but very poor teeth. He saw
himself as a soldier-reformer, injecting his demoralized countrymen
with his own vigour and building a new and gleaming society on the
débris of the old regime. But to others he seemed a fair specimen
of what Professor Denis Brogan has called the 'unidea'ed' politician,
the pursuer of power for its sake or for its fruits—a type not confined
to Arab politics. Part of the interest of his career lies in the fact that
this noisy and inefficient dictator, lacking a clear view of social or
political organization, concluded an alliance in the last weeks of his
life with one of the rare 'thinkers' in Arab politics, a Lebanese
visionary and revolutionary called Antun Sa'ada. The relationship
was ultimately fatal to both of them.

8

Antun Sa'ada and his Party

ANTUN Sa'ada's father, Dr Khalil Sa'ada, was a member of the Greek Orthodox community in Lebanon who went to Egypt at the close of the nineteenth century where he is best remembered as the author of a two-volume English-Arabic dictionary. At the turn of the century he emigrated to Latin America, taking with him a belief in Syrian nationalism which had been a leading political idea in Beirut in the 1890s. He started a magazine in Brazil in which his son, born in 1904, made his first experiments in journalism.

Antun came to the Near East as a young man in the late 1920s and worked on the Damascus newspaper *al-Ayyam*. But Syria under the French was suffocating and intellectually poverty-stricken, so he soon moved to the more congenial atmosphere of Beirut. He had no money or profession, and supported himself meagrely by giving private lessons in German. The American University of Beirut was an intellectual centre of the town and Sa'ada, although never formally attached to the college, often found his way to the staff common room where tea was served at 4 p.m. He wore a full beard like a priest and attracted a certain amount of ridicule on account of his appearance and the obstinate insistence with which he defended his views. He talked for hours in the common room, went swimming with the students, and gathered his first disciples.

On 16 November 1932 Sa'ada founded a secret society of five, bound by a solemn oath of loyalty to himself, which he called *al-Hizb al-Suri al-Qawmi*, the Syrian National Party, but known more widely by its French name of Parti Populaire Syrien, or PPS.[1] Some months later, detecting signs of 'anti-party' activity among his confederates, he dissolved the group, reforming it on the same day

---

[1] *Qawm* means 'people' and *qawmiya* was a term used to mean 'nationhood' or 'nationalism'. But the French authorities mistranslated *qawmi* as 'populaire', so that the party came to be known as the Parti Populaire Syrien. The word 'Social' was later added to the party's name so that its official designation became the Syrian Social Nationalist Party.

with only two members. By 1935 it had overspilled the university campus and recruited several thousand devoted followers in Syria and Lebanon into a rigidly hierarchical regional organization under Sa'ada's absolute authority. It emerged that year from underground, held its first plenary conference, and immediately engaged the attention of the French mandatory authorities. On 10 December 1935 Sa'ada and other party leaders were arrested and jailed.

What were Sa'ada's views?

At the outset of my nationalist consciousness [he wrote later], when I began to give serious thought to the revival of our nation against the background of the irresponsible political movements rampant in its midst, it became immediately clear to me that our most urgent problem was the determination of our national identity and our social reality. . . . I became convinced that the starting point of every national endeavour must be the raising of this fundamental question: *Who are we?* This was the question which preoccupied my mind from the very beginning of my social-nationalist thinking. . . . After extensive research I arrived at the following conclusion: *We are Syrians and we constitute a distinct national entity.*[2]

The first principle of the party was then formulated as follows: 'Syria belongs to the Syrians who constitute a nation complete in itself'.

But this doctrine of Syrian nationalism was embellished with a good deal of metaphysics: Sa'ada spoke of the 'general will of the Syrian nation' seeking Freedom, Duty, Discipline, and Power; he preached the existence of an 'organic correlation' between the nation and its geographical homeland; of the 'organic unity' of Syrian society, based not on race or blood, but the result of the

long history of all the people who have settled in this land, inhabited it, interacted and finally become fused into one people. This process started with the peoples of the neolithic age . . . and continued with the Akkadians, Canaanites, Chaldaeans, Assyrians, Aramaens, Ammorites and Hittites.[3]

The party's fifth principle defines the territory in which this society took root:

The Syrian homeland is that geographic environment in which the Syrian nation evolved. It has natural boundaries which separate it from other countries extending from the Taurus range in the north-west and

[2] *The Principles of the Syrian Social Nationalist Party*, by The Leader (n.d.), p. 7.
[3] Ibid. p. 14.

s.s.—6

the Zagros Mountains in the north-east to the Suez Canal and the Red Sea in the south and includes the Sinai Peninsula and the Gulf of Aqaba, and from the Syrian sea (Mediterranean) in the west, including the Island of Cyprus, to the Arch of the Arabian Desert and the Persian Gulf in the east. This region is also called the Syrian Fertile Crescent, the Island of Cyprus being its star.[4]

The homeland and its inhabitants are said to be linked by an 'indissoluble bond'.

The common stocks, Canaanite, Chaldaean, Aramaean, Assyrian, Ammorite, Mitanni, and Akkadian, whose reality and blending are an indisputable historical and scientific fact, constitute the ethnic-psychological-historical-cultural basis, whereas the regions of natural Syria (the Fertile Crescent) constitute the geographic-agricultural-economic-strategic basis of Syria's unity. . . . In short, a remarkable home for a remarkable nation.[5]

Sa'ada expounded his theories at length in a book, *The Rise of Nations*, which he started in prison and published in Beirut in 1938.[6] In it he explores the notion of the collective will of a nation and dismisses language, race, or religion as a proper basis for nationhood; he reiterates that the 'land is the nation' and supports his argument with long digressions into ancient history and numerous quotations from obscure sociological works. The vibrant style, the utter conviction of tone, the learned references, the stringing together of abstract nouns, the appeal to 'sociological facts', the claim to be in possession of truths denied to others, were typical of the man. So also was the violent intolerance towards opponents:

All those who deny that Syria belongs to the Syrians and that the Syrians constitute a nation complete in itself, are guilty of the crime of stripping the Syrians of their right to sovereignty over their own homeland. The Syrian Social Nationalist Party, in the name of the millions of Syrians yearning for freedom and struggling for life and progress, declares such people to be criminals.[7]

One of his disciples, Sami al-Khuri, summarizes his views as follows:

Following certain prehistoric geological upheavals, the earth was divided into a number of distinct geographical zones, inhabited by distinct com-

---

[4] Ibid. p. 22. The 'geographical homeland' as defined by the party in the 1930s made no mention of Cyprus and listed the Tigris as the eastern boundary. It was extended in 1947 to include Cyprus and the whole of Iraq (see A. Sa'ada, *al-Ta'lim al-suriyya al-qawmiyya al-ijtima'iyya*, 4th ed. (1947), p. 18).
[5] *The Principles*, pp. 17 and 23.   [6] Sa'ada, *Nushu' al-umam* (1938), pt. 1.
[7] *The Principles*, p. 9.

munities, geographically independent of each other. . . . In time, man's relationship to the earth became not simply one of habitation but of positive interaction with the natural environment. Man began to leave his mark on nature as well as to be moulded by her. Each geographical zone was distinguished by certain characteristic features. It followed that the interaction between man and nature which took place in each zone differed from community to community. These differences were sharpened by the varied civilizations which sprang up. The result was the growth of special features in each society. Extended and developed in time, these special features came to represent what Sa'ada calls the spirit of a society or a nation. Natural boundaries formed frontiers which prevented the population of each zone from spreading and thus imprinted a single way of life on them. In this way they came to form a single society permeated with the same spirit. This unity of national spirit and its permanent manifestations make up the social unit.[8]

Society', Khuri continues,

in its spirit and characteristics, forms a unit in which we cannot distinguish between the human element—the flesh of the structure—and the land—the base on which the structure is erected. . . . This recognition of the working dynamic of society and its continuity in action is the heart of Sa'ada's belief. . . .[9]

Sa'ada's geographical determinism might be dismissed as an example of that 'half-baked infatuation with general ideas characteristic of young intellectuals in countries remote from centres of civilization'.[10] His pseudo-science cannot have made many converts; few members of his party read his long and abstruse book. But he relied less on argument than on organization. What was attractive was the accent on youth, the rigid discipline, the Fascist conception of the role of the leader, as well as the simple thesis that 'natural Syria' was a great nation which had played, and would play once more, a great role in history. Sa'ada was perhaps the first Arab to produce a wholly indigenous version of the youth formations which flourished in Italy and Germany in the 1930s. From the start, the para-military side of the party assumed great importance. French rule being at its most repressive, it was felt that freedom could be obtained only by force of arms. Sa'ada provided an outlet for the resentment of youth against the Mandate and the compromises of its elders; by insisting on order and discipline, struggle and service, he stiffened its devotion to national ideals.

[8] Sami al-Khuri, *Radd 'ala Sati' al-Husri*, pp. 51–52.   [9] Ibid. p. 57.
[10] Isaiah Berlin, *The Hedgehog and the Fox* (1954), p. 7.

In terms of practical politics, the party stood for the separation of Church and State and the abolition of confessionalism; it opposed all local separatism, including that of the Lebanese: 'The Syrian Social Nationalist cause will not be fulfilled unless the unity of Syria is achieved.'[11] It disputed the thesis that the Arabic language could serve as a basis for nationalism—'The world of the Arabic language is not one nation, just as the world of the English or the Spanish language is not one nation'[12]—or that Islam could fulfil this function —'Religion is not national, it is against nationalism. In both Christianity and Islam all believers are brothers, without difference of race or nationality'.[13] It stood for the abolition of 'feudalism' and for the 'organization of the national economy on a basis of productivity'. But it opposed the growth of trade unions and the notion of class struggle. These principles not unnaturally attracted the hostility of the Communists and of left-wing movements such as the Ba'th; Lebanese nationalists found its views on nationalism too broad, Arab nationalists found them too narrow; to the Mandatory it represented an organized threat to its authority; others found that it too closely resembled European Fascism.

The Ba'th leader Michel 'Aflaq sums it up as follows:

> The whole movement was an odd mixture of modernism, of scientism, with something extremely old, even archaeological; with a resurrection of the local past and grudges a thousand years old. Among the many movements of Arab rebirth, this was one which aborted and lost itself in an unhealthy romanticism, due perhaps to the fact that Sa'ada's mind was directed towards the past. It was also an extreme right-wing movement, preaching a sinister philosophy of order, a synthesis of the interests of employers and employees, deliberately playing down the rights of the working class on the pretext that to acknowledge them would lead to anarchy.[14]

Sa'ada's trial in 1936 created considerable publicity for the party. He was far from penitent: when his name was called out in court as Antoine Sa'ada he gave no reply until 'Antun' had been substituted for the gallicized 'Antoine'. When charged with conspiracy against the state, he threw back at the prosecutor that it was the French themselves who were the conspirators since they had signed the Sykes–Picot Agreement.[15] Later he petitioned the High Commis-

[11] *The Principles*, p. 24.   [12] Sa'ada, *Nushu' al-umam*, p. 173.   [13] Ibid. p. 374.
[14] Michel 'Aflaq to the author, Beirut, 7 Jan. 1961.
[15] Dr 'Abdallah Sa'ada (no relation of Antun), president of the Syrian Social Nationalist Party, to the author, Beirut, 1 Dec. 1960.

sioner for a Syro-Lebanese union which led to renewed repression of the party by the authorities. Towards the end of 1938 he left Lebanon, visited Italy and Germany briefly, and reached South America before the outbreak of war. The French accused him of broadcasting over Radio Berlin during the war and of receiving German subsidies, but the charges remained unproved. Nine years later, on 3 March 1947, he returned to Beirut from Brazil to renew his agitation for a Syrian fatherland. The war had not blunted his enthusiasm; on the contrary, further research into ancient history had convinced him that Cyprus and the whole of Iraq must be included in the homeland, and the party's fifth principle was in consequence duly amended.

Saʿada inspired devotion as probably no other leader in Arab politics has done. Men who knew him at this time describe him as a sort of intellectual dictator: authoritarian, magnetic, immensely fluent, with a brilliant superficial knowledge of a great many subjects. He had strong views and knew where he stood on every single issue; there was no such thing as intellectual freedom in his company and no possibility of convincing him in argument. He gave his disciples no alternatives save conversion or expulsion from the party. Even resignation was not tolerated: Saʿada would issue a pre-dated decree expelling the culprit, an ugly reason would be fabricated and a press campaign launched to blacken his name. But even Saʿada's victims continued to venerate him. If, however, his movement is to be judged by results, it was a failure and his political judgement appears less commanding than his intellect.

Early in June 1949 armed clashes occurred in Beirut between Saʿada's men and their chief local rivals, another para-military body known as the *Phalanges Libanaises*—founded in 1936 by a young and able Maronite, Pierre Jumayyil—self-appointed champions of Lebanese independence in the face of the threat from Saʿada's 'natural Syria'. Saʿada's growing power and militancy were causing the Government concern and it is possible, as the PPS allege, that the authorities deliberately incited the *Phalanges* to launch an armed attack on their newspaper offices and printing works in an attempt to destroy Saʿada. But he fled unhurt from the building and went into hiding. His party offices were then raided by the police, the Government claiming to have seized plans of barracks and public buildings and documents to prove that he was conspiring to seize power with Zionist support. Several arrests were made but Saʿada fled across the frontier to Syria. He now had no alternative but armed revolt.

Za'im's successful *putsch* in Damascus in March 1949 had perhaps spurred Sa'ada to think in terms of seizing power himself in Lebanon as a first step towards his pan-Syrian union. Opposition politicians in Lebanon had traditionally sought support in Damascus against their own Government and Sa'ada made the mistake of taking the same road. He met the Syrian dictator, was befriended and encouraged. Together they reviewed plans for a coup in Lebanon. Each thought he could put the other to work: Za'im saw in Sa'ada an instrument for bringing down the Lebanese Premier and veteran nationalist Riyad al-Sulh, who had been a close friend of Shukri al-Quwatli and whom he suspected of plotting his own downfall. Trouble in Lebanon might give him a pretext to march in. He accordingly offered Sa'ada both men and arms and presented him with a silver pistol in token of his friendship. Sa'ada saw in Za'im a vehicle for his own ideology, to be discarded when the time came to take over Syria. He therefore accepted arms (from the gun-racks of the Syrian *gendarmerie*) but refused the men, not wishing to give Za'im an occasion to dictate terms to him in Lebanon.[16]

In the first week of July his men launched a series of small assaults against isolated police posts in the Lebanese mountains, while he declared war on the Beirut Government from the 'Headquarters of the First Popular Social Revolution'. It was a quixotic enterprise. The party leadership later claimed [17] that these were no more than diversionary tactics to draw off the Lebanese forces so that a massive attack could be delivered elsewhere. But before this feint could be carried out the movement was decapitated.

On the night of 6 July Sa'ada was delivered by the Syrian authorities to two Lebanese envoys, the police chief Amir Farid Shihab and Nur ul-Din Rifa'i, who were believed to have instructions to convey him to the Syro-Lebanese frontier and kill him as he 'attempted to escape'. But reluctant to have Sa'ada's blood on their hands, they agreed to confront the Lebanese Government with its responsibilities and took him under arrest to Beirut. It was decided to interrogate, try, and sentence him on the spot—all of which took place inside twenty-four hours. A military court, sitting *in camera*, convicted him of high treason and he died by firing squad at dawn on 8 July 1949. All Damascus newspapers reproduced a Syrian Government state-

[16] Ibid.   [17] Ibid.

ment to the effect that Sa'ada had been apprehended on Lebanese soil, but this was not believed.

Sa'ada had gambled and lost. Any independent judiciary would have condemned him, but he was not given a free trial or allowed to defend himself. The Government waived normal judicial procedure and cut him down in a moment of panic. The party was dissolved on 16 July and its members were hounded by the police. The exact nature of the bargain whereby Za'im betrayed Sa'ada is still unknown. It has been variously suggested that the Lebanese Premier, Riyad al-Sulh, 'bought' him from Za'im and that Egypt was induced to put pressure on the Syrian dictator to hand him over. It may not have been a coincidence that shortly afterwards Za'im signed an economic agreement with Lebanon ending a long period of dispute. Moreover, had Za'im backed Sa'ada to the end, he would have been forced to intervene directly in Lebanon with possible permanent damage to the delicate political structure of that country. This was a possibility which few of the interested Great Powers could countenance. It may be assumed that they were not unhappy at the destruction of a fanatical right-wing movement which threatened their interests as well as the stability of the area.

Worshipped when alive, Sa'ada was now 'deified'. His betrayal and the swift savagery of the sentence passed on him made him a martyr. He had been ready to face death for his ideas and this caused a great impression. Stirred by the circumstances of his death, by contempt for Za'im and hostility to the Lebanese Government, young Syrians flocked to the party. Its ranks were swollen by refugees from police repression in Lebanon and it also enjoyed considerable support among army officers. But although secular and anti-separatist in its teachings, the movement relied at bottom on confessional and minority support: Christians, Druzes, Kurds, Alawis, and minorities of all sorts, faced with the Sunni Muslim majority, saw a welcome alternative to Arab nationalism in Sa'ada's militant secular pan-Syrianism.

The PPS played a prominent and often violent role in Syrian politics over the next few years, but its strength was often exaggerated outside the country and by western observers inside it. It rarely dared give full and public expression to its central doctrine of a 'Syrian nation'. No political leader or Government in Syria could openly profess any creed but that of Arab nationalism: public opinion would tolerate nothing else. Although running counter to public sentiment, the PPS continued to exist in the shadows by virtue of its good organization as a *parti de cadres*, only flourishing when the political mind of the public was distracted or engaged by other issues. At the moment of Sa'ada's death it probably enjoyed the most genuine current of favourable opinion in its history, comparable only to its revival nine years later during the Lebanese civil war of 1958. On Sa'ada's death, the honorary title of *al-Amina al-ula*[18] was bestowed on his widow, Juliette al-Mir, while effective leadership passed to one of his disciples, Georges 'Abd al-Massih, who rallied the faithful and swore to avenge him.

[18] 'First trustee'.

9

Hinnawi's Counter-Coup

DESPITE its author's failings, Husni al-Za'im's coup d'état sprang from a long accumulation of popular grievances, radically transforming the procedures and principles of Syrian political life. It came as close to an expression of a public judgement on the situation as the poverty of Syrian political thinking and institutions then allowed. No such claim can be made for the cleverly engineered conspiracy which overthrew Za'im five weeks after Sa'ada's execution.

Most sources agree that the Iraq Government, displeased with Za'im's attitude and his pro-Egyptian policy, and impatient to see established in Damascus a government more friendly to itself, was ready to pay to bring him down. Iraq was in touch with a group of Syrian officers and politicians who included the commander of the First Brigade, Colonel Sami al-Hinnawi, his brother-in-law, As'ad Tallas, his second in command, Lieut-Colonel Alam al-Din Qawwas, as well as Captain Muhammad Ma'ruf of Army Intelligence, and a Syrian air force pilot, Captain 'Isam Mraywad, who had a plane standing by to fly the conspirators to Baghdad in case of failure. If Hinnawi was Iraq's choice to overthrow Za'im, it was a bad one. He commanded the main armed force in southern Syria and therefore had the physical means to carry out a coup, but he had none of the qualities required to help him to remain in power and he never assumed effective political leadership of the revolt. He may have been the unwitting agent of Iraqi ambitions and of Za'im's other enemies inside Syria.

The Socialist leader Akram al-Hawrani had his own reasons for planning Za'im's downfall. He and his officer friends had been Za'im's earliest and most effective supporters, but they had been driven into opposition by the dictator's alliance with the Barazi clan—Hawrani's traditional enemies in Hama. Za'im suspected Hawrani's army friends—and principally Colonel Bahij Kallas and Major

Adib al-Shishakli—of disloyalty and dismissed Shishakli from the army early in August 1949.

The only conspirator to leave a written record of the events, Lieutenant Fadlallah Abu Mansur,[1] alleges direct Iraqi complicity but his own role in the plot was only that of an executioner at the end of a long chain of command so that his account is of greater interest on the unfolding of the coup than on its preparation. He was selected to pull the trigger because he too had his own reasons for killing Za'im: he was a member of the PPS and a devoted follower of Sa'ada. He had, moreover, two other qualifications for the task: he commanded an armoured car company of Syria's First Brigade which held the Syro-Israeli armistice line within easy reach of the capital. He was also a member of the warlike and separatist Druze community in southern Syria which was traditionally faithful to Hashimite Amman.

When planning his own coup some months earlier, Za'im had secretly met the Druze notable Hasan al-Atrash, who had promised him Druze support against Quwatli,[2] but once in power Za'im had veered towards Egypt and Saudi Arabia and had lost Druze allegiance. Now, suspecting the Druze of conspiring against him in league with the Hashimites and the People's Party, Za'im sent strong forces to garrison the Jabal Druze and intimidate its inhabitants. Both Fadlallah Abu Mansur and his superior officer Major Amin Abu Assaf, the armoured battalion commander who was also a Druze, saw in this move a threat to their homes and families. They were further alarmed when Za'im ordered the armoured battalion to proceed to the Jabal and place itself at the disposal of the local garrison commander, Major Husni Jarras. This they interpreted as a threat to their commands.

Hasan al-Atrash later related that he met Hawrani at this time, who proposed that Za'im should be eliminated and that Druze officers should effect this.

I disagreed [Hasan al-Atrash said], arguing that it would be enough to arrest and depose him. But Hawrani went behind my back and secured the co-operation of a number of Druze officers, most of whom had PPS connexions. Being both Druze and PPS enthusiasts, they thus had two reasons for seeking revenge.[3]

Apart from these specific enemies there was besides a genuine current of revulsion against Za'im among nationalist officers for

---

[1] Abu Mansur, p. 83.
[2] Hasan al-Atrash to the author, Beirut, 21 Oct. 1960.   [3] Ibid.

deviating from the reformist aims of the revolution, and against his Prime Minister, Muhsin al-Barazi, who was blamed for leading him astray.

Za'im's order to the armoured battalion to proceed to the Jabal Druze drove the conspirators to action: if they allowed the armour to pass outside their control they were doomed. To gain time, Colonel Hinnawi moved the column to Qatana, within twenty miles of Damascus, on the pretext that the armoured cars, recently withdrawn from the front, needed servicing. A week later, a few hours before dawn on 14 August 1949, the column moved on the capital to re-enact the *coup de force* which had brought Za'im to power four and a half months earlier. Small detachments of two or three vehicles made for the houses of the Prime Minister, the military police chief, Major Ibrahim al-Husayni, the army, *gendarmerie* and police headquarters, the telephone exchange, radio station, and central bank. Lieutenant Fadlallah Abu Mansur led a task force of six armoured cars through the silent streets to the presidential residence; disarming a motor-cycle patrol he deployed his troops around the building. The Circassian guard commander had been bribed to be absent and his men surrendered without resistance. Fadlallah shot his way in and confronted Za'im in pyjamas in the hall. He struck him in the face and, significantly, charged him with the crime of betraying Antun Sa'ada. Za'im was bundled into an armoured car and taken to a prearranged rendezvous where he was joined some little time later by Muhsin al-Barazi, who had been arrested at the same time. Captain Mraywad then informed Fadlallah that the High Command had sentenced Za'im and Barazi to death and ordered him to carry out the sentence on the spot. They were then shot, and the news of the coup was announced to the public at seven that morning.

RAPPROCHEMENT WITH IRAQ

The immediate effect of Hinnawi's *putsch* was to put Syria back into play in the inter-Arab game and to reopen the debate on her international alignments which Za'im had momentarily closed by his hostility to Jordan and Iraq and his understanding with Egypt and France. The late summer and autumn of 1949 saw a further development of the trends already noticed in the first weeks of Za'im's rule and clarified the motives and interests of the principal parties concerned. Some of these were betrayed in the immediate reactions to the coup: King 'Abdallah and Nuri al-Sa'id sent congratulations as

well as emissaries to the new colonel in Damascus; Egypt heard the
news of the Marshal-President's assassination with consternation and
the court went into mourning for three days; Tass and Radio Moscow
reported that the 'War Council which tried and condemned Za'im
included British officers', while the usually responsible *Le Monde*
attributed the coup to the 'clan of Stirling, Frere, Spears, Glubb and
company for whom a truly national regime in Syria is an anomaly
which must be removed . . .'[4]—all British officials concerned with
the area.

On the morning of 14 August Colonel Hinnawi's Higher Military
Council issued a communiqué accusing the 'tyrant Za'im and his
servile clique' of having delivered the country 'to anarchy and abuse',
of having conducted a foreign policy 'offensive to certain Arab neighbours and promoting a return of the supporters of the Mandate', of
having falsified the referendum returns, of establishing a police
regime and of plundering the state treasury. Hinnawi was a simple
soldier with few political ambitions who had served without distinction in the Ottoman army and with the *Troupes spéciales*. His first
move was to lift the ban on political parties (with the exception of the
Communists and the right-wing Socialist Co-operative Party) and to
hand over power to 'loyal and independent patriots'.

The army which had, with Za'im's help, escaped from civilian
control knew how to unseat governments but had not yet acquired
the self-confidence and political skill to enable it to take its place in
the political arena as a powerful independent force. When it was not
the unwitting instrument of forces inside and outside the country, it
appears to have conceived of its role as a sort of extra-political
guardian of the nation's vital interests. It was not long to be so
modest. One of the dominant themes of the next few years was the
contest for power between the army and the divided politicians who,
seeking friendships in the army to use against their civilian rivals,
only speeded their own surrender of day-to-day decision-making to
the ever more ambitious and domineering officers.

This, however, was not the case with Hinnawi. He announced the
army's retirement from politics and called on the veteran Hashim
al-Atasi, the finest symbol of Syria's struggle against the French
Mandate, to form a Government[5] in which the People's Party

---

[4] *Le Monde*, 16 Aug. 1949.
[5] Prime Minister, Hashim al-Atasi; Foreign Affairs, Nazim al-Qudsi (PP); Nat.
Economy, Faydi al-Atasi (PP); Interior, Rushdi al-Kikhia (PP); Finance, Khalid
al-'Azm (Ind.); Justice, Sami Kabbara (Ind.); Agriculture, Akram al-Hawrani

immediately secured the key posts: Rushdi al-Kikhia at the Ministry of the Interior, Nazim al-Qudsi at the Foreign Ministry, and Faydi al-Atasi at the Ministry of National Economy. The B'ath leader Michel 'Aflaq was given the Ministry of Education in recognition of his increasing hold over the student body, while Akram al-Hawrani, whose harnessing of the discontented peasantry had made him a powerful man in north-central Syria, became Minister of Agriculture. Some of Hinnawi's army friends, whom Za'im had forcibly retired, were reinstated, such as Adib al-Shishakli, who was given the important First Brigade command. The Independent Khalid al-'Azm became Finance Minister. The National Party, poorly represented in the cabinet by the Minister of State, 'Adil al-'Azmeh, was not ready to make a come-back. Its old leaders, Quwatli and Mardam Bey, were discredited and abroad; those remaining in Syria, such as 'Abd al-Rahman Kayyali and Sabri al-'Asali, had no great following. Moreover, the party as a whole was too closely identified with those pro-Egyptian, anti-Hashimite tendencies against which the planners of Hinnawi's coup had rebelled. Early in September 1949 a new electoral law[6] was published granting the franchise to all men and women over 18 (although women had to hold a primary-school certificate to be eligible) and elections for a Constituent Assembly were announced for mid-November. The Atasi Ministry declared itself to be a provisional Government with the sole mission of restoring constitutional life.

The People's Party now tasted power for the first time: it controlled the Presidency and dominated the cabinet; it had been given office by army *putschists* overtly favourable to Iraq; As'ad Tallas, the influential brother-in-law of Colonel Hinnawi, became Under-Secretary for Foreign Affairs and actively sought an agreement with Baghdad, while, to spur quick and decisive action, protagonists of union in both Iraq and Syria had before them the dismal results of procrastination and excessive caution afforded by the Syrian-Iraqi negotiations in the first weeks of Za'im's rule. The pro-Iraqi trend was, moreover, to be reinforced from an unexpected direction: on 29 September the National Party, hitherto fiercely hostile to both Fertile Crescent and

---

(non-party); Education, Michel 'Aflaq (Ba'th); Defence, Gen. 'Abdallah 'Atfi; Public Works, Majd al-Din al-Jabiri (Ind.); Ministers of State, 'Adil al-'Azmeh (NP) and Fath Allah Asyun (PP).
[6] The law provided for a Chamber of 108 deputies each representing 30,000 citizens and comprising 86 Muslim deputies, 15 Christians, 1 Jew, and 6 tribal representatives.

Greater Syria, issued a manifesto calling for union with Iraq—a sudden volte-face which looked like a piece of calculated cynicism on the part of Sabri al-'Asali designed to steal the clothes of the People's Party and profit by a movement which then appeared to enjoy popular support.

With the ground so prepared and the public fully alerted by a grand debate in the press on the possibility of a rapprochement with Iraq, the climax was provided by the Iraqi Regent himself, Prince 'Abd ul-Ilah, the man whose ambition to revive the throne of Syria provided much of the drive for union from the Iraqi side. Returning from London to Baghdad on 5 October, he landed at Damascus and spent an hour and a half at the airport, which was bright with the flags of Syria and Iraq and loud with the two national anthems. In addition to the Prime Minister, Atasi, his cabinet, and Colonel Hinnawi, he was also received by Faris al-Khuri and Sabri al-'Asali, who handed him a copy of the National Party's new policy statement in favour of Iraq. 'Abd ul-Ilah made no official statement but it was widely believed that his visit was intended to test public opinion on the union issue. 'The Regent', as the People's Party leader, Nazim al-Qudsi later remarked bitterly, 'believed in a policy of *mazahir* or show; he thought he could rally the Syrians just by appearing in their midst'.[7]

The debate on relations with Iraq continued to dominate all other issues in the month before the 15 November elections but the cabinet, internally divided and subject to conflicting external pressures, lapsed into indecision. 'My Government', the aged Premier repeated, 'is purely transitional. It cannot commit the country to any long-term policy which is likely to have a decisive effect on its future.' Only a properly elected parliament, representing the will of the people, could pronounce on the project.

Opponents of the union meanwhile mobilized their forces. Within the cabinet 'Aflaq and Hawrani, faced with the pro-Iraqi tendencies of the majority People's Party, formed a two-man opposition. 'Aflaq said later:

Rushdi al-Kikhia at the Ministry of Interior attacked us whenever he could. I am sure he rigged the November elections. At all events I was not elected outright but was placed *en ballotage*[8] after the first round when I

---

[7] Nazim al-Qudsi to the author, Aleppo, 3 Nov. 1960.
[8] A candidate who did not obtain the required proportion of votes in the first round could be elected on the second ballot, which was decided by simple majority. Between the two ballots the candidate was described as *en ballotage*.

thought it best to withdraw. Hawrani only won in Hama with the help of his officer friends. An anti-Iraqi group which arose in the army at about this time set itself to discredit the People's Party with all the means at its disposal. It included some officers who adopted this course out of conviction; others bought over by such powers as Saudi Arabia which had reason to fear an Iraqi-Syrian rapprochement. Other officers were in turn bought by Iraq. But the army as a whole was anti-Iraqi.[9]

The Syrian branch of the Muslim Brothers, organized into an Islamic Socialist Front early in November 1949, also came to the defence of the Republic against Iraqi ambitions. Its candidates had done well in Damascus in the 1947 elections and it had emerged as a considerable political force in opposition to Za'im. On 11 November its revived party newspaper, *al-Manar al-Jadid*, published an election manifesto in which it called for stronger bonds between Arab states, the upholding of their independence against foreign interference and a united front *vis-à-vis* 'imperialist plots'. The National Party decided to boycott the elections and a large proportion of the electorate abstained. Party discipline was loose and the affiliations of many candidates unclear, so that each newspaper carried different election results according to the source of its subsidies.[10] The Constituent Assembly met for the first time on 12 December and elected the People's Party leader Rushdi al-Kikhia as its President or Speaker. 'Aflaq resigned from the Atasi cabinet shortly after the elections and was followed by Hawrani early in December.

OBSTACLES TO AN IRAQI-SYRIAN UNION

The People's Party, claiming 51 seats out of a House of 114, could well have interpreted its clear lead over all opposition as a mandate to press ahead for an agreement with Iraq. Why then did nothing come of it? Part of the explanation must lie with the People's Party itself. It was pro-Iraqi, and its Aleppo merchant support looked to Mosul and Baghdad rather than to Damascus; but faced with the need for decisive action, its position appeared less clear-cut. Its desire for unity with Iraq was checked by two main reservations: first, it was

[9] Michel 'Aflaq to the author, Beirut, 13 Jan. 1961.
[10] 100 candidates were elected on the first round; 7 placed *en ballotage*; and 7 returns declared invalid. The independent Beirut newspaper *L'Orient* (18 Nov. 1949) reported the following results: People's Party 43; Independents close to the PP 20; Independents 22; Ba'th 1; National Party and friends (although the party officially boycotted the elections) 13; PPS 1. Damascus newspapers such as *Alif Ba'* (22 Nov. 1949) added the Islamic Socialist Front 4, and Tribal Representatives 9.

unwilling to sacrifice Syria's republican regime for a monarchy under
'Abd ul-Ilah, and secondly, it was concerned lest Iraq's treaty with
Britain be extended to Syria in the event of a union. These were no
more than the objections of all opponents of the union project, who
denounced it as 'bartering Syria's independence for a throne chained
by treaty to the British'. Opinion of all shades was determined that
Syria, so recently freed from French rule, should not fall under the
tutelage of another imperial Power. But such was the timidity and
vacillation of the People's Party leaders that it was never quite clear
whether they genuinely shared these objections or to what extent
they considered them open to compromise. Neither of these difficulties would have been insuperable had a genuine political will for
union existed in both Syria and Iraq.

'We stood for Arab unity but we were never pro-Hashimite',
Nazim al-Qudsi later declared.[11] 'This was a fabrication of our enemies which King Sa'ud and the public came to believe. We did not
want an Iraqi king. We were given the damning label of being pro-
Hashimite while others collected the Iraqi subsidies!' This may well
have been the truth but all that can be said is that opinion at the time
held the party to be irretrievably committed to Iraq—and that meant
to Britain. The party wanted union with Iraq but was hamstrung by
reservations for which its opponents and the public did not even give
it credit.

Secret negotiations with Baghdad had taken place throughout this
period, conducted on the Syrian side by a ministerial committee comprising Nazim al-Qudsi, Akram al-Hawrani, Khalid al-'Azm, and
'Adil al-'Azmeh and presided over by the Prime Minister, Hashim
al-Atasi. In subsequent months the Egyptian press published alleged
details of the talks[12] but a full account must await the opening of state
archives. Saddiq Shanshal, a leader of the Iraqi Istiqlal Party who
played an active role in these exchanges, explained the position as
follows:

The Iraqi envoys, on instructions from the Regent, advocated the unity
of both countries under one throne, but the Syrians wanted unity of the
peoples. Their view was that there should be a joint parliament in which
the Syrian and Iraqi peoples would be represented. Defence, Foreign
Affairs and Economics would be handled in common, while on all other

[11] Nazim al-Qudsi to the author, 3 Nov. 1960.
[12] See al-Ahram (Cairo), 30 Dec. 1949 and 4 Feb. 1950, quoted by Khadduri, in
Frye, Near East and the Great Powers.

issues each country would enjoy full local autonomy. This was the plan agreed on by Atasi's ministerial committee to which the Iraq Government, after much hesitation, finally consented. But the Syrians then demanded assurances on one essential point: they wanted to be certain that, in the event of union, Iraq's treaty with Britain would not be extended to them. Nazim al-Qudsi, the Foreign Minister, put the question officially to the British chargé d'affaires in Damascus. He received no reply. It was clear to the Syrian Government at the time that any agreement reached with Iraq could be upset overnight by the army. They told me plainly that unless Britain gave the required assurances the army would overthrow the Government in the name of national independence.[13]

This suggests a number of other reasons for the collapse of the union hopes. Strong elements in the Syrian army, and particularly Hawrani's friends such as Colonel Adib al-Shishakli, growing in importance and now commanding the First Brigade, were opposed to it. They were republicans, they wanted no tie with the British, and they were, moreover, afraid of taking second place in a stronger Iraqi army. It may also be assumed that France and Saudi Arabia, traditional enemies of an Iraqi-Syrian union, used their influence in and out of the army to prevent a step in that direction. The United States did not favour any change of the Arab map which was opposed by their friends in Saudi Arabia. Israel, in turn, was hostile to any concentration of Arab strength.

There remains the question of Britain's attitude. The Syrian public was convinced that Britain was scheming to bring union about and this belief was undoubtedly one reason why it was so fiercely opposed. But was this view well founded? The great weight of evidence suggests that, at this time at least, it was not. The paradox of the situation is that although the belief was widespread, it was held by virtually no one on the inside. Michel 'Aflaq, for example, had this to say:

Britain never really wanted union between Syria and Iraq. She disliked Za'im because he seemed to her an instrument of French policy and she may have had a hand with the Iraqis in bringing him down. But it is, *a priori*, difficult for us to believe that an imperialist Power will ever seek to unite two Arab countries. Setting up a friendly government in Damascus was perhaps a means of bringing Syria within Britain's sphere of influence without surrendering anything in return. But a union of the two countries would have meant certain changes in Iraq: Britain would have been under pressure to share with other Powers her privileged position there; all those

[13] Saddiq Shanshal to the author, Baghdad, 15 July 1960 and 25 Apr. 1961.

political and economic interests which had become identified with the *status quo* would have been disturbed. The evidence suggests that British policy aimed at securing a Syria friendly to herself and to Iraq, but stopping short of union. This policy could never be openly admitted as it would have wounded too many nationalist susceptibilities and lost its authors valuable support.[14]

Khalid al-'Azm held much the same view: 'The British never really wanted union. They were uncertain of being able to harness the effervescent side of the Syrian character. Nuri pretended he was for it but at bottom he thought like an Englishman.'[15] In the opinion of Dr Nagib al-Armanazi, Syrian ambassador in London in 1948–9 and in 1955–6, Britain opposed the union partly because of her prior engagement with France whereby Syria remained a French preserve, and partly because she did not wish to compromise her good relations with Saudi Arabia.[16] The National Party leader, Sabri al-'Asali, related that

in 1949 many politicians of all parties had private discussions with Iraq on the question of unity and they were agreed to push ahead with it. But the Iraqi politicians were puppets in the hands of the British who did not really want union. I remember being visited in Damascus in 1949 by a British diplomat from the Baghdad Embassy on his way through Syria. 'Arab unity', he said to me, 'is like a train. We shall neither try to push it nor stop it, but if we see it gathering speed, we might even jump on board.'[17]

How strong was the will to unite in Baghdad itself? The evidence suggests that few politicians in Iraq took the union project seriously. 'Abd ul-Ilah alone, particularly on the approach of King Faysal's majority, was consumed with desire for Syria, but he seemed incapable of seeing through an effective plan to achieve his ambition. The Syrian issue came to engage the best part of his attention, and it seems probable that Nuri al-Sa'id and his colleagues only espoused the cause to the extent of creating an engrossing foreign diversion for him. Nuri may have considered the bribe-money expended in Syria well worth it if the Regent's attention was thereby diverted from domestic affairs. Senior Iraqi officials later suggested to the author that Nuri and the Regent had their differences over Syria and that it was largely Nuri's restraining influence which accounted for Iraq's

[14] Michel 'Aflaq to the author, 13 Jan. 1961.
[15] Khalid al-'Azm to the author, Damascus, 8 Nov. 1960.
[16] Dr Nagib al-Armanazi to the author, Damascus, 9 July 1961.
[17] Sabri al-'Asali to the author, Damascus, 9 Nov. 1960.

wavering attitude. At the time of Hinnawi's regime, in particular, Iraq waited for the initiative to come from Syria. Iraqi politicians such as Fadil al-Jamali appeared to be more enthusiastic than Nuri about Hashimite ambitions in Syria, at times exploiting Nuri's doubts to intrigue against him with the Regent. Indeed, their enthusiasm for union with Syria may have been influenced by their desire to win the Regent's backing on the internal political scene. But Nuri's knowledge of Syrian politics was more profound than either the Regent's or Jamali's. He could assess more accurately the extent of Syrian support for the project. In contrast, 'Abd ul-Ilah was too impatient to listen carefully to other people and his information was limited.

The change of Government in Iraq in December 1949, shortly after the Syrian elections, illustrates to what extent the Syrian issue had become a pawn in the Iraqi political game. Nuri al-Sa'id, the Iraqi Premier, was unpopular in Syria, where he was thought to be more faithful to Britain than to the Arabs. The People's Party leaders felt that his tenure of office was an obstacle to union as few Syrians cared to envisage a future under his rule. The Iraqi statesman Husayn Jamil has explained how, early in November 1949, Nazim al-Qudsi suggested to the Iraqi Regent that it would be wise, if their union plans were to mature, to replace Nuri by a more acceptable figure such as 'Ali Jawdat or Jamil Midfa'i.[18] In mid-November the Regent therefore approached 'Ali Jawdat about the possibility of forming a Government. After discussions with the National Democrats, Kamil Chaderchi, Muhammad Hadid, and Husayn Jamil, and with the Istiqlal leaders, 'Ali Jawdat succeeded in forming a cabinet which included Jamil on 10 December—two days before the first session of the Syrian Constituent Assembly. After the ceremonies of cabinet-making, the ministers went in a body to the palace for the traditional meeting with the Regent. Jamil relates that the very first subject broached by 'Abd ul-Ilah was to request them to invite Nazim al-Qudsi to Baghdad. Nine days later, however, on 19 December, Colonel Adib al-Shishakli seized power in Damascus and the Regent overnight lost all interest in the 'Ali Jawdat Government. Looking back, the Iraqi-Syrian union seemed doomed long before this third coup took place because of the forces ranged against it, but the Syrian army chiefs felt they had to make quite sure.

[18] Husayn Jamil to the author, Baghdad, 28 Apr. 1961.

The Third Coup d'État
by Shishakli

COLONEL Adib al-Shishakli, the author of Syria's third *putsch*, was shrewder, tougher, and politically more agile than either of his predecessors. He was also more durable, dominating Syrian politics for the next four years. He moved his tanks on Damascus on 19 December 1949 to defend Syria's republican regime and save her from British influence and union with monarchical Iraq. But too much ideological content should not be read into the bloodless coup which was carried out with such practised ease only a week after the first session of the Constituent Assembly which emerged from the mid-November elections.

The preceding months were overshadowed, as has been seen, by the issue of the projected Iraqi-Syrian union: Hashim al-Atasi's transitional Government was awaiting the results of the elections before committing the nation to a decision of such consequence. The victory of the People's Party, therefore, led people to expect an immediate step in the direction of Iraq, a view reinforced by the election of the party leader, Rushdi al-Kikhia, to the Presidency of the new Chamber on 12 December. Two days later, the out-going Premier, Hashim al-Atasi, was elected temporary Head of State with special legislative and executive powers pending the promulgation of the constitution. But once again hopes of union did not materialize.

The occasion for the first clash between pro- and anti-union forces was a quibble over the wording of the oath which was to be taken by the Head of State and by members of the Constituent Assembly. A draft had been prepared by three deputies well known for their Hashimite sympathies—Husni al-Barazi, Hasan al-Hakim, and Zaki al-Khatib—by which jurors pledged themselves before God 'to respect the laws, safeguard the independence of the Fatherland, its sovereignty and the integrity of its territory, to preserve the public purse and work towards the achievement of the union of Arab countries'. But this text made no mention of Syria's republican regime, an omission opponents of the union were quick to seize upon and from which they drew sinister implications. Akram al-Hawrani and 'Abd al-Baqi Nizam al-Din led the opposition in the Chamber, being supported by the Islamic Socialist Front leader, Mustafa al-Siba'i, and by such anti-Iraqi dissidents from the People's Party as 'Abd al-Wahab Hawmad, who together formed a Republican Front to press the attack. But the People's Party and its following of 'Independents' commanded an easy majority and the text of the oath was approved unamended on 17 December.

The Chamber had, in effect, voted for union. Moreover, Colonel Sami al-Hinnawi, the Chief of the General Staff, was known to be a pliant instrument in the hands of his pro-Iraqi entourage. As there seemed no further obstacle to an immediate agreement with Baghdad, Akram al-Hawrani and Colonel Adib al-Shishakli felt impelled to intervene. Their careers, if not their lives, were at stake and they had no time for the tactics of a debating society. Involved at close range in the contest, they did not appreciate—few people did at the time— the strength of the forces ranged against the union and the half-heartedness of many of its supporters.

On the night of the vote, Akram al-Hawrani visited in their barracks Major Amin Abu Assaf and Captain Fadlallah Abu Mansur, the two Druze officers who had carried out Hinnawi's coup and who still commanded the First Brigade's armour.

You alone [he told them] can save the country and put an end to the decline. History will record your achievements and appreciate your work. If you hesitate even for a few days the opportunity will be lost. An imperialist army will enter Syria behind the screen of an Iraqi army. It will again enslave and humiliate our country.[1]

The officers, won over by this appeal, pledged their support for the conspiracy. The following day Hinnawi, smelling mutiny, decided to replace the armoured battalion commander by Major Subhi Ibara, a man of undoubted loyalty whom he sent to battalion headquarters with a military police escort. But that night Major Ibara was seized by Shishakli's men and the armoured vehicles rolled once more into

---

[1] Abu Mansur, p. 96.

the capital to arrest General Hinnawi,[2] his brother-in-law As'ad
Tallas, the military police chief Muhammed Ma'ruf, the head of the
deuxième bureau, Mahmud al-Rifa'i, and a number of other senior
officers.

On the morning of 19 December Colonel Shishakli issued a communiqué informing the nation that the army had been compelled
to act to put an end to the conspiracies of the Chief of the General
Staff as well as a number of 'professional politicians' who, in con-
nivance with foreign elements, threatened 'the security of the army,
the structure of the state and the republican regime'. The army
commanders had overnight changed sides on the question of Syria's
future.

SHISHAKLI AND HAWRANI

Adib al-Shishakli and Akram al-Hawrani, twin partners in the
coup, had been childhood friends in Hama. They grew up into two
of the most determined and able leaders of their generation. Born in
1909, Shishakli first attended an agricultural school before deciding
on a career in the *Troupes spéciales*. He was commissioned in 1930,
but deserted in May 1945 to take part with Hawrani in the rising
against the French. They were members in early manhood of the
PPS at a time when Sa'ada's movement seemed one of the most
effective counters to the Mandate, but were no more than militant
nationalists with few theoretical or ideological views. Both men led
bands of irregulars in January 1948 in attacks against Jewish settlements in Palestine. Shishakli, one of the more successful Syrian
commanders in the Palestine campaign, was often seen at his headquarters in the Safad area surrounded by radical politicians who spent
their time at the front growing beards and talking revolution before
returning to Damascus as heroes. In retrospect, the two men seem
the only prominent figures to have survived the 1949 coups. Shishakli
was the young officer chosen by Za'im to command the armoured
column which overthrew Quwatli's regime in March, while Hawrani
became Za'im's close adviser on the morrow of his coup. They later
quarrelled with him and Shishakli was retired from the army with
the rank of Lieutenant-Colonel on 6 August 1949. He was reinstated

---

[2] Hinnawi was released from prison on 7 September 1950, only to be shot dead in
Beirut on 31 October by Ahmad Hersho al-Barazi, in revenge for the execution
of his cousin Muhsin al-Barazi. Ahmad was condemned to death by the Beirut
Military Tribunal but the sentence was commuted to one of 18 years' imprisonment
and the payment of £L25,000 to Hinnawi's family.

two weeks later and given command of the First Brigade when Hinnawi took over with Hawrani's help. But, as has been seen, the two veterans, faced with what they thought was the imminent delivery of the country to Nuri al-Sa'id and the Iraqi Regent, used their technique of revolt and seized power on their own account.

Hawrani had by this time severed his ties with the PPS but had not yet allied himself with the Ba'th. He alone among Syrian politicians had a devoted personal following in the army but, on the Damascus political stage, he felt the need for a party machine. He therefore decided to revive his Arab Socialist Party, which in the mid-1940s had served as a screen for his PPS allegiance, and published in January 1950 a party programme which represented the evolution and refinement of his early rebellion against the landed 'feudalists' of Hama. It called for the distribution of estates to the poor—'the source of all power, all authority, all sovereignty'; a foreign policy 'free from all foreign influence'; the suppression of religious confessionalism; the emancipation of women; free primary and secondary education; compulsory military service; the setting up of armament industries; the opening of agricultural, trade, and technical schools, and, finally, the establishment of a 'republican, constitutional and parliamentary regime' in the Arab nation as a whole.

Shishakli and Hawrani represented the anti-Iraqi trend in Syrian politics for reasons which, in Hawrani's case, dated at least as far back as the quashing of the Rashid 'Ali movement in Iraq and the restoration of 'Abd ul-Ilah by British arms in 1941. To them the Regent and Nuri, with their cautious social policies and imperial attachments, seemed the exact equivalent of everything they had fought against in Syria. They had, moreover, no intention of being ruled from Baghdad. But to what extent could they claim to be champions of Syrian independence against encroachments from *all* sides? They disliked Iraq but could they save Syria from the pressure of rival influences?

Shishakli has sometimes been represented as a champion of Syria's sovereignty. But in Michel 'Aflaq's view he did not deserve the title:

Although he opposed union with Iraq, he was deeply committed to the Saudis, the Egyptians, and the French, and his independence was just as limited. French spokesmen, in particular, spoke of Shishakli as the champion of Syrian integrity, but this was because he played their game of opposing Baghdad and thus the British.[3]

[3] Michel 'Aflaq to the author, Beirut, 13 Jan. 1961.

There seems no doubt that, even if Shishakli and Hawrani carried out their coup independently of any outside influence, they knew to whom they could appeal for support when the time came. In this sense the Syrian coups were more than just the explosive protest of popular leaders and politically-minded officers against an unrepresentative and incompetent system; they were equally the product of the rival ambitions of Syria's Arab neighbours and the conflicting policies of the Great Powers in the area.

By their *putsch* of 19 December, carried out in the face of a hostile Chamber and an indifferent public, Shishakli and Hawrani demonstrated that they were unburdened by constitutional doubts and had a sound if crude view of where power lay: tanks spoke a language more forceful than parliamentarians. On the Damascus political scene, however, they were outsiders, representing the extra-parliamentary pressure groups of the army and the 'left' but uncertain of their authority and enjoying only grudging recognition from the old stalwarts. Moreover, Shishakli's ambitions seemed at this stage relatively modest: the army was in his view no more than an arbiter to whom appeal could be made to call the politicians to order in moments of national crisis; it was not in itself an instrument of government. Indeed, his first move was to leave 'the direction of the country to its legitimate rulers' and allow them to carry on the traditional business of cabinet-making, not fully appreciating to what extent this had been disturbed by the successive military interventions of the past few months.

The convulsions of 1949 were followed by two years of confused groping for a political formula which would express the new pattern which had emerged from the coups. The politicians did not immediately grasp the new restrictions on their powers and continued to play their disorderly parliamentary game, drafting constitutions, issuing manifestos, intriguing with foreign Powers, as if refusing to admit that the final word must now rest with the General Staff. Shishakli himself encouraged this illusion by the caution with which he exercised his ultimate authority. He would not make Za'im's rash mistake of shouldering full responsibility for government too early and so exposing himself to public opprobrium. He was a cool-headed soldier with a gift for intrigue and management of men, preferring to allow the politicians to play themselves out in exhausting internecine struggles, harassing them, meanwhile, by the slow but relentless encroachments of the army. This is, at all events, how it seemed. A fairer estimate may be that he was himself uncertain of his own strength and of the amount of fight left in the civilians; the long months of 1950 and 1951, in which he remained in the background, were a period of necessary preparation and training before assuming full powers. One of the main themes of the period was the unfolding contest between the army and the politicians, but the fact that the final outcome was never in doubt lent an air of unreality to much of the politicians' effort.

EGYPT'S DIPLOMATIC SUCCESSES

Another theme was Syria's perennial problem of external alignments. Hashimite hopes were sadly checked by Hinnawi's overthrow, but they were not extinguished. Egyptian diplomacy, however, was not idle during the same period and scored two notable successes which contrasted with the misdirected fever of Iraq and her supporters. It will be recalled how, to promote the cause of union with Syria, the Iraqi Regent had replaced Nuri al-Sa'id as Premier by 'Ali Jawdat al-Ayubi in December 1949, but that Shishakli's coup later that month had prevented the change from bearing fruit. 'Ali Jawdat meanwhile had appointed as deputy Premier Muzahim al-Pachachi, an Iraqi politician then well liked in Egypt, who was sent to Cairo to smooth out differences between the two countries over Syria. Pachachi, without consulting his cabinet and in opposition to the manifest will of the Regent, initialed a 'gentleman's agreement'[4] whereby Iraq and Egypt undertook not to interfere in Syrian affairs for a period of five years. The agreement contained prohibitions against 'direct' and 'indirect' interference and made specific reference both to the Greater Syria and Fertile Crescent schemes.

Pachachi returned to Iraq from Cairo on 31 January 1950, at about 3 p.m. The Regent immediately summoned ministers, including such members of the opposition as Salih Jabr, Saddiq Shanshal, and Mahdi Kubba, to a meeting that afternoon at the Rihab Palace. Pachachi's agreement with Egypt, which the Iraqi cabinet then heard about for the first time, came under heavy fire from the Regent and the opposition leaders. That same evening, the Regent got in touch with a number of Independents in the cabinet, who took their orders from him but on whom the Government's majority depended, and asked them to withdraw, leaving 'Ali Jawdat's ministry no alternative

---

[4] Text in 'Abd al-Razzak al-Hasani, *Tarikh al-wizarat al-'Iraqiyya*, viii (1955), pp. 136-7.

but to resign.[5] The Pachachi agreement was consequently repudiated, and the new Iraq Government of Tawfiq al-Suwaydi announced its intention of including the Syro-Iraqi federal project in its programme. The Syrian and Iraqi peoples, the Premier told the Senate in February 1950, have an 'imperative need to unite'. The incident merely served to illustrate the deplorably unsettling effect which the Syrian issue had on internal Iraqi politics, and Egypt's more coherent and effective tactics.

Egypt's second diplomatic success was even more striking. Supporters of an Iraqi-Syrian merger had argued in 1949 that only such a union could make an effective stand against Israeli expansionism. When, that autumn, the leaders of the People's Party, backed by Colonel Hinnawi, seemed on the point of reaching an agreement with Baghdad, Egypt countered by proposing a multilateral Arab collective security pact—known as the Treaty of Joint Defence and Economic Co-operation—which would co-ordinate the defences of all Arab states and so make unnecessary any bilateral agreement such as Iraq and Syria proposed. Advanced by Egypt at an Arab League meeting in October 1949, the pact was finally approved by the League Council on 17 April 1950.[6] It pledged collective support for any member faced with aggression; it provided for consultation in the event of an external threat and for co-ordination and consolidation of armed forces; it set up a permanent military commission to draw up plans for collective defence, as well as a ministerial Joint Defence Council to supervise their execution. Provision was also made for economic co-operation.

On two points the pact moved a step beyond the Arab League Charter: contracting states agreed to be bound by decisions of the Council adopted by a two-thirds majority (Art. 6); they also undertook 'to conclude no international agreement which may be inconsistent with the present Treaty' and 'in their international relations to pursue no course which may be incompatible with the purposes of the present Treaty' (Art. 10). The pact was portrayed as a step towards greater integration between Arab states and an expression of their will to stand together. In fact it reflected nothing more than Egypt's traditional policy, already embodied in the League, to obstruct any regional Arab grouping, notably that of Iraq and

---

[5] Husayn Jamil to the author, Baghdad, 28 Apr. 1961.
[6] See Fayez A. Sayegh, *Arab Unity* (1958), pp. 142–51 for a discussion of the pact's provisions.

Syria, to defend the territorial *status quo* in Arab Asia and thus secure for herself the dominant role as the single most powerful Arab state.[7]

This inter-Arab rivalry on which the pact was erected is illustrated by the fact that Iraq and Jordan did not sign until 2 February 1951 and 16 February 1952 respectively, and that dates of formal ratification ranged from 31 October 1951 to 11 October 1953. It need hardly be said that, although the Defence Council of the pact held a number of perfunctory meetings, no attempt was made to implement its provisions: no joint general staff was set up, no troops allocated, and no co-ordination achieved in any military field. Militarily the pact remained for five years a dead-letter, only to be resuscitated by Egypt—particularly its crucial Article 10 with its prohibition of divergence in foreign policy—as a weapon against Iraq in the struggle over the Baghdad Pact in 1954–5. However, its Egyptian authors had never meant it as a military instrument, but rather as a means of containing Iraq and of reaffirming the principle of the independence of each Arab state which was first underwritten by the League. To this extent it served its purpose.

DECLINE OF THE PEOPLE'S PARTY

The dominant position of the People's Party was shaken but not destroyed by Shishakli's coup. He robbed it of the military backing which Hinnawi had provided and set up the General Staff as a rival authority to the Constituent Assembly, where the party had a commanding majority. Any Government must henceforth strike a balance between the claims of the Assembly, jealous of its prerogatives, and an increasingly enterprising and self-confident army. It was some time before such a formula could be found and before the politicians had explored and even grasped the new restrictions on their powers. This was reflected in the difficulties of forming a Governemnt on the morrow of the coup. Between 20 and 23 December several vain attempts were made: by the Independents, Khalid al-'Azm and Sami Kabbara, by the leaders of the Republican Front, Akram al-Hawrani and 'Abd al-Baqi Nizam al-Din, by the Islamic Socialist Front leader, Mustafa al-Siba'i, and by Shakir al-'As, a prominent member of the People's Party. On Christmas eve the deputy leader of the People's Party, Nazim al-Qudsi, formed a ministry dominated

---

[7] See the *Bourse égyptienne*, 27 Oct. 1949, for an Egyptian acknowledgement that this was the role intended for the pact at its inception.

by his own followers.[8] But the army objected, the Head of State Hashim al-Atasi offered to resign, and Qudsi was forced to withdraw the following day, ending the life of the briefest Government in Syrian history. Finally, on the night of 27 December, Khalid al-'Azm drew up a compromise list[9] after long consultations. Hawrani, the army's appointee, took over the Defence Ministry; the Ministry of the Interior went to an Independent, while the People's Party, who had dominated the cabinet a month earlier, had now to be content with four secondary portfolios. The first task of the new Government was to issue a decree retiring General Hinnawi and promoting Colonel Anwar Bannud as Chief of Staff. Shishakli, the real master of the situation, preferred the less publicized position of Deputy Chief.

'Azm was a realist and his policy statement to the Chamber on 4 January 1950 clearly indicated Syria's new orientation; he pledged himself to defend her independent republican regime and promised his Government's support for the Arab collective security pact, then under negotiation in Cairo. In default of a clear line from the People's Party, it was left to a number of pro-Hashimite independents, such as Husni al-Barazi, Munir al-'Ajlani, and Hasan al-Hakim, to clamour for 'an absolute and total' Arab union, beginning with a federation of those countries most directly threatened by Israel: Iraq, Jordan, Syria, and Lebanon. But these outdated appeals raised no echo in the Assembly and 'Azm's policy was approved on 7 January by 93 votes to 6 with 1 abstention. The following day Colonel Shishakli set off on a journey to Cairo and Riyad to repair the breach caused by the Hinnawi interlude. He was followed in February by the Minister of National Economy, Ma'ruf al-Dawalibi, who secured a $6 million interest-free loan from Saudi Arabia and the promise of a further £5 million from Egypt. This was the price for underwriting Syria's independence from the Hashimites.

The National Party and its agile secretary-general Sabri al-'Asali also demonstrated this sensitivity to the change of climate: at a

---

[8] Prime Minister & Foreign Affairs, Nazim al-Qudsi (PP); Defence & Nat. Economy, Faydi al-Atasi (PP); Justice, Zaki al-Khatib (PP); Education, Hani al-Siba'i (PP); Interior, Ahmad Kanbar (PP); Public Works, Muhammad al-Mubarak (Isl. Soc. Front); Finance, Shakir al-'As (PP); Agriculture, Mahmud al-'Azm (Ind.); Health, Georges Shalhub (Ind.).

[9] Prime Minister & Foreign Affairs, Khalid al-'Azm (Ind.); Defence, Akram al-Hawrani (Rep. Front); Agriculture, 'Abd al-Baqi Nizam al-Din (Rep. Front); Nat. Economy, Ma'ruf al-Dawalibi (PP); Justice, Faydi al-Atasi (PP); Education, Hani al-Siba'i (PP); Health, Fath Allah Asyun (PP); Interior, Sami Kabbara (Ind.); Finance, 'Abd al-Rahman al-'Azm (Ind.); Public Works, Muhammad Mubarak (Isl. Soc. Front).

congress in Homs the party retracted its statement in favour of union with Iraq (issued in the previous autumn when such views were fashionable) and reaffirmed its loyalty to the Republic. On 27 January 'Asali led a party delegation to Egypt to make peace with the veteran exiles Shukri al-Quwatli and Jamil Mardam and ingratiate himself once again with the Arab League and the Egyptian authorities. Quwatli, who had not ceased to plan his return to power since his overthrow by Za'im in March 1949, saw in this visit the revival of his party and the reawakening of his hopes.

The People's Party, meanwhile, opposed by the army, by Hawrani, by the Ba'th, and by its reanimated rivals of the National Party, sought to exploit its one remaining asset, namely its majority in the Constituent Assembly. Nazim al-Qudsi packed the thirty-three-man commission which was to draft the constitution with his own party members, but the draft text was widely criticized when it was published in April.[10] There was no quarrel over Article 1, which declared Syria to be a sovereign, parliamentary republic, but Article 3, which proclaimed Islam the religion of the state, was the subject of a violent dispute in the press between conservative Muslims and the defenders of a secular state. The Ba'th newspaper reported that 235 university students had petitioned the Head of State calling for the suppression of all confessional distinctions. The Christian communities were also deeply concerned and most Easter sermons dwelt on the subject. 'You must struggle', the Greek Catholic Patriarch told his congregation, 'to prove that right is on your side and that you are not refugees in your own country.' The Islamic newspaper al-Manar disputed the arguments put forward by the Christian communities, extolling the spiritual values of Islamic legislation. Article 5 declared that Damascus was to be the capital with the qualification that this was not irrevocable. This was seized upon by Qudsi's opponents who saw in it a conspiracy by the People's Party 'to transfer the seat of Government to Aleppo on the first possible occasion'.[11]

At the height of the controversy, on 25 April, Hawrani resigned from the cabinet declaring that he was opposed to no fewer than fifteen articles of the new constitution and that the Government had not been consulted in the drafting. Relations between the Government and the Constituent Assembly betrayed, he said, 'a total lack of concordance'. But the constitutional issue was only a symptom of

---

[10] French trans. in L'Orient (Beirut), 20 Apr. 1950.
[11] al-Barada (Damascus), 18 Apr. 1950.

the underlying struggle between the People's Party, entrenched in its authority as the electors' choice, and the extra-parliamentary forces of the army, Hawrani, and the Ba'th, who claimed to be more truly representative of public opinion. Hawrani may have been reluctant to face a trial of strength in parliament which he knew he could not win. His resignation may also have been due to an instinct to quit before the collapse of the 'Azm Government, which had run into an economic storm largely on account of a deterioration of relations with Lebanon.

The dispute with Lebanon concerned the long-standing problem of customs policy and organization. Under the Mandate, customs administration, together with a number of other departments such as posts and telegraphs, the control of concessionary companies and the production of tobacco, fell under the immediate control of the High Commissioner as they were considered matters of common interest to all parts of the Mandate territories and could not therefore be wholly controlled by the Governments of the different regions.[12] In 1937 the Syrian and Lebanese Governments agreed on the principle of separate customs administrations but failed to agree on the proportion of customs revenues to be allotted to each state. In 1938 the Syrian Government imposed a tax on Lebanese products and Lebanon retaliated, but the measures were never effectively carried out and the dispute remained unresolved during the war. By the end of 1944 France had formally handed over the customs administration to a joint Syro-Lebanese Conseil Supérieur des Interêts Communs, but its operations were never harmonious and ended in disagreement in February 1948. Colonel Husni al-Za'im negotiated an agreement with Lebanon in July 1949 (some alleged it was linked with his betrayal of Antun Sa'ada), but it was short-lived and soon ceased to operate. Plans for the construction of a port on the Syrian coast of Latakia to free Syrian trade from dependence on Beirut excited nationalist opinion to press the Government to put an end to an 'association by which the interests of four million Syrians are sacrificed on the altar of Lebanese commerce'. The Lebanese Government had, moreover, become unpopular in Syria at this time because of its repressive measures against the PPS following Sa'ada's execution. Khalid al-'Azm then proposed an economic union between the two countries but, when Lebanon rejected this proposal since the economics of the two states were not complementary but clashed,

[12] See Hourani, *Syria and Lebanon*, pp. 171, 222, and 289, and Longrigg, p. 357.

the Customs Union was dissolved in March 1950. The immediate result was a wave of higher prices on the Syrian market, bringing home to the public the harmful consequences of the rupture. 'In Syria we are living through the worst days in our history', a Damascus newspaper wrote on 1 May 1950.

Our trade is at a standstill, our industry is paralysed, our farmers cannot find buyers for their produce, our independence is in danger, our Republic is threatened, our Constituent Assembly allows itself to be distracted by petty disputes, our Government is a medley of conflicting tendencies, the country is being pillaged. We are looked upon as prey by Turkey, Iraq, Transjordan, and even by the Jewish gangsters. All these people are encouraged by the Russians, the British, the Americans and the French. . . .[13]

Mounting economic difficulties, the bitter controversy over the constitution, the lack of harmony between the General Staff, the Chamber and the cabinet, together with the resignation of both Hawrani and Faydi al-Atasi, brought down Khalid al-'Azm's Government on 29 May.

The army [Shishakli declared that same day in a speech to the troops] will prevent at all costs a recurrence of the comedy for which Syria has been the stage and which nearly destroyed her . . . As God is our witness, the army wants only to safeguard Syria's independence and the republican regime.[14]

The next day, following a lengthy conference between the army chiefs and Head of State, Nazim al-Qudsi was asked to form a Government. It was significant that the army took a hand in naming the Premier-designate, but the man chosen was the majority leader in the House. Qudsi, in turn, made important concessions. He formed his cabinet on 4 June[15] but was forced to appoint an army officer, Colonel Fawzi Selu, Minister of Defence. He also gave an undertaking that his cabinet would take no decisions of policy; it was to be a transitional administration which would keep the wheels of government turning pending the approval of the new constitution. The People's Party which was in power was in effect powerless. Qudsi had by these expedients concluded a truce with the General

---

[13] al-Fayha (Damascus), 1 May 1950.   [14] Ibid. 30 May 1950.
[15] Prime Minister & Foreign Affairs, Nazim al-Qudsi (PP); Interior, Rashad Barmada (PP); Defence, Col. Fawzi Selu; Nat. Economy, Shakir al-'As (PP); Education, Farhan Jandali (PP); Public Works, Georges Shalhub (PP); Justice, Zaki al-Khatib (Ind.); Finance, Hasan Jabbara (non-parliamentarian).

Staff. He had bought off the immediate hostility of the army but was faced in the summer and autumn of 1950 by a still more violent opposition from the supporters of the former President, Shukri al-Quwatli. It was part of the continuing irony of Syrian politics in the years before the union with Egypt that the National and People's Parties, the two traditional groups which had sprung from the National Bloc and which shared a common interest in the maintenance of the old order, should yet have remained locked in battle to the end, to the sole advantage of the radical forces by which they were both threatened.

Sabri al-'Asali, a clever lawyer and political temporizer, was the moving spirit behind the regrouping of pro-Quwatli forces. He went to the length of linking the National Party to the Socialist Co-operative Party, an extremist organization,[16] to form an opposition Patriotic Front. On 26 June a bomb exploded in the parliament building which the Government blamed on the National Party. Rushdi al-Kikhia, People's Party leader and President of the Chamber, denounced from the tribune the National Party's 'campaign of defamation' against the Constituent Assembly.

The National Party [he said] is for ever accusing us of all sorts of crimes. Its press labels us 'traitors' and 'agents of foreign interests'. But is it treason to want a federation or union with a brother country? Yes, we stand for federation or union [with Iraq]. We have said so and we say so now. But we have taken the trouble to define the union to which we aspire. It must not encroach on our sovereignty or independence. Where else but in union can a small country like ours find salvation? We are accused of being the enemies of the Republic. But the new constitution which is now being drafted will maintain the Republic. The National Party is not above changing sides. It did not hesitate in the past to give its unconditional support to union. It decided later that it was in its interest to disown this policy. We leave it to public opinion to judge between its attitude and ours.[17]

On 7 August Quwatli, exiled in Alexandria, breaking his silence for the first time since his overthrow by Za'im, called on all Syrians to defend their independence. This was the signal for which his

---

[16] The Socialist Co-operative party was founded in 1948 by Faysal al-'Asali whose attacks on the army during the Palestine War had been one of the contributory causes of Za'im's coup (see above, pp. 41-42). Faysal, a young energetic eccentric, organized his party as a right-wing terrorist force, preaching pan-Islam, living ascetically and drilling secretly in mountain hideouts. Imprisoned by Za'im, he was released by Hinnawi and was elected to the Chamber as his party's sole representative in the November 1949 elections.

[17] L'Orient (Beirut), 1 July 1950.

3. King Saʿud and President Shukri al-Quwatli at a banquet in Damascus.

4. The Regent of Iraq, ʿAbd ul-Ilah; President Hashim al-Atasi of Syria; King Faysal of Iraq; and the Syrian People's Party leaders, Rushdi al-Kikhia and Nazim al-Qudsi

5. Colonel Husni al-Zaʿim

6. Colonel Adib al-Shishakli

supporters were waiting. They called a strike in the Damascus *suks*, organized demonstrations, and held a mass meeting on 5 September —the day the Chamber was to vote on the constitution—condemning the regime and denouncing the decision of the Constituent Assembly to turn itself into a legislative body for a period of four years, which was, in effect, a move to perpetuate the People's Party rule. But the new constitution was duly approved, the veteran Hashim al-Atasi was elected President of the Republic, and Nazim al-Qudsi formed a new cabinet.[18] Quwatli, meanwhile, with Egyptian and Saudi support, continued to publicize his claim to be the one man who could stand up to the Hashimites abroad and the colonels at home.

While this duel continued between the National and People's Parties, a parallel contest was taking place between the army and a number of militant pro-Hashimite Independents, such as Munir al-'Ajlani and Hasan al-Hakim. On 2 August 'Ajlani dared to launch an attack on the army in the Chamber. 'The army', he said, 'busies itself with everything: with smuggling, with police duties, with the Ministry of the Interior, with the secret police, and even with the surveillance of members of this Assembly.'[19] He had himself been 'honoured' by its attention on his return from a visit to Jordan. The army retorted a few weeks later by issuing a warrant for 'Ajlani's arrest on charges of conspiring with Jordan against the security of the state. He was tried by military court but was acquitted, the prosecutor seizing the occasion, however, to denounce the Greater Syria project, for which King 'Abdallah continued to campaign, as a 'national crime' aimed at 'crushing Syria's independence and the republican regime in favour of colonialism'. Hasan al-Hakim, another persistent critic of the army's encroachment on public affairs, resigned from the Government in October.

Scattered acts of violence in the second half of 1950 continued to testify to the fragmentation of political authority and to the struggle for power. On 31 July Colonel Muhammad Nasir, commander of the Syrian air force, was murdered near Damascus. A 37-year-old graduate, he was considered Shishakli's most serious potential rival. Baghdad, Cairo, and Beirut newspapers reported that he named the

---

[18] Prime Minister & Foreign Affairs, Nazim al-Qudsi (PP); Interior, Rashad Barmada (PP); Defence, Col. Fawzi Selu; Nat. Economy, Farhan al-Jandali (PP); Public Works, Ahmad Kanbar (PP); Agriculture, 'Ali Buzo (PP); Health & Welfare, Georges Shalhub (PP); Justice, Zaki al-Khatib (Ind.); Min. of State, Hasan al-Hakim (Ind.).
[19] *Alif Ba'* (Damascus), 3 Aug. 1950.

head of the *deuxième bureau*, Ibrahim al-Husayni, and his deputy, 'Abd al-Ghani Qannut, as his assailants before he died, but the Syrian Defence Ministry forbade all press comment. The two men, whose names recur in the margins of Syrian history, were later acquitted for lack of evidence. On 12 October an unsuccessful attempt was made on Shishakli's life which led to the uncovering of a terrorist organization known as the *Phalanges de la Rédemption Arabe*,[20] eleven of whose members were arrested and charged with crimes including the placing of bombs in a Syrian synagogue, the attempted murder of Lt-Colonel W. F. Stirling,[21] an assault against a Jewish school in Beirut, placing bombs in the British and United States legations in Damascus, an attack on the Jewish quarter in Damascus, an explosion at the local UNRWA office, and the attempted murder of King 'Abdallah and Colonel Adib al-Shishakli. A number of political figures were said to be implicated, including Ahmad al-Sharabati, a former Defence Minister who had been discredited by the Palestine War, and Nasha't Shaikh al-Ard, brother of King Sa'ud's private physician who, it was alleged, had been channelling Saudi funds to the terrorists. These men were later acquitted, but Syria's relations with Egypt and Saudi Arabia suffered as it became plain that these states were promoting Quwatli's return to power and that this campaign in favour of the former President cloaked the revival of much that had been disreputable and violent in the old regime.

The year following Shishakli's coup saw, therefore, a steady decline of the People's Party. Qudsi had been Premier since June 1950 but a soldier sat in his cabinet as Defence Minister and controlled the *gendarmerie*. The party still dominated the Assembly which, after the promulgation of the constitution, had transformed itself from a constituent into a legislative body. But power was increasingly passing to forces outside parliament. The party found itself threatened not only by the army, by Hawrani, by the Islamic Socialist Front and the Ba'th, but also by a sharp revival of its old National Party rival. It was further embarrassed by the open pro-Hashimite advocacy of

---

[20] *Kata'ib al-fida' al-'Arabi*, founded by four young terrorists including Husayn Tawfiq and Hani al-Hindi. Tawfiq had been accused of the murder of a former Egyptian Minister, 'Uthman Amin; he escaped from a Cairo jail and took refuge first in Jordan and then in Syria where the authorities refused Egypt's request for his extradition.

[21] A correspondent of *The Times* and former British political agent for tribal affairs, who had settled in Damascus after the Second World War. On 6 November 1949 he was attacked at home by three gunmen and wounded in the chest. See his autobiography, *Safety Last* (London, 1953).

'Independents' like Munir al-'Ajlani which only served to put the army on its mettle. But the party's weakness and ultimate failure were due above all to the contradictions of its external policy: its leaders sought union with Iraq while simultaneously proclaiming in all honesty their attachment to Syria's republicanism and independence. They wanted a union—but without Nuri, 'Abd ul-Ilah, or the treaty with Britain. These aims were not realistic and their pursuit laid the party open to charges of vacillation or plain deception. They divided their friends and were misrepresented by their enemies. Egypt, in the meantime, further reinforced the *status quo* by the conclusion of the Arab collective security pact. In this political turmoil a further source of conflict was to be introduced: the efforts of the western Powers to organize the Middle East for defence against the Soviet Union. Within the two arenas of both internal Syrian and inter-Arab politics, the global aspect of this problem was often neglected. The issue was adapted to the Arab scene, serving to underline local conflicts and providing local rivals with an additional stick with which to beat each other.

Middle East Defence, 1951

T HE Arabs have often been reproached for not sharing the world-wide anxieties which drove the western Powers to seek to erect a Middle East defence system after the Second World War. Their indifference to the threat from the Soviet Union was considered naïve and symptomatic of their political immaturity in much the same way as was the wartime alliance of some of them with Nazi Germany. British and American policy in the Middle East was largely governed by such 'cold war' preoccupations as the Communist coup in Czechoslovakia, the Berlin blockade, the need to secure oil supplies for European reconstruction, the collapse of Chiang Kai-shek, and the Korean War—all located outside the area.[1] Western planners believed that they must be ready to resist attack anywhere on the periphery of the Communist bloc and particularly in areas both vulnerable and important such as the Middle East. But Arab concerns were parochial: they thought more of containing Israel than inter-national Communism; of ejecting British troops from their territory than of enlisting their aid 'in defence of freedom'; they were more concerned with the 'intra-regional' struggle for Arab leadership—the fratricidal feuds between the newly independent Arab states—than with the need for a united front against an external threat. These differences in political and defence objectives partly explain western failure to secure Arab co-operation in defence planning. The fears of Britain and the United States tended to make them insensitive to the detail of Arab politics and to what was going on in and between the Arab states. This led them to misjudge the Arab mood, to make errors of timing in advancing their defence proposals, and to take sides, even if unwittingly, in inter-Arab conflicts. They seemed too often to view the Middle East through the binoculars of their own interests and see it as an annex to European diplomacy or as just another 'cold war'

[1] See Elizabeth Monroe, 'Mr Bevin's "Arab Policy" ', in *St Antony's Papers*, ed. A. H. Hourani, no. 11, pp. 9–10.

battlefield, but only too rarely in terms of its own indigenous tensions. Western Middle East defence plans were, in fact, superimposed on the complications of Arab politics, which had been insufficiently explored. This was a blunder as it was precisely on the local level of stresses and strains in individual Arab countries that these grandiose schemes foundered. The West's objective was to defend its Middle East interests in the light of certain global commitments. These were the terms of reference within which the defence plans were drafted. The concern of this study, however, is not with world-wide strategy or with the motives and anxieties of the Great Powers, but rather with the narrower problem of the impact of some of these plans on internal politics in various Arab states, particularly Syria, seeing that it was in this parochial setting that the issue was often ultimately decided.

ARAB NEUTRALISM

It is sometimes said that the West discovered Arab neutralism when 'Abd al-Nasir went to Bandung in April 1955 and bought Communist arms that summer. But neutralism was plain for everyone to see in Syria in 1950–1: many of the new leaders had advocated it long before the Egyptian revolution and some of those who did not were displaced because of the hostility to western defence proposals. Syria's neutralism was an emotion which sprang from a number of grievances: there was the bitter experience of the French Mandate, the resentment at the defeat in Palestine and the West's part in the creation of Israel; this was aggravated by opposition to the project of an Iraqi-Syrian union under British tutelage, by a real fear of modern warfare, and by the widespread view that independence was a fiction and that Syria was at the mercy of the Powers. In January 1950 Akram al-Hawrani's Arab Socialist Party published its programme calling for a foreign policy 'free from all foreign orientation or influence'.

The Arab-Israeli dispute then seemed in danger of breaking out once more into armed conflict: Britain had resumed arms deliveries to Egypt, Iraq, and Jordan, while Israel was buying military equipment where she could and increasing small-arms production. The rumour spread that Britain and the United States were putting pressure on the Arabs to come to terms with Israel as a prerequisite for peace and stability in the Middle East. A bitter chorus arose that the Arabs would a thousand times prefer to fall into the arms of

Russia than a prey to Israel. The Islamic Socialist Front took up the cry: at a rally in Damascus on 12 March one of its leaders, Shaikh Mustafa Siba'i, declared:

> We are resolved to turn towards the eastern camp if the Democracies do not give us justice. . . . To those who say that this eastern camp is our enemy we would answer: when has the western camp been our friend? . . . We will bind ourselves to Russia were she the very devil.[2]

This was one of many similar outbursts. It is worth recalling that the Islamic Socialist Front, unlike the Muslim Brothers in Egypt, far from being a highly organized para-military, political instrument was, in reality, an authentic mouthpiece of the Syrian masses who were and remain both Muslim and fervent.

On 25 May 1950, a month before the outbreak of the Korean War, Britain, France, and the United States issued their Tripartite Declaration in a bid to keep the Palestine frontier quiet.[3] They declared their 'unalterable opposition to the use of force or threat of force between any of the states in the area' and made the supply of arms conditional on an undertaking of non-aggression. These terms were eventually accepted by Egypt, Syria, Iraq, Jordan, Lebanon, and Israel, and governed the supply of arms to the Middle East until 1955. The Korean War overshadowed the rest of the year. Of all the Middle East states, only Turkey came out openly on the side of the United Nations and decided to send an armed contingent to Korea. Arab opinion was quick to establish a parallel between Zionist and North Korean 'aggression', and to compare United Nations behaviour on both occasions. Several Arab newspapers were openly jubilant at the reverses of the United Nations armies, seeing in them a just retribution for the Organization's support of Israel. By her abstentions in the Security Council, Egypt regained in the Arab world some of the prestige she had lost in the Palestine War, while a politician of the Syrian People's Party and future Premier, Shaikh Ma'ruf al-Dawalibi, declared that the only way to prevent a third world war was to sign a non-aggression pact with the Soviet Union.[4] Not

---

[2] Quoted by Pierre Rondot, 'Les États Unis devant l'Orient d'aujourd'hui', *Orient*, no. 2, Apr. 1957, p. 41.
[3] Text in Hurewitz, ii. 308–9. The Declaration may also have been intended to prevent punitive action against Jordan, which had absorbed Arab Palestine against the fierce opposition of Egypt and Saudi Arabia. The Jordanian Parliament formalized the annexation on 24 April 1950.
[4] Walter Z. Laqueur, *Communism and Nationalism in the Middle East* (1956), p. 256.

unnaturally, the western view was that events in the Far East only made more urgent the need to organize the Middle East for defence.

GENERAL ROBERTSON AND MR MCGHEE

This western preoccupation with Middle East defence was reflected in the crowded military and diplomatic timetable of the early months of 1951. British and American service chiefs held a series of conferences in Malta in January and March, and were joined in April by French and Italian admirals; General Sir Brian Robertson, Commander of British Middle East land forces, toured Arab capitals in January and February; the Comptroller of the French Army, General Valéry, visited Damascus in January, while French Middle East envoys met in Beirut in April under the chairmanship of M. Couve de Murville, ambassador in Cairo. In February Mr G. C. McGhee, American Assistant Secretary of State for Near Eastern, South Asian and African Affairs, presided over a conference of United States envoys in Istanbul. A final statement noted with satisfaction 'the further progress Turkey, Greece and Iran made during the past year in building up their own defences'[5] and it was hoped that other countries of the region were becoming more conscious of the need to make their individual contribution to the general security of the region. But this sanguine hope was not confirmed by Mr McGhee himself when he toured the area in February and March.

In the weeks before General Robertson's visit to Damascus on 7 February, the Ba'th, Hawrani's Arab Socialist Party, and the Islamic Socialist Front all called for a 'policy of strict neutrality towards the two world camps'. On 20 January an explosive charge was placed in the British consulate in Aleppo, while the Ba'th brought students out in protest demonstrations in Damascus, Homs, Hama, Der'a, and Deir ez-Zor. A Ba'th manifesto declared on 24 January that

the Arab nation fighting to free itself from Anglo-French-American imperialism . . . warns the Arab League against making any gesture of adhesion to one or other of the two blocs; it holds to a genuine neutralism which will prevent Western imperialism making the Fatherland a strategic base and exploiting its oil resources for military ends. . . .

Damascus university students petitioned the Premier to keep General Robertson out of Syria, while a workers' delegation delivered a protest note to the British legation.

[5] *New York Times*, 22 Feb. 1951.

An official communiqué issued after the General's visit said that neither side 'had sought or given any undertaking', but Syrian sources later reported to the author that the General had asked for the use of roads, railways, and ports in the event of hostilities. He had argued that Britain needed Syria as a friendly link between the strong British forces stationed on the Suez Canal and forward positions in Iraq close to the Soviet border. Some Syrians who met the General found confirmation for their view that Britain wanted Syria's friendship, but feared that her instability might be exported to Iraq: she would have liked to see Syria in her sphere of influence but stopped short of promoting a Syro-Iraqi union. An objection raised by the Syrian authorities was that to allow a British force free passage from the Canal to the Euphrates would mean opening the Palestine frontier and collaborating with Israel. This could not be thought of.

Mr McGhee's visit to Damascus in March gave the Syrians a foretaste of that missionary fervour in support of a global crusade which later came to be associated with Mr Dulles. Neutralism, he told them, worked only for the enemy, but he was happy to note that it was in retreat. There could be no neutrality between aggressors and defenders of freedom. Salah al-Din Bitar, the Ba'th secretary-general and future Syrian Foreign Minister, thought this a 'gratuitous statement which did not reflect the real sentiments of the eastern peoples. They believe their interests lay wholly in neutrality'. Very shortly after Mr McGhee's departure, the residence of the United States Minister in Damascus was slightly damaged by a bomb explosion.

Some of these reactions were no doubt Communist-inspired, but western observers tended to believe that they all were and did not grasp the indigenous roots of Arab neutralism. Men like Hawrani, 'Aflaq, Bitar, or the leaders of the Islamic Front were not fellow-travellers and were not obeying Communist directives. The West had been their enemy for the whole of their political life, and their instinct was to keep out of Great Power conflicts. Salih Harb, the Egyptian chairman of the Society of Muslim Youth, writing to the Arab League secretary-general, said that

the Arab peoples, after all they have suffered, will not accept to be sold in the name of democracy on the British imperial market. . . . What is left of Arab pride inherited from our great ancestors compels us to ask you, in the name of the Arab peoples, to proclaim the most absolute neutrality. We wish neither to support Communism nor to defend imperialist democracy.[6]

[6] *al-Misri* (Cairo), 22 Jan. 1951.

Hawrani's early PPS affiliations had made him a confirmed anti-Communist while the Ba'th leaders, although brought up on Marxism, had long since been disillusioned and had been conducting a bitter feud with their local Communists since the last years of the war. The Ba'th and the Communist Party competed, after all, for the same following.

Hasan al-Hakim, an old friend of the Hashimites,[7] was one of the few public men in Syria openly to advocate a pro-western policy in 1951.

Let us voluntarily join the western camp [he argued] before we are forced to do so by events, for our collaboration will then earn us no gratitude. Neutrality is utopian. For good or ill, we shall be involved in international events. Our weakness allows us no escape.[8]

But these views found no echo in the younger generation: 200 university students addressed a message of protest to the President declaring that 'the Syrian people have no wish to fight side by side with their executioners . . .'[9]

THE FALL OF NAZIM AL-QUDSI

This public debate which racked the country in the early spring of 1951 served to underline certain local political conflicts. Nazim al-Qudsi, the People's Party secretary-general, had been Premier since the previous June but his authority and that of his party had been fatally undermined. He had failed to stand up to the army and was increasingly harassed by the Ba'th and the revived National Party. The Minister of the Interior, Rashad Barmada, was engaged in a contest with Colonel Fawzi Selu, the Defence Minister, for the control of the *gendarmerie*. Neither side felt it could give way: stripped of the *gendarmerie*, the Government would lose all physical means of enforcing its will throughout the country; but without it the army was unsure of controlling future election results. Qudsi's hands were tied by Shishakli, but he continued to press for an Arab federation—in effect a federation with Iraq. In January 1951 he called on the Arab League to examine what preliminary steps would be necessary to bring about such a federation. These manoeuvres

---

[7] 'King 'Abdallah offered me the title of Pasha on several occasions but I invariably replied that I could not afford it' (Hasan al-Hakim to the author, Damascus, 10 Nov. 1960).
[8] *al-Insha'* (Damascus), 18 Feb. 1951.
[9] *al-Sha'b* (Damascus), 13 Mar. 1951.

came to nothing, and served only to confirm army suspicions that the People's Party was conspiring with the Hashimites.

The situation was brought to a head by a foreign policy debate in the Chamber on 5 March. Qudsi was wavering and indecisive: 'Our external policy', he declared, 'will be governed by the constant evolution of the international situation . . .' In his vain search for a formula of association with Iraq, he could not afford to preach neutralism, but nor did his party allow him to take up a clear pro-western position like that of Hasan al-Hakim and Munir al-'Ajlani. He was driven to a milk-and-water compromise which satisfied nobody. Akram al-Hawrani did not spare the Government:

> I, too, stand for Arab unity [he mocked the People's Party], but I don't want an English or an American Arabism. I believe in Arab socialism, but I reject Communist socialism . . . I should like to adapt a saying from the French revolution which describes our situation: Arab unity, what treachery and what crimes are committed in thy name![10]

Four days later, on 9 March, Nazim al-Qudsi resigned. 'This is not a ministerial crisis but a constitutional crisis', a party spokesman said, but it marked in effect the failure of the party's policies at home and abroad. Qudsi himself held the French in part responsible for his downfall. He later explained:

> They found it unbearable that we should work for Arab unity. They were also afraid that we might seek to take over the French-controlled Banque de Syrie et du Liban. My Government had been the first to nationalize foreign enterprises in the Middle East. We took over French water and electricity companies in Aleppo, a French electricity company in Homs, British electricity and transport companies in Damascus, and the French tobacco monopoly. The French then thought that we had designs on the Banque.[11]

TROUBLE ON LAKE HULA

Syria was without a Government for eighteen days after Qudsi's fall. Fighting broke out with Israel during this interregnum on the malarial, sparsely settled banks of the Jordan, below Lake Hula, which the Syrian-Israeli armistice agreement had made into a demilitarized zone. The Israelis started drainage works in the Hula basin, claiming that the whole area had been awarded to them by the General Assembly's resolution of November 1947. They planned to

---

[10] *al-Insha'*, 6 Mar. 1951.
[11] Nazim al-Qudsi to the author, Aleppo, 3 Nov. 1960.

settle thousands of immigrants in this strategic area. Syria protested against this 'flagrant violation of the July 1949 armistice convention'. On the home front, the impact of the incident was to convince the army of the disloyalty of the People's Party in provoking a crisis at this dangerous moment, completing the divorce between them. Relations were further strained when the People's Party refused to serve under Khalid al-'Azm in a Government of National Union. When, therefore, Qudsi managed to form a Government on 23 March, the army imposed its veto; Qudsi was forced to withdraw, and Rushdi al-Kikhia, the party leader, resigned in protest from the Presidency of the Chamber. Khalid al-'Azm ended the long crisis on 27 March by forming a ministry primarily of Independents, to which Hawrani and the army gave their blessing and in which Colonel Fawzi Selu served once more as Defence Minister.[12] But 'Azm was immediately faced with the open hostility of the People's Party, which used every device afforded by its control of the Chamber to obstruct his Government. He had no chance of finding a compromise, as he had done in 1950, between the rival claims of the Assembly and the General Staff, and was driven into total reliance on—and therefore servitude to—the army.

Continued violence on the Israeli frontier at Lake Hula absorbed the public's attention, allowing the People's Party and the fringe of vociferous pro-Hashimites to revive their campaign for Arab union— 'if not a total union of all Arab states at least a partial one'—as the sole defence against the Israeli menace. The Iraqi Minister in Damascus was quick to take up the theme: the first step, he told the press, was 'to bring together those countries linked by history, geography and common interests . . .'. He accused the opponents of a limited Arab union of 'throwing a spoke in the wheel of the Arab cause'. Khalid al-'Azm retorted by reminding foreign envoys that the Foreign Ministry would always be glad to hear their views direct. 'As for throwing a spoke in the wheel of a federation for two', he added, 'the whole carriage in my view has been wrecked and swept away by the storm at the end of the year before last' (a reference to Shishakli's coup in December 1949).

A renewed outbreak on the Israeli frontier caused Syria to summon

[12] Prime Minister & Foreign Affairs, Khalid al-'Azm (Ind.); Interior, Sami Kabbara (Ind.); Agriculture & Justice, 'Abd al-Baqi Nizam al-Din (Rep. Front); Finance, 'Abd al-Rahman al-'Azm (Ind.); Education & Nat. Economy, Ra'if al-Mulki (Ind.); Health & Public Works, Sami Tayyara (Rep. Front); Defence, Col. Fawzi Selu.

an emergency meeting of the Arab League Council in Damascus on 14 May and to appeal to Egypt and Iraq for aid. This seemed a heaven-sent occasion for Iraq to provide a practical demonstration of her brotherly interest and concern for Syria.

At this very moment at which I am speaking [Nuri al-Sa'id told the Iraqi Chamber on 16 May], our anti-aircraft batteries are crossing into Syria to help her against Zionist air aggression. Our units, batteries and fighters will stay on Syrian soil, under Syrian command, as long as is necessary.

Iraq's swift response contrasted with Egypt's reticence.[13] Iraqi troops paraded through Damascus on 17 May to the immense satisfaction of all those eager for closer ties with Baghdad. Hasan al-Hakim and Munir al-'Ajlani, tireless propagandists for the Hashimite cause, paid tribute to Iraq in the Chamber as the only Arab state to have come to Syria's defence. The Egyptian press feared that Iraq's aid was a bid to unite the Fertile Crescent by force,[14] while the French Minister in Beirut, M. Clarac, conveyed to the Iraq Government France's concern at the dispatch of troops to Syria.[15] Everyone was behaving very much as one might have expected.

Iraqi troops had made the People's Party bolder. All that summer it ran a campaign against the Prime Minister accusing him of 'favouring the imperialist activities of the Banque de Syrie and encouraging Syrian and foreign capitalists to exploit the people'. These charges carried some weight in view of 'Azm's 'big business' connexions and close ties with France (he had been ambassador in Paris and, earlier still in 1941, Premier under the Mandate). The People's Party brought the work of the Chamber to a standstill, attacking the Government in session after session and refusing to vote additional credits for defence or allow salary increases for civil servants. 'Azm's attempt to dissolve parliament was opposed by President Atasi. On 30 July all official business was halted as Syria's 17,500 civil servants struck for higher wages and better working conditions. No mail was collected or delivered, no telephone services operated, and the

[13] *L'Orient* (Beirut) reported on 16 May 1951 that the Egyptian Minister of the Interior, Mohammad Salah al-Din, had said in answer to a question in the Senate that Egypt would not intervene in the Syrian-Israeli dispute and would take 'no decision which would make her incur unnecessary risks'. But the Minister denied making these remarks when he attended the Arab League meeting in Damascus on 14–19 May.
[14] See the Cairo newspapers *al-Ahram*, 18 May 1951; *al-Nida'*, 22 May 1951; *al-Muqattam*, 24 May 1951.
[15] *Le Monde*, 24 May 1951.

country was virtually cut off from the outside world. 'Azm's Government resigned that same night. But the People's Party which brought him down could not itself hope to replace him because of the army's opposition. The choice of Hasan al-Hakim as Premier-designate, an outspoken supporter of the Hashimites and the West, was therefore all the more surprising. On the day he was approached to form a government, Shishakli flew to Riyad to secure payment of the outstanding instalments on the Saudi loan to Syria and to confer with Ibn Sa'ud about the situation in Jordan following King 'Abdallah's murder on 20 July. Cabinet-making had to await his return on 9 August, pointing once more to the real source of ultimate decision.[16]

HASAN AL-HAKIM'S MINISTRY

Hasan al-Hakim later explained how he came to power:

Relations between the army and the governing People's Party had reached breaking-point. A solution had to be found. The People's Party asked President Atasi to call on me to resolve the crisis. I reminded the President that my reputation for independence even among 'independent' deputies, and the fact that I was well known as pro-Hashimite and pro-western, might be used against me to the detriment of stable government. But he proceeded to assure me that a majority in the Chamber, led by the People's Party, favoured my appointment. I accordingly took office and set about working on the most pressing problems. These were three in number: a grain shortage—I was told that our stocks would only last a fortnight—, the civil servants' strike, and the budget deficit. On the first, we approached a number of countries and received an offer of 50,000 tons of wheat from the Turkish Ambassador. As for the civil servants, I first tried to convince their leaders that a salary increase was out of the question at the moment. I could not give away something I did not have. My duty was to tax-payers as well as to them. But these arguments were of no avail. I then prepared a draft bill which provided for the dismissal of striking civil servants and made them ineligible for further employment even by private firms. I only had recourse to these stern measures when reason failed. I would not submit to the temptation of cheap popularity. When I was in office, the secret funds available to the Prime Minister for propaganda were returned to the Treasury untouched, to the indignation of several journalists who had been

[16] Prime Minister & Finance, Hasan al-Hakim (Ind.); Foreign Affairs, Faydi al-Atasi (PP); Interior, Rashad Barmada (PP); Health, Fath Allah Asyun (PP); Nat. Economy, Shakir al-'As (PP); Defence, Col. Fawzi Selu; Public Works & Communications, Hamid al-Khuja (Rep. Front); Education, 'Abd al-Wahab Hawmad (PP); Justice, 'Abd al-'Aziz Hasan (Rep. Front); Agriculture, Muhammad Mubarak (Isl. Soc. Front).

in the habit of deriving their income from this source. The budget deficit
was more difficult to deal with as the army was unwilling to see its own
budget cut in any way. I then adopted the stratagem of delaying the
presentation of the full budget from month to month, getting parliament
instead to approve a series of *douxièmes* (or monthly instalments), each so
adjusted as to allow the overall budget to balance. In this way I avoided a
head-on clash with any department.[17]

It did not escape notice that when Hasan al-Hakim made his ministerial statement in the Chamber on 13 August, he found it expedient
to pass over Syria's need to unite with her neighbours and to co-
operate with the West. Instead he declared that the republican regime
was the 'foundation of Syria's existence and the secret of its rebirth'.
Abroad, the Government's policy would be 'friendship towards all,
within the limits of our national interest and the framework of the
U.N. Charter and international law'. In this way he placated the
army and won his vote of confidence. Later Hasan al-Hakim said:

> My relations with Shishakli were good and I had no real occasion to
> resent his interference in Government. I made no secret of my western and
> Hashimite sympathies, but he must very soon have been convinced that I
> was planning nothing underhand. I was, after all, a Hashimite sympathizer
> in the sense that my ties were with Faysal I and 'Abdallah. I had little
> contact with the new generation of 'Abd ul-Ilah, Husayn, or Faysal II,
> and I took no part in the various conspiracies on their behalf. I believe
> Shishakli came to have confidence in me and even approached me on
> occasions to ask if I had any criticisms of the army.[18]

It was a Ba'th deputy, Jalal al-Sayyid from Deir ez-Zor, who on
24 September raised in the Chamber the issue of military intervention in public affairs. 'Governments', he said, 'come to power and
fall against the will of the Chamber and even without its knowledge.'
The People's Party leader, Rushdi al-Kikhia, then delivered the main
onslaught. He said that his party had only lent its support to Hasan
al-Hakim after receiving an undertaking that the Government would
tolerate no interference in its affairs and would exercise its full
sovereignty. The Government had promised to recover from the
army control over internal security forces. External policy was at
present dictated without regard for the national and Arab aims laid
down in the constitution. 'I should like to say frankly that our
patience is just about exhausted. If we find ourselves unable to give

---

[17] Hasan al-Hakim to the author, 10 Nov. 1960.   [18] Ibid.

the nation what it hopes for and desires, we shall leave this Chamber in a body.' This empty ultimatum was the party's only recourse against the strangulation of its political powers.

THE 1951 DEFENCE PROPOSALS

The bombs, demonstrations, and neutralist manifestos which greeted western generals and statesmen on their exploratory visits to the Middle East in 1951 did not deflect them from pressing on with their defence plans. Only the main dates in this timetable[19] need be recalled here before turning to the impact of these plans on Syria. On 18 June 1951 Saudi Arabia agreed to renew for five years the lease of the United States base at Dhahran. On 20 September the Council of the North Atlantic Treaty Organization recommended the accession of Greece and Turkey to the alliance, while the British, French, Turkish, and United States Governments set to work on a plan for a Middle East defence organization which they prepared to present to Egypt in a bid to 'internationalize' the Suez base. On 13 October the four Powers invited Egypt to join an allied Middle East command 'as a founder member . . . on a basis of equality and partnership'. An accompanying British note, however, made the evacuation of the Canal Zone base conditional on Egypt's acceptance of the plan. It was immediately rejected.

Its authors had betrayed an astonishing insensitivity to Egyptian and Arab opinion. Egypt's claims were simple: total evacuation of British troops and the union of Egypt and the Sudan under the Egyptian crown. They had been restated by the Prime Minister, Nahas Pasha, in the Speech from the Throne in November 1950. The existing reasons for intransigence were reinforced by the grievance with the British over Palestine to which Muslim and Arab fellow feeling in Egypt responded. Egypt refused to support the United Nations action in Korea until her own claims had been met. Mobs attacked the British and American embassies in August 1951, the anniversary of the signing of the Anglo-Egyptian Treaty of 1936 which, in Egyptian eyes, had been negated by the British ultimatum to Faruq in February 1942. On 8 October Nahas Pasha tabled

---

[19] See *Anglo-Egyptian Conversations on the Defence of the Suez Canal and on the Sudan*, Egypt No. 2 (1951), Cmd. 8419; Egypt, Min. of Foreign Affairs, *Records of Conversations, Notes and Papers Exchanged between the Royal Egyptian Government and the United Kingdom Government, March 1950–November 1951* (1951); John C. Campbell, *Defense of the Middle East* (1960), pp. 39–48; Tom Little, *Egypt* (1958), pp. 182 ff.

decrees in the Chamber of Deputies for the unilateral abrogation of the 1936 treaty, the abolition of the Anglo-Egyptian Condominium Agreement, and the proclamation of Faruq as King of Egypt and the Sudan. Egypt and the Wafd were plainly committed to a policy of neutralism. But less than a week later, on 13 October, as if oblivious to these developments, the British, French, Turkish, and American ambassadors presented their Governments' proposals to the Egyptian Foreign Minister.

THE IMPACT ON SYRIA

On the same day in Damascus, envoys of the four Powers informed the Syrian Foreign Minister, Faydi al-Atasi, of the joint note to Egypt. No request was made for Syria to join: the communication was for information only. But this was a nuance which the Syrian public did not appreciate. Thousands of demonstrators marched in protest after the Friday prayers, led by the Islamic Socialist Front leader, Muhammad al-Mubarak, Minister of Agriculture in Hasan al-Hakim's Government. Telegrams were sent from 'the people and Muslim organizations gathered in the Mosque of the Umayyads' to the Prime Minister, the Security Council, to Muslim and Arab states and to a number of foreign Powers, pledging support for the Egyptian cause—'which is the cause of all Arabs and Muslims'—and denouncing the 'imperialist plot of common defence'. The sequence of events which then followed is related by the Prime Minister, Hasan al-Hakim:[20]

As parliament was rising on 22 October, a number of deputies asked the Foreign Minister for a statement on the western defence plans which he promised to make at the next sitting. The cabinet met the following day, but Faydi al-Atasi was absent, and only appeared briefly as the meeting was breaking up at about 3.00 p.m. I noticed he was carrying a sheaf of notes and inquired what statement he intended making in the Chamber. He replied that he would simply list the main points of the western proposals. I said firmly that I could see no reason for discussing the plan. I instructed him merely to tell the Chamber that we had not been asked for our views and that the communication made to us was for information only.

At about 5 p.m. that afternoon Faydi al-Atasi rose and, to my indignation, delivered a long and detailed attack on the western defence plans ('Our participation in a system of common defence', he said, 'can only be

[20] To the author, 10 Nov. 1960.

7. Khalid al-'Azm   8. President Shukri al-Quwatli   9. Faris al-Khuri

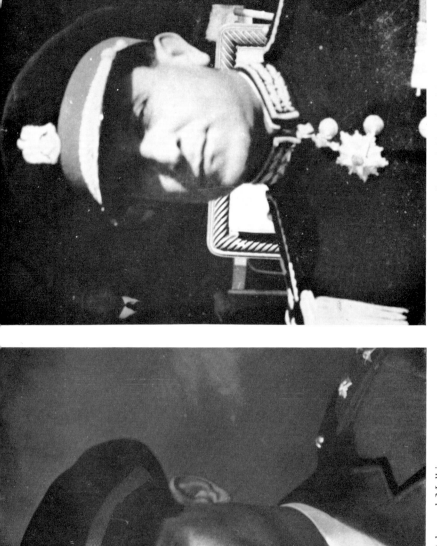

11. General Shawkat Shuqair

10. Colonel 'Adnan al-Malki

justified by a clear and real national interest. But I have sought in vain for such an interest. . . . Common defence supposes an enemy against whom it is directed. . . . But in what way are we threatened by the enemy aimed at by this project? What evil has this enemy done us?' It was the West which had created Israel, and so on. . . .) During a brief adjournment, I approached the President of the Chamber, Nazim al-Qudsi, and told him of my intention to speak. But he advised me to delay my rebuttal of Atasi for a day or two so as not to aggravate matters. I reluctantly agreed, but I prevented the broadcast of Atasi's speech which he had been trying to arrange.

HASAN AL-HAKIM'S FALL

The following day, 24 October, I submitted my resignation to the President on the grounds that I could no longer remain in office in the face of open dissension within my Cabinet. I agreed, however, to stay on for a brief transitional period to allow for the smooth transfer of power to a successor Government. It was then that I began to suspect that Faydi al-Atasi's speech was a manoeuvre by the People's Party to bring me down. I had settled the problems of grain supplies, the civil servants' strike and the budget deficit, and they were eager to assume power once more. I waited from 24 October to 10 November, during which time Qudsi postponed meetings of the Chamber. I then presented to the President my resignation in writing telling him that I could wait no longer in the present ambiguous situation. I sent a copy of my letter to Qudsi, appending a refutation of Faydi al-Atasi's views. I argued that a common defence plan would allow us to strengthen ourselves militarily and economically and would be a substitute for the various treaties by which individual Arab states were bound. My resignation opened a long crisis which was finally resolved by Shishakli. . . .

It was only six years later that my suspicions of a People's Party intrigue, involving the President of the Chamber, were confirmed. Ma'ruf al-Dawalibi, the party secretary-general, wrote an article in al-Ayyam in September 1957[21] in which he launched a retrospective attack on the common defence proposals. He revealed that the party as a whole had opposed the project and had instructed the Foreign Minister to attack it in the Chamber. Thus the People's Party which had put me in power later stabbed me in the back because I had refused to be a puppet in its hands and act as a shield between it and the military authorities.

The fall of the Hakim Government illustrated the entanglement of foreign and domestic issues which is characteristic of weak countries. The question of the western defence proposals had been put to work

[21] al-Ayyam (Damascus), 24 Sept. 1957, no. 6225.

in internal politics. The People's Party had seized the occasion to overthrow Hakim, who had outlived his usefulness to it, and, by its onslaught on the western plans, silenced those critics who accused it of secret ties with Britain. As Hakim hinted above, and as all the protagonists were aware, the issue of Syria's eventual participation in a western defence system had been grafted on to more pressing local problems—the contest between the People's Party and the National Party, between these two traditional factions and the rising power of Hawrani and the Ba'th, between sticklers for the constitution and those who believed the army had a role to play in politics, between defenders and opponents of union with the Hashimites and, perhaps most immediate of all, between the People's Party and the General Staff. Two days before Hakim's fall, the Minister of the Interior, Rashad Barmada, had resigned in protest against the Defence Minister's refusal to transfer the *gendarmerie* to his department. The fate of the western defence plans could not be separated from the outcome of these parochial, overlapping battles.

For nineteen days Syria was without a Government. The People's Party, misjudging its powers, stuck fast to principle: it would not participate in the Government unless the *gendarmerie* passed to the Ministry of Interior, unless the Defence Ministry was given to a civilian and the constitution applied in both letter and spirit. But these were just the issues on which Shishakli could not give way without forfeiting his control of the political process. His patience with the People's Party had grown thinner over the past two years, worn by cabinet instability and by the party's irritating flirtation with Baghdad at a time of conflict and uneasy truce on the Palestine frontier. Shishakli was convinced the party was committed to destroying Syria's independence by selling out to Iraq and robbing the army of its key role in the nation's affairs.

In consequence, candidate vainly succeeded candidate as Premier-designate. Finally, Ma'ruf al-Dawalibi managed to form a cabinet on 28 November.[22] He was in many ways a good candidate: he was a member of the People's Party but of anti-Hashimite sentiment; he was a shaikh, which reassured conservative Muslim opinion; he

---

[22] Premier & Defence, Ma'ruf al-Dawalibi (PP); Justice, Munir al-'Ajlani (Ind.); Education, Hani al-Siba'i (PP); Interior, Ahmad Kanbar (PP); Agriculture, Muhammad Mubarak (Isl. Soc. Front); Foreign Affairs, Shakir al-'As (PP); Finance, 'Abd al-Rahman al-'Azm (Ind.); Nat. Economy, 'Ali Buzo (PP); Health, Muhammad Shawwaf (PP); Public Works & Communications, Georges Shahin (PP, non-parliamentarian).

advocated land reform, the expansion of educational facilities, and the redistribution of wealth, which placed him among the 'progressive' *avant-garde*; he was in the mainstream of the neutralist current by having been one of the first in the Arab world to call for a non-aggression pact with Russia and arms purchases from the east to break the western arms monopoly. His motto was 'More friends and no enemies for Syria', but the American press described him as the most outspoken anti-American Arab leader. At home, he opposed the army's dictation of policy. He therefore took over the Defence Ministry himself and gave the People's Party the lion's share of the other cabinet appointments.

SHISHAKLI'S SECOND COUP

Shishakli warned Dawalibi that the cabinet list he presented was not acceptable and would force him to dissolve parliament—a situation he appeared genuinely to wish to avoid. But Dawalibi would not compromise. So Shishakli struck again. On the night of 28–29 November he ordered the arrest of the Prime Minister, members of the Government, the People's Party secretary-general, Nazim al-Qudsi, as well as a number of Hashimite sympathizers such as Husni al-Barazi. A communiqué dated 29 November informed the nation that the army had taken over responsibility for security and public order. In a proclamation broadcast that morning Shishakli accused the People's Party of responsibility for all three coups d'état. He said that the Syrian army believed that the People's Party did not really represent the people. The army believed that the party's main objective was to conspire against the country's independence, to destroy its army and restore the monarchy.

Later that morning, Shishakli summoned five deputies representing the Ba'th, the Arab Socialist Party, the Islamic Socialist Front, the Republican Front, and the PPS and informed them of the measures taken during the night. He then suggested to the President that the arrested politicians might be released if Dawalibi agreed to resign and parliament were dissolved—the only way of breaking the entrenched power of the People's Party. Two vice-presidents of the Chamber approached Dawalibi in prison with these terms: he rejected them on 30 November but, still under arrest, agreed to resign on 1 December. The following day the aged Hashim al-Atasi called on Hamid al-Khuja to form a Government, dissolve the Chamber, and carry out new elections. But this programme was bitterly opposed by the People's Party. Faced with a stalemate, the President resigned. Shishakli then assumed by military decree the functions of Head of State and the same day dissolved the Chamber. On 3 December he conferred full legislative and executive powers on Colonel Fawzi Selu together with the functions of Head of State, Prime Minister, and Minister of Defence. Selu was to be assisted by the secretaries-general of the various ministries. Shishakli himself stepped back out of the limelight.

Hasan al-Hakim's view was that:

> even at this stage, Shishakli was not convinced of the army's ability to run the country. He seemed extremely reluctant to become President, prefer-ring to remain in the background. Selu was put in as a first step and, when this seemed to work, Shishakli himself took over later. It is important to note these tentative, precautionary moves when weighing up what were Shishakli's ambitions. My own view of him is that he was not ambitious to become President as many people believed: the situation and the office were in a sense forced upon him. Had he wanted to provoke a crisis he could have done so much earlier. . . .[23]

The army had swept aside all pretence at a parliamentary regime and assumed full powers. But this could only be a temporary solution. At Shishakli's elbow stood Hawrani, and farther back, in the shadows, was the PPS, which now sought to benefit from Shishakli's former membership of the movement and from the political vacuum which he had created. The Ba'th did not like military regimes, but could not but applaud the eclipse of the traditional conservative parties. The People's Party still had supporters in the country, but they were silenced and bewildered by a head-on clash with the army. The party had claimed to stand for constitutional government and democratic procedures against the encroachments of the army. But it was com-promised in the public eye by its link with Iraq and by its ties with 'feudal' interests. Its talk of reform was not radical enough to be convincing. Its defence of the constitution may well have been genuine, but as a working principle in Syrian politics it lagged behind public opinion which wanted a 'progressive' rather than a 'demo-cratic' regime. Politically-minded young men in the professions, the army, and at the university wanted a Government which would defend their interests as a nation and as a class. They were less concerned with the niceties of democratic rule.

---

[23] Hasan al-Hakim to the author, Damascus, 10 Nov. 1960.

All these groups—and Syria's anxious neighbours—waited to see what the army, long the real master of the situation, would do with the powers it had now publicly assumed. The controversy over western defence plans gave way to more intimate, domestic worries, overlooked for the most part by western observers. The *New York Times* sententiously warned its readers that another spectre was haunting the Middle East,

the same specter that the 1848 Manifesto said was haunting Europe—communism. In Syria the deposed Premier wanted to deal with Russia. In the whole Middle East the ultimate dilemma is communism or Western democracy. We say that the answer must be Western democracy because if it isn't the West probably cannot survive. . . .[24]

It is doubtful whether Shishakli saw the problem in this light.

[24] *New York Times*, 30 Nov. 1951.

12

Military Dictatorship

WHEN Syrians come to weigh the benefits and rigours of military rule they think of Adib al-Shishakli: he gave them their first extended experience of government by soldiers. Husni al-Zaʿim's brief, spirited, and extravagant regime lay somewhere between political gangsterism and musical comedy. His successor, Sami al-Hinnawi, was a mere puppet. Of Syria's three military dictators, only Shishakli can be said to have meant business. His was the dominant, if sometimes veiled, influence on Syrian affairs from his first coup in December 1949 to his fall in February 1954. His long tenure of power was marked by profound changes in Syria's political life with far-reaching implications for the whole post-war history of that country.

The dictator in Shishakli was slow to reveal itself. The last two chapters have shown what caution this veteran conspirator exercised before emerging as uncontested master after his second coup in November 1951. For two years he had played cat and mouse with the People's Party, harrying it by repeated army intervention in the process of government, so sapping its authority as to reduce its leaders to impotence and to make a mockery of parliamentary rule. It was to a large extent under the umbrella of army protection that Akram al-Hawrani, Shishakli's closest civilian associate, emerged into national politics first to harass and then to persecute the landlords of central Syria. The Baʿth, in turn, could not fail to profit in this period from the clash between the army and the more traditional political groups. But for all civilian politicians, the lesson which had to be learned was how to live with the army and how to find a place for it in the political arena as one force among many; in the event, the army's domestication was secured by inviting it to share fully in civilian political disputes. Thus Shishakli's rule made the Syrian army an unashamedly political instrument. It was not properly to 'return to its barracks' until the union with Egypt in 1958—and then only for the brief life of the United Arab Republic.

Shishakli's army grew not only in political experience but also in size and strength. Neither Za'im nor Hinnawi had had time to remedy the weaknesses which the Palestine War had so agonizingly revealed: the army was undermanned, under-trained, and under-equipped. Shishakli, with French aid, did a great deal to turn it into a modern fighting force. He made important changes: he retired many of the older men whose minds had been formed with the *Troupes spéciales* and promoted young nationalist officers to positions of responsibility. Many of these, sent for training to France, Italy, West Germany, Britain, and the United States, returned better equipped to fill the senior posts to which he appointed them. Shishakli liked the society of young men and was to be seen nightly at the centre of an admiring bantering circle in the Damascus officers' club, a luxurious relic of the French Mandate which the Syrian army made its own.

But more important than his popularity was the fact that he was, for much of his rule, without a serious rival; and as the uncontested head of the army, he united it about himself, preventing its incursion into politics from developing into factionalism. No army chief after his fall was to enjoy the same authority. Indeed, many of the young officers who were his special favourites—such as Shawkat Shuqayr, Amin al-Nafuri, Ahmad 'Abd al-Karim, 'Abd al-Hamid Sarraj, Ibrahim al-Husayni, Tu'meh al-'Awdatallah, Ahmad al-Hunaydi, and Burhan Adham—were to make much of the political running in the years after his eclipse, but never as a concerted team. The suicidal division of the army into rival factions was, as we shall see, one of the prime causes of the union with Egypt.

Even after his second coup in late November 1951 Shishakli, with characteristic circumspection, did not assume any formal title of political leadership. He chose instead to rule through Colonel Fawzi Selu on whom he conferred by decree the functions of Head of State, Prime Minister, and Minister of Defence. Selu, sober and reliable, served in effect both as figure-head of the regime and as political Chief of Staff, while Shishakli retained the flexibility and freedom from scrutiny of a Commander-in-Chief behind the lines. Commissioned into the *Troupes spéciales* at 19 in 1924, Selu rose steadily to command the Homs military academy immediately after the departure of the French in 1946. He made his name as head of the Syrian delegation to the armistice talks with Israel after the Palestine War and then sat as Defence Minister in civilian cabinets from June 1950 to

November 1951. Selu was Shishakli's choice for seeing through the numerous reforms which, as absolute ruler, he felt it his mission to initiate.

But Shishakli was no more of a sophisticated political thinker than his predecessors. He believed in order and discipline, on the view that states could be run on much the same lines as armies. The radical elements in his ideas were provided by Hawrani who, sharing in his victory over the People's Party, had in the early months come to be the ideological mouthpiece of the regime. The two childhood friends from Hama had 'arrived'; in all Syria there was no one more powerful. But in spite of their great astuteness they were amateurs in the business of government. Their 'programme for workers and peasants' announced in January 1952 was well-intentioned but ill-prepared. Its central provision, the Decree for the Distribution of State Lands (no. 96 of 30 January 1952), was inapplicable because both the area and the location of the unregistered lands were unknown.[1]

This piece of legislation was preceded by a campaign of violence and intimidation against landowners in central Syria in the summer of 1951. Encouraged by Hawrani, villagers attacked members of such families as the Barazis, keeping them off their land and sniping at their houses. Hawrani launched his 'The land belongs to the Peasant' movement which provoked Communist opposition as they felt he was stealing their thunder. In telegrams to the central Government, landowners appealed for help against 'the Arab Socialist Party whose principles resemble the destructive principles of Communism, namely attacks and disturbances which paralyse agricultural production and sow dissension in the country'. The climax of Hawrani's campaign was a three-day 'anti-feudalist' rally in Aleppo in mid-September 1951. Attended by thousands of *fellahin* from all parts of Syria, this rural demonstration, the first of its kind in the Arab world, opened with a great parade of peasants through the streets carrying banners demanding land reform.

Hawrani's ideas were based on his experience in the Homs–Hama areas of central Syria where large landlords held a monopoly of the good land and took an excessive share of the produce. His legislative programme might have been more effective had it aimed at the resettlement of poor peasants on state irrigation schemes, rather than at limiting the size of properties in the rapidly developing dry-farm-

---

[1] See Warriner, pp. 101–5, for a discussion of the law's inadequacies, its subsequent amendments and meagre results.

ing zones of the north, thereby running the risk of checking invest-
ment of risk capital there without benefiting new settlers.

Shishakli's regime seemed set to discredit its predecessors by its
own activity. Many of its measures, often intensely chauvinistic in
tone, were aimed at curbing the influence of foreigners, religious
leaders, and minority racial groups. Government control was extended to foreign as well as to Syrian private schools; the opening of
new missionary schools was prohibited; the receipt of funds from
abroad for educational purposes had to be approved by the Ministry
of Education. Youth groups and clubs were forbidden all political
activity, while scouting and sporting associations were reorganized
by decree so as to eliminate all suggestion of an exclusive confessional or racial membership. Religious teachers and mosque func-
tionaries were ordered to wear a turban and a standard costume;
cafés and other places of entertainment were forbidden them. On the
first day of Ramadan, 24 May 1952, police patrols were ordered to
arrest anyone seen publicly breaking the fast.

Foreigners were subject to much stricter surveillance and were not
allowed to buy property. Relations with foreign countries came under
watchful scrutiny; the use of code in all non-diplomatic correspon-
dence was forbidden; the Syrian University, the Arab Academy, and
the Antiquities Department lost the right to correspond directly with
foreign establishments; indeed, officials of any ministry or public
body had to pass their foreign mail through the Foreign Ministry.
The receipt of money from foreigners for propaganda purposes was
made a criminal offence, punishable by fines and imprisonment. Entry
into Syria was denied to beggars, madmen, prostitutes, extraditable
criminals, and anyone 'likely to disturb public security and peace'.

To quell any opposition, the Government in mid-January 1952
ordered the dissolution of the Syrian branch of the Muslim Brotherhood, closing its offices and schools throughout the country. Similar
repressive measures were taken against Faysal al-'Asali's Socialist
Co-operative Party. Civil servants and trade unionists were prohibited from taking part in political activity, a measure which was
followed in April by a general ban on all political parties. A number
of senior civil servants were then purged, while schoolmasters and
university lecturers refusing to take an oath of loyalty to the regime
were dismissed. 'There can be no more orderly country in the
Middle East', reported *The Times*. Its correspondent estimated that
Shishakli's autocracy, run by directors-general of ministries answer-

able to Colonel Selu, had in its first six months of rule issued decrees at the rate of one and a quarter a day.[2] The local press, appreciating the necessity for strict self-censorship, approved Shishakli's measures without reserve, encouraging him to make even more daring innovations. Some papers campaigned for a 'single national costume' while others demanded that women should, like men, do their military duty to the Fatherland or be drafted into labour corps on the model of Hitler's Germany. The abundant rain, promising bumper crops, was attributed to the divine favour which the leader had deserved by his wisdom and integrity.

Shishakli had, within six months, set up a highly centralized dictatorship, silencing his critics by traditional police methods as well as by the sheer momentum of his 'reforms'. With the politicians out of action and a devoted army behind him, he had found Syria an easy country to govern. Foreign observers who appreciated that road traffic was now orderly and public transport uncrowded hinted that a new Atatürk had arisen in the East. In the half-year before it was robbed of the limelight by the Egyptian revolution of July 1952, Syria held the centre of the Middle East stage.

SHISHAKLI'S ARAB POLICY

Iraq was dismayed at Shishakli's assumption of full powers. His hostility to the Hashimites and their friends in Syria was notorious, so that his second coup dashed all hopes of an Iraqi-Syrian *entente*. Indeed, the eclipse of the People's Party and the final triumph of the Syrian army seemed a death-blow to Iraqi ambitions, accounting perhaps for the hysteria with which Iraq heard the news. Iraqi politicians called for intervention to save Syria from 'this high-handed rebel', while the cabinet decided to withhold recognition, appealing to other Arab states to do likewise. These manoeuvres were in vain: by 6 December 1951 all other Arab states had recognized the *fait accompli* in Damascus and ten days later, on 17 December, the representatives of Britain, France, the United States, and Turkey called on Colonel Selu, the Head of State, to inform him of their countries' recognition. With this overture, the four Powers hoped, no doubt, to interest Shishakli in their plans for an allied Middle East Command which Egypt had so forcefully rejected two months earlier.

Shishakli was not opposed to a general rapprochement between

[2] *The Times*, 30 May 1952.

Arab states and Atlantic Powers on a basis of equality, but he was not ready to go so far as to accept a limitation of sovereignty within a western-inspired defence system. He wished to get arms but understood that the key to this lay in Cairo; he was being supplied by France but realized that he could not widen his contacts until a solution had been found to the Anglo-Egyptian dispute. Moreover his associates, Hawrani and others, were doctrinaire neutralists to whom any agreement with the West was a betrayal, an attitude which may have governed Shishakli's systematic refusal of United States Point IV aid. He also feared infiltration and unofficial activities by Point IV technicians.

It is traditional with Syrian rulers, the legitimacy of whose regime may be in doubt, to send envoys to neighbouring states to plead their cause, or indeed to go in person and thus demonstrate the stability of their home base. On 19 March Shishakli and Selu, much to Baghdad's irritation, were the guests of King Tallal in Amman; the following week they crossed the mountains into Lebanon, where their way had been smoothed by the conclusion of a Syro-Lebanese economic agreement which ended a two-year breach. On 8 April Shishakli left for Saudi Arabia, where he visited oil installations and the Prophet's tomb, as well as conferring at length with the king. All his visits, he declared, were aimed at 'strengthening fraternal relations between the Arabs'.

Arabism was a slogan which Shishakli used warily in the early months of his regime, less because he was unaware of its appeal than on account of his semi-clandestine relations with the PPS since Arab nationalism conflicted with the party's central doctrine of a 'Syrian' nation. With Shishakli as undisputed ruler, the PPS sought to benefit from the vacuum which he had created around himself by the dissolution of such political parties as the Ba'th and the Arab Socialist Party. They presented themselves to Shishakli as a well-organized political force in an alliance of expediency rather than of principle.

Although the PPS never dared give full and public expression to their pan-Syrian objectives, there was a moment early in 1952 when the relationship seemed to flourish. To please them, Shishakli in a number of speeches put the accent on Syria and passed over the issue of Arabism. A leading party member, 'Isam al-Mahaiyri, later to become secretary-general of the movement, sometimes accompanied the dictator on his journeys as companion and journalist, a connexion from which the party drew some little comfort. But this trend did not last: in the heady months of Shishakli's ascendancy the role of Arab leadership offered too many rewards. Arabism was the only cause to which the Syrians would respond. 'Syria is part of the Arab world and the Syrian people constitute a part of the Arab nation', Shishakli declared in a traditional profession of faith at the Aleppo staff college in May.[3] Syria, he promised, would be the 'Prussia of the Arab states', the 'fortress of steel' from which the spark of liberation would fly to the whole Arab world.

THE ARAB LIBERATION MOVEMENT

With the growth of Shishakli's political ambitions appeared the need for an instrument with which to realize them. In the two years between his first and second coup he had been an influential figure in the background exercising the veto rather than wielding executive power. When he swept aside the civilian politicians and emerged as all-powerful, Colonel Selu provided him with that screen between himself and direct executive responsibility which his cautious instincts and scant experience of government demanded. Now a number of circumstances dictated a further step into the open: Selu had run the country with apparent ease since December 1951; the political parties were in eclipse after their dissolution; Syria, prosperous and orderly, seemed destined to play a paramount role in Arab affairs. Shishakli could not escape the conclusion that he must now lead in name as well as in fact; he must build a political machine, establish his regime on a constitutional basis and become President. But the path to legitimacy is a dangerous one: Shishakli's downfall is perhaps to be traced to his attempted transition from military ruler to elected President, in the course of which he lost touch with the army and, by fighting the politicians on their own ground, allowed them to unite against him.

A Council of Ministers was set up by decree on 8 June 1952, 'to assist the Head of State in the exercise of his legislative and executive powers'. The following day Colonel Selu formed a cabinet.[4] Two months later, on 2 August, another decree created the office of Vice-Premier which Shishakli filled, retaining his duties as Commander-

---

[3] al-Barada (Damascus), 22 May 1952.
[4] Prime Minister & Defence, Col. Fawzi Selu; Foreign Affairs, Zafir al-Rifa'i; Finance, Sa'id Za'im; Nat. Economy, Munir Diab; Education, Sami Tayyara; Health & Social Affairs, Dr Murshid Khatir; Agriculture, 'Abd al-Rahman al-Hunaydi; Justice, Munir Ghannam; Public Works & Communications, Tawfiq Harun.

in-Chief. On 25 August, when every Middle East regime was feeling the wash from the tidal wave of the Egyptian revolution, Shishakli inaugurated the Damascus headquarters of the Arab Liberation Movement, a mass one-party rally which he hoped would give his regime the broad, popular base it required.

> The Arab Liberation Movement [he declared] is not a new party to be added to the list of old parties to confuse the nation and divide its forces. It is a loyal and sincere attempt to regroup the good elements from all parties and all classes, to forge them into a single powerful bloc, fully capable of restoring the nation's confidence, and give the country a voice which is listened to and respected.

Many dictators have spoken this language.

A 31-point programme, couched in flamboyant terms, described the Arab national home as stretching from the Taurus to the Gulf of Basra and from the Mediterranean to the Atlantic. It called for compulsory military service, the emancipation of women, progressive taxation, the reform of land tenure, the settlement of nomadic tribes, the establishment of trade and agricultural schools, and full employment. But the document was more a pious declaration of principle than a legislative programme. Shishakli launched his movement in Aleppo on 24 October after a triumphant entry into the city at the head of a parade of 1,000 cars. He declared:

> Our country is the home of the Arab idea. . . . I invite you to join the progressive Arab Liberation Movement which is destined to grow until it embraces the whole Arab Fatherland . . . Our movement is the expression of the revolt of the Arab conscience in Syria. The flame of this revolution is spreading to all Arab countries to bring down the frightened leaders who, by their weakness, committed a crime against the Arabs of Palestine. . . .[5]

To carry this message abroad, Shishakli ordered a vast expansion of Syrian broadcasting services. His regime pioneered the use of radio propaganda as a weapon in inter-Arab disputes:[6] long before 'Abd al-Nasir's 'Voice of the Arabs' came to dominate Arab broadcasting, Damascus radio set the pace for those slanging-matches which are perhaps the most characteristic feature of relations between Middle Eastern states.

[5] al-Barada, 23 Oct. 1952.
[6] Mainly responsible was Ahmad 'Isseh, Shishakli's able Director of Radio. He was one of a trio of close advisers, wielding great power, who were familiarly known as the 'Three Graces'. The other two were Shishakli's private secreatry, Qadri al-Qal'aji and his Director of Information and Propaganda, Nazih Hakim.

The Arab Liberation Movement was ideologically of hybrid growth, borrowing ideas from many different sources. It preached militant Arab nationalism and advocated 'progressive' social and economic policies. Shishakli claimed, in much the same terms as 'Abd al-Nasir was later to use for Egypt, that Syria had been chosen by destiny to free the Arab nation from colonialism, poverty, ignorance, and internal division. In matters of organization the movement was modelled on the PPS. Party militants could be seen marching in and out of their Damascus headquarters greeting each other with raised-arm salutes. Some officers were attracted to it, but no politician of note joined its ranks in spite of considerable pressure by Shishakli to do so. Like many a monolithic movement, allowing no rival, it had no grass-roots in voluntary association, and was no adequate substitute for the political parties to which the Syrian electorate had grown accustomed. But these weaknesses were not at first apparent.

The regime's first anniversary, which was celebrated in Damascus in December 1952 with the biggest military parade in living memory, was marred only by an incident in which a tank skidded into a dense crowd killing fifty-two people. The press took up the theme of Syria's new army, 'an armoured giant of iron and steel', evoking the glorious days of the Middle Ages when Umayyad troops paraded through the city 'on their way to fresh conquests'. Damascus, Shishakli declared, was 'the capital of Arabism today, the heart of the Arab nation where lies Saladin, liberating hero of Palestine'.[7] A year after his second coup, he seemed unshakably secure.

SHISHAKLI AS PRESIDENT

The triumphal arches had barely been dismantled when the first cracks appeared in Shishakli's edifice. Confident of his home base, he visited Cairo on 11 December 1952, where he was applauded standing beside General Nagib, exchanging congratulations on the revolutions which their respective armies had carried out. He wished also to sound the Free Officers on the question of continued Egyptian support for Syria in the face of Iraqi hostility. In this sense, his mission resembled Husni al-Za'im's visit to King Faruq in April 1949. He reminded his hosts that only when Cairo and Damascus had been united by Saladin were the Crusaders defeated.

He returned to Damascus on 16 December to face what was, in effect, a revolutionary situation. Most reports agree that he was met

[7] al-Barada, 4 Dec. 1952.

at the airport by Lieut-Colonel 'Adnan al-Malki, a prominent young officer, who presented him with three urgent requests: the dissolution of the Arab Liberation Movement; the ending of public subscriptions for the army because of allegations that these funds were being diverted to the Movement; the restoration of political freedoms and party political life. Shishakli, who was a good tactician, agreed to the conditions, congratulating Malki on the extent of his following which he ventured to suggest must be extensive. Malki, swallowing the bait, produced a list of officers, political figures, and university professors who shared his objectives. Shishakli promptly jailed them all. He may not have been entirely unprepared for the crisis as other reports suggest that he was urgently recalled from Cairo by his chief of security, Lieut-Colonel Ibrahim al-Husayni.

On 24 December the General Staff announced the uncovering of a plot against the regime and the arrest of a number of officers who 'had allowed themselves to be trapped by subversive ideas spread by certain extremist politicians'. The communiqué added that the accused had been spreading tendentious reports to the effect that the Government was about to join a western Middle East defence scheme and had agreed to settle Palestinian refugees in Syria. A week or two later, at the turn of the year, Akram al-Hawrani and the two Ba'th leaders, Michel 'Aflaq and Salah al-Din Bitar, crossed secretly into Lebanon to avoid arrest and repeated the charges to the Beirut press. Shishakli, therefore, faced a movement of disaffection both in the army and among the men who had been his closest civilian supporters.

The process is familiar whereby a dictator, in the enjoyment of unfettered power, loses touch with his early associates. With increasing confidence, Shishakli had become less accessible. He visited the Officers' Club less frequently and the devotion of his young admirers cooled. He began to groom himself for the Presidency. As his own political ambitions became more pronounced, there loomed the danger of the army's involvement in politics and the desirability of returning it to its barracks and of cutting down its privileges. The officers came to see in him a different man from the popular hero of the early days. Indeed, they came to see him less often.

Shishakli's break with Hawrani, 'Aflaq, and Bitar was a turning-point in his and their careers. He lost the support of what were, in different measures, perhaps the most astute and the most principled men in Syrian public life, while they, united in opposition to his autocracy, entered then into a partnership which was to change the future of the country. In a statement to the Lebanese newspaper *al-Dustur* on 4 January 1953, Hawrani accused Shishakli of 'smothering liberties, muzzling the press and persecuting opponents of the regime'. The Syrian leader, he added, was an accomplice of western defence plans: 'How else can one explain the roads and strategic airfields now being built with the tax-payers' money? And the port of Latakia? And the conventions that are being signed with oil companies?' In Damascus the three fugitives were described as 'secret agents of imperialism', but Lebanon refused the demand for their extradition—in spite of pressure from Shishakli who closed the frontier for twenty-four hours and broke off economic talks. They were, however, finally asked to leave Lebanon in June 1953.

In a bare month—December 1952 to January 1953—things had so changed that a regime which had seemed solid now looked shaky. *Le Monde*, in a dispatch from Damascus on 20 January, wrote that the shadow of civil war hung over the town. Prisons were full of suspects, several people had taken flight, while unrest had spread from the army to the university which had gone on strike for the first time in many months. The incidents shook Shishakli's nerve. He never trusted his fellow men; now he became obsessively suspicious, moving about irregularly and not daring to sleep at home for fear of assassination. But in the spring of 1953 a period of greater stability encouraged him to press ahead with his plans for establishing his regime on a constitutional basis.

The press had for some weeks been hinting at a republican presidential system on the United States model when the draft of a new constitution was published on 21 June. It was also announced that a referendum would be held on 10 July to approve the constitution and that a President would be elected on the same day by direct suffrage. Shishakli himself expounded the main provisions of the constitution in a broadcast, stressing the advantages of presidential rule. He said: 'This draft is more progressive than all the constitutions in the Middle East and even some in the western world; it contains nothing inconsistent with our potentialities or with the real condition of our people.' It laid down that the President, 'elected by the people by universal, secret and equal suffrage', must be a Syrian by birth and would be assisted by ministers appointed by and responsible to him—and not to parliament. Article 1 reiterated that Syria was an Arab, democratic, and sovereign republic, but dropped the term 'parliamentary' from the earlier text. The draft also put an obligation on the state to 'seek to bring about the unity of the Arab nation'.

A Homs newspaper, *al-Suri al-Jadid*—the only opposition organ of the period—printed a manifesto signed by twenty-five lawyers denouncing the referendum as a 'form of Caesarism', but this did not prevent Shishakli's election as President and the ratification of the constitution by overwhelming majorities.[8] Five days later, on 15 July, Shishakli formed a cabinet of lawyers, businessmen, and land-owners, chiefly remarkable for the absence of names formerly associated with Syrian public life.[9] Fawzi Selu, his usefulness at an end, was retired amid rumours of disagreement with Shishakli, while General Shawkat Shuqayr was appointed Chief of Staff. On 30 July a new electoral law, replacing that of September 1949, made provision for a Chamber of only 82 deputies—69 Muslims, 9 Christians, and 4 tribal representatives—each representing 50,000 inhabitants.

Elections were fixed for 9 October, while a decree outlined the conditions for party activity: party statutes must be 'democratic' and contain no suggestion of a secret or para-military association; their avowed aims must not conflict with the objective of Arab unity; there must be no racial or confessional grouping nor should membership be exclusively recruited from any one such group; the army, the police, civil servants, and the student body were barred from all political activity. Eventually, the elections took place quietly amidst public indifference, only the Arab Liberation Movement and the PPS taking part. The other parties were either barred or preferred to boycott the proceedings. The Arab Liberation Movement, as was to be expected, swept the board, securing 60 out of 82 seats, while the PPS won only one, a striking commentary on their lack of public following in spite of their association with the dictator. The remaining seats were accounted for by tribal representatives and Independent candidates.

The new Chamber met for the first time on 24 October to hear the President deliver the Arab nationalist credo which is *de rigueur* on such occasions:

[8] The constitution was approved by 861,152 votes against 2,713 out of an electorate of 995,417. Shishakli, standing as the only presidential candidate, was declared elected by a fractionally larger majority.
[9] President & Premier, Adib al-Shishakli; Interior, Nuri Ibish; Justice, As'ad Mahasin; Health & Social Affairs, Dr Nazim al-Qabbani; Agriculture, 'Abd al-Rahman al-Hunaydi; Foreign Affairs, Khalil Mardam; Finance, Georges Shahin; Defence, Brig. Rifa't Khankan; Public Works & Communications, Fath Allah Asyun; Economy, 'Awn Allah al-Jabiri; Education, Anwar Ibrahim.

By our Syrian Fatherland [he declared] we mean the current official name for that country which lies within the artificial frontiers drawn up by imperialism when it still had the power to write Arab history. But our real Fatherland is the Arab nation which stretches to the heart of the world . . .[10]

Ma'mun al-Kuzbari, a lawyer of standing who eight years later was to head the first Syrian Government after the break-up of the UAR, was elected Speaker.

Three days earlier Hawrani, 'Aflaq, and Bitar returned to Syria under a general amnesty proclaimed by Shishakli after his election to the Presidency.

Shishakli's Government [Salah al-Din Bitar said later] was an illegal regime which he sought to legitimize by means of elections. But only about five per cent of the electorate actually went to the poll. It was then clear that Shishakli was politically finished. He was isolated. The people had learned that, in the long run, military rule could offer them nothing. The way was open for the political parties to join forces to call for an end to dictatorship and for a restoration of the political and other liberties which Shishakli had suppressed.[11]

Shishakli's long tenure of power is not to be explained by the efficiency of his secret police, still less by the originality of his political ideas or the success of his constitutional experiments. He was not a great statesman or reformer, but neither was he a monster of repression. Indeed, even his personal motives are hard to track down: was it power-hunger alone or was he inspired by reformist ideals later perverted? If one reason were to be given for his durability, it may well be the fact that the late 1940s and early 1950s saw the consolidation of Syria's great post-war agricultural boom.[12] Huge tracts of virgin land, idle for centuries, were brought rapidly into cultivation in the rainfed belt which extends in the north-west of the country from Aleppo to the Iraq border across the Euphrates and Jazirah provinces. In the years 1943–53 grain production doubled while cotton production increased nearly tenfold. No other Middle East country could boast such a strikingly rapid rate of expansion. The level of output per head in Syria, measured in the main crops, far outdistanced that of Egypt or Iraq. But Syrian Governments, pursuing a policy of *laisser-faire*, could not claim the credit. The expansion of dry-farming was almost entirely due to the enterprise

[10] *al-Barada* (Damascus), 25 Oct. 1953.
[11] Salah al-Din Bitar to the author, Damascus, 23 Sept. 1960.
[12] See Warriner, pp. 71–112.

of Syrian merchants, mainly of Aleppo, who used risk capital to mechanize agriculture. The principal contribution of Shishakli's regime to this pattern of development was the foundation of the Cotton Bureau[13] in 1952, when the rapid expansion in cotton had been checked by falling prices, crop diseases, and over-cultivation. The Bureau sold improved seed and enforced a number of other control measures. The year of Shishakli's fall—1954—marked a post-war peak both in the total area under cultivation in Syria and in the production figures for the main crops. While, therefore, it may have been prosperity which kept Shishakli in power, it was not general hardship which deprived him of it.

[13] Ibid. p. 74.

13

The Overthrow of Shishakli

A STUDY of Shishakli's downfall reveals more about the intricacies of Syrian politics than a survey of his years in power. Dictators stultify the process of politics by censoring opinion and driving dissent underground. The blanket which they cast over the political scene is only torn aside when their enemies emerge to challenge them. Thus the events which led to Shishakli's flight from Damascus on 25 February 1954 are more instructive than the preceding years of authoritarian rule. But the men who overthrew him were not all impatient democrats. Their motives were both pure and impure: patriotism and hatred of tyranny were reinforced by hopes of personal gain and inducements from abroad.

THE FIRST ASSAULT

'My enemies', Shishakli used to say, 'are like a serpent: the head is the Jabal Druze, the stomach Homs, and the tail Aleppo. If I crush the head the serpent will die.' Shishakli had good reason to fear the Druzes. They were a compact, inbred community of southern Syria, traditionally resistant to rule from Damascus. Their close links with Jordan made them a vehicle for Hashimite influence in Syria. The ease with which they could slip to safety across the border contributed to their factiousness. The celebrated Druze leader Sultan Pasha al-Atrash had sought asylum with King 'Abdallah after the collapse of the 1925 revolt against the French, only returning to Syria when amnestied in 1936. Britain had developed a certain connexion with some Druzes families—a relationship far less extensive than the long-standing ties which Russia had with the Greek Orthodox community in the Levant and France with the Maronites but which may have gone some way to explaining why the Druzes were on good terms with Britain's Hashimite friends.

The Jabal was integrated into Syria in 1945, losing the near-autonomy it had enjoyed under the Mandate. This did not make for easy relations with post-war Syrian Governments. Indeed, Druze complicity in the conspiracy against Shishakli was only one incident in a long history of feuding with Damascus. In 1947 President Quwatli made a bid to curb the power of the Atrash family in the Jabal. Enlisting the aid of King Ibn Sa'ud (by persuading him of Druze plans to make King 'Abdallah king of Syria) Quwatli encouraged the Druze peasantry to rise against its Atrash landlords. The embattled share-croppers, organized in a movement called the *Sha'biyyun*, set fire to Atrash houses in half a dozen villages and called on Sultan Pasha in his stronghold of al-Quraya to surrender. But the veteran Sultan held a council of war and summoned his fighting men who, led by Hasan al-Atrash, defeated the rebels in a pitched battle near the village of Baqqa. Amir Hasan claims[1] that the Syrian Defence Minister, Ahmad al-Sharabati, awaited the outcome with a battalion of government troops twenty miles away, ready to occupy the Jabal once the Atrashes had been driven out. But with the failure of the rebellion, Sharabati withdrew his troops to Damascus, leaving the Druzes to make their peace between themselves.

This abortive intrigue against the Druzes weakened Quwatli's position and contributed to the success of Za'im's coup d'état. But, as has been seen,[2] Za'im in turn aroused Druze hostility on assuming power and Druze officers were prominent among the conspirators who overthrew him. Shishakli's relations with Sultan Pasha were never cordial. They worsened when Mansur, one of Sultan's sons, was arrested for taking part in a Ba'th demonstration against Shish-akli. According to Shishakli's Chief of Staff, General Shawkat Shuqayr, information reaching the dictator in the months before his fall pointed to plans by his opponents at home and abroad to start a revolt in the Jabal which would then spread to the whole country.[3]

The town of Homs, fief of the Atasi family—and the 'stomach' of Shishakli's serpent—was the main opposition centre to him through-out his rule. How the Atasis had joined the newly-formed People's Party in 1948, opposing Quwatli's National Party and promoting closer ties with Iraq, has already been described. Great landed families such as the Atasis still retained at that time a considerable hold over the countryside, although they were soon to lose control of the central Government to the army and were beginning to see

---

[1] Hasan al-Atrash to the author, Beirut, 21 Oct. 1960.   [2] p. 74 above.
[3] Gen. Shawkat Shuqayr to the author, Beirut, 18 Dec. 1960.

their economic supremacy challenged by a small group of industrial-
ists[4] and by a class of 'merchant-tractorists'[5] who were opening up
the virgin lands of the north-east to mechanized agriculture. By the
early 1950s the traditional pattern of power had been disturbed but
had not yet suffered the assaults of the post-Suez years. Indeed,
the popular ex-President, Hashim al-Atasi, whose family, retainers,
and friends dominated the town of Homs and much of the surrounding country, was not a figure with whom Shishakli dared openly to
clash. Under his patronage Homs was enabled to publish *al-Suri
al-Jadid* (The New Syrian), the only opposition newspaper then
appearing.

It was in that city that representatives of all parties and groups
hostile to Shishakli met secretly on 4 July 1953, to put their signatures
to a National Pact which was, in effect, a pledge to bring the dictator
down. The National and People's Parties, the Ba'th, the Communists,
and a number of influential 'independents' all agreed to unite in a
common effort to overthrow him. Shishakli's attempts to legitimize
his regime by the ratification of a constitution and by his election to
the Presidency encouraged his opponents to emerge from underground. They agreed that each province of Syria should prepare for
its own liberation, but that the signal for revolt throughout the
country would be a rising in the Jabal Druze.

The Druze leader, Hasan al-Atrash, recounts what then took
place in the Jabal:[6]

In mid-1953 the National Party leader Sabri al-'Asali sent word to me
to say that we must join forces to save the country from dictatorship. Our
meeting marked the beginning of the movement against Shishakli. We
started to marshal our forces in the Jabal while the politicians in turn held
a series of secret meetings to organize an effective opposition. The climax
of these contacts was the signature of the pact of Homs.

There then occurred a grave error of timing. Before our preparations
were ready, the Ba'th caused anti-Shishakli tracts to be distributed in the
Jabal—perhaps in a bid to seize the leadership of the opposition movement.
Their action, by alerting the authorities, brought disaster upon us. Acting
swiftly to forestall a revolt, Shishakli arrested a Druze delegation which was

---

[4] Notably an industrial group known as *al-Khumasiya* (The Five) in which the
leading associates were Badr al-Din Diab, 'Abd al-Hadi Rabbath, 'Abd al-Hamid
Diab, Muhammad Adil Khuja, and Anwar Qutub, with interests in cotton, cement,
sugar refining, soap, glass, petroleum, etc.
[5] The phrase is Doreen Warriner's (pp. 71 ff).
[6] Hasan al-Atrash to the author, 24 Oct. 1960.

then in Damascus (and included myself) and sent strong forces to the Jabal. Sultan Pasha was virtually besieged in his own house at al-Quraya.

My arrest and this display of force caused the Druzes to demonstrate against the Government in our capital of Suwayda. Shishakli interpreted this as the first move in a prearranged plan to overthrow him and determined to nip the revolt in the bud. He sent armoured units to occupy the city. He also made much of the slanderous charge that we were hand in glove with Israel by displaying Israeli arms captured at the front as if they had been seized in the Jabal. Provoked in this way, the whole south of the Jabal gathered at al-Quraya. It was more of a mob than a military force but the government troops, frightened perhaps at their numbers, closed in on them and suffered a number of casualties before falling back.

The army was by then thoroughly roused against the villagers. It regrouped at Suwayda and started to massacre the population. Heavy weapons were used and some atrocities committed. The army then occupied the whole of the Jabal and the Druze leaders escaped across the frontier to Jordan. We heard that Kamal Jumblat [the Lebanese Druze leader] was ready to march to our aid from across the mountains, but the passes were thick with snow. . . .

The events in the Jabal here described by Amir Hasan reached their climax in the last week of January 1954. They had been accompanied by strikes and student demonstrations in the principal Syrian cities. Aleppo—the 'tail' of Shishakli's serpent—had set the pace. It was not only the stronghold of his old enemies, the People's Party, but also the home, as is north Syria as a whole, of numerous racial and religious minorities against whom many of Shishakli's 'reforms', aiming at the creation of a homogeneous Arab-Muslim state, seemed directed. Kurds, Assyrians, Armenians, Alawis, and Christian minorities of all sorts were harried by a swarm of decrees ordaining that hotels, cafés, and cinemas be given purely Arabic names, that Arabic be the language spoken at all public meetings, festivals, or celebrations, that Muslims sit in equal numbers with non-Muslims on all committees of minority organizations, whether cultural, social, or athletic, and that the spiritual heads of minority communities be banned from addressing public meetings outside their own places of worship.

Early in December 1953 students clashed with police in Aleppo and shops closed in sympathy with the demonstrators.[7] The Homs opposition newspaper *al-Suri al-Jadid* reported that teachers and

[7] Disturbances started when students attempted to set fire to the American college in Aleppo in protest against a school play which they alleged expressed anti-Arab sentiments.

pupils had been wounded and that Aleppo lawyers had struck in protest against police brutality. The issue snowballed. The arrest of three Aleppo lawyers brought students into the streets in Homs and Hama as well as Damascus, where several arrests were made and university lectures suspended.

It was then that this unrest ignited into violence in the Jabal as described above, leading Shishakli to believe that his enemies were about to strike at him. He forestalled them by ordering the arrest of two dozen leading politicians[8] on the night of 27–28 January and by confining the revered but by now openly rebellious Hashim al-Atasi to his house in Homs. A state of emergency was declared while senior army commanders were appointed Deputy Governors in the Aleppo, Homs–Hama, and Jabal Druze *muhafazas*. In Damascus itself the Chief of the General Staff, General Shawkat Shuqayr, became Deputy Governor while Shishakli retained the governorship.

The politicians struck back with an impassioned manifesto issued in the name of the National Front calling on the people to rise and rid themselves of the dictator and the 'vermin' about him, while Hashim al-Atasi appealed to member states of the Arab League to intervene before they too were 'contaminated' by the Shishakli poison. On the same day, 28 January, the Damascus and Aleppo bar associations issued sharply worded protests against the arrests, while Shishakli broadcast an appeal to the 'noble Syrian people' warning them against 'saboteurs who had abused constitutional freedoms, excited the population to sedition and exploited the patriotism of students'. Tempers then cooled. By 31 January the Government was claiming that order had been restored throughout the territory. Early in February outgoing press censorship was lifted, as was the curfew in the Jabal; the Syro-Lebanese frontier which had been momentarily closed was reopened and the Government started talks with the detained political leaders in an attempt at a reconciliation. To many observers Shishakli appeared to have weathered the storm.

THE ROLE OF IRAQ

This pause in the assault on Shishakli gives an occasion to set Syria's internal disturbances in a wider context: it is no secret that his

---

[8] The arrested men included Sabri al-'Asali of the National Party; Rushdi al-Kikhia, 'Ali Buzo, Shakir al-'As, Faydi and 'Adnan al-Atasi of the People's Party; Akram al-Hawrani; the Ba'th leaders Michel 'Aflaq and Salah al-Din Bitar; the Amir Hasan al-Atrash, and a number of Damascus university professors active in politics such as 'Abd al-Wahab Hawmad, Rizq Allah Antaki, and Munir al-'Ajlani.

domestic opponents had foreign friends. As has been seen, Syrian coups are often the work of a temporary coalition of men within the country supported by outside sympathizers. Inspired by widely different motives, the conspirators unite in the desire for change. Much of the evidence suggests that the insurrection against Shishakli was encouraged and financed by Iraq.

It was part of the logic of Arab politics that Shishakli's internal enemies should find support in Baghdad, where he was seen as the main obstacle to the expansion of Hashimite influence in Arab Asia. Since his first coup in December 1949, he had rebuffed Iraq's advances, hounded her friends in Syria and, in the name of Syrian independence, forged close links with Saudi Arabia. His second coup in November 1951 had driven the pro-Iraqi People's Party from office. All these were good reasons for Baghdad to desire his downfall. But only the Iraqi Regent's strong personal interest in Syria can fully explain the eagerness with which Iraq welcomed the appearance of the first cracks in the Syrian monolith.

'Abd ul-Ilah had watched the consolidation of Shishakli's regime with mortification and disquiet: his own future was uncertain as his regency was due to end on 1 May 1953, with the accession of Faysal II. The 'throne of Syria' which he dreamed of securing for himself seemed, therefore, all the more desirable. It had needed dogged ambition to keep his hopes alive in 1952, the year of Shishakli's unchallenged supremacy, but they had revived when the Syrian dictator came under attack at home. Shishakli's opponents of all political complexions found encouragement in Baghdad for their seditious plans.

Iraq's involvement, which was not widely understood at the time, was revealed four years later, in 1958, when General Qasim's revolutionary Government brought to trial servants of the former regime. It was then made clear in evidence brought before the court that numerous Syrian politicians had been in intimate contact with the Iraqi Government, in many cases receiving regular payments from it.[9] Shishakli's suspicions of Iraq were not, therefore, without

[9] Some embarrassment was caused by disclosures made during the Baghdad trials. Sabri al-'Asali, to take one example, was forced to resign from the vice-presidency of the UAR when it was revealed that he had received 15,000 dinars from Iraq during the campaign against Shishakli. (See his statement to al-Ahram (Cairo) on 7 Oct. 1958, as well as Muhammad Hasanayn Haykal, Maza gara fi Suriya? (What happened in Syria?), a series of articles in al-Ahram from 13 Oct. to 1 Dec. 1961. See also BBC, no. 793, 13 Nov. 1961.) Ma'ruf al-Dawalibi, Syrian Premier for 24 hours before being overthrown by Shishakli in 1951, stated in a letter to the Presi-

foundation. A detailed plan existed for an armed invasion of Syria from Iraq which General Ghazi al-Daghistani, Deputy Chief of Staff of the Iraqi army, admitted at his trial having inherited from his predecessor early in 1954.[10] This 'Plan X' is believed to have been drawn up in 1953 by the Iraqi military attaché in Damascus, 'Abd al-Mutallib al-Amin.

In view of her considerable influence in Iraq at the time, Britain could scarcely have been ignorant of what was being planned. She did not, at any rate, escape the accusation of having encouraged the assault on Shishakli. As early as 21 April 1953 Le Monde declared that

we are witnessing manoeuvres, very probably inspired by Great Britain, to rouse Syria's Arab partners against her. . . . It is not the first time that Syria's internal peace is disturbed by foreign intrigue or that Britain has attempted to draw in to her sphere of influence this key piece on the Middle East chessboard.

But the alacrity with which the French press sprang to defend Shishakli as a 'champion of Syrian independence' was not unconnected with the fact that France had recovered, under his regime, some of her influence in her former mandated territory. On 17 October Le Monde reported the formation in Baghdad of a 'Free Syrian Government' headed by Colonel Muhammad Safa[11] and renewed its accusations against Britain—charges which Shishakli was himself to make against a 'foreign Power' when his regime was near collapse early in 1954.[12]

The Syrian press, enlarging on these accusations, discerned behind the disturbances a British plot to set up a puppet Government in Damascus which would commit Syria to a Fertile Crescent federation; join with Israel in a regional defence pact; and isolate Egypt and Saudi Arabia—all of which, the reports alleged, would benefit British as opposed to American interests in the Middle East.[13] That some of these fantasies were believed bears witness to the credibility of Syrians and to the incoherence of British Middle East policy.

dent of the Baghdad court, which was read out during Fadil al-Jamali's trial, that Nuri and the Regent had offered him financial and military assistance against Shishakli at a meeting in Baghdad in the summer of 1953, but that he had refused (see BBC, no. 663, 25 Sept. 1958).

[10] See Iraq, Min. of Defence, *Mahkamat al-Sha'b* (1958), i. 276.

[11] Safa was one of the officers retired by Shishakli after the abortive coup against him in December 1952.

[12] See his statement to *al-Gumhuriya* (Cairo), 2 Feb. 1954.

[13] See, in particular, *al-Fayha* (Damascus), 3, 4, and 9 Feb. 1954.

The early 1950s saw a steep climb in Iraq's oil output, from 6 million tons in 1950 to 30 million in 1954. Britain's prime interest was in a stable and friendly Syria which would ensure the safety of the Iraq Petroleum Company pipelines to the Mediterranean. She had no real interest in a Syro-Iraqi union which would have been fiercely opposed by the Saudis, the Egyptians, and the French as well as by radical Arab nationalists everywhere. It would, moreover, have meant exporting Syria's problems to Iraq. But Britain had obligations of friendship to the Hashimites: having rescued the Iraqi Regent in 1941 and built him up into a considerable figure after the war, she could not oppose too openly his designs in Syria. Indeed, she was the more inclined to fall in with Iraqi plans as she was facing mounting difficulties in Egypt. She may not have fully appreciated the growing gulf which divided Arab nationalists from the Hashimite family. Iraq, with her great rivers and soaring oil wealth, seemed in British eyes a strong candidate for Arab leadership. Her friendly ruling house, Nuri's statesmanship, and the British connexion seemed further powerful assets when the situation was weighed in London. But viewed from an Arab capital these were just the counts on which Iraq was disqualified for Arab leadership.

Thus whatever the real or imagined role of the Great Powers, the conspiracy against Shishakli took shape with Iraqi aid in the autumn of 1953 exploding, as has been described, into overt unrest in January 1954. Early that month the Iraqi Premier, Fadil al-Jamali, seeking to exploit the anti-Shishakli trend in Syria, put before the Arab League a plan for a federal Arab union to be brought about by stages starting with Syria, Iraq, and Jordan. His Foreign Minister made a proposal whereby Iraq would finance the creation of an Arab army from her oil revenues. But both Egypt and Saudi Arabia were suspicious of these proposals and Syria dismissed them as a fresh incarnation of the Fertile Crescent project which Shishakli had opposed throughout his political career.

This brusque rejection angered Iraq and strengthened the resolution of her Syrian friends. The Iraqi press castigated the Syrian dictator as 'an instrument in the hands of French imperialism' and called on other Arab states to intervene. The chairman of the Foreign Affairs Committee of the Iraqi Chamber, Sadiq al-Bassam, urged the Premier to call an immediate meeting of the Arab League 'because the Syrian affair is not just an internal question but one which concerns all the Arabs'. Two days later, on 4 February, Syria demanded the recall of the Iraqi military attaché in Damascus 'for actions exceeding the scope of his official duties'. His payment of subsidies to Syrian politicians and newspapers had, in fact, become notorious.

On the same day in Beirut, leaders of the Druze community in Lebanon met in congress to inform world opinion and the Red Cross of the massacre of their Syrian co-religionaries. Kamal Jumblat delivered a fiery attack on Shishakli, to which the Damascus authorities replied by closing the frontier on 6 February.

Violently at odds with both Iraq and Lebanon, Shishakli found strong support in Egypt where both President Nagib and Anwar al-Sadat, a prominent member of the Revolutionary Command Council, urged the Syrians to close their ranks against 'imperialist agents and their filthy British backers'. But Saudi Arabia was Shishakli's principal support in the face of Iraqi pressure. Shaikh Yusuf Yasin, the man mainly responsible for Saudi foreign policy, detested Iraq and directed an ever growing proportion of Saudi Arabia's mounting oil revenues to preventing an Iraqi-Syrian *entente*. It was largely due to the mediation of the Saudi ambassador in Damascus, Shaikh 'Abd al-'Aziz ibn Zayd, that the Syro-Lebanese frontier was reopened twenty-four hours after its closure.

Tension was subsiding in the Syrian capital. The Lebanese Premier, 'Abdallah al-Yafi, visited the city with an offer of mediation after the Iraqi Premier, Jamali, had travelled to Beirut on a conciliatory mission. The Syrian parliament met from 8 to 10 February to voice routine accusations against Iraq, the British, and their *agents provocateurs*, but the crisis seemed past. The public awaited in a quieter mood the outcome of the talks between Shishakli and the detained opposition leaders whose release was expected daily.

There is no longer any doubt [*Le Monde* declared on 23 February] that the Syrian conspirators acted in concert with forces outside the country. The latent conflict between the regime and the opposition cannot alone explain the gravity of recent events. It now seems well established that the supporters of the Fertile Crescent—the union of Syria with Iraq and Jordan—sought to exploit internal difficulties in order to overthrow Shishakli, who is known as a bulwark of Syrian independence. Their skill lay in shuffling the cards and in disguising as an internal crisis what was in effect a manoeuvre against Syria's independence . . . But General Shishakli has emerged victorious from this new trial of strength.

Two days later, his enemies mounted their swift and decisive assault on him.

THE ARMY REVOLT

Shishakli was overthrown by a military insurrection. His principal civilian opponents were in jail and the frontiers quiet when at 6.30 a.m. on 25 February 1954 Captain Mustafa Hamdun of the Aleppo garrison broadcast the first call to revolt, appealing to Shishakli to leave the country to avoid bloodshed.

This is not a communiqué [he declared], but an avowal, an undertaking and an appeal. It is an avowal of the situation to which the army and the people have been reduced by a handful of evil men. . . . It is an undertaking to wash clean the shame and disgrace suffered by the army, to restore its noble virtue and to return it to its barracks in discipline. . . . It is finally a call to arms and to honour. . . .

An hour or two before this mutinous declaration—which complacent Damascus at first dismissed as an Israeli broadcast—Major Faysal al-Atasi, chief staff officer of the 2nd division stationed at Aleppo, arrested his commanding officer, Colonel 'Umar Khan Tamir, as well as the *muhafiz* of Aleppo and the leading local members of Shishakli's Arab Liberation Movement. Tanks, on his orders, took up positions in the main streets while troops occupied the Post Office, the broadcasting station, and government buildings. At about 8.30 a.m. Colonel Amin Abu Assaf, the 3rd division commander stationed at Deir ez-Zor, publicly rallied to the insurgents.

Each of these three chief conspirators, Faysal al-Atasi, Amin Abu Assaf, and Mustafa Hamdun, represented an important faction in the coalition which opposed Shishakli. Major Atasi, a nephew of the former President, Hashim al-Atasi, stood for the centre of rebellion at Homs; the Druze Abu Assaf represented the Jabal which had borne the brunt of Shishakli's repression; finally, Captain Hamdun, a native of Hama, was a close friend and political disciple of Akram al-Hawrani. The army, then, was acting as an instrument of sectional civilian interests, but it was reinforced by its own distinct motives for revolt: Shishakli's attitude towards it had changed. As he sought to legitimize his regime, so he ceased to regard the army as an élite corps and, by trimming its privileges and powers, attempted to restore it to something like its normal, more modest, position in the life of the nation. This trend had been bitterly resented by most officers outside the President's immediate entourage who, in addition, saw their careers and promotions governed by the whims of the dictator's favourites.

By 9 a.m. the commander of the west coast Latakia garrison, Major 'Abd al-Jawad Raslan, had joined the uprising, followed a few hours later by Colonel Mahmud Shawkat, commanding the Homs–Hama region of central Syria. In Aleppo Major Atasi summoned the foreign consuls to inform them of the gains made by the insurgents. An ultimatum addressed that morning to Shishakli called on him to leave Syrian territory by 9 p.m. or face trial for high treason. The mutinous officers further announced that they had agreed to ask Hashim al-Atasi to return to the Presidency from which he had resigned following Shishakli's second coup in November 1951.

The whole country north of Damascus was up in arms: in the early afternoon the commanders of the Aleppo, Deir ez-Zor, Latakia, and Homs–Hama garrisons put their names to a proclamation addressed to all newspapers in the Arab world declaring that the Syrian army, free from all personal or political ambition, had risen in answer to the people's call to restore legitimate and democratic government. In the early evening Colonel 'Umar Qabbani, commanding the Hawran garrison in southern Syria, rallied in turn to the insurrection. Ten thousand of Shishakli's best troops were pinned down in the Jabal Druze. Damascus stood alone.

General Shishakli spent the morning in conference with his civilian advisers and headquarters staff. They are believed to have decided[14] that the forces at his disposal—which included the bulk of Syria's armour and heavy artillery based on Qatana and Qabun—should take up defensive positions, moving in to attack only in the event of an armed intervention by Israel or by a neighbouring Arab state. No troops were to be withdrawn from the Israeli frontier. These decisions were reached before the Aleppo ultimatum had been delivered or word had reached Shishakli that the Hawran and Homs–Hama garrisons had gone over to the rebels. These matters were considered at a sombre meeting in the afternoon at which a majority of Shishakli's colleagues enjoined him to resign. This advice was accepted.

At 10 p.m.—the insurgents having agreed to extend their time-limit by one hour—the President left Damascus for Beirut and exile. Damascus radio broke the news at midnight, following the announcement with the closing paragraph of the letter of resignation which

14 *al-Hayat* (Beirut), 26 Feb. 1954.

Shishakli had addressed on his departure to the President of the Chamber, Dr Ma'mun al-Kuzbari.

Wishing [Shishakli wrote] to avoid shedding the blood of the people whom I love, of the army for which I have sacrificed everything, and of the Arab nation which I have sought to serve in sincere devotion, I submit my resignation from the Presidency to the beloved Syrian people who elected me and who gave me their confidence, in the hope that my gesture will serve the cause of my country. I pray God to preserve it from all ill, to make it united and invincible and to lead it to the heights of glory.[15]

Why did Shishakli not stay and fight it out? With a virtual monopoly of tanks and heavy guns he had more than an even chance of mastering the rebel garrisons. Damascus radio did not quote earlier passages from his letter of resignation in which he explained that he could easily have crushed the rebels but only at the cost of splitting the army—'our own flesh and blood'—and weakening Syria's defence in the face of the enemy on the frontier. These reasons may well have carried weight with him. He may also have been led to believe that if it came to a fight the insurgents would call on the Iraqi army, thus throwing open to Baghdad that doorway into Syria which it had been his dedicated policy to keep closed.[16]

Moreover, Shishakli's temperament was not combative. He had been an able commander in the Palestine War but in politics his instinct was to defeat his enemies by intrigue rather than frontal assault. He may have calculated that his best chance was to feign defeat and retire to Beirut before springing back upon the rebels in the unguarded moment of triumph. He may again have wearied of power, holding that with money in foreign banks and an assured home in Saudi Arabia he would do well to retire with life and dignity while there was yet time. The Syrian has an undeserved reputation for violence. The truth is that more often than not in Syrian conflicts both sides, whatever their threats, conspire to stop short of bloodshed.

THE INTERREGNUM

Confusion followed Shishakli's sudden departure on 25 February. The insurgents had not yet closed in on Damascus where supreme authority lay with the Chief of the General Staff, General Shawkat

[15] *Cahiers*, xxix (1954), p. 74.
[16] The insurgents' relations with Baghdad after the start of the uprising, or indeed with the 'Free Syrian Government' of Col. Safa, are not clear.

Shuqayr. His first move was to broadcast an appeal for calm; then, shortly after midnight, when Shishakli can scarcely have reached Beirut, he went in person to Mezze prison to release the score of prominent politicians who for the previous month had impotently watched the development of the crisis from behind bars. But there were other contenders for power in the Syrian capital that night.

Two key officers of the Damascus garrison, the military police chief, Captain 'Abd al-Haq Shehade, and the commander of a local armoured unit, Captain Husayn Hiddeh, refused to concur in the swift collapse of Shishakli's regime. They had too great a stake in it to see it supplanted without a fight[17] and had strongly opposed the majority decision recommending Shishakli to resign. They found a cautious ally in Dr Ma'mun al-Kuzbari, the President of the Chamber, who called parliament into session on 26 February and read the fallen dictator's letter of resignation to those few deputies who were bold enough to venture out of doors.[18] Invoking Articles 86 and 89 of the constitution, Kuzbari then declared himself acting President of the Republic, relinquishing his own presidency of the Chamber to Sa'id Ishaq, the Vice-President. The session was then adjourned until the following morning.

But at 8.15 p.m. that evening, Damascus radio broadcast a communiqué which sounded like a call to counter-revolution. Signed by General Shawkat Shuqayr, it pledged the backing of the General Staff for the acting President and 'opposed any change or overthrow of the regime not brought about by legal means'. It later emerged that Captains Shehade and Hiddeh had issued the statement in General Shuqayr's name after first kidnapping him.

While this last-ditch stand was being prepared the Aleppo insurgents were getting restive. They broadcast two proclamations on 26 February demanding a clean break with the past and sent planes over Damascus with tracts accusing the officers of the armoured unit of threatening the nation with civil war and calling on the citizens

[17] Shehade may have had more specific fears. Shortly before the Second World War a crank called Sulayman Murshid had proclaimed himself God and founded a politico-religious cult near Latakia. He had been used by the local French political officers to sabotage the 1936 treaty which provided for the integration of the Alawi and Druze areas into the Republic of Syria. Shukri al-Quwatli had had him hanged. Murshid's son tried to revive the movement under Shishakli. Shehade was sent to investigate and killed him in a brawl. He may have feared that the case would be reopened after Shishakli's fall. He was, in fact, brought to trial later and condemned to death *in absentia* on 11 November 1954.
[18] 46 members were present.

to rise against the Kuzbari–Shuqayr faction. Their appeal was heard. As parliament met on the morning of 27 February, student demonstrators, joined by phalanxes of Druzes, Communists, and Muslim Brethren, took the Chamber by assault, withdrawing only when Sa'id Ishaq had assured them that the House had just agreed on its own dissolution. General Shuqayr, by this time released, issued a communiqué declaring the Chamber dissolved and investing Dr Kuzbari with provisional executive and legislative powers 'pending final arrangements to be made in agreement with the authorities of the country'.[19]

But the rebels were still not satisfied. At noon the five insurgent area commanders issued a fresh ultimatum addressed to Kuzbari calling on him to resign forthwith, as neither the army nor the people recognized the legality of the regime which he was seeking to perpetuate. Insurgent columns were rumoured to be moving on Damascus. To avoid a clash, General Shuqayr then decided to treat directly with the rebel commanders who had gathered at Hashim al-Atasi's house in Homs. After consulting the politicians whom he had released from prison, he drove to Homs late on 27 February and spent the night in hammering out a political solution. He returned to Damascus at dawn and broadcast a communiqué declaring that he had reached agreement with the political leaders and the insurgent chiefs to restore power to its rightful holders.

This was the signal for a great explosion of anger in the city against Shishakli and the group of men still faithful to him who had entrenched themselves in the Damascus radio building. Demonstrators attacked the building in mid-afternoon on 28 February, only to be thrown back by tear gas and small-arms fire. But braving the curfew they reassembled in their thousands and renewed their assault later in the day. As troops fired volley after volley into the advancing crowd, the director of the station, Ahmad 'Isseh, one of Shishakli's ablest advisers, escaped from the building with a strong bodyguard. Swept aside by these events, Dr Kuzbari submitted his resignation to General Shuqayr, while Captains Shehade and Hiddeh, surrendering at last, left that night for Europe as the newly-appointed military attachés in London and Paris. On the following morning, 1 March 1954, Hashim al-Atasi entered Damascus in triumph at the head of a procession of 400 cars before climbing to the presidential palace on the hill above the city.

[19] *al-Bina'* (Beirut), 27 Feb. 1954.

SHISHAKLI IN EXILE

Adib al-Shishakli spent his first night of exile in the Saudi Arabian embassy in Beirut. He was due to leave at dawn the following morning but the swarm of journalists and photographers who had taken the airport by storm awaited him in vain. The situation in Damascus was confused. Messages reached Shishakli from his supporters urging him to return. The Lebanese authorities, aware of Druze hatred of him, feared that an attempt might be made on his life while on Lebanese soil. There is strong evidence to suggest that the Iraqi authorities were prepared to go to considerable lengths to prevent his reinstatement in Damascus. On orders from Baghdad, the Iraqi embassy in Beirut is understood to have reached an agreement with Lebanese Druze leaders for Shishakli's liquidation. It would be put about that the Druzes were avenging themselves for the massacre of their co-religionaries in the Jabal.

But President Camille Sham'un of Lebanon, anxious to avoid a disturbance, gave the Iraqis assurances that Shishakli would depart promptly on the morrow, and the plot was called off. The Saudis also let Shishakli understand that he could leave their embassy only for Saudi Arabia. On 27 February, accompanied by the Lebanese Director of Security, the Chief of Police, and the Chief of the General Staff, Shishakli was taken under heavy escort to Beirut international airport where he boarded a Saudi royal aircraft for Riyad.

'Shishaklism' did not long survive him as a political force in Syria. Freed from authoritarianism, the country heaved a great sigh of relief and vowed never again to submit to military rule. But for months and even years after his departure Damascus lived in grudging awe of him: the mention of his name or the rumour, periodically taken up in the Arabic press, of his passage through a neighbouring airport, was still enough to raise a flutter.

His political legacy only gradually became clear. The army, fully roused to political ambition, was never again properly to return to its barracks until the union with Egypt four years later—and then only for the brief life of the UAR. Tainted by its tenure of power, it was also infected by complicity in the long conspiracy against Shishakli. A politician like Sabri al-'Asali, to take one example, whose collusion with Iraq was known to the officers, thereby signed away on that account part of his freedom of action. The army, in fact, became

inextricably wedded to politics and came to reflect civilian factionalism in its own structure. Revolution, George Orwell remarks somewhere, is a corrupting process. It is not merely that 'power corrupts';
so also do the ways of attaining power. Much had also changed on
the civilian party front since the army's first intervention in politics
four years earlier. As the 1954 elections were shortly to reveal,
ideologically-based parties, ramifying underground, had known
better than their more traditional rivals how to take advantage of
Shishakli's dictatorship.

   But Shishakli's considerable achievement was to give Syria a strong
Government during a period of transition in Middle East affairs. He
took Syria out of the fierce play of inter-Arab politics, protecting her
in the early 1950s both from Hashimite expansionism (to which
Iraq's mounting oil revenues of £2 million in 1950 and £67 million
in 1954 were giving teeth) and from the impact of revolutionary
Egypt. His own pan-Arab pretensions were not of serious consequence, undermined as they were by his own confused thinking and
the poverty of his domestic resources. He was above all a Syrian
nationalist who resisted pressure not only from his neighbours but
also from Great Powers, refusing to co-operate in their attempts to
organize the area for defence to the extent of refusing Point IV aid.
His fall left Syria unprotected in the coming battle between Egypt
and Iraq over the Baghdad Pact.[20]

---

[20] Adib al-Shishakli was shot dead near his farm at Ceres, in the state of Goias,
Brazil, on 27 September 1964. He was 55 and had been living in Brazil since 1960.
His assassin was identified as Nawas al-Ghazali, a Druze, whose motive was thought
to be revenge for Shishakli's repression of the Jabal Druze ten years earlier.

14

The Ba'th and the Communists

THE parties of the left in Syria are of special interest as dynamic instruments of change. Their political action drew its force from a body of ideas which may be said to have transformed the attitudes and ways of thinking of a whole generation of Arab youth. Ideologically the Ba'th and the Communists had much in common, but as contenders for power they had long been bitter rivals, uniting only at brief moments of crisis when they had cause to fear 'imperialism' or domestic 'reaction' more than each other. A study of their growth and interaction throws light on the origins of radical Arab nationalism as it developed after the Second World War. Their leaders had been active since the 1930s but it was not until Shishakli's fall in 1954 that they secured the political recognition to which they were entitled by their impact on the public mind.

ORIGINS OF THE BA'TH

Two young Syrians, Michel 'Aflaq and Salah al-Din Bitar, the one a Christian and the other a Muslim, became inseparable when students in Paris from 1929 to 1934.

Before going to France I was simply a nationalist ['Aflaq said later], I had been greatly influenced by my father who had taken an active part in the struggle against the French and had been imprisoned several times. Nationalism was our local reality, but Bitar and I discovered socialism in France. On our return we were eager to pass on these ideas to a new generation.[1]

They did not for some years devote themselves wholly to politics. Instead 'Aflaq began teaching history and Bitar physics in a Damascus secondary school. Students were the most politically conscious members of the community, providing fertile ground for their ideas. In 1935 they helped found and edit a left-wing weekly called *al-Tali'a*

[1] Michel 'Aflaq to the author, Beirut, 3 Jan. 1961.

(Vanguard) which was frankly revolutionary in its views on literary, social as well as political questions.

Both men have described their experiences at this time:

> In 1928 (before we went to Europe) we saw nationalism simply as a struggle between the nation and the colonizer. . . . In the country those who helped the foreigner were called traitors and those who opposed them nationalists. . . . Then we went to France and found support among Communists for the nationalist cause. . . . We read the great liberal thinkers of the West and acquired a picture of an enlightened society, free from misery and corruption. We discovered that we were suffering not only from national wounds inflicted by the foreigner but also from social wounds because our society was sunk in ignorance and falsehood. We then understood that the struggle against the colonizer had to be waged by the people as a whole. . . .
>
> We returned to Syria to find that the national leaders were men who could not see beyond their economic and family interests . . . To be effective, the struggle against the colonizer had to involve a change of mind and of thought, a deepening of national consciousness and of moral standards; it was related to the nation's intellectual and moral life.[2]

FLIRTATION WITH COMMUNISM

It was then, in the early 1930s, that 'Aflaq and Bitar first made contact with the local Communist Party, which consisted at the time of 'two or three young men in prison and two or three others on the run'.[3] They remained on intimate and friendly terms until 1936. 'We were then Marxists with few reservations', 'Aflaq explained.[4]

The Communists were being persecuted by the authorities and we admired them and sympathized with them for it. They were vigorous in attacking foreign colonialism and seemed to us to give life and movement to our old stagnant Arab society. But I was suspicious of their dogmatic views since I had learned my socialism from André Gide and Romain Rolland ['noble souls, far above Communist factionalism', as he says in another context].[5]

'Aflaq greatly admired Gide. He was himself a poet and as a young man had written some promising short stories. Politics, he confided, were a refuge for an unsuccessful writer. He showed little interest in Marxist economics, but like Gide and Rolland saw Communism

---

[2] Salah al-Din Bitar and Michel 'Aflaq, al-Qawmiyya al-'arabiyya wa mauqafuha min al-shuyu'iyya (1944).
[3] Ibid. p. 15.   [4] Michel 'Aflaq to the author, Beirut, 3 Jan. 1961.
[5] Bitar and 'Aflaq, p. 13.

as a way of life, a metaphysical cure which would end war and exploitation. Like them again he was far too individualistic ever to join the Communist Party. 'They later claimed that I had held a card', he said, 'but you may be sure that had any such documentary proof existed they would have exploited it to the full.'[6]

'Aflaq's flirtation with Communism ended in 1936,[7] when he was disillusioned by Communist tactics following the formation of the Popular Front administration in France. While pressing for some relaxation of the Mandatory regime, the Communists stood nevertheless for its retention. This caused sharp disappointment. At home 'Aflaq had his first taste of the opportunism of the local party which now emerged noisily from underground.

The Syrian Communist Party [he wrote] became nothing more than an executive tool of its French parent party and of the French Government in general. . . . It began to recruit members from among confessional and ethnic minorities, among all those who opposed Arab nationalism. . . . It dropped its revolutionary demands and lent its weight to the French colonial regime. . . . Indeed, its very existence became dependent on France's continued hold over Syria. . . . It forgot its real enemies and concentrated instead on attacking Franco, Chiang Kai-shek, Mussolini, and other enemies of France and Russia, while allying itself to political and social reaction at home.[8]

It was also about this time that books and articles first appeared describing what conditions were really like in the Soviet Union. In Gide's *Retour de l'URSS* 'Aflaq and Bitar found echoes of their own reservations.

Some thinkers whose sincerity cannot be doubted [they wrote] visited Russia and reported that she had not kept to her principles, but that she was instead pushing ahead for the sake of self-aggrandisement. Like other states, she put her national interests first, making use of Communist propaganda to weaken her rivals. All this led us to ask: If a Great Power like the Soviet Union looks only to her own interests, should not we Arabs, as a young nation, follow her example and pursue an independent policy, seeking our own interests above all else? These events caused in us a spiritual and intellectual crisis which interrupted our writing and political activity for about two years. This was the case because we were not politicians who don a different garment to suit each occasion and disguise their

[5] Bitar and 'Aflaq, *al-Qawmiyya*, p. 13.   [6] Michel 'Aflaq to the author.
[7] 'If I am asked for a definition of socialism', he wrote in 1936, 'I shall not look for it in the works of Marx and Lenin' ('Aflaq, *Fi sabil al-ba'th* (1959), p. 22).
[8] Bitar and 'Aflaq, *al-Qawmiyya*, p. 8.

mistakes with specious argument. We wanted above all to explain things to ourselves; and to explain to ourselves and to the nation something more profound than politics—namely the Arab mind and soul.[9]

FULL-TIME POLITICAL WORK

By 1940, after two years of reflection, 'Aflaq's ideas were taking shape. He and Salah al-Din Bitar, while continuing to teach at the Tajhiz, the principal government secondary school in Damascus, started weekly political meetings for small groups of students in their homes on Friday, the Muslim day of prayer. They issued their first tract in January 1941, which was followed by six or seven others in February. They were directed both against the French and the National Bloc leaders whom they accused of shilly-shallying with the Mandatory Power. Rashid 'Ali's revolt in Iraq of May 1941 gave them occasion to demonstrate their devotion to the wider Arab cause. They launched a 'Victory in Iraq' movement, raised money for Rashid Ali, and formed committees of young people who were ready to afford him armed support. The revolt which was short-lived provided the impetus which set the Ba'th on its militant path.

'Aflaq and Bitar gave up teaching at the end of 1942 to devote themselves to full-time political work. They proceeded to build up their organization in the last years of the war and in the immediate post-independence period. Secondary schoolchildren and university students were mobilized for political agitation; clandestine sheets were published; a beginning was made at organizing the 'street' and *suk* for strike action. The party of the Arab Ba'th emerged as an officially constituted political movement after the departure of the French in 1946. In that same year, the party newspaper, *al-Ba'th*, first appeared. In 1947 the first party congress was convened at which the party programme was adopted. The first executive committee consisted of Michel 'Aflaq—known as *al-'amid*, the dean or *doyen*— Salah al-Din Bitar as Secretary, Jalal al-Sayyid, and Wahib al-Ghanim. Branches were later formed in Jordan and Iraq and small groups sprang up in Lebanon and at Cairo university.

The transition from war to peace was a time of sharp struggle on the internal political front. Although split by personal squabbles, the National Bloc stayed in power. The Ba'th, supported by Akram al-Hawrani, campaigned for free and universal suffrage which they secured at the 1947 elections, their supporters staging a march on

[9] Ibid. pp. 8–9.

parliament. But their campaign for a secret ballot was not successful until 1954 when, as will be seen, it proved of great value to them, particularly in the villages of central Syria. The party can, therefore, rightly claim to have pioneered democratic procedures in Syria. But in 1944–5 it was still fighting a lone battle with slender organization. Sabri al-ʿAsali at the Ministry of the Interior suppressed press and other freedoms and sent Salah al-Din Bitar to a detention camp at Palmyra, in the Syrian desert. ʿAflaq stood as a candidate at both the 1943 and 1947 elections but failed to get a seat. The vote was, in the latter case, rigged, the regime using the army to influence electors and intimidate opposition candidates.

In June 1944 the Baʿth leaders issued their first full-length assault on the Communists, whom they were finding increasingly dangerous opponents. They wanted above all to expose as false the Communist claim to be working for Arab national interests. The following précis of some of their arguments[10] is interesting for their insight into Soviet motives at such an early date:

What is Soviet Arab policy?

i. There can be no doubt that Russia has more regard for the interests of her wartime allies than for the Arabs.

ii. Russia may be expected to back France in the Middle East to counter-balance the influence of the Anglo-Saxon Powers.

iii. Will Russia sacrifice her French ally for Syria? No: witness the mutual support which the French authorities and the Syrian Communist Party lend each other.

iv. Both Turkey and Iran do not like to see the Arabs strong. Russia is deeply interested in both these countries. Is she more likely to back them or the Arabs?

v. One can expect nothing from Russia except the exploitation of Arab interests in the cause of Soviet world domination. All smaller nations must fall into line.

vi. The Communists say that they do not want to import Marxism into Syria but only to join in the struggle for national independence. We Arab Nationalists reply that we do not need the aid of a foreign party dependent on a foreign Government.

vii. The Communists claim to provide a solution for our social and economic problems, but the Arab Nationalist, responding to the call of his own people, is alone qualified to undertake reforms. His guide will be the eternal mission of the Arab Nation.

[10] Bitar and ʿAflaq, *al-Bath waʾl-hizb al-shuyuʿi* (1944).

viii. *Conclusions*

The Syrian Communist Party will oppose Arab interests whenever these conflict with or diverge from Soviet interests.

We are not against the Soviet Union. We make a sharp distinction between the Soviet Union as a state and the local Syrian Communist Party. The Arabs see no necessity to oppose a great state like the Soviet Union which, from its inception, has shown sympathy for countries fighting for their independence. Our aim is to establish friendly relations with the Soviet Union by means of official inter-governmental treaties and not through the medium of the local Communist Party.

Communism triumphs where there is muddled thinking and weakness of national spirit. But the well-informed Arab cannot be a Communist without giving up Arabism. The two are mutually exclusive. Communism is alien and foreign to everything Arab. It will remain the greatest danger to Arab nationalism so long as the latter is unable to give a systematic, coherent and overall definition of its aims. . . .

BA'TH DOCTRINE[11]

What, then, was the doctrine which 'Aflaq hammered out in the war years? One of his earliest associates, recalling the 1940–1 period, put it schematically: "Aflaq outlined three objectives for his movement: Arab unity, freedom and socialism. These we called the 'Trinity'. We used to meet secretly in each other's houses to listen to him expound his ideas.'

'Aflaq acknowledges two main intellectual debts: the first is to the Marxism of his Paris students days; the second to German theories of a romantic and idealistic nationalism which he embraced in the late 1930s. 'We learned from German philosophy that there is

[11] The doctrine of the Ba'th did not spring intact from 'Aflaq's mind in the early 1940s but has been evolving from the 1930s to the present day. While the accent was on socialism in the mid-1930s, nationalism came to the fore after 1936 with occasional lapses into fanaticism; but on the whole 'Aflaq's nationalism was of a humanitarian brand. The seizure of power by the party in Iraq and Syria early in 1963 caused a further evolution with what appeared to be a drift towards Marxism, later moderated after the party's overthrow in Iraq in November 1963. See *Nidal al-ba'th fi sabil al-wahda al-huriyya al-ishtirakiyya* (collection of party documents from 1942 onwards), i: *Dar al-Tali'a* (1963); 'Aflaq, *Fi sabil al-ba'th* and *Ma'rakat al-masir al-wahid* (1958); 'The Constitution of the Arab Ba'th Party' in Sylvia G. Haim, ed., *Arab Nationalism* (1962; see also Mrs Haim's Introduction, pp. 61–72); Yitzhak Oron, 'The History and the Ideas of the Arab Socialist Renaissance Party', *The New East*, ix (1959); Simon Jargy, 'Declin d'un Parti', *Orient*, no. 11, 1959; Gebran Majdalany, 'The Arab Socialist Movement', in W. Z. Laqueur, ed., *The Middle East in Transition* (1958).

something deeper than external events or economic relations in explaining the march of history and the growth of society. This is what modified our materialistic philosophy. . . .'[12] Believing that 'Nationalism is a living and eternal reality',[13] 'Aflaq adopted the motto 'One Arab nation with an eternal mission' as the central slogan of his ideology. It was to become the party's rallying cry.

A strong dose of metaphysics was injected into the three objectives of unity, freedom, and socialism. The struggle for unity is not conceived simply in straightforward pan-Arab terms as the elimination of divisive political boundaries; it is seen as a regenerative process leading to the reform of Arab character and society. This can only come about when Arabs free themselves from all regional, religious, and communal loyalties; liberate themselves from all 'ambivalence', and submit to the eternal values of mankind. Unity, therefore, is not merely a clear-cut political objective: it is a search for the 'treasure of hidden vitality', the moral and spiritual founts of nationalism.

Freedom is conceived both as personal freedom—'freedom of speech, freedom of assembly, freedom of belief, as well as artistic freedom'[14]—*and* as national independence—freedom from colonialism, the liberation of subject peoples. Socialism, in turn, is considered the handmaid of nationalism; it is 'a necessity which emanates from the depth of Arab nationalism itself. Socialism constitutes, in fact, the ideal social order which will allow the Arab people to realize its possibilities and to enable its genius to flourish. . . .'[15] In 'Aflaq's view, socialism is less a set of recipes for solving specific social and economic problems than an instrument for the moral improvement of the people at large. In western Europe, he argues, the state is in the service of the bourgeoisie; western socialism, reflecting the needs of dispossessed classes, is therefore bound to be both materialistic and anti-nationalistic. But Arab socialism is the very opposite: it is both spiritual and identified with nationalism, because it involves the genius of the entire people. 'Socialism is the body, national unity is the spirit'. Political unity is hailed as a creative force which will, of itself, inspire a socialist society. Unity is, in fact, not conceivable without a 'progressive' content. This mystical marriage of nationalism and socialism is 'Aflaq's peculiar message.

The Ba'th do not believe that their aims can be secured by gradual

---

[12] Bitar and 'Aflaq, *al-Qawmiyya*, p. 17.
[13] Ba'th constitution, 'General Principles', art. 3 (Haim, pp. 233–4).
[14] Ba'th constitution, Second Fundamental Principle.
[15] Ibid. General Principles, Art. 4.

and piecemeal reform. They advocate a *bouleversement*, an over-turning only less violent than a Communist revolution, but an organic change none the less.

The Party of the Arab Ba‘th is revolutionary [states Article 6 of the constitution]. It believes that its main objectives for the realization of the renaissance of Arab nationalism or for the establishment of socialism cannot be achieved except by means of revolution and struggle. To rely on slow evolution and to be satisfied with partial and superficial reform is to threaten these aims and to conduce to their failure and their loss.

But, once again, ‘Aflaq makes clear that the aim of revolution is not just the realization of a political programme, but ‘something truer and deeper’. ‘By revolution’, he writes, ‘we understand that true awakening which it is no longer possible to deny or to doubt, the awakening of the Arab spirit at a decisive stage in human history. . . .’[16] And again, ‘Revolution, then, before being a political and social program, is that prime propelling power, that powerful psychic current, that mandatory struggle, without which the reawakening of the nation is not to be understood.’[17]

‘Aflaq, as Sylvia Haim has put it,

considers politics as a means of effecting a change of heart among the Arabs, in fact of instituting the reign of love among them. . . . It is for this reason that he proclaims . . . that ‘Nationalism is love before everything else’. It is only when the Arabs love one another, their nation, and their soil with an absolute and unquestioning love that they will find salvation, and that their weaknesses and difficulties will fall away from them. This uncompromising vision of a superhuman and transformed life as the end of political action gives Aflaq a stature which other Arab nationalist writers do not possess.[18]

‘Aflaq’s three objectives—national unity, freedom, and socialism—are, in his view, indissolubly fused; none can be fully achieved without the others; all depend on the people and on faith in their eternal regenerative powers. But all are, in turn, only means to the ultimate end of the mission of the Arab nation in the world.

They ask us, Brethren, what do you mean by the mission, *the eternal Arab mission*? The Arab mission does not consist in words which we proclaim, it does not consist in principles to be incorporated in programs, it

---

[16] ‘Aflaq, ‘Aspects of Revolution’, in *Fi sabil al-ba‘th*, quoted in Haim, p. 244.
[17] Ibid. pp. 244–5.   [18] Ibid. Introd. pp. 71–72.

does not constitute matter for legislation. All these are dead, counterfeit things. . . .

It is our life itself, *it is to agree to experience this life with a deep and true experience, great and massive in proportion to the greatness of the Arab nation, in proportion to the depth of suffering undergone by the Arabs, in proportion to the great dangers which threaten its continued existence. This living and true experience will bring us back to ourselves, to our living realities; it will make us shoulder our responsibilities and will set us on the true path* in order that we may fight these diseases and these obstacles, these counterfeit conditions, in order to fight social injustice, class exploitation, and the eras of selfishness, bribery and exploitation, in order to combat tyranny, the falsification of the popular will, and the insults to the dignity of the Arab as a citizen and a man; *for the sake of a free society in which every Arab will regain consciousness of himself, of his existence, his dignity, his thinking, and his responsibilities.* The experience in which our struggle takes place is that of the Arab nation dismembered into different countries and statelets, artificial and counterfeit; we struggle until we can reunite these scattered members, until we may reach a wholesome and natural state in which no severed member can speak in the name of all, until we can get rid of this strange and anomalous state. Then will it be possible for the Arabs to unite, for their spirit to be upstanding, their ideas clear, their morality upright; then will there be scope for their minds to create, for they will have become that wholesome natural entity, one nation. This wholesome and true experience, struggling against the existing conditions until we return to the right state, such is the Arab mission. . . .[19]

The constitution of the Ba'th Party makes no mention of Islam, but 'Aflaq has not neglected its close connexion with Arab nationalism.[20] Islam is, to him, yet another manifestation of the eternal genius of the Arab nation to be accepted and adhered to as a civilization or national culture if not as a religion. In fact, he 'explicitly represents Islam not as a divine revelation but in part as a response to Arab needs at the time of Muhammad and in part as a foundation of Arabism'.[21] Islam, he says, was an Arab movement the reflexion of a renewal and maturing of Arabism. There is no fear, he argues, that nationalism will clash with religion, 'for, like religion, it flows from the heart and issues from the will of God; they walk arm in arm, supporting each other, especially when religion represents the genius of the nationality and is in harmony with its nature.'[22]

[19] Ibid. p. 248.
[20] See 'Aflaq, 'Dhikra al-rasul al-'arabi' (The anniversary of the birth of the Arabian Prophet), 2nd ed. (1943), in *Fi sabil al-ba'th*.
[21] Haim, p. 62.   [22] Ibid. p. 243.

Critics object that the Ba'th never moved beyond inspirational rhetoric to produce detailed social and economic programmes. But the party's role was, none the less, immensely important in the immediate post-war generation. The major problems then facing the Arabs were how to free themselves from foreign influence and save themselves from unwilling involvement in Great Power disputes. Almost a decade before 'Abd al-Nasir, the Ba'th leaders became the most consistent and inflexible anti-colonialists and 'neutralists' of the Arab world.

The Ba'th trinity of slogans—unity, freedom, and socialism—meant, in effect, a simultaneous assault on 'reaction' at home and 'imperialism' abroad. In the Arab East the party was among the pioneers of the idea, which has since passed into Afro-Asian thinking, that freedom from foreign control, if it is to be durable and effective, must be accompanied by a thorough overhaul of traditional attitudes and social organization, by a national rebirth or resurrection (ba'th). This cannot be achieved by surface remodelling following western recipes. Genuine reform must spring from the roots of Arab national consciousness and from faith in the Arab people themselves.

We saw colonialism as an effect rather than a cause: an effect of the deficiencies and distortions in our society ['Aflaq said in a speech in March 1957]. This view now seems natural and simple to you. . . . But when we started our movement fifteen years ago, this sort of language was difficult to understand or accept. The unreal atmosphere created by earlier political movements concealed from the people the true nature of the problem. Their leaders, whether professional or amateur politicians, did no more than play at politics. . . . They could not see that our local difficulties were allied to a general world problem; they would not agree that our struggle against colonialism was part of our social struggle at home; nor did they understand that the problem facing us in all Arab countries was the same, that its divisions were artificial and that, in the heart of the people, lay a guarantee that these artificial divisions would disappear and that the truth that we were one nation would become self-evident.[23]

The Ba'th, therefore, provided the Arab national movement with a dynamic, home-grown ideology and with specific moral and political aspirations at a time when it was beguiled by other creeds. In Syria—that 'great railway junction'[24] for the movement of ideas throughout

---

[23] 'Aflaq, Fi sabil al-ba'th, p. 207.
[24] H. Lammens, La Syrie et sa mission historique (1915), p. 15.

the Arab world—the Ba'th was in competition with two other élite ideological parties, the Communists and the PPS. The first were thinly disguised agents of a foreign Power, the second preached a mystical pan-Syrianism, fiercely opposed to the claims and assumptions of Arab nationalism. The Ba'th had also declared war on the National and People's Parties, which it considered the entrenched forces of conservatism and stagnation. All these were its rivals. Its achievement was to marry radical ideas of social justice and democratic political procedures to the fifty-year-old dream of Arab unity which, at bottom, is perhaps the only political idea to which the Syrian public will always remain faithful. Alone among the warring voices of his rivals, 'Aflaq declared in noble and eloquent terms that this was the main stream of Arab nationalism, a claim which, whatever the party's setbacks, is probably still true today.

ALLIANCE WITH HAWRANI

These, then, were the views which 'Aflaq and Bitar finally came to hold after much heart-searching before uniting with the Hama deputy Akram al-Hawrani, in November–December 1952. Something of Hawrani's career has been described: his assault on the great landowners of central Syria; his friendships in the army; his role in the 1949 coups d'état and his break with Shishakli which marked the beginning of the decline in the dictator's fortunes. The merger of Hawrani's Arab Socialists with 'Aflaq's Ba'thists dates from their flight together across the mountains from Shishakli's tyranny. 'Our common opposition to Shishakli was one factor in our decision to unite', 'Aflaq later explained.[25] 'We were also looking forward to the period of party warfare which would follow his downfall. We felt the need to join forces against our principal opponent at the time, the People's Party.'

In character and appearance, 'Aflaq and Hawrani were very different. To his 'admirers', a correspondent of *The Times* wrote, 'he ['Aflaq] is not only an influential but a saintly figure, once described as "The Ghandi of Arab nationalism"—a pale, slight man of painful shyness, deep sincerity and debilitatingly frugal habits.'[26] Hawrani is a natural leader; spirited, courageous, eloquent, and sly; a lean, humorous man without a trace of humbug, he devotes himself to politics with aggressive single-minded energy. He enjoys power, and

[25] Michel 'Aflaq to the author, Beirut, 13 Jan. 1961.
[26] *The Times*, 'Arab Ideals and Reality', 8 July 1959.

what distinguishes him from his contemporaries is a clear unmuddled sense that there is no point in being in politics without obtaining it. His enemies fear and detest him while some of his more tender-minded friends shake their heads over his alleged lack of principle. He lives simply, as an undoctrinaire practical socialist with few material possessions. The assets he brought to the alliance were a talent for political action, his disciples in the army, and a powerful home base in Hama which, as the 1954 elections were to prove, he had built into an electoral stronghold. There were, no doubt, occasions in later years when both Hawrani and 'Aflaq regretted the merger, but it is doubtful whether either alone could have changed the course of Syrian history in the way they eventually did.

KHALID BAQDASH AND THE COMMUNIST PARTY

The Communist Party of Syria and Lebanon was founded in the mid-1920s but remained weak and proscribed, its activities virtually restricted to demonstrations on May Day and 7 November, until the Popular Front coalition came to power in France in 1936. These were the formative years.[27] One of its earliest members was Fu'ad al-Shamali, an Egyptian of Lebanese origin, who arrived in Lebanon sometime between 1922 and 1924 after being expelled from Egypt by the British for Bolshevik activities. He settled in the village of Bikfaya and set about forming a union of tobacco workers.

At about the same time another young Lebanese, Yusuf Yazbek, then a translator in the immigration department of the port of Beirut, drew attention to himself on account of his socialist views. The occasion was the death of Anatole France. Yazbek, in an appreciation of the French writer, wrote that 'the friend of the peasants and the workers' was no more. His article appeared in a Lebanese newspaper, al-Ma'rad, on 19 October 1924, and was noticed by Joseph Berger, a member of the Communist Party of Palestine who came to Lebanon in November to find out who this promising young man might be. He brought with him a copy of the article in which he had underlined the tell-tale phrase in red. What, he asked Yazbek, had he meant by describing Anatole France as 'the friend of the workers and the peasants'?

Yazbek confessed his socialist leanings, a meeting was held in

[27] Sami Ayyub, *al-Hizb al-shuyu'i fi suriyya wa lubnan, 1922–58* (1959), pp. 57–63; Qadri al-Qal'aji, *Tajribat 'arabi fi'l-hizb al-shuyu'i*, pp. 45–47; Laqueur, *Communism and Nationalism*, pp. 141 ff.

Bikfaya, followed by another in Beirut attended by Berger, Yazbek, Shamali, and other sympathizers. At this gathering Berger revealed that he was a Bolshevik and that he had been delegated by the Communist Party of Palestine, on a recommendation from the Communist International, to found a branch outside Palestine.

A difference then developed almost at once between Berger and the Lebanese representatives, who objected to being a branch of the Palestine party and wanted to form an autonomous party of their own. This they did after a second meeting, calling their movement the Lebanese People's Party which, on 30 April 1925, submitted an application to the government for licensing. Shortly afterwards, Yazbek and Shamali made contact with an Armenian Communist-inspired group calling itself Spartacus and headed by Artin Madoyan. The two movements agreed to merge in 1925 to form the Communist Party of Syria and Lebanon. The first provisional Central Committee consisted of Yusuf Yazbek, Fu'ad al-Shamali, Artin Madoyan, Hekazon Boyadjian, and Elias Abu Nadir.

But in 1926 the French mandatory authorities stepped in and arrested Yusuf Yazbek and Artin Madoyan. All party activity was frozen until their release in 1928 when, under the leadership of Fu'ad al-Shamali, the party extended its activities to Tripoli and Damascus as well as to some country towns.

A new recruit to the party in 1930 was a young Kurdish law student from Damascus called Khalid Baqdash. He was then aged 18 but by 1932 he had succeeded in ousting Shamali from the leadership in circumstances which remain obscure. He was also expelled from the university for political activity before taking his degree. For the next twenty-five years he was one of the leading Communists of the Arab world, renowned both for his dedicated political talent and for his skill at evading arrest. His closest associates at the start were Artin Madoyan and Rafiq Rida, who were later joined by Nicola Shawi and Farjallah al-Hilu. This group of men remained in active command of the party until the Syrian-Egyptian union when Baqdash fled to Eastern Europe, Rida defected, and Hilu died under torture in a Syrian jail.

Baqdash was tall, broad and exuberant, but his popularity in Syria was not due solely to his personal appeal or to his role as a Communist leader of dedicated outlook and great resource: it also reflected certain special features of Middle Eastern society. The fact that he was a Kurd ensured him a following on ethnic and religious grounds. He also commanded respect as a leading member of a numerous, power-ful, and tightly-knit social unit: his was one of the largest families in Damascus where men prefer to lend their support to the head of a family or clan rather than to an individual leader. His books, pam-phlets, and speeches reveal a well-trained and subtle rather than an original mind.[28] But he nevertheless stood out from among most Syrian politicians for his skill in debate, his ability to disarm oppo-nents, and for the doctrinal coherence of his views. Compared to the Socialist leader Akram al-Hawrani, he was as professional to amateur.[29]

Imprisoned by the French authorities in 1931 and 1932, Baqdash first went underground before going abroad. In 1935 he led the Syrian delegation to the Seventh Congress of the Communist Inter-national in Moscow where he underwent in the middle 1930s a period of training.

The formation of the Popular Front government in France in 1936 set him working seriously to establish his party on a sound footing. The party organ *Sawt al-Sh'ab* (Voice of the People) was allowed to appear legally in 1937. In November of that year Baqdash led a Syrian Communist delegation to France, which was followed by a return visit to Syria in May 1938 by two French Communist deputies who addressed mass meetings in Damascus. But conditions were not long to remain so favourable. With the collapse of the Popular Front, the Syrian Communist Party found itself once more in opposition to the French authorities. The Nazi-Soviet Treaty of August 1939 completed its discomfiture, although the Syrian party leaders did in fact volunteer to fight for France on the outbreak of war. These three brief years, 1936-9, gave the party its first opportunity for sustained above-ground activity. Cadres were formed and the party member-ship increased tenfold, from 200 to about 2,000 in each of the two Levant states.

The party was outlawed in September 1939 and its leaders arrested soon afterwards. But the Allied occupation of Syria in May 1941, followed two months later by Hitler's attack on the Soviet Union, led to their release and to the resumption of full-scale Communist activity that winter. The period 1942-8 marked the party's second phase of legality. *Sawt al-Sh'ab* reappeared from its Beirut office and

---

[28] I am greatly indebted to Prof. Hanna Batatu of the American University of Beirut for information regarding the Syrian Communist Party and for help in compiling the list of Baqdash's publications found in the bibliography.
[29] See Jacques Rastier, 'À la recherche de socialism syrien', *Orient*, no. 4, 1957, p. 171.

a number of 'front' organizations—notably Antun Thabit's Anti-Fascist League in Lebanon—were revived and grew in popularity as it gradually became evident who was going to win the war. After the proclamation of Syria's independence in 1943, the Syrian and Lebanese Communists acquired a separate independent status although they remained linked in a single Central Committee. But on 23 July 1944 their autonomy was confirmed by the creation of separate Central Committees.

The party line throughout the war was to collaborate with 'national reformist elements' in the struggle against Fascism and in the movement of national liberation and revival. This involved putting revolutionary class demands into cold storage and emphasizing instead the party's 'national character'. At the 1943 election, for instance, the first to be held after the formal proclamation of Syrian independence, Baqdash campaigned on the following innocuous platform:

i. Independence and Freedom for Syria;
ii. National unity and the regrouping of the people in the cause of national independence;
iii. The creation of truly representative institutions;
iv. Strengthening economic and cultural ties with other Arab states;
v. Strengthening relations with other countries on a basis of justice and equality.[30]

By such tactics Baqdash established excellent relations with Quwatli and the National Bloc leaders; members of the Government listened to his speeches on such ceremonial occasions as May Day, so much so that by the end of the war the party had achieved a position of considerable power and prestige. Baqdash realized that in the absence of a large Syrian proletariat his best hope lay in a friendly bourgeoisie manoeuvred from behind the scenes by the Communist Party.

Pro-Soviet sympathies reached their peak when the Soviet Union recognized Syrian and Lebanese independence in July 1944, and when the Soviet ambassador smuggled the Syrian Prime Minister out of the country in his car in the 1945 crisis. But after the departure of the French in April 1946, the Syrian Communist Party lost ground to other political groups, although it continued to announce loyalty to the cause of national independence. One of the reasons why it always tended to side with the French was the belief that if France

[30] Khalid Baqdash, *Election Manifesto*, 7 June 1943.

were eliminated the door would be opened to the British and British-backed schemes for Fertile Crescent unity. Moreover, because of its close links with the French Communist Party, it also proclaimed on every occasion that the liberation of the proletariat in Syria was indissolubly linked with the fate of the French working class. The *coup de grace* was the Soviet vote at the United Nations, in November 1947, in favour of a Jewish state, followed by Soviet recognition of the State of Israel in May 1948. Such action was indefensible so far as the Syrian public was concerned. The party was dissolved in January 1948 and was driven underground by the first military coup in March 1949.

It continued to publish its clandestine newspaper, *Nidal al-Sha'b* (The People's Struggle), in spite of Husni al-Za'im, and vilified both the military dictators and the Western Powers in a flood of tracts and manifestos. The Syrian Partisans of Peace were the main Communist front in 1950–1: they held a country-wide convention in 1950 and their periodical, *al-Salam* (Peace), appeared during 1951. They also staged demonstrations against imperialism during the visit to Damascus of General Sir Brian Robertson. After first opposing Shishakli, the Syrian Communist Party gradually came to consider him a lesser evil than the People's Party and its pro-Iraqi schemes. Many of its energies were thereafter directed against Shishakli's enemies and in particular against the Ba'th. This, in part, reflected a change in the party line which chose between 1948 and 1953 to regard most national movements as enemies of Communism. There was to be no further collaboration with 'national reformist elements' until after Stalin's death. Communist leaders did, in fact, join the conspiracy against Shishakli in late-1953 and called at the 1954 elections for a national front of all 'enemies of feudalism, reaction and imperialism'. But how they fared in their third period of legitimacy, from 1954 to 1958, in the new conditions of political freedom must be left to another chapter.

15

Free Elections (1954)

THE Syrian elections of September 1954, held seven months after Shishakli's downfall, drew up the internal battle order for the next four years. Hailed as the first free elections in the Arab world, they provided a valuable gauge of public opinion at a critical moment in what was perhaps the most politically sophisticated of all Arab countries. They represented Syria's return to parliamentary rule. But since little of importance has happened in the Arab world over the past thirty years without the legal and constitutional assemblies having first been sent on holiday,[1] this return was of less significance than the opportunity which the elections presented to judge the comparative strength of the rival forces on the Syrian political scene.

One major issue overshadowed the election campaign: whether or not Syria should join a western-sponsored Middle East defence pact. A continuing theme of this book has been the two-way interaction between the internal power struggle in Syria and conflicts on the wider stage of Arab politics together with, on a still higher plane, Great Power policies in the area. In 1954 these outside contests became fiercer. The proposed Baghdad Pact split the Arab world so that Syria, caught in the cross-fire, was all the more disturbed. The details of this great defence debate which burst upon the Arab world in 1954–5 must be left to the next chapter. All that need be said here is that the fate of the Baghdad Pact was, in a very real sense, decided on the plane of internal Syrian politics. Shishakli's fall in 1954, and the subsequent elections, mark Syria's involvement in the international Power battle: 'The rivalries of the Powers were no longer played out across the passive body of a powerless, ancient world.'[2]

[1] See Jacques Berque, 'L'Univers politique des Arabes', *Encyclopédie française*, xi (1957).
[2] A. H. Hourani, *A Vision of History* (1961), p. 144.

SABRI AL-'ASALI'S MINISTRY

The first move of Shishakli's successors was to pronounce his long tenure of power illegal. His 1953 constitution was set aside and the 1950 text reinstated. As if to erase from memory the immediate past, the new Head of State, Hashim al-Atasi, first accepted the resignation of Dr Ma'ruf al-Dawalibi, the Premier whom Shishakli had displaced by his second coup in December 1951, before calling on the National Party secretary-general, Sabri al-'Asali, to form a Government. Over the next four years 'Asali was never long out of the Prime Minister's office. His career illustrates, more clearly perhaps than that of any other prominent Syrian politician, the conflicting pressures to which Syria was subject and the divided loyalties which resulted.

Born in Damascus in 1903, 'Asali took his law degree on the eve of the 1925 insurrection against the French, in which he took part. In the late 1920s and 1930s he practised as a lawyer, and helped to found and direct a noisy nationalist pressure group called the League of National Action before joining the National Bloc in 1936. He sided with Vichy in 1940–1 and was interned by the Allies on their invasion of Syria. He was elected to the Syrian Chamber in 1943 and was re-elected in 1947, becoming secretary-general of the National Party. He served in several post-war cabinets—mainly at the Ministry of the Interior—and was closely associated with the failures and abuses of President Quwatli's regime. The political repression for which he was then responsible earned him the enmity of the emergent Ba'th Party, while his sudden conversion to belief in union with Iraq in 1949, earned him the scorn of the People's Party leaders.

In the uncertain years of military dictatorship, 'Asali was eager to insure himself with all Syria's powerful neighbours. He therefore maintained secret contact with Iraq while remaining on close terms with the exiled Quwatli and his Egyptian and Saudi backers. He was prominent in the conspiracy against Shishakli, accepting Iraqi subsidies, but this mercenary complicity made him vulnerable to the threat of exposure by his fellow conspirators, notably in the army. A further complication was the fact that he was a senior partner in a prosperous law firm which counted such prominent American companies as Tapline among its clients. At bottom he was an old-style politician, without programme, principle, or ideology, whose frequent subsequent appearances as Prime Minister were less an indication of his political weight than of the fact that he was acceptable, as a pliant, compromise candidate, to both right and left wings in the Chamber. His speech was a flood of Arabic rhetoric concealing an agile mind.

On 1 March 1954 'Asali formed a coalition[3] of the National and People's Parties, stiffened by such prominent Independents as the Druze leader Hasan al-Atrash, and the Hama landowner 'Abd al-Rahman al-'Azm. The Syrian Chamber was recalled a fortnight later, but once again, in an attempt to erase the past, it was not Shishakli's parliament which reassembled but an earlier assembly, elected on 15 November 1949, packed by the People's Party and dissolved by Shishakli on 2 December 1951.

The striking feature of 'Asali's transitional cabinet was its exclusion of Akram al-Hawrani and the Ba'th, in spite of their record of opposition to Shishakli and their part in bringing him down. It was rumoured that Hawrani had demanded the Ministry of the Interior and had been refused. Both he and 'Aflaq went immediately into opposition, denouncing the coalition as reactionary and declaring that there could be no confidence in elections held under its auspices.

FERTILE CRESCENT PROSPECTS

Iraq's deep involvement in the conspiracy against Shishakli and her unconcealed joy at his overthrow aroused all the familiar suspicions that yet another bid would now be made to bring about a union of the Fertile Crescent.

Conditions seemed propitious. Fadil al-Jamali, an enthusiastic unionist, was Prime Minister of Iraq. Egypt's attention was distracted by her negotiations with Britain over the Canal Zone base and by the struggle between 'Abd al-Nasir and Nagib within the Free Officers' junta. Saudi Arabia was also weakened by internal change following the death of King 'Abd al-'Aziz ibn Sa'ud in 1953. His son, King Sa'ud, had neither his character nor ability. In Syria itself Shishakli, Iraq's main enemy, had fallen while the People's Party, Iraq's main friends, enjoyed a moment of triumph with the restoration of their parliamentary dominance and their seats in the cabinet. This was some redress for the trials they had suffered at the hands of the army

---

[3] Prime Minister, Sabri al-'Asali (NP); Nat. Economy, Fakhir al-Kayyali (NP); Public Assistance, Muhammad Sulayman al-Ahmad (better known by the literary pseudonym of Badawi al-Jabal) (NP); Min. of State, 'Afif al-Solh (NP); Defence, Ma'ruf al-Dawalibi (PP); Foreign Affairs, Faydi al-Atasi (PP); Public Works, Rashad al-Jabri (PP); Interior, 'Ali Buzo (PP); Agriculture, Hasan al-Atrash (Ind.); Justice, 'Izzat al-Saqqal (Ind.); Finance, 'Abd a-Rahman al-'Azm (Ind.); Education, Munir al-'Ajlani (Ind.).

—an army which was now divided and disturbed. The left, in turn, had not yet fully recovered from its persecution by the dictator. Indeed, this was perhaps the last occasion on which determined action in favour of a Fertile Crescent union might have been effective. Considerable pro-Hashimite sentiment still existed in Syria at that time. Many influential men, particularly in the north of the country, thought of union with Iraq in *patriotic* Arab terms—in spite of the British presence there. 'Abd al-Nasir was only just beginning to preach that all ties with foreigners were treacherous and that Arabs should unite only with Arabs. Iraq's image had not yet been tarnished by the repression and excesses of the final four years of the old regime. Before the Baghdad Pact, before the Czech arms deal and before Suez, it was still possible to advocate a union of the Fertile Crescent without being labelled a reactionary traitor to Arabism. Why, then, were these uniquely favourable circumstances not exploited?

The failure was one of will. Union did not come about because no one wanted it strongly enough. The men most closely concerned were themselves undecided. The People's Party was divided on the issue: as in 1949, few of its leaders were prepared to accept with equanimity the possibility of rule by 'Abd ul-Ilah and the threat of an extension to Syria of Britain's treaty relations with Iraq. These doubts blunted their resolution. In Iraq, Jamali's enthusiasm was matched by Nuri's caution. Baghdad, its hopes so often disappointed by recurrent Syrian coups d'état, had grown wary of Syrian instability and deeply suspicious of Syrian politicians who clamoured for money but rarely delivered the goods.

Courted from all sides—from Saudi Arabia, France, Egypt, and Turkey as well as from Iraq—many Syrians realized that to unite with Iraq would stem the flood of gold. It would be to kill the goose that laid the golden eggs. To a large extent this reasoning explains why Iraq was sometimes successful at helping to overthrow a Syrian Government but was never able to press home the advantage to the point of negotiating a union with the successor administration. Iraq and the Syrian conspirators had planned that Shishakli's overthrow would be followed by a vote in the Syrian Chamber in favour of union. But once in the saddle, the Syrian politicians preferred to resume their highly lucrative game of extracting money from all sides. Moreover, Iraq's former vacillation was infectious: Baghdad had failed to act when Colonel Hinnawi came to power in 1949; these past hesitations made the Syrians themselves now pause.

Active British support for an Iraqi-Syrian union might at this stage have been decisive. But Britain had still not departed from her widely misrepresented neutrality towards the project. France, as has been seen, considered Syria a legitimate and exclusive sphere of influence to be defended at all costs against Iraqi—and British— encroachments. She saw in both Za'im and Shishakli champions of Syrian independence—that is to say of her interests—and supported them accordingly. Up to 1954 Britain tacitly concurred with French pretensions: she did nothing to promote Hashimite ambitions in Syria although she could not openly oppose them. She had no enthusiasm for a merger of Syria with either Iraq or Jordan, realizing that it might both disturb her special position in these Hashimite states and arouse the fierce hostility of France, Egypt, and Saudi Arabia which, under Ibn Sa'ud, had been one of Britain's staunchest Arab friends for over thirty years. None the less, the fact that Britain was popularly thought to want a Fertile Crescent union under Iraqi leadership helped, no doubt, to defeat the scheme—an ironical outcome which she may not have found unwelcome. Her real aims were more modest. British interests lay simply in a friendly Syria, providing safe transit for Iraqi oil to the Mediterranean. But in a few months the Baghdad Pact was to force her openly to take sides in the contest between Iraq and Egypt—a contest the outcome of which was principally to turn on the control of Syria's foreign policy. But by then the opportunity, if such it was, of an Iraqi-Syrian *entente* had been missed.

While Syria's relations with Baghdad never blossomed into a political union, her relations with Cairo were at the time still less cordial. Nationalists in Syria and throughout the Arab world did not then trust 'Abd al-Nasir. The Istiqlal in Iraq and the Ba'th in Syria sided with Nagib against him.[4] This was largely because Nasir was thought to be pro-American and to be soft towards the British in the negotiations over the Canal Zone. He was also suspected of planning to establish an authoritarian military regime as opposed to a democratic system with political parties. The high point of resentment against him was reached with the conclusion of the treaty with Britain, which was followed by the trial of the Muslim Brotherhood. Within this general context there were numerous more specific incidents which served to disturb Syria's relations with Cairo, of

[4] See Majdalany, 'The Arab Socialist Movement' (in Laqueur, *Middle East in Transition*, p. 340 n.2).

which perhaps the most important concerned Mahmud Abu'l-Fath, a well-known Egyptian newspaper proprietor who escaped to Damascus in mid-May 1954 after being sentenced in Egypt to fifteen years' imprisonment and to the confiscation of his property. Abu'l-Fath stood for democratic principles, freedom of expression, and an uncompromising attitude towards the British.[5] His newspaper, *al-Misri*, had been the official mouthpiece of the Wafd which had abrogated the 1936 Treaty. In Syria he was warmly welcomed. The Prime Minister and members of the Government attended banquets in his honour while the Syrian press renewed its attacks on the Egyptian junta for its treatment of him. All requests for his extradition were refused although he did, in fact, leave Syria shortly afterwards for Baghdad, where Nuri al-Sa'id later granted him Iraqi nationality.

The Syrian press had a further occasion to attack the Free Officers when an Egyptian military attaché was caught smuggling articles of clothing between Beirut and Damascus, although subsequent investigations revealed that his operations were of a trivial nature. When, in yet another connexion, it was announced that Major Salah Salim, a leading member of the Egyptian junta, would shortly visit Damascus, the Syrian Government made it clear that the initiative for the visit had come from Cairo, not Damascus. Angered, Cairo called the visit off.

Torn between Baghdad and Cairo, the Syrian Premier 'Asali was not sure which way the wind was blowing. He had accepted subsidies from Iraq in the conspiracy against Shishakli, but his National Party had long had close ties with the rival camp of Saudi Arabia and Egypt, whence Quwatli himself was shortly expected to return. He thought it best to keep in with both sides. When student demonstrators, organized by the Ba'th, petitioned President Atasi to remove the Prime Minister and save Syria from a union with 'a neighbouring, imperialist enslaved country', the Government pledged itself not to commit the country to any long-term alignment before the elections.

But the habit of conspiracy with Iraq did not die easily. On 8 June, only three days before the fall of his Government, 'Asali held a secret meeting at the Lebanese mountain resort of Brummanah with Mikhail Ilyan, a rich, pro-Iraqi National Party politician, and the Iraqi leaders Jamali and Baban. According to evidence submitted at

[5] See Ahmed Abul-Fath, *L'Affaire Nasser* (1962).

the Baghdad trials which followed the Iraqi revolution in 1958, the
four men discussed the possibility of bringing about a Fertile
Crescent union by means of an Iraqi armed attack on Syria.[6]

'ASALI'S FALL

'Asali's coalition Government lasted 100 days but it was brought
down before it could conduct the elections for which it had been
formed. It was weak, partial, and divided, displaying few of the skills
required to effect the delicate transition from military dictatorship to
parliamentary rule. Its first weeks in office were disturbed by an
impassioned public debate on the question of the return from exile
of the former President, Shukri al-Quwatli. Quwatli's friends saw in
him the finest flower of the nationalist struggle against France; to his
enemies he was a bumbling politician of the old school whose
feebleness and tolerance of corruption had led to the collapse of
Syria's young democracy.

On 9 April 1954 a delegation of Syrian notables, Muslim leaders,
and Greek Orthodox prelates called on Quwatli in Alexandria to
invite him to come home. His opponents retorted with street demonstrations and a violent campaign throughout Syria. 'Those who call
for the return of Shukri al-Quwatli', one left-wing newspaper wrote,
'surround him with an odour of sanctity as if he were Christ Himself.
In fact, he plans to return to the Presidency as the "High Commissioner" of a Saudi-Egyptian mandate and as the instrument of
American policy.'[7]

The Government faced another storm over a bill to make Shishakli's former colleagues, as well as civil servants promoted by him,
refund to the state salaries earned during his regime. This punitive
measure was politically inept. It had the unexpected effect of rallying
Shishakli's former supporters in indignant defence of their legitimate
rights, and of reviving his Arab Liberation Movement as a political
force determined to contest the elections. Leaders of the Movement
met at the house of Ma'mun al-Kuzbari, the former Speaker, to
draft a manifesto[8] in which they threw back at 'Asali's Government
its accusations of political illegitimacy. The Government then
threatened to bring Shishakli himself to trial but, to its embarrassment, he declared that he would be glad to place himself at the

---

[6] See evidence submitted at Fadil al-Jamali's trial on 20 September 1958 (BBC,
no. 661, 23 Sept. 1958).
[7] al-Ra'i al-'Amm (Damascus), 22 Apr. 1954.
[8] See al-Barada (Damascus), 8–9 June 1954.

disposal of the Syrian courts, seeing he had nothing of which to be ashamed. The proposal was then hurriedly dropped.

The Government was given little rest. It was accused of packing the civil service with nominees of the coalition parties, and of planning to amend the electoral law to ensure its return to power. Furious protest was aroused by its decision to suspend all newspaper licences and request newspaper proprietors to reapply within a fortnight for permission to publish. Two factors were perhaps decisive in bringing 'Asali down. The first was his suspected flirtation with the United States, which ran counter to a strong neutralist current in Syria. When, for instance, General Arthur Trudeau, American Deputy Chief of Staff, visited Damascus on 8 May, it was rumoured that he had come to negotiate a military assistance agreement such as Iraq had concluded with the United States in April. The Government denied any such intention but the damage was done.

Finally, the Syrian army, so long at the centre of affairs, did not take easily to the role of silent docility which was now expected of it. It was on bad terms with the civilian Defence Minister, Ma'ruf al-Dawalibi, who had clashed with army chiefs in the past; the officers resented his attempts rigidly to enforce the 'return to barracks' and to bring the General Staff under strict civilian control. Army pressure behind the scenes was widely held to have been a major factor in forcing 'Asali to resign on 11 June.

GHAZZI'S ELECTORAL PROCEDURE

'Asali was succeded by Sa'id al-Ghazzi, a respected Damascus lawyer of independent mind who formed a non-partisan Government on 19 June,[9] in the face of a new threat of an army coup.[10] Ghazzi immediately declared his total impartiality in domestic affairs and his intention to maintain fraternal relations with all Arab states within

[9] Prime Minister & Defence, Sa'id al-Ghazzi; Finance & Foreign Affairs, 'Izzat al-Saqqal; Justice and Nat. Economy, As'ad Kurani; Education & Agriculture, Nihad al-Qasim; Interior, Isma'il Quli; Public Works, Communications, Health & Public Assistance, Nabih al-Ghazzi.

[10] Col. Muhammad Safa and a number of other officers were arrested on 19 June on a charge of plotting to seize power with the aid of a foreign Power. In 1952–3 Col. Safa had carried on a campaign against Shishakli from Baghdad under the name of the Free Syrian Government. It is probable that Iraq, irritated at 'Asali's failure to press for union, had encouraged Safa to bring matters to a head. On the eve of his arrest Safa told a Homs paper: 'I have never been in the pay of any country but Syria. I am no more Iraqi or Saudi than I am British, American or French. I have no political ambitions. . . . "Free Syria" which was formed in Iraq was not a Government but a resistance movement against dictatorship which operated with the support of all true Syrians and on orders from H. E. the President, Hashim al-Atasi' (al-Suri al-Jadid (Homs), 18 June 1954).

the framework of the Arab League, without committing Syria to any international undertaking. His Government's first and only task would be to conduct free and fair elections in accordance with a new electoral law which he proposed to draft in collaboration with the Chamber. This clear statement of intention and his past record won him general confidence. The Ba'th trusted him and he was skilful enough to secure the army's loyalty by appointing General Shawkat Shuqayr, the Chief of Staff, as Defence Minister.

Ghazzi set about his task with vigour. Elections were fixed for 20 August. The Syrian constitution provided for a single Chamber of Deputies elected for a four-year term.[11] Within ten days of coming to power, Ghazzi had secured parliamentary approval for a new electoral law abolishing Shishakli's bill and restoring the 1949 law with amendments. It provided for a Chamber of 142 deputies, each representing 30,000 persons. Any literate male citizen over thirty years of age could stand as a candidate. All male citizens over eighteen years were given the vote, as well as all women citizens of the same age holding an elementary-school certificate.

The basic electoral unit was a *qada*—comparable to a French *arrondissement*—usually returning 2 or 3 deputies, although centres of high population density such as Aleppo and Damascus returned 14 and 12 deputies respectively. To be elected on the first round, a candidate had to receive at least 40 per cent of the votes cast. If any seats then remained unfilled, a second round would be held a week later, open to candidates who had received more than 10 per cent of the votes cast on the first round. A simple majority was then sufficient for election.

Government in Syria is highly centralized. This made it possible for the authorities to control elections through the provincial officials of the Ministry of the Interior. The levers of this control were the *gendarmerie*, the *muhafizes* and the *qaimaqams*—comparable to *prefets* and *sous-prefets* in France. They supervised the registration of voters, the passing on of the eligibility of candidates and the actual conduct of voting, as well as a mass of administrative machinery which governed the lives of ordinary citizens. Their approval was necessary to secure a commercial licence, a certificate of birth or of marriage; they watched over the assessment and collection of taxes; it was well-nigh

[11] For some of the details in this chapter on Syrian electoral procedure, I am indebted to an unpublished paper by Professor Ralph Crow of the American University of Beirut entitled 'A Study of Political Forces in Syria based on a survey of the 1954 elections', May 1955.

impossible to secure a loan from the agricultural bank without their backing. It was natural that these officials tended to side with influence and vested interest in the countryside. In particular, the poor and ill-educated *gendarmes* were often bought off by such indirect means as gifts at harvest time or occasional invitations to dinner at the landlord's house. It was not to their advantage to interfere with the 'natural forces' at work in the community.

To break this collusion with local interests, Ghazzi transferred every *muhafiz* and *qaimaqam* to a new post one month before the elections. A trusted non-political figure took over the Ministry of the Interior and the *gendarmerie*, while civil servants were reminded that all political activity was forbidden them by law. The army voluntarily agreed to confine itself to barracks during polling.

Quite as important as these safeguards was the institution of a secret ballot. Ghazzi laid down a voting procedure which he hoped would be cast-iron. It was as follows: the voter presented his identity card at the polling station where it was checked against the voters' registration lists. He was handed an envelope supplied by the Government and signed by the chairman of the electoral committee. He then entered a secret voting booth and put his ballot—which was supplied by the parties, by the candidates, or made out by himself— in the envelope, sealed it and deposited it outside in the ballot box in full view of the electoral committee.

This procedure alone represented a revolution in Syrian, as indeed in Arab, electoral practice. It was adopted on the insistence of the Ba'th and in the face of opposition from the People's and National Parties, who argued that a largely illiterate population made nonsense of such niceties. These parties also did their best to obstruct the civil service purges and transfers of officials which Ghazzi had set in motion. On 29 July, three weeks before the poll, the People's Party announced its intention to boycott the elections, complaining that the army was once again interfering in politics. It may have thought that the trend in the country was running against it. The National Party followed suit, forcing the Government to reconsider its original date of 20 August and to put back the elections to 24 September when all parties agreed to take part.

THE CAMPAIGN

In the following weeks each party and political faction refurbished its programme, checked its cadres, and planned its election tactics.

Some account has already been given of the principal political groups: the National and People's Parties, twin heirs of the old Nationalist Bloc; the Ba'th representing the concerted radical, pan-Arab forces of 'Aflaq and Hawrani; the Communist Party; the Muslim Brethren; the pan-Syrian PPS or Syrian National Social Party; Shishakli's Arab Liberation Movement and Faysal al-'Asali's extremist Co-operative Socialist Party. As the struggle for power in Syria over the next few years was largely conducted under party banners it is worth attempting a brief appraisal of their comparative strength on the eve of the elections.

The National Party

Shukri al-Quwatli's return from exile on 7 August raised the spirits of his National Party supporters. The party announced that the former President would take no direct part in the campaign except to issue general directives, but it clearly regarded him as a major elec-toral asset. Quwatli called a conference at his house on 3 September to which he invited large numbers of politicians, former colleagues, journalists, presidents of professional associations and chambers of commerce, the rector of the university, and other notables. Address-ing them on the necessity for national unity, he urged them to set up a National Congress run by a multi-party committee. 'I have not returned from Egypt to add a new party to the existing list, or to present my own candidature', he declared; 'I have come to appeal to your consciences to work in union for a stable regime in Syria.' But his appeal carried little weight and the Congress was still-born. The People's Party was deferential but reserved; the Ba'th cool and the Communists hostile. Powerful Independents such as Khalid al-'Azm, who was spoken of as Quwatli's main rival for the presidency, were not invited to join. The general public was indifferent, finding it puzzling that so much fuss should be made around a man who stood for an old order generally held responsible for Syria's subsequent upheavals.

The National Party had, in effect, been in retreat since 1947. It had lost ground to the People's Party at the elections that year, had then been further weakened by the exile of its leaders after Za'im's coup, and was virtually disbanded under Shishakli. But the effects were less fatal than it might seem because the party had never attempted to recruit a permanent mass membership bound by ideology or party discipline. It consisted almost solely of the candidates themselves, deriving its influence from their nationalist record, personal prestige, wealth, and social standing.

The Damascus lawyer Sabri al-'Asali was secretary-general, while two rival presidents, Dr 'Abd al-Rahman Kayyali and Lutfi al-Haffar, presided respectively over the Aleppo and Damascus branches. Other influential party members included Mikhail Ilyan, Suhayl al-Khuri, and Majd al-Din al-Jabiri. It controlled two newspapers, *al-Kabas* (The Flame) in Damascus and *al-Shabab* (Youth) in Aleppo.

Under Quwatli's leadership, the party had fiercely opposed Hashimite expansionism in the post-war years. It had stood for Syrian independence against all attempts at Fertile Crescent unity. But by 1954 this was no longer its unanimous policy. A pro-Iraqi wing led by Lutfi al-Haffar demanded a rapprochement with the People's Party, while Kayyali led a group faithful to Quwatli and his Saudi and Egyptian friends. In 1955 the Baghdad Pact brought these differences into the open, splitting the party.

Its campaign propaganda was virtually restricted to reminding the public of its patriotic achievements under the Mandate. No attempt was made to outline a programme except for a speech by Sabri al-'Asali in Aleppo on 9 July in which he announced the party's conversion to a 'new' form of socialism—'Not a socialism which robs men of their property but one which allows the workers to enjoy the fruits of their efforts'[12]—a definition which the left-wing press greeted with mocking disbelief. Most of the party's energies went into drawing up lists of candidates and in seeking electoral alliances with the People's Party. But differences between them ran too deep, and in all major constituencies both parties put forward rival lists. Many of the National Party leaders had long been on friendly terms with Britain, a relic of wartime days when General Spears lent them British support against the French, but at the elections they were suspected of enjoying the backing of the United States (it was recalled that Sabri al-'Asali was the Tapline lawyer) and of Saudi Arabia.

The People's Party

The People's Party approached the elections warily. Its leaders were afraid that the vote would show up how much their stock had fallen since the formation of the party in 1947–8. In the years of military dictatorship they had fought and lost two major campaigns:

[12] *al-Shabab*, 11 July 1954.

the first in favour of a Syrian-Iraqi union; the second against the army in defence of constitutional government. Weakened by their long duel with Shishakli and, by 1954, divided over what to do about Iraq, the party was in poor shape to contest the elections.

But it had retained some major assets to set against these handicaps. It was essentially a regional political force based on Aleppo and Homs. It could count on these strongholds, however poor its following and however uncertain its organization in other parts of the country. Its leaders also enjoyed a greater reputation for personal integrity than their National Party rivals. Less rapacious in office and less active in dispensing patronage, they had what Syrians call 'clean names'. Their party statutes displayed an awareness of social and economic problems, although this was not supported by any detailed programme. Like the National Party, their chief electoral asset was not an ideology or a party machine but the personal standing and authority of their leading members. These were, in Aleppo, Rushdi al-Kikhia, Nazim al-Qudsi, Ma'ruf al-Dawalibi, Ahmad Kanbar, and 'Abd al-Wahab Hawmad; in Homs, Faydi al-Atasi, Hani al-Siba'i, and 'Adnan al-Atasi; in Damascus, 'Ali Buzo, Shakir al-'As, Rashad Jabri, and Nassib al-Bakri. They controlled three newspapers: the courageous Homs daily, al-Suri al-Jadid (The New Syrian), which had led the opposition to Shishakli, al-Sha'b (The People) in Damascus, and al-Nazir (The Guardian) in Aleppo.

During the election campaign the party avoided the controversial question of relations with Iraq, stressing instead the defence of Syria's independence and republicanism. This no doubt reflected its own differences of opinion. Some of its campaign funds were popularly believed to have come from Iraq, while its enemies made much of the alleged contacts between the Iraqi military attaché and some of its members.

The Ba'th Party

The Ba'th emerged in strength from the underground to which Shishakli had driven it to throw itself into the election campaign. Michel 'Aflaq and Akram al-Hawrani consolidated the alliance which they had forged in exile by becoming joint presidents of a revitalized party which was said to have a nucleus of 6,000 registered members. 'Aflaq and his close associate, Salah al-Din Bitar, had a large following among young people in Damascus and the Jabal Druze. Hawrani's stronghold was in the countryside around Hama. He also had many friends in the army who stiffened the party, enabling it to stand up to such disciplined ideological rivals as the PPS on the right and the Communists on the left.

In the months before the elections, Hawrani made tremendous efforts to rouse peasants and workers against their traditional masters. Peasant organizations and labour unions were set up. Everything was done to bring home to agricultural workers that they had rights. The party hired lawyers and sought out cases where landlords had struck or insulted their tenants. The party provided the legal counsel and took the cases to court. With Ghazzi's neutral Government in power, traditional forces on the defensive, and the public enthusiastic for democratic government, the courts gave justice. The party newspapers played up these incidents and publicized them all over the country. They were avidly followed in the villages.

Hawrani hired large numbers of trucks, filled them with his supporters, and rode into villages on campaign ventures. He was usually met with force by the landlord's men and frequent battles occurred. But it was this show of force which overcame the reticence of the peasants and caused them to throw in their lot with him. In extreme cases landlords found it dangerous to enter their own villages and in one instance a village school was destroyed because it had been built by the landlord and became a symbol of his dominance.

In the mid-1950s about three-quarters of the Syrian population could be classified as rural-settled.[13] The peasantry was 'village organized', living in small, tightly-integrated villages, bound by strong family and community pressures, rather than in scattered farms. The bus and the motor car had introduced a new mobility since the Second World War, but a large percentage of the urban population still retained official residence in the villages, to which they had to return for voting purposes. Hawrani's tactics attacked this rural social structure at its foundations and the provision of a secret ballot, for which the party had long campaigned, allowed it to reap the political rewards of its action.

Alone of all Syrian political parties, with the exception of the Communists, the Ba'th had a detailed programme and a party line on each of the great issues of the day. It opposed all foreign influence in the Arab world—whether political, economic, or cultural. It was anti-Iraqi, anti-Hashimite, anti-western—but also anti-Soviet. Throughout the campaign it refused all forms of co-operation with the Com-

[13] See Warriner, p. 82.

munists in spite of Khalid Baqdash's repeated appeals for a 'National Front'. When Iraq announced her military assistance agreement with the United States in April 1954, the Ba'th joined Kamal Jumblat's Lebanese Progressive Socialist Party in a joint declaration of neutralism.[14]

At a vast rally in Aleppo on 8 July Salah al-Din Bitar outlined the party's objectives. It would fight for two pieces of legislation: a labour code to protect the worker from arbitrary action by his employer, and a bill to define relations between peasants and landowners. Bitar also spoke of land reform, industrialization, income limitation, and the struggle against the domination of foreign capital.

The party's meetings were lively and well attended, seemingly unaffected by attacks on it as atheistic by the Shaikhs and doctors of Quranic law. Its newspapers were *al-Ba'th* (Resurrection) in Damascus and *al-Tarbiya* (Education) in Aleppo.

The Communist Party

Shishakli's fall coincided with a change in Communist tactics towards national movements all over the world. Whereas between 1948 and the early 1950s Moscow was on the whole hostile to national movements, unless Communist in character, after Stalin's death the Soviet authorities came to see more clearly that 'national reformist movements' in dependent or formerly dependent territories had an important role to play in the anti-'imperialist' struggle. Communists were accordingly encouraged to collaborate with nationalist parties—whatever their class character or their social and economic programmes—in patriotic anti-'imperialist' fronts.[15]

In Syria this change in the party line led Khalid Baqdash to call on all 'enemies of feudalism, reaction and imperialism' to join forces and contest the elections as a united 'National Front'. He appealed primarily to the Ba'th and to such prominent non-party but 'progressive-minded' politicians as Khalid al-'Azm. At first he met with little success. 'Azm was already looking left for potential political support but he was not yet ready for an overt alliance, while the Ba'th had until then been vigorously anti-Communist although strongly influenced by Marxist ideas. Common enemies were later to bring them together, but at the time of the 1954 elections the Communist Party had to fight alone. Although tolerated by the

[14] *al-Ba'th*, 9 May 1954.
[15] See below, pp. 230 ff. for a fuller treatment of this subject.

authorities, it was not legally recognized as a political party so that several of its men campaigned as 'national union' candidates.

The party had little mass following in 1954, but Baqdash's charm and confidence led people to overestimate its strength. Its support came mainly from the professional classes—lawyers, university lecturers, doctors, and engineers, notably those educated in France. It also had a following among junior civil servants and, surprisingly, among Muslim women who saw in Communism a liberating force and a promise of equal rights with men. But it was far outdistanced by the Ba'th in the two most powerful extra-parliamentary pressure groups: the army and the student body. It had only just begun to recruit members in the small urban proletariat and had made no significant headway among the peasantry.

A number of Damascus newspapers habitually reflected the Communist point of view, notably the clandestine *Nidal al-Sha'b* (The People's Struggle), which appeared irregularly, and the fellow-travelling weekly *al-Tali'a* (Vanguard). But the party line was more authoritatively stated in the Beirut weekly *al-Akhbar* (The News).

The Syrian National Social Party (PPS)

The PPS, in 1954, was a well-drilled, minority party whose impact on Syrian affairs bore no proportion to its numbers. It had been too closely associated with Shishakli to enjoy much popular support at the elections which followed his downfall. Its pan-Syrian doctrine ran counter to the Arab nationalism which most Syrians embraced. Banned in Lebanon in June 1949 after the execution of its founder,[16] the PPS transferred its headquarters to Damascus under the leadership of Georges 'Abd al-Massih. It enjoyed at the time a brief moment of popularity which was reflected in the election to the Chamber of its secretary-general 'Isam al-Mahaiyri. But even at its peak, in 1949–50, it could not claim a mass following.

Its importance in 1954 lay in the fact that it attracted the attention of some western officials by denouncing the 'Red Peril' and otherwise adopting the slogans of the extreme western right wing. In April 1955, eight months after the elections, it was to discredit these views and, by implication, the whole western position, by assassinating the deputy chief of the Syrian army, Colonel 'Adnan al-Malki. But an

[16] See ch. 9.

account of this disastrous intervention in Syrian politics—the so-called 'Malki affair'—must be left to another chapter. The party's views were reported in the Damascus newspaper *al-Bina'* (The Edifice) until the suppression of the party in April 1955. The newspaper later reappeared in Beirut.

The Muslim Brethren

The Syrian branch of the Muslim Brethren did not contest the elections as a political party. It merely lent its weight in support of candidates whom it considered 'good Muslims' or to those who opposed the West. It pleaded for solidarity among Muslims and for a return to the Quran and Islam as the basis of national life. But, unlike its Egyptian parent body, it did not succeed in using this Islamic approach as a political instrument for rallying the youth of the country in a highly-disciplined, para-military mass movement. Its influence was widespread, but diffuse and politically ineffective. It was scorned by sophisticated opinion generally. Its views were given publicity in its newspaper *al-Manar* (The Lantern), in weekly sermons in the mosques and in Friday religious broadcasts over Damascus radio. Its leaders were Shaikh Mustafa al-Siba'i, Muhammad Mubarak, and Ma'ruf al-Dawalibi (who was also a leading member of the People's Party).

The Brethren's main political contribution in 1954–5 was, perhaps, to influence the Syrian public against the Egyptian revolution. Representatives of the movement from Syria, Iraq, Jordan, and the Sudan met in conference in Damascus following Nagib's dismissal by 'Abd al-Nasir in February 1954 and launched a campaign against the Egyptian Free Officers.[17] Themselves recently freed from army dictatorship, Syrians did not look kindly on Egypt's military regime. The Egyptian junta became still less popular with its repression of the Muslim Brethren. The Syrian public did not appreciate how different were the Brethren's fanatical terrorists in Egypt from their own mild and devout shaikhs. The continued Syrian press attacks, together with the anti-Egyptian activities of refugee members of the Muslim Brethren, caused Egypt to recall her ambassador from Damascus early in November. Indeed, one of the main tasks of Egypt's next envoy to Syria, Mahmud Riyad, who arrived in January 1955, was to stem this wave of anti-Egyptian sentiment which, as he discovered, was a major handicap that Egypt had to overcome when

---

[17] See Husaini, *Moslem Brethren*, pp. 134–5.

bidding for Syrian support against Iraq in the battle over the Baghdad Pact.

The Co-operative Socialist Party

This right-wing, pan-Islamic movement consisted of the personal devotees of an eccentric but spirited young Syrian named Faysal al-'Asali. His vigorous attacks on the army[18] during the Palestine War had landed him in jail when Za'im seized power in March 1949. This setback cooled the ardour of some of his disciples, but did not prevent him standing as a candidate at the 1954 elections—and getting elected. His principal lieutenants were Rashid al-Dakr and Sayf al-Din Ma'mun, while two newspapers, *al-Barada* (the name of the river which flows through Damascus) and *al-Insha'* (Creation), often echoed his views.

The Arab Liberation Movement

Shishakli's Arab Liberation Movement, although dissolved after his fall, re-emerged when its members were threatened with punitive measures by the authorities. It continued to function, therefore, more in self-defence than as an active political force. On foreign policy it was thought to lean towards the West, and particularly towards France, with whom Shishakli had had special ties. The Movement's leading members were Ma'mun al-Kuzbari, 'Abd al-Hamid al-Khalili, and Subqi Duq al-Bab, while the newspaper *al-Fayha'* (The Verdant, one of the traditional names of Damascus) generally gave the Movement its support.

The Independents

In spite of the multiplicity of Syrian political parties, Independents captured no less than half the seats in each *muhafaza*—with the exceptions of Aleppo, Homs, and Hama, where party candidates predominated. These non-party men usually represented traditionalism in its purest form: they were landowners, businessmen, tribal and minority leaders, or the heads of the largest and most powerful families. They derived their support from local factors, and their repeated success at elections bore witness to the strength of traditional forms of loyalty as much as to the weakness of party organization. Skilfully manipulated, the Independents could, by virtue of their number, play a commanding role in the Chamber. Some Indepen-

[18] See above, ch. 5.

dents were pro-Hashimite, like Hasan al-Hakim or Munir al-'Ajlani; others, such as the Premier, Sa'id al-Ghazzi, genuinely wished to remain outside party disputes; others still, such as the millionaire Khalid al-'Azm, hoped to harness to their advantage the 'progressive', neutralist trend in the country.

THE ELECTIONS

The elections were held in two rounds, on 24–25 September and 4–5 October, in conditions of exceptional freedom and orderliness. The frontiers were closed during polling, troops were confined to barracks, while police and *gendarmerie* patrolled the main towns in strength. This is not to say that candidates and electors were free from all pressures—merely that such pressures were very much reduced. Of the 142 seats in the Chamber, 99 were filled on the first round and 43 on the second with the following results:

1954		*1949*[19]	
Independents	64	Independents (including 9 tribal representatives)	31
		Independents friendly to the People's Party	20
People's Party	30	People's Party	43
Ba'th	22	Ba'th	1
National Party	19	National Party	13
PPS	2	PPS	1
Co-operative Socialist Party	2	Co-operative Socialist Party	1
		Islamic Socialist bloc	4
Arab Liberation Movement	2		
Communist Party	1		
Total:	142	Total:	114

The outstanding features of these results were the emergence of the Ba'th, the halving of the strength of the People's Party, Khalid Baqdash's election as the first Communist deputy in the Arab world, and the return of a vast floating mass of Independents, outnumbering all the organized groups.

The backbone of the Ba'th success was Hawrani's sweeping

[19] The 1949 figures are given only as a rough guide: no exact comparison is possible. In 1949, party boundaries were fluid and candidates' affiliations unclear; the Chamber then consisted of 114 members against 142 in 1954; the National Party officially boycotted the election although many of its members stood; in 1954 no Islamic party contested the election.

victory in Hama where he and his friends captured five seats, routing a rival list of Independents headed by a popular and powerful young landowner, 'Abd al-Rahman al-'Azm.[20] 'Azm had the backing of all the landowning families in the area. He bore a name traditionally held in great respect. Almost alone of the young men in his milieu, he was open-minded and highly educated. But he made one bad mistake. Under pressure from his conservative supporters, he agreed to include in his electoral list the name of Husni al-Barazi, a man who as former Premier and Governor of Aleppo had the reputation of being both tough and corrupt. 'Azm was warned that Barazi's inclusion might prejudice his own chances, but he had given his word and could not go back on it.

One of Hawrani's closest associates gave the author the following account of Ba'th strategy in Hama:

The basic situation was that the countryside was for Hawrani while Hama itself was in the hands of the 'feudalists'. The atmosphere in the town was very tense before the elections. The landowners behaved with great violence, beating up and intimidating any suspected Ba'th supporter. Our strategy in the weeks before the poll was to act weak and not fight back but to call on the authorities to restore order, demanding only the application of the law.

The landowners thought they had won. Ten days before the elections they called out all their supporters following a great beating of drums in all the quarters of the town. We continued to bide our time until two days before the poll when, making a supreme effort, we threw everything we had got into organizing a mass demonstration, bringing in peasants from outlying villages, and rallying all our supporters. The result was some of the biggest crowds the city had ever seen. Public opinion was impressed and the elections were carried.

That the young upstart Hawrani with his peasant votes and low-class army friends should have unseated the representatives of all that was once great and honoured in Hama was the extent of the revolution to which the results pointed. Other important Ba'th successes were Wahib Ghanim's election in Latakia and Salah al-Din Bitar's victory over the PPS secretary-general 'Isam al-Mahaiyri in Damascus.

Michel 'Aflaq did not stand. The election results were as much

[20] Ba'th list: Akram al-Hawrani, 'Abd al-Karim Zuhur, Faysal al-Rikabi, Sa'd al-Khani, Khalil Kallas.
    Independents: 'Abd al-Rahman al-'Azm, Ra'if al-Mulki, Husni al-Barazi, Khudr al-Shishakli, Adib Nassur.

his triumph as Hawrani's: they were the fruits of a decade of patient indoctrination. No other Syrian could rival his influence with the generation which grew to manhood in the late 1940s and early 1950s. But he had no taste for the more direct forms of political action. His chosen forum was a circle of disciples or a classroom. He could not inflame crowds and, at moments of stress, preferred solitude in the Lebanese mountains to the political passions of Damascus. With the Ba'th electoral success, 'Aflaq had, in a sense, completed one stage of his work. He was a thinker rather than a political figure and it was now up to others to give practical expression to his ideas. Increasingly after 1954, Hawrani the tactician took over the day-to-day direction of the party.

The People's Party reverse marked the end of a long phase in Syrian-Iraqi relations. Hope had now to be abandoned of uniting the Fertile Crescent by a majority vote in the Syrian Chamber. Iraq and her friends in Syria were driven to revise their strategy: only force, they felt, could now decide the issue. It was, therefore, the outcome of the Syrian elections as much as the Baghdad Pact the following year that opened a new phase of violent conspiracy. Iraq's enemies saw the setback to the People's Party as a guarantee of Syrian integrity in the face of Hashimite expansionism. 'This latest popular ballot is less a victory for the Independents than for independence itself', *Le Monde* declared.[21] But although its overall representation was halved, the People's Party demonstrated once again its hold over Aleppo and Homs. Twenty-two of its thirty seats were won in these two *muhafazas*, where the party leaders scored impressive personal victories—Rushdi al-Kikhia, Nazim al-Qudsi, and Ma'ruf al-Dawalibi in Aleppo and the Atasis in Homs.

Khalid al-'Azm, heading an Independent list, won a sweeping victory in Damascus. Many voters had coupled his name on the ballot paper with that of Khalid Baqdash, the Communist leader. But the massive vote for the 'two Khalids' was due less to a genuine leftist trend in the country than to a popular reaction against what was thought to be American pressure on the Syrian Government. Whether this allegation was true or false is less important than that it was believed. It was said, for instance, that the United States Government had demanded Baqdash's exclusion from the elections; that American interests wanted to build a Coca-Cola plant in Syria; that Syria was under pressure to accept Point IV aid—which Syrian

[21] *Le Monde*, 11 Oct. 1954.

opinion identified with colonialism; that American aid in building a modern airport at Damascus was made conditional on the acceptance of certain secret clauses; that rejection of these had caused Pan American Airlines to lead an exodus to Beirut where an international airport was built instead. These were some of the reports then put about. They resulted in quite a strong current of anti-American and anti-western feeling, from which such men as Akram al-Hawrani, Khalid al-'Azm, and Khalid Baqdash all benefited. Ma'ruf al-Dawalibi, who was known for his dislike of the Anglo-Americans, polled more votes than any other candidate. American opinion seemed blind to everything except Khalid Baqdash's success; *Newsweek*, for example, declared in its October issue that Syria had become the Communist leader of the Arab world.

Not only did the elections demonstrate that the old social order had not stood up to the convulsions and military coups of the previous years. They also marked the triumph of neutralism in Arab opinion. The men whom the elections revealed as the most powerful and dynamic in Syrian politics were all committed to rejecting treaties, pacts, and indeed any formal tie with the West. This warning, ignored in London and Baghdad, was noted in Cairo and Moscow. On 25 October, the morrow of the elections, the Cairo daily *al-Ahram* used some of its heaviest type to headline the news that 'Syria rejects all pacts with the West'. 'Abd al-Nasir, who had signed the Anglo-Egyptian evacuation agreement a week earlier, must have found encouragement and inspiration in Syria's election results.

16

The Baghdad Pact and its Enemies, I

THE Baghdad Pact had a profound effect on every level of Arab politics. It was intended for a dual purpose: as a military weapon against the Soviet Union and as a political instrument of British and Iraqi power in the Arab world. The effectiveness of its first role has yet to be tested, but its second was seen to be a failure almost before its signature. Crippled from the start by Anglo-American disagreement, the Pact foundered on the rock of Iraqi-Egyptian rivalries. But to appreciate its impact on Arab affairs, some account must first be given of the defence debate which raged in the Middle East for a year or more before its conclusion on 25 February 1955. This was the context in which 'Abd al-Nasir's Arab policy took shape, which was to become the dominant theme in the area over the next four years.

ANGLO-AMERICAN DIFFERENCES

Although Britain and the United States were agreed on the importance of defending the Middle East against Communist expansion, they often differed on how this should be done. No exact account of their disagreements can be given in the absence of official documents; but it is clear that failure to concert their policies contributed to the poverty of the arrangements that were ultimately made.

To state their differences in the broadest possible terms, it may be said that while both were agreed on the global strategy of 'containment', Britain was further concerned to salvage what she could from a once dominant position in the Arab world. She therefore preferred to think in terms of a western-sponsored regional defence organization in which her existing treaty rights and military facilities in certain Arab states could be retained under a new multilateral formula. This contrasted with the American view of Middle East defence, which tended to be impatient of Britain's acquired positions and to envisage a rampart of non-Arab states hard up against Russia's southern flank.

But this distinction was not always so clear-cut. The Americans, too, would have liked to see the Arabs join a collective system if this could have been arranged. Indeed, in the original western plan of 1950–1, Britain and the United States joined with France and Turkey in an abortive attempt to induce Egypt to join a defence system and give a lead to the Arab world.[1] It was only later, during the Anglo-Egyptian negotiations over the Suez Canal Zone base in 1952–4, that Anglo-American policies were seen to diverge. An item in the British case was that a settlement should be conditional on Egypt's agreement to participate in a Middle East defence organization, but this was a point the Americans were less inclined to press. As Eden put it:

. . . American policy in general seemed to be conditioned by a belief that Egypt was still the victim of British 'colonialism', and as such deserving of American sympathy. It also appeared to be influenced by a desire to reach a quick solution almost at any cost and by a pathetic belief that, once agreement was reached, all would be well. These considerations, combined with a horror of unpopularity and fear of losing their influence with the new regime, particularly on the part of the United States Embassy in Cairo, and also an apparent disinclination by the United States Government to take second place even in an area where primary responsibility was not theirs, resulted in the Americans, at least locally, withholding the whole-hearted support which their partner in NATO had the right to expect and which would have been of great, if not decisive, influence on our negotiations.[2]

Anglo-American differences emerged clearly when the new Republican Administration turned its attention to Middle East defence early in 1953. This fresh American initiative may conveniently be dated from Mr Dulles's tour of the Middle East and South Asia in May. At the start he was plainly still exploring the possibility of Arab participation in a collective system. Colonel 'Abd al-Nasir, who met him at that time, is reported as saying that the Secretary of State's 'conversation was all about military objectives and the means by which to face any possible aggression from outside'. 'Abd al-Nasir continued:

---

[1] See above, ch. 11.
[2] *The Memoirs of the Rt Hon. Sir Anthony Eden, KG, PC, MC*, iii: *Full Circle* (1960), pp. 256–7. Eden makes plain his distrust of the U.S. ambassador in Cairo, Mr Jefferson Caffery (p. 252).

I told him my opinion frankly. I told him that there would be no aggression from outside for the simple reason that methods of modern warfare with its nuclear weapons have changed the whole art of war, and rendered any foreign aggression a remote possibility. I then added that internal fronts were of highest priority as regards defence and security. I also told him that he could by his own ways and means exert pressure over any Arab Government, to join the Western camp and give them military bases on its own territory, but this would be of no avail when the decisive experience came. I also added that he would find that the Government which submitted to their pressure would be divorced from its popular support, and would be unable to lead the people. Leadership, therefore, would be to leaders unknown to them. Besides, the military bases obtained under pressure would be of no use when they were needed. This was because there would be tens of bases working against this base.[3]

These arguments were not lost on Mr Dulles. He made it plain on his return to the United States that in his view a Middle East defence organization was 'a future rather than an immediate possibility'. But whereas the Arab states were too much engrossed in local quarrels to wish to join in defence against the USSR, the 'northern tier of countries' was aware of the danger and should be strengthened 'to resist the common threat to all free peoples'.[4] This was a clear judgement in favour of a forward defence strategy and against a system in depth in Arab territory.

The Americans may have been encouraged in this view by their successes on the northern fringes of the Arab world in the six years preceding Mr Dulles's tour.[5] Turkey had been receiving American aid since 1947. The relationship was further consolidated by the electoral victory of the Turkish Democratic Party in May 1950; by Turkey's participation in the Korean War, and by her admission to NATO in February 1952. Her role as an anti-Communist bastion was unquestioned. In Iran American influence had greatly increased as a result of the oil crisis. Musaddiq's fall in August 1953 and his succession by the pro-western Government of General Zahedi was followed by a large influx of American aid. When a settlement of the oil dispute was reached, American interests acquired a substantial stake in the Iranian oil industry. Farther east, in Pakistan, Mr Dulles found himself acclaimed: massive American wheat shipments had averted a famine on the eve of his arrival.

[3] 'Abd al-Nasir in an interview with journalists of the *New York Times*, 3 Nov. 1959 (*President Gamal Abdel-Nasser's Speeches and Press Interviews, 1959*, p. 600).
[4] *New York Times*, 2 June 1953 (RIIA, *Survey, 1953*, pp. 115–17).
[5] See Rondot, in *Orient*, Apr. 1957, p. 37.

These, then, were the principal 'northern tier' countries whose 'interrelated defences' the United States hoped to strengthen. Turkey and Pakistan were already allied by a treaty of friendship of 26 July 1951.

From both countries vital Russian targets could be more quickly reached than from any other base on the southern Russian flank. If to these countries Persia could be joined, there would come into existence the essential geographical basis for military defence and retaliation against the USSR. If, further, the USA were to be associated in some way with these countries, that geographical basis could be furnished with material means and the effect would be the extension into central Asia of the lines of anti-Russian containment, which were fixed at their western end in the Atlantic.[6]

The shape of this American design emerged gradually throughout 1953 and in the early months of 1954 to the accompaniment of protests from India, the Soviet Union, China, and Afghanistan. But Mr Dulles was not to be deflected; a Turco-Pakistani agreement was signed on 2 April 1954, followed on 19 May by a military aid agreement between the United States and Pakistan.[7] Suggestions that Iraq was being pressed to join the Turco-Pakistani pact seemed confirmed by the announcement of 25 April that she too was to receive American military aid.

The Americans had so far made all the running—but in the face of mounting British resentment. It was even reported that Britain had advised Iraq to delay joining the pact.[8] Indeed Britain was 'at pains to make clear that she had been informed but not consulted on U.S. plans'.[9] The causes of British vexation are not far to seek. In both Iraq and Pakistan, Britain considered the 'primary responsibility' to be hers: she did not welcome America's uninvited incursion. In the case of Iraq there was the more specific question of the fate of the Anglo-Iraqi Treaty of 1930 which was due to expire in 1957. An attempt to renew it in 1948 had ended in violent anti-British demonstrations in Baghdad. In the event of Iraq joining an American-dominated 'northern tier' alliance, the Anglo-Iraqi Treaty would, in due course, lapse. There would be little justification for its renewal or its renegotiation. Britain's long-standing position in Iraq would be threatened.

---

[6] RIIA, *Survey, 1953*, p. 117.
[7] For preliminary steps and further details see ibid. p. 121 and *1954*, pp. 203 ff.
[8] *Scotsman*, 21 Apr. 1954.   [9] RIIA, *The Baghdad Pact* (memo., 1956), p. 3.

Britain was also concerned at the impact of the American initiative on Commonwealth opinion—notably in India—and on Egypt. The Egyptian leaders were known to oppose Iraqi membership of a western defence system. It was feared that rumours of Iraq's adherence to the Turco-Pakistani alliance might adversely affect the Anglo-Egyptian negotiations which had then reached a critical stage, and might further reduce the already slender hopes of future Egyptian membership of a defence organization.

But to grasp the full measure of British disquiet it should be recalled that it was precisely at this moment, in April 1954, that the battle of Dien Bien Phu reached its final phase: a French collapse in Indo-China with far-reaching consequences was threatening. Mr Dulles was then attempting to press the United Kingdom into an *ad hoc* coalition, ready to intervene, which might develop into a South-East Asia defence organization.[10] Eden's view was that intervention might well bring the world to the verge of war and would be militarily ineffective. Moreover, he believed that the long-term issue of collective security should be clearly distinguished from the immediate question of 'united action' and would require 'the most careful thought and study, particularly on the question of membership'.[11] In any event, nothing should be done which might prejudice the outcome of the Geneva Conference on Indo-China which was due to open at the end of the month.

Mr Dulles's reaction was to take steps 'to settle the question of membership [of the proposed security pact] in advance, on his own terms'.[12] He convened a meeting on 20 April in Washington of the ambassadors of the United Kingdom, Australia, New Zealand, France, the Philippines, Thailand, and the three Indo-Chinese Associated States with the object of setting up an informal working group to study the collective defence of South East Asia. The United Kingdom refused to attend, Eden concluding his instructions to the British ambassador with the words:

Americans may think the time past when they need consider the feelings or difficulties of their allies. It is the conviction that this tendency becomes more pronounced every week that is creating mounting difficulties for anyone in this country who wants to maintain close Anglo-American relations. . . .[13]

---

[10] Eden, *Memoirs*, iii. 95 ff; RIIA, *Survey, 1954*, pp. 21 ff.
[11] Eden, *Memoirs*, iii. 96.   [12] Ibid. p. 98.   [13] Ibid. p. 99.

A Chatham House survey commented:

There was . . . said to be a certain restiveness in official quarters at the method of Mr Dulles's announcement of his policy and a tendency to regard it as tantamount to putting pressure on his allies by facing them with the choice of either adopting a policy they had not approved, or publicly repudiating a course of action propounded by the American government.[14]

Some of this irritation undoubtedly overspilled into the British assessment of the proposed 'northern tier' alliance. As one senior British official remarked: 'Dulles thought he had invented the Northern Tier. He was a great believer in blocs no matter who belonged.'

On the conclusion of the Anglo-Egyptian agreement in October 1954, Britain felt free to regain the initiative in the Middle East. Nuri al-Sa'id, the Iraqi statesman who had stood for the British connexion, provided the opportunity. 'I was delighted', Eden writes, 'to hear at the end of 1954 that Nuri es-Said, the Prime Minister of Iraq, was working on a plan to strengthen the Arab League pact, by the inclusion of Turkey and with the help of the United Kingdom and the United States.'[15] This was a distinct alternative to Mr Dulles's plan. Whereas the 'northern tier' alliance was a forward defence line up against Russia's borders composed of non-Arab states —Turkey, Iran, and Pakistan—with the possible addition of Iraq as a junior partner, Nuri's rival project shifted the centre of gravity of the defence system back to the Arab world. It provided for extensive Arab participation—all the signatories of the Arab collective security pact—and gave Iraq the key role of a central pivot or connecting link between these Arab states on the one hand and Turkey and the western Powers on the other. Finally, the whole scheme was to be launched under British rather than American sponsorship.

No doubt there were visions in London of taking in harness the Arab collective security pact under friendly Iraqi leadership in much the same way as, a decade earlier in 1945, Britain had hoped to control the Arab League under Egyptian leadership. It seemed, for a moment, as if Nuri had hit upon a statesmanlike formula which would both satisfy Arab nationalist opinion and perpetuate the British presence in the Arab world behind the screen of a multilateral association. It was in this sense that the project may be said to have been designed

[14] RIIA, *Survey, 1954*, p. 30.   [15] *Memoirs*, iii. 219–20.

as a political instrument of British and Iraqi power in the area. The nucleus of this design was the Iraqi-Turkish pact of mutual co-operation of 24 February 1955, known as the Baghdad Pact. It was not altogether surprising that the Americans, whose elaborate northern-tier plans were thus bypassed, were piqued. 'My difficulty in working with Mr Dulles', Eden writes somewhat disingenuously, 'was to determine what he really meant. . . . Nor could I understand the prolonged coolness of American policy towards the Baghdad Pact in its most critical period. . . .'[16]

EGYPT'S ARAB POLICY

Nuri al-Sa'id's grandiose scheme of a regional alliance of Arab states, stiffened by the adherence of their northern neighbours and underpinned by the western Powers, was defeated by Egyptian opposition. It offended against every canon of Egypt's Arab policy as this had evolved since the 1940s and as the revolutionary junta was in process of reshaping it.

'Abd al-Nasir relates in his illuminating little book, *Falsafat al-thawra* (The Philosophy of the Revolution) written in 1953, how the 'first elements of Arab consciousness' began to filter into his mind when, in protest against the Balfour Declaration, he marched out of school with his fellow students on 2 December each year. But he adds: 'When I asked myself at that time why I left my school so enthusiastically and why I was angry for this land which I never saw, I could not find an answer except the echoes of sentiment.' At the military school, and then when studying Mediterranean defence problems at the staff college, he began to see the issue more clearly. Finally, 'when the Palestine crisis loomed on the horizon I was firmly convinced that the fighting in Palestine was not fighting on foreign territory. Nor was it inspired by sentiment. It was a duty imposed by self-defence.'[17] 'Abd al-Nasir's reaction was that of an Egyptian patriot.

We were fighting in Palestine [he writes], but our dreams were in Egypt. Our bullets were aimed at the enemy lurking in the trenches in front of us, but our hearts were hovering round our distant Mother Country, which was then a prey to the wolves that ravaged it. . . . We spoke of nothing but our country and how to deliver it.[18]

[16] Ibid. pp. 63–64.   [17] Jamal 'Abd al-Nasir, *Falsafat al-thawra*, pp. 56–57.
[18] Ibid. p. 12.

The first impact on Egypt of the Palestine War was indeed to lay bare the decay at home rather than promote the cause of Arab solidarity. When the Egyptian army marched, there was a strong feeling in Egypt that this was a specific mission which concerned all the Arabs, but that once that mission was fulfilled the army could return to the homeland and life would continue as before. Defeat, with its attendant conviction that Egypt had been betrayed by her allies, strengthened the trend towards isolationism. The luckless Arabs should be left to go to the wall. To Egypt, unlike Jordan and Syria, Israel did not at the time seem a pressing danger; Sinai lay between them like a great protective sand shield. Even after the Egyptian revolution in 1952 there was a pronounced 'Egypt First' trend among the Free Officers: it was felt that an Arab policy was a luxury Egypt could ill afford; she should cut herself off from the turbulence of Arab politics and concentrate on internal problems.

'Abd al-Nasir was almost alone in standing out against this trend. Unlike many of his compatriots, the main lesson he derived from the Palestine War was the interdependence of the Arab countries and the need to mobilize their joint resources against imperialism and Israel. He sets out with great clarity how he arrived at this conclusion.

After the siege [of Falouga] and the battles in Palestine I came home with the whole region in my mind one complete whole. The events that followed confirmed this belief in me. As I pursued the developments of the situation I found nothing but echoes responding to one another. An event may happen in Cairo today; it is repeated in Damascus, Beirut, Amman or any other place tomorrow. This was naturally in conformity with the picture that experience has left with me: One region, the same factors and circumstances, even the same forces opposing them all. It was clear that Imperialism was the most prominent of these forces; even Israel itself was but one of the outcomes of Imperialism . . . Imperialism is the great force that throws around the whole region a fatal siege a hundred times stricter and more cruel than the siege around us in Falouga . . . I thus began to believe after these facts became established within me, in one common struggle and repeat to myself, 'As long as the region is one, and its conditions, its problems and its future, and even the enemy are the same however different are the masks that the enemy covers its face with, why should we dissipate our efforts?' The experience of what followed on 23rd July increased my faith in a united struggle and its necessity. The secret of the picture began to reveal itself and the darkness which shrouded its details began to disappear.[19]

[19] Ibid. pp. 62 ff.

Palestine, then, brought home to 'Abd al-Nasir the need for Arab solidarity. With less cynicism but greater ambition, he reached the conclusion to which 'Ali Mahir, King Faruq, and Nahhas Pasha had come before him—that Egypt's interests lay in identifying herself closely with the Arabs of Asia. This lesson, derived from his personal experience, served to underscore the Arab policy which he inherited from his predecessors, embodied in the Arab League Charter of 1945 and the Arab collective security pact of 1950. These two instruments, with their provision for Egyptian primacy over a group of smaller, less powerful, and less advanced Arab states, were an important part of a political legacy. But, as *Falsafat al-thawra* reveals, Nasir was soon convinced that Egypt had a still more ambitious role to play. Her 'theatre of activity'—the vital sphere in which she could play an active role—was wider than that of the Arab states. 'Abd al-Nasir's now famous conclusion was that the facts of history and geography had placed Egypt at the intersection of three circles, those of the Arab, African, and Muslim worlds.

I do not know why I always imagine that in this region in which we live there is a role wandering aimlessly about seeking an actor to play it. I do not know why this role, tired of roaming about in this vast region which extends to every place around us, should at last settle down, weary and worn out, on our frontiers beckoning us to move, to dress up for it and to perform it since there is nobody else who can do so.
Here I hasten to point out that this role is not a leading one. It is one of interplay of reactions and experiments with all these factors aiming at exploding this terrific energy latent in every sphere around us and at the creation, in this region, of a tremendous power capable of lifting this region up and making it play its positive role in the construction of the future and humanity. . . . We, and only we, are impelled by our environment and are capable of performing this role.[20]

This was the tenor of 'Abd al-Nasir's thinking when, in the winter of 1953-4, events forced the Egyptian leaders to think out and define their position unequivocally. Mr Dulles's 'northern tier' was taking shape, threatening to engulf Iraq; the first heady proposals for a grouping of uncommitted, newly-independent Asian and African states were being discussed; Egypt herself was on the threshold of an agreement with Britain which would complete her independence and free her foreign policy from the pressure of foreign troops garrisoned on her territory; her young leaders, for the first time since they came

[20] Ibid. pp. 55 f., 73.

to power, were driven to look beyond the Nile Valley and to discover afresh the Arab world around them.

In late December 1953 Colonel 'Abd al-Nasir and the whole team of Egyptian negotiators at the Anglo-Egyptian talks—'Abd al-Hakim Amir, 'Abd al-Latif Baghdadi, Salah Salim, and Mahmud Fawzi— held a series of meetings to thrash out Egypt's new policy line. They were joined early in January by the Egyptian ambassadors to the United Kingdom, the United States, the USSR, India, and Pakistan, who had been recalled for consultations. The press and radio described the meetings, which continued almost without interruption into early February, as 'a comprehensive and decisive revision of Egypt's foreign policy'. It was made clear that Egypt's approach to renewed talks with Britain would be subordinated to the policy that was then being evolved.[21]

A key session was held on 9 January, after which it was announced that Egypt's foreign policy would be based on the following principles:

1. The establishement of an Arab bloc, free from imperialist influence, to protect the interests of Islamic, Asiatic and African peoples;
2. The conclusion of a treaty binding these peoples together;
3. The establishment of an African bloc which would include all African countries still under the imperialist yoke.[22]

Indian and Soviet views on neutralism weighed heavily on the conference. The Egyptian ambassador in Moscow, General 'Aziz al-Masri, arrived in Cairo declaring 'Neutrality means peace and Russia wants peace'.

But at this early stage Egypt's neutralism was more an expression of her desire for complete national independence than the militant weapon it was soon to become in the Arab world as a whole. The Arab News Agency reported on 27 January that, on returning to their posts, the Egyptian ambassadors would carry 'crucial instructions' on Egypt's policy, but that this policy would not be a neutral one 'in the true sense of the word', because it would be based on the principle of refusing to accept 'any sort of co-operation other than one based on a full recognition of her rights, sovereignty, and national prestige'.

This was confirmed by Major Salah Salim, the 'Voice of the Revolution', at a press conference on 10 February called to mark the end of the series of meetings:

[21] *Mideast Mirror*, 2 Jan. 1954, p. 2.   [22] BBC, no. 431, 15 Jan. 1954.

As to Egypt's policy, call it neutrality or what you like. Some may differ on the definition of the word neutrality; but what concerns us, and what we cannot disagree on, is that we will oppose and will not co-operate in any way whatsoever with anyone who opposes our dignity and freedom. We will co-operate with and support all who assist and support us. I hereby announce that Egypt has taken practical steps to improve co-operation in all its forms with the states of the world, in the east and in the west equally. We will not discriminate between one state and another, except in the measure of its response to our demands and its support of us in the economic and political fields, which respect our Egyptian nationality; we will not tag along behind anyone. In short, we desire to live in freedom and will struggle to do so. No one can blame us for struggling until we attain a freedom for which we will never bargain, however big the bargain may be.[23]

'For the first time in history', Cairo radio declared, 'Egypt has a defined policy . . .'.[24] The hardening of Egypt's attitude was reflected in an expansion of her broadcasting services. The 'Voice of the Arabs' service had been on the air for half an hour a day since 4 July 1953, but it was expanded on 4 January 1954 to one hour and three-quarters, becoming the chief anti-'imperialist' transmission from the Middle East. 'Cairo must always remain in the service of the Arabs and of Arabism and Islam', it declared. 'The Voice of the Arabs speaks for the Arabs, struggles for them and expresses their unity; it has no object but Arabism and no hope in anyone but the Arabs. It struggles for nothing but the glory and independence of the Arabs. . . .'[25] It was the only transmission from an Arab country openly directed to the Arabs as a whole. Six months later, on 4 July 1954, the service was further expanded to four hours a day on both short and medium waves, when it also started broadcasting in Swahili: 'Egypt's geographical situation requires her to work for the liberation from all forms of imperialism of the African continent through which the Nile flows. . . .'[26]

The announcement of the Turco-Pakistani agreement on 2 April drew a brief but unequivocal comment from 'Abd al-Nasir: 'No Arab country should join the alliance. It is a defensive pact which ignores the interests of the Middle East, and at the same time aims at frustrating the work of the Arab League.'[27] But as Iraq edged towards this alliance, Egyptian opposition hardened:

[23] BBC, no. 440, 16 Feb. 1954.   [24] BBC, no. 441, 19 Feb. 1954.
[25] BBC, no. 430, 12 Jan. 1954.   [26] BBC, no. 480, 6 July 1954.
[27] BBC, no. 465, 14 Apr. 1954.

Every Arab now realises the glaring fact that the West wants to settle in our land for ever. The West wants to remain the master of the world so that it may colonise, enslave and exploit it. The West will give Iraq military equipment, but what for? Is it to strengthen proud Iraq so that she may liquidate the step-daughter of imperialism and the principal enemy of the Arabs, Israel? No, it is to lead her to death in the front lines of the next world war in order to immortalise the Western colonization of Iraq.[28]

In the face of this threat, Egypt's Arab policy then entered a more aggressive phase which began with a tour of the Arab world by Major Salah Salim. Cairo radio described him as 'flying from one Arab city to another trying to unite the Arabs and smash the chains of imperialism and slavery'. The message which he preached in Saudi Arabia, the Yemen, and Lebanon was that it was time relations between Arab states were established on a new basis of a unified Arab policy on all major issues. The first priority was a unanimous Arab repudiation of all foreign military alliances.

Egypt [Cairo radio declared] has one clear and unequivocal policy, to support actively the unity of the Arabs so that they can face aggression, injustice and subjugation as one man.

The 'Voice of the Arabs' calls on the Arabs to stand in one rank in face of imperialism, to expel the British, to cleanse the land of Arabdom from this plague, to obtain with their own money and to make for themselves arms which will repulse aggression, and to maintain peace and justice.

No-one would refuse honest aid from abroad; but the Arabs can do without any pennies and bullets which bring enslavement and put back the clock of Arab progress. Aid of this kind is not based on respect for mutual interests and for the rights of people to freedom and independence. This, O Arabs, is the policy of Egypt.[29]

Up to mid-1954, the new Egyptian regime was still very much of an unknown quantity to other Arab states. To the outside world it was not yet clear which of the many rival forces, both domestic and foreign, competing for the control of the Egyptian revolution, had gained the upper hand. The Free Officers who had carried out the revolution were busy establishing themselves at home and had had very few contacts with other Arab states. The world outside the Nile Valley was unfamiliar territory which they explored with caution and reluctance. But it was in these circumstances that 'Abd al-Nasir took the bold step of making Arabism Egypt's *official* policy. Arab

[28] BBC, no. 471, 4 June 1954.   [29] BBC, no. 279, 2 July 1954.

solidarity under Egyptian direction was wedded to non-alignment. This was the policy which Egypt urged the Arabs to adopt: Arabs must unite only with Arabs.

> Compatriots ['Abd al-Nasir declared on 23 July 1954, the second anniversary of the Egyptian revolution], Egypt has started a new era of relations with the Arabs—an era based on true and frank fraternity, facing up to and thinking out problems and endeavouring to solve them. The aim of the Revolution Government is for the Arabs to become one Nation with all its sons collaborating for the common welfare . . . The Revolution also believes that the weight of the defence of the Arab states falls first and foremost on the Arabs and they are worthy of undertaking it.[30]

It was an over-simplification to suggest, as did some western observers, that Egypt was then only concerned to strengthen her hand in negotiations with Britain, and that once these were satisfactorily concluded she would fall into line with the West. On the contrary, the anti-western themes of Cairo comment were throughout represented as an expression of concern for other Arab, Muslim, and Asian peoples rather than a call to them to support Egypt over the Suez Canal Zone or other questions. Egypt was feeling her way towards the heady doctrine of *total* freedom from European tutelage. Indeed, the negotiations with Britain opened new vistas for Egypt: 'Instead of the old choice between subjection and autonomy within the British sphere, she now had a choice between autonomy and real independence.'[31] The agreement demonstrated that Egypt could and did choose independence: Britain was compelled to evacuate the Canal Zone without securing Egypt's consent to join a western-sponsored collective defence system.

Indeed, when the Anglo-Egyptian agreement was initialed on 27 July, Egypt was at pains to make clear to the Arabs that her policy remained unchanged: she believed the defence of the Middle East was best left to the states of the region themselves and that any alliance with the western Powers would be a 'mask for colonialism'.

> The Anglo-Egyptian agreement is no alliance [Cairo radio explained]. The 'Voice of the Arabs' can emphasise that Egypt today has one alliance for which it works and in which it believes. It is the alliance of the Arab collective security pact. It is the hope around which Egyptian policy centres. It is the Arab alliance in which all Arabism should crystallise and

[30] BBC, no. 486, 21 July 1954.
[31] Hourani, 'A Moment of Change: The Crisis of 1956', *A Vision of History*, p. 132.

which should be established on a firm basis. . . . No alliances with the West but with you, O Arabs.[32]

The young Egyptian rulers were at this time much influenced by Indian neutralism[33] which, under the impact of the Korean War, had evolved from its origins in Hindu pacifism and tolerance into an international mediating force, throwing its weight impartially on the side of peace, and peace through negotiation.

New to freedom itself, India saw the pattern of Western alliances in Asia as an infringement of this freedom, as a warning that, once again as in the imperial period, Asians were to be used as pawns in the great game for world power and that it was possible that control through foreign bases, reinforced by economic domination, might prove as effective as the old territorial occupation.[34]

This was precisely Egypt's view. To both India and Egypt, non-alignment seemed a guarantee of sovereignty as well as a means of escaping involvement in the conflicts of international Power blocs. Indeed, Egypt's objections to Iraq's membership of a western-sponsored pact in 1954–5 re-echoed, in more virulent terms, the arguments India had advanced against Pakistan's membership of SEATO in 1953. But in Egypt's case, non-alignment had to be fitted into a context of inter-Arab politics. To retain her dominant role in Arab affairs, she had to 'sell' neutralism to *all* the Arab states; she could allow no dissentient voices. Any alternative policy was a direct challenge to her. Egyptian policy was therefore based on two inter-related equations: first, that non-alignment was the main guarantee of independence; and second, that the Arabs should rely for their defence on themselves alone. A third tacit conviction was that this form of Arab solidarity based on the Arab League and the Arab collective security pact was the best assurance of continued Egyptian leadership.

IRAQ'S ARAB POLICY

The first challenge to these ideas came from Iraq. Her rulers—Nuri al-Sa'id and the Regent 'Abd ul-Ilah in particular—did not believe in neutralism; the threat of Russian expansionism was too real; Britain's acquired position in Iraq as founder and mentor of the state was too great; they had no faith in the armies of their

---

[32] BBC, no. 498, 7 Sept. 1954.   [33] See RIIA, *Survey, 1953*, p. 118.
[34] Michael Edwardes, *Asia in the Balance* (Penguin Books), p. 113.

Arab neighbours, while their links with Turkey and Persia on their northern and eastern frontiers were in many ways as intimate.

Moreover they heartily disliked both the Arab League and the Arab collective security pact, which seemed to them little more than instruments for Egyptian interference in Arab Asia—an area which Iraq considered her legitimate sphere of influence. For a decade Egypt had used the League to contain Iraq on the Tigris and prevent the union of the Fertile Crescent to which the Hashimites were so much attached. Indeed, Egypt's resolute entry into Arab affairs after the Second World War had robbed vintage Arab nationalists such as Nuri, comrades in arms of Faysal I, of the dominant role they would no doubt otherwise have played. Egypt had imposed her own pattern of relations on the Arab world at the expense of Nuri's grand design. (Few men were more unpopular in Iraq than the former secretary-general of the Arab League, 'Abd al-Rahman 'Azzam, considered too docile a servant of Egyptian policy.)

There was little chance, then, that Iraq would respond favourably in 1954 to the call of the young revolutionaries in Cairo for Arab solidarity within the framework of the Arab collective security pact. Nuri was not satisfied that Iraq could be defended without stiffening from the western Powers and the collaboration of her non-Arab neighbours. He further understood the need for close co-operation with Turkey and Iran in order to contain the Iraqi Kurds and thus ensure Iraq's internal unity (a consideration some of his successors have failed to grasp). But, perhaps more to the point, Nuri saw in the defence debate a chance of wresting from Egypt the initiative in Arab affairs.

Steeply mounting oil revenues had made him bolder and had enhanced Iraq's standing in the Arab world; in Syria Shishakli's fall had created new opportunities for Iraqi diplomacy; in Egypt the junta faced a difficult year. Its leaders were young and untried; General Nagib's resignation in February and subsequent return to power suggested internal tensions; Arab opinion everywhere was disturbed by the Free Officers' long and bitter struggle with the Muslim Brotherhood. Even the trimphant conclusion of the Anglo-Egyptian negotiations was not without problems for 'Abd al-Nasir and his colleagues: they found themselves victims of the anti-British propaganda on which their public had grown up. Egyptian opinion would never tolerate a new alliance with the western Powers: independence would first have to be *seen* to be real; a transitional period free from all links with Great Powers would be necessary before Egypt could even contemplate taking part in a western-sponsored Middle East defence organization—even were she then to feel so inclined.

All this Nuri must carefully have weighed. But, he argued, if Iraq were to become the lynch-pin in a collective defence system, she would benefit from a flood of western arms, money, and equipment, other Arab states would follow her lead, the Middle East would be safe from Communism, and Egypt would be faced with the bleak choice of isolation or of tagging along as a junior partner.

Viewed in this light, Nuri found Mr Dulles's northern-tier *entente* not wholly satisfactory. For one thing Britain was opposed to Iraq's joining it, and loyalty may have been enough to dissuade Nuri from doing so. But there was a still more powerful reason: the forward strategy of the northern tier did not provide for extensive Arab membership. If Iraq were to join the Turco-Pakistani alliance, she would be cut off from the Arabs rather than leading them. Nuri's problem, then, was to devise a formula in which Iraq would be the pin holding together the Arab states, their northern neighbours, and the western Powers. These were the ideas he turned over in his mind in the summer of 1954 after the initialing of the Anglo-Egyptian agreement in July.

THE SARSANK CONVERSATIONS

The first confrontation of Egyptian and Iraqi policies took place in the third week of August 1954 at Sarsank, a mountain resort in northern Iraq. The Egyptians proposed the talks. Their side was led by Major Salah Salim, chief spokesman of the revolutionary Government, accompanied by Mahmud Riyad, who shortly afterwards, in January 1955, became Egypt's envoy in Damascus. The two men were the leading architects of Egypt's Arab policy. Major Salah Salim gave the following account of what took place:[35]

I flew to Mosul in mid-August and then continued by car to Sarsank where I met King Faysal, the Regent, Nuri al-Sa'id, and the other Iraqis. I talked with each of them separately and with all of them together.

Their main worry was a possible military threat from Russia. They reminded me that their borders were very close to the Caucasus, only some 300 or 400 miles. They were also concerned about the problem of Palestine and about what could be done there. They said they were very weak.

[35] Salah Salim to the author, London, 12 Apr. 1960.

They congratulated me on the success of our negotiations with the British, adding that they would like to do the same as their treaty with Britain was shortly to expire. They spoke a great deal about their weakness and about how Britain and the West were the normal sources of arms. 'There is no hope whatsoever of getting more arms and of building up a real army except by concluding a pact with the West as Pakistan and Turkey have done', Nuri told me.

Nuri also raised his fears of Turkey. He said Turkey had always wanted to seize Mosul, as she had secured Alexandretta from Syria. It was essential to build up a real position of strength to resist Turkish ambitions.

They then spoke of the indirect Communist threat from neighbouring countries such as Iran and from underground Communist activity in Iraq itself. They said: 'We are a realistic government unlike your former governments of the Pashas. We should like to co-operate with you.' Finally, Nuri ended his statement of their position by saying: 'I should like to do something for Palestine before I die.'

I replied that we in Egypt had struggled a long time to achieve real independence. But having secured it, we now believed that we should avoid all foreign ties, particularly with Great Powers. We had made alliances in the past—for example our treaty with Great Britain in 1936. But the powerful partner had exploited the treaty to limit the freedom of the weak partner. In all the twenty years of the alliance, the British had only helped us create a force of some 10,000–20,000 men, equipped with rifles for parades. They had never helped us build up a real army fit for war. They had sent us military missions which, instead of training our troops, had themselves become the real commanders and interfered in our internal affairs. The British ambassador was the real power in the country; he could dismiss cabinets and appoint Prime Ministers.

The British had, in fact, interfered in every branch of our lives. I told them that our people still remembered this interference and knew why it was so. It was simply that the British were more powerful than we were and that they had interests in the area. In such an alliance there could be no question of real independence.

In conclusion, I told them that we in Egypt had decided that it would now be far better to have a transitional period free from all foreign obligations during which we could observe how we were treated by Britain and the West. If they treated us as sovereign states, then we might in the future change our minds. But we were resolved at present to refuse all ties with Great Powers. We aimed at full, unconditional independence.

In reply to Nuri's fears about Turkish designs on Mosul, I merely said that if the West gave Turkey its support, there was little that Iraq could do. Conversely, if the West did not want Turkey to acquire Mosul, she would never do so.

As for Communism, I told Nuri frankly that his policy of making pacts with the West was the best way of strengthening the Communist underground in Iraq. Not only would his policy induce the Communists to redouble their activities inside the country, but it would also allow them to represent the Government as puppets in the hands of the Great Powers and, with this argument, win over the nationalists to their side.

'Your nationalists are much the same as ours', I told them. 'They want complete independence. They are sick of British interference in their internal affairs. They will inevitably be influenced by Communist propaganda. The problem in Iraq is how to secure the confidence of the nationalists, because if you lose their confidence you will have lost the battle inside your country. The arms you are seeking from the West may in fact be used by the nationalists against you.'

The Regent then spoke up to say that conditions in Iraq were quite different from those in Egypt. He was convinced that the officers were loyal to the throne and to the Hashimite family. He listed the many benefits which the officers enjoyed: they were given villas, their pensions were generous, and they received a full year's salary as a bonus on retirement. He spoke on this subject for half an hour. 'Faruq', he said, 'treated his officers very badly. That is why you carried out your revolution.'

But I retorted: 'We did not overthrow Faruq for higher salaries. We revolted because we are nationalists. We wanted to free the Government from foreign influence. Freedom cannot be bought with villas, salaries, and allowances. I tell you frankly that if you want your Government and Throne to be stable, you should adopt a policy which will give your country real independence.'

They then asked how they could strengthen their army if they adopted our policies and, in reply, I made certain proposals.

I said: 'Let us call all the Arab countries to a conference and together set up a real defence organization. If Cairo and Baghdad agree to this, all the others will follow. If we, in fact, set up a purely Arab pact in this decisive region of the world, with a combined headquarters, a common defence strategy, and joint plans for training, for building roads, aerodromes, and so on . . . If we then went together, as one unit, to the Western Powers and said to them: Here is a regional organization in accordance with Articles 51 and 52 of the UN Charter. You have many interests in the area. We want you to help this organization by giving it arms so that it may repel aggression from any quarter. Our people would not be suspicious of a purely Arab organization of this sort.

'But if, after we had done all this, the West refused to give us arms, we should have to think again. But you may be sure that uniting in such a workable organization would give us tremendous power. At present the West is playing us off against each other. But if we combine, we shall be in a far stronger position to meet our various defence and economic needs.'

'Consider Israel', I added; 'our people know that Israel could never have been established without western help. How can we now convince them to join forces with those who allowed Israel to become a source of continuous aggression against us?'

Nuri al-Sa'id appeared convinced by my arguments. He said: 'We accept your proposals in general', adding that he would visit Cairo in mid-September on his way to London and would then discuss the details with 'Abd al-Nasir and myself.

I left the conference room thinking I had been highly successful. I was full of hope and returned to Cairo elated. . . .

Major Salim's account sins only by omission. He fails to mention two points, the one trivial, the other a matter of substance, which together destroyed the fruits of his mission and undermined any agreement he might have thought he had reached with Nuri al-Sa'id.

The first was an unguarded statement, unconnected with the principal issues discussed at Sarsank, which he let slip at a press conference in Baghdad on 19 August. A journalist asked him to define Egypt's attitude towards bipartite unions between Arab states. This was a clear reference to the burning issue of a Syrian-Iraqi union which Egypt had systematically opposed in the past. What would be the attitude of Egypt's new revolutionary Government? Salah Salim replied: 'Egypt does not oppose any kind of union. If two or more Arab peoples wish to unite in some form, Egypt does not object. It is possible for us Arabs to agree on the defence of our countries and the preservation of our existence.'[36]

Major Salim did not realize the implications of his reply. He was preoccupied, as the latter part of his answer suggests, with questions of Middle East defence which had dominated the Sarsank conference. But Arab opinion immediately took him to mean that Egypt had withdrawn her objections to Nuri's Fertile Crescent plan. The Syrians were indignant that their future should have been discussed at talks from which they were absent, while King Sa'ud was beside himself. Egypt was forced to issue a denial that she had offered Iraq her support in a plan to annex Syria. A wholly artificial storm was raised which distracted attention from the major issues at stake and poisoned the atmosphere for future negotiations.

The point of substance on which Major Salah Salim was less than fully explicit concerns the nature of the agreement on Middle East

[36] BBC, no. 494, 24 Aug. 1954.

defence reached at Sarsank. He was right in saying that Nuri had agreed on the need to strengthen the Arab collective security pact. But he failed to mention that he had himself consented that Britain and the United States should be consulted at every stage and their support requested. It was later revealed that the following resolution had been agreed upon:

> The parties have agreed that it is necessary to reconsider the collective security pact with the object of strengthening it and making it a strong and effective means of enabling the Arab countries to cope with any danger threatening themselves. Each of the parties will study this matter and conduct the necessary talks with the USA and Britain in this regard. During the second half of September another meeting will be held in Cairo between Egypt and Iraq in order to review the results of the contacts with the USA and Britain, and in order to resume discussions. Thereafter, the two parties will jointly meet with the representatives of Britain and the USA to discuss the subject, preliminary to submitting the matter to the other Arab countries with a view to reaching a comprehensive agreement.[37]

Salah Salim had been outmanoeuvred. He had thought to win Nuri over to the notion of a purely Arab pact but instead had himself assented to linking an Arab defence organization to the western Powers. Indeed, before leaving Baghdad for Cairo after the Sarsank talks, he had gone so far as to contact the United States and British chargés d'affaires—the respective ambassadors being absent from Iraq at the time—to discuss the matter with them and to inform them that he would get in touch with the American and British ambassadors in Cairo.[38] He had gone beyond his brief, illustrating how uncertain and tentative in 1954 was the notion of Arab independence *wholly* free from western tutelage.

He found, on his return to Cairo, that 'Abd al-Nasir did not share his satisfaction at the results of his mission. Soon the Arab press was speculating freely on reports of a split in the junta concerning the Sarsank conversations: early in September Major Salim was said to have gone 'on leave', only to be recalled to his duties two days later. His brother, Gamal Salim, telephoned Nuri to deny rumours of

---

[37] Quoted by Nuri al-Sa'id in a broadcast on 16 December 1956 defending his Arab policy in the period of bitter Iraqi-Egyptian recrimination which followed the Suez war (see BBC, no. 126, 18 Dec. 1956). 'Abd al-Qadir Hatim, director of the Egyptian Dept. of Information, replied to Nuri on 20 December (see BBC, no. 130, 27 Dec. 1956).
[38] BBC, no. 126, 18 Dec. 1956.

disagreement in the Council of the Revolution, but the divergence was real none the less, as the Egyptians themselves later admitted:

> After Salah Salim's return to Cairo, President Gamal 'Abd al-Nasir opposed the idea of seeking advice from Britain and the U.S.A. on a matter 'purely within our prerogative rights' and said that to consult America and Britain meant entering into negotiations with the two countries.
>
> On 7th and 9th September, President Gamal 'Abd al-Nasir received Nagib al-Rawi, the Iraqi Ambassador to Egypt, and the Ambassador said on this occasion . . . that Nuri al-Sa'id would not visit Egypt as previously agreed on with Salah Salim until Britain and America had been consulted on the question of strengthening the collective security pact. President 'Abd al-Nasir pointed out to the Ambassador that the idea of seeking advice from Britain and America 'is inconsistent with our independent policy. Our discussions in this respect are being conducted with Iraq, as the British answer is well known to us. Their only way to strengthen the collective security pact is through their participation in this pact. They told us that, and we have rejected it since 1953.'
>
> The Iraqi Ambassador said: 'Your failure to contact the British and Americans will prevent Nuri al-Sa'id from visiting Egypt and consequently prevent the resumption of discussions.'
>
> The President replied that Nuri al-Sa'id was free to take any decision he might wish but it was in the general interest that discussions should be resumed and that Nuri al-Sa'id should be present as he had promised, so that the Arab cause might be furthered.[39]

Salah Salim's mission to Sarsank had failed.

THE NURI–NASIR MEETING

Nuri Sa'id's visit to Cairo on 15 September 1954 shattered any remaining illusions of an Iraqi-Egyptian agreement and marked the opening of a more violent phase in the defence debate. The following is Salah Salim's own account of what took place:

> 'Abd al-Nasir and I met Nuri at the airport. I then accompanied him to the Semiramis Hotel where he asked me to come up to his room. He entered and closed the door. 'I am sure you are having a lot of trouble with 'Abd al-Nasir over the Sarsank proposals', he said. 'I am ready to help you against 'Abd al-Nasir'. I spent more than an hour with him swearing that there had been no trouble of any sort and that 'Abd al-Nasir would repeat to him ever word I had said.
>
> We all met again at 'Abd al-Nasir's that evening. Nuri began to speak. He spoke for two hours. None of us understood a word. He had the

[39] 'Abd al-Qadir Hatim's reply to Nuri al-Sa'id (BBC, no. 130, 27 Dec. 1956).

supreme ability of speaking for hours without conveying any sense. He went on and on and on. I looked at ʿAbd al-Nasir and he looked at me. Impatient at last, ʿAbd al-Nasir intervened to say: 'I really cannot understand. Please tell me in brief what you want to say.'

Nuri then quite simply spoke as follows: 'I cannot depend on the Arabs to defend my country. If I tell my people and my foreign friends that I am going to depend on the Syrian, Saudi, and Lebanese armies to defend Iraq, they will say "Nuri, you are a fool!" The only way to defend my country is to make an alliance with the West. I well understand your suspicions of the British, but I am going ahead right away.'

ʿAbd al-Nasir then replied with just a few words: 'Well, Nuri, I gave you my advice. You are, of course, free to do whatever you wish. We shall continue with our policy and the future will judge between us.'[40]

The official Egyptian version of this encounter, as broadcast by ʿAbd al-Qadir Hatim on 20 December, gives some further details:

Nuri al-Saʿid: '. . . From whom can we obtain arms if there is no link between the British and the collective security pact?'

ʿAbd al-Nasir: 'So the purpose is British participation in the collective security pact. The British have asked us a number of times to conclude an alliance with them. We have rejected the offer and have informed them that the collective security pact is the only basis for organising the defence of the Arab countries.

'Contact with the British will lead to one of these replies: either the conclusion of bilateral agreements between the Arab countries and Britain; or the admission of Britain and Turkey to the Arab collective security pact . . . For these reasons, any fresh discussions with them will lead only to a reiteration of these requests, and would thus result in the beginning of diversified negotiations with Britain, which negotiations we can do without.' The President added: 'We must not only think about defence against foreign aggression. We must equally consider the question of safeguarding our independence from the designs of imperialism.' President ʿAbd al-Nasir then made this statement of policy:

'Our intention is to conclude the evacuation agreement, and we feel that matters will not crystallise until two years after the British evacuation of Egypt. Egypt needs two years after the evacuation to think the matter over and determine the policy she will follow. For this reason I cannot possibly agree to any of these proposals. We want to enjoy independence and exercise our minds at a time when we are independent. This needs a period of two years after the evacuation.'

[40] Salah Salim to the author, London, 12 Apr. 1960.

Nuri replied: 'Iraq cannot possibly do anything to conflict with Egypt's plan to secure independence ... but the collective security pact is mere ink on paper, and another means [of defence] must be found.'[41]

NURI'S ALTERNATIVE PLAN

It was now clear that Iraq and Egypt could not agree, but Iraq's next move was uncertain. Nuri planned his strategy over the next month: first in London, where he spent three weeks immediately after his visit to Cairo, and then in Istanbul, where he remained from 8 to 19 October. It was during these visits that he advanced to both British and Turks his proposed alternative to the northern tier alliance: this was the plan, which Eden so warmly welcomed,[42] to strengthen the Arab collective security pact by the inclusion of Turkey and the help of Britain and the United States.

The first move was to draw Turkey away from the Turco-Pakistani alliance and bring her into closer contact with the Arab states. This was no new initiative but, in the minds of both Nuri and the Turkish Foreign Minister, was the continuation of earlier post-war efforts at a rapprochement between the two countries. Nuri had himself, when out of office in 1946, negotiated a treaty of friendship and *bon voisinage* with the Turks which the Iraqi parliament had approved the following year, in June 1947.[43] It was therefore natural that he should look once more towards Turkey; but it is worth recalling that the 1947 treaty was opposed at the time by Arab nationalists on the grounds that it might involve Iraq against her will in a conflict with the Soviet Union and that it implied recognition of Turkey's annexation of Alexandretta.

The notion of a new Turco-Arab alliance appealed, however, to the Turkish Democratic Party leaders who had come to power in May 1950 and who had greatly reinforced their position at the May 1954 elections. The Foreign Minister, Fuat Köprülü, was thought to be inspired by a vision of a vast grouping of all Arab—if not all Muslim— states under Turkish leadership. The first hint of this new policy came in a suggestion at the end of October that Iraq was not now expected to join the Turco-Pakistani alliance but that the Turkish Government was instead considering the conclusion of bilateral agreements with individual Arab states.[44] At the opening of the new

[41] BBC, no. 130, 27 Dec. 1956.   [42] See above, p. 191.
[43] See Majid Khadduri, *Independent Iraq* (London, 1951), pp. 346–7.
[44] Beirut radio on 31 October quoting Turkish sources (BBC, no. 515, 5 Nov. 1954).

session of the Grand National Assembly on 1 November, President
Bayar laid emphasis on Turkey's improved relations with the Arab
states, particularly Iraq and Egypt, and looked forward to further
developments in this field.[45]

Egypt had not yet clearly grasped Iraq's intentions. All that was so
far visible of Nuri's grand design was a Turco-Iraqi rapprochement.
Not to be outdone, and to ensure herself against any surprises, Egypt
in turn set about wooing Turkey. Her ambassador in Ankara declared
on 31 October that

the necessary ground has been prepared for the establishment of close
co-operation between Turkey and Egypt as the two great republics of the
Middle and Near East. The opening of official negotiations in this connexion in the near future has been agreed upon. . . . Close co-operation between Turkey and Egypt, as well as becoming a great source of strength
for the Egyptians, will also constitute a support for the Arab world. . . .
To put it briefly, the Turkish-Egyptian alliance will constitute a tremendous force in the Near East with a total population of fifty million.[46]

President 'Abd al-Nasir himself lent weight to the campaign in a
much-quoted preface to a book entitled *Turkey and Arab Policy*:
'No matter what has happened between us and Turkey in the past or
the present, we belong to each other', he wrote. 'Its father and our
father were brothers in history. . . . If Turkey is safe, we are safe, and
if we are sufficiently strong to make the enemy think twice, Turkey
will be safe. . . '.[47]

Many observers saw in this brief Egyptian-Turkish honeymoon,
following close on the signature of the Anglo-Egyptian agreement,
grounds for supposing that Egypt was looking westwards. But it was
no more than a precautionary move in Egypt's contest with Iraq: she
had no wish to be outmanoeuvred on the Arab plane by a combination of Turkey and Iraq. Indeed, her relations with Turkey quickly
soured when it became clear that the latter was being used as a decoy
to lure Egypt into a western-sponsored defence system. By the end
of the year the honeymoon was over and the Turkish ambassador had
been expelled from Cairo.[48] As the Turkish Premier, Adnan Menderes, commented on 27 December, 'those living in a certain region

---

[45] For President Bayar's speech see BBC, no. 516, 9 Nov. 1954.
[46] BBC, no. 515, 5 Nov. 1954.
[47] Reported by Ankara radio (BBC, no. 524, 7 Dec. 1954).
[48] There were also personal reasons for the worsening of relations: the Turkish
ambassador had personally insulted 'Abd al-Nasir in a scene at the Opera House
and had been declared *persona non grata*.

must not fall prey to the illusion that by uniting only among them-selves they can live in security'.[49]

But the Egyptian leaders held fast to their policy. No document is more characteristic of the fire and gusto with which they staked their claim to Arab leadership than the 'Voice of the Arabs' clarion call on 19 October 1954—the night of the evacuation agreement.

Dear Arab brothers in Jordan and Iraq, in the south of the Arab penin-sula, in North Africa, and in Palestine, raise your heads from the imperial-ists' boots, for the era of tyranny is past. Egypt has started to free herself from imperialism's shackles. Tonight the evacuation agreement will be signed. Raise the heads that are bowed in Iraq, in Jordan and by the Arab on the outskirts of Palestine. Raise your head, my brother in North Africa. The sun of freedom is rising over Egypt and the whole of the Nile Valley will soon be flooded by its rays. Raise your heads to the skies.

The start of Egypt's liberation from imperialism's shackles has come. Raise your heads, and see what is happening in Egypt. There you will find no despotic monarch, no feudalism, no weak army. See how Egypt's revolution has freed the nation from the imperialist forces on the Canal. Watch Egypt kicking out the king and his minions; watch her executing her great irrigation projects; watch her breaking the blockade and building ammunition and aircraft factories. Listen to her when she says there can be no alliances except with the Arabs. Watch her as she forces the occupier to evacuate the base on the Suez Canal . . .

Egypt achieved all this in only two years. Think what Egypt can do for you now that evacuation has been achieved. You, brother with the bowed head in Iraq, brother on the outskirts of Palestine and in North Africa, you must remember the past two years and imagine the next two years, in Egypt; you will then raise your head in pride and dignity. In Iraq, your Arabism and your Habbaniya will be liberated by the liberation of Egypt. The imperialists will be driven to work for your friendship instead of sniffing at your hostility. Raise your head now, my brother, for victory has been won for you by your Egyptian Arabs.[50]

But in spite of these vibrant appeals, the Egyptian leadership was not yet resolutely anti-western. The evacuation agreement led to a surface improvement in Anglo-Egyptian relations; British envoys were on cordial terms with leading members of the junta. There was, at the time, an ambiguity in Egyptian thinking: she preached un-compromising Arab independence under her leadership, but still looked to the West as a source of arms and as a possible future part-ner—after the expiry of the 'transition period'. This ambiguity was

[49] BBC, no. 530, 31 Dec. 1954.   [50] BBC, no. 511, 22 Oct. 1954.

reflected in conflicting resolutions unanimously approved at a meeting of Arab Foreign Ministers in Cairo in December 1954.

The resolutions were:

1. That no alliance should be concluded outside the fold of the Arab collective security pact.
2. That co-operation with the West was possible, provided a just solution was found for Arab problems and provided the Arabs were allowed to build up their strength with gifts of arms.[51]

The Arab states refused, in effect, to acknowledge that adopting Egypt's policy (as expressed in the first resolution) would in any way conflict with co-operation with the West. Commenting on this Foreign Ministers' meeting, Major Salah Salim said:

> It is striking to recall that they unanimously agreed that all Arab states were ready to co-operate with the West. Egypt signed the declaration. But to sweeten the pill for public consumption, Egypt insisted on including in the joint statement on co-operation some such phrase as 'provided a just solution is found for Arab problems'. There followed a long discussion, some delegates wanting to know what was meant by 'Arab problems'. Did it mean, they asked, that no co-operation was possible until a just solution to *all* Arab problems had been found? It was made quite clear in the subsequent discussion that no such thing was intended. It was agreed that the solution of Arab problems might take a long time, but that co-operation with the West could start immediately.[52]

There was a failure to grasp or a refusal to face the implications of Egyptian policy: that by demanding absolute freedom from all foreign ties—not only for herself but for the whole Arab world and Africa—Egypt must inevitably clash with British interests.

This state of innocence lasted only a few weeks. Nuri al-Sa'id had drawn up his defence plans with the British and the Turks and was impatient to put them into effect. Adnan Menderes visited Baghdad and, on 13 January 1955, issued with Nuri the famous joint communiqué announcing the early conclusion of a mutual defence pact. Iraq was at pains to point out that 'the Turkish-Iraqi agreement has no connexion with the Turkish-Pakistani pact' and to urge Egypt 'to be in the forefront of Arab states to join'.[53]

---

[51] BBC, no. 130, 27 Dec. 1956.
[52] Salah Salim to the author, London, 13 Apr. 1960.
[53] Burhan al-Din Bashayan in a statement to *al-Akhbar* (Cairo), 15 Jan. 1955 (see BBC, no. 535, 21 Jan. 1955).

Egypt's reaction was pained surprise, followed by indignation. Nuri's initiative was immediately recognized as a challenge to her supremacy. As Salah Salim put it:

It was clear that the battle between our policy and Iraq's would be joined over Syria. The issue was quite simply this: If Iraq and Turkey got Syria on their side, Jordan and Lebanon would soon follow and Egypt would be completely isolated. We should then be faced with little choice but to yield. We decided to fight back. We therefore immediately summoned all Heads of State from the Arab League countries to a conference in Cairo on 22 January to discuss this important matter. . . .[54]

The Baghdad Pact itself was not formally signed until a month later, but Syria had, in the interval, made her decisive choice.

[54] Salah Salim to the author, London, 12 Apr. 1960.

17

The Baghdad Pact and its Enemies, II

IF Syrian politics have so far seemed parochial, the Baghdad Pact gave them a wider significance. This was because Syria enjoyed what amounted to a casting vote on the Pact's future: had she applied for membership, other Arab states would have followed; in the event, her abstention and hostility 'froze' the alliance, isolating its only Arab member, Iraq. The battle over the Baghdad Pact underlines Syria's pivotal status: just as she was the focus of rivalries between Arab states, so she was also the hinge on which turned more grandiose pieces of Great Power diplomacy. Her choice against the Pact was made in the weeks immediately preceding its signature on 25 February 1955, but this decision had been foreshadowed by the strong neutralist trend at the September 1954 elections.

Until then Syrian politics had reflected little more than the feuds of her Arab neighbours. She had been the target for repeated but poorly-sustained Hashimite interventions countered and held in check by Saudi Arabia and Egypt, the one hostile as ever to Hashimite expansionism, the other opposed to an Iraqi-Syrian merger because it would have meant the rise of an Arab Power strong enough to challenge her. Shishakli's dictatorship gave Syria some protection from these external pressures; but, by an illuminating coincidence, he fled into exile on the same day, 25 February 1954, as 'Abd al-Nasir first ousted General Nagib in Egypt. A strong Government dedicated to the defence of Syrian independence had fallen in Damascus at the very moment when Egypt, under 'Abd al-Nasir, embraced a more coherent and dynamic Arab policy.

Syria's return to parliamentary life took place, therefore, in conditions more complex than the hitherto familiar pattern of Hashimite probe and Saudi-Egyptian counteraction. While these disputes for local dominance remained the Arabs' main concern, wider cold war issues were grafted on to them so that inter-Arab conflicts acquired a new ideological colouring as well as greater virulence. In Syria, the debate over the Baghdad Pact provided the political occasion for the neutralist 'left' to seize the initiative and translate into national policy the gains it had scored at the elections.

FARIS AL-KHURI'S GOVERNMENT

Two broad groups confronted each other in the new Syrian legislature which first met on 14 October 1954 to elect its officers. On the right stood a loose uneasy coalition of the National and People's Parties together with a group of about ten Independents led by Munir al-'Ajlani calling themselves the Liberal bloc—in all some sixty deputies. But it was the least stable of alliances, rent by personal rivalries and ancient feuds and bound by no common political principle. Conservatives had suffered reverses at the elections but their acquired position was still strong: habit had caused them to be regarded as the government party. The Head of State, Hashim al-Atasi, was thought of as a sort of life patron of the People's Party. It was also no surprise when Nazim al-Qudsi, the People's Party leader, was elected President of the Chamber.

The left of the Assembly was more spirited but equally heterogeneous. It consisted of the Ba'th, led by Akram al-Hawrani, the 'progressive' millionaire Khalid al-'Azm and his group of about thirty Independents calling themselves the Democratic Bloc, and the redoubtable Communist, Khalid Baqdash—once again some fifty to sixty deputies. Poised between these two groups were a number of men of uncertain political colouring: tribal representatives, members whose first allegiance was to Islamic organizations and, finally, a handful of former associates of General Shishakli.

On 14 October, then, the President accepted the resignation of Sa'id al-Ghazzi, the non-party Premier who had so scrupulously conducted the elections, and called on Khalid al-'Azm, the outstanding victor at the polls, to form a Government. But 'Azm could only rally a majority so slender that it would have been at the mercy of one or two defectors; after ten days of fruitless manoeuvre he admitted defeat. The experiment demonstrated that 'Azm and the Ba'th were too weak to form a Government so long as the National and People's Parties and Munir al-'Ajlani's group refused to serve with them in a coalition. Only by splitting their opponents could the left hope to make a bid for power.

The President's choice then fell on the distinguished Protestant jurist and statesman, Faris al-Khuri, one of the last of the old guard of Syrian nationalists whose lives had been spent working, first against the Turks and afterwards against the French, for the independence of their country. At 77 he had a reputation for moderation and political wisdom. But he too was unable to form a Government of national union, the Ba'th and 'Azm now refusing to take part. He was thus forced to rely heavily on the National and People's Party in drawing up his cabinet list[1] on 29 October, only to be denounced by the left for 'deliberate and premeditated deviation from the popular trend revealed at the elections'. To placate the opposition, Faris Bey declared his ministry's opposition to all foreign alliances. He was induced to say further, in the turbulent debate which followed his statement of policy, that he would refuse even to consider a 'pledge, pact or agreement' with a foreign state. But this profession of neutralism was unconvincing in view of his known pro-western sentiments, and his opponents awaited his first departure from it to bring him down.

ARAB PREMIERS' CONFERENCE

Egypt summoned the Arab Premiers to a conference in Cairo on 22 January 1955 to censure Iraq for her declared intention of concluding a security pact with Turkey. The battle over the Baghdad Pact had entered its final phase. More than a confrontation of policies, it was a trial of strength for Arab leadership on Egyptian ground. Colonel 'Abd al-Nasir, for whom this was the first meeting of Arab states he was to attend, called on each Premier to make his position clear. Those present included the Syrian Premier, Faris al-Khuri, the Lebanese Premier, Sami al-Solh, the Jordanian Premier, Tawfiq Abu'l-Huda, and the Amir Faysal of Saudi Arabia. The Foreign Ministers of Egypt, Syria, Lebanon, and Jordan were also present. Nuri al-Sa'id refused to attend, advancing reasons of ill-health. But after repeated appeals from the conference, he agreed to dispatch Fadil al-Jamali, a former Premier, accompanied by the Vice-Premier, Ahmad Mukhtar Baban, and the Deputy Foreign Minister, Burhan al-Din Bashayan, who arrived in Cairo on 26 January.

Premier, Faris al-Khuri (Ind.); Foreign Minister, Faydi al-Atasi (PP); Interior, Ahmad Qanbar (PP); Defence, Rashad Barmada (PP); Justice, 'Ali Buzo (PP); Finance, Dr Rizq Allah Antaki (PP); Public Works & Communications, Majd al-Din al-Jabiri (NP); Health, Badawi al-Jabal (NP; alias for Muhammad Sulayman al-Ahmad); Nat. Economy, Dr Fakhir al-Kayyali (NP); Education, Dr Munir al-'Ajlani (Ind.); Agriculture, 'Abd al-Samad Ftayah (Tribal Rep.).

Major Salah Salim gives this account of what took place:

Talk was frank and lively as each side outlined its position. The Syrians were equivocal. Their representatives, the aged Faris al-Khuri and his Foreign Minister Faydi al-Atasi, agreed not to commit Syria to any foreign alliance, but they would not go so far as to condemn Nuri al-Sa'id. They maintained that he was quite free to do as he pleased in his country. They said Iraq should not be treated as an accused party and that they had not come to Cairo to indict anyone.

But we said to the Syrians: 'You must make your position clear. After all, the Turco-Iraqi announcement contains an invitation to you.' They replied that they had received no formal invitation and could not be expected to frame their policy in reaction to what appeared in the press.

We then asked them whether they would agree to sign a joint declaration to the effect that we Arab Governments rejected all ties with foreign pacts. But they refused, maintaining that such a statement would do Iraq harm. The Lebanese sat on the fence and said little. The Jordanians, who were at the time in a pro-Saudi and anti-Iraqi phase, sided with us as, of course, did Saudi Arabia.

Jamali repeated all the arguments I had heard at Sarsank about Communism and about how vulnerable they were. The discussion became heated with delegates shouting at each other. At one point Jamali cried, 'I am not here to be insulted by foreigners'. But we retorted, 'There are no foreigners here but only brother Arabs'. No agreement was reached.[2]

Cairo radio had throughout kept up an intensive barrage of propaganda against the Pact, but as the conference moved towards stalemate in the last week of January, a new and more violent note of personal invective was heard:

Today the peoples and states of the Arab League are witnessing a new barefaced treason, the hero of which is Nuri al-Sa'id. His insistence on this alliance, his challenge to the Arab peoples and his trifling with their most sacred rights is an act of treachery against Arabism far more damaging to the Arab League than anything done by Israel or Zionism. . . .[3]

This onslaught, the first in a series of increasing savagery directed at Nuri personally, marked the final burial in Arab politics of the world of the *redingote* and of graceful courtesies. Men of an elder generation such as Sa'dallah al-Jabiri, founders of the Arab League, would not have abused their political enemies in this fashion.

The week also saw the end of the brief Turco-Egyptian honey-

² Salah Salim to the author, London, 12 Apr. 1960.
³ Cairo Radio, 30 Jan. 1955 (BBC, no. 539, 1 Feb. 1955).

moon. On 25 January Cairo radio introduced the theme that any alliance with Turkey, 'the friend of Israel', necessarily meant an indirect alliance with Israel itself, and the betrayal of the Arab cause. Nuri had become 'the ally of the ally of Israel'.

To break the deadlock at the Cairo conference, the Arab Premiers decided on 30 January to adjourn their meetings for a few days while a four-man delegation visited Nuri in Baghdad. It consisted of the Lebanese Premier, the Jordanian and Syrian Foreign Ministers, and Major Salah Salim, who gives the following account of what took place:

> Pretending to be ill, Nuri received us in pyjamas and dressing gown. The other three remained silent while I repeated the Egyptian argument. That evening I was visited at my official residence by several Iraqi elder statesmen such as Tawfiq al-Suwaydi and others. Each of them came separately and spoke against Nuri and his mania for pacts.
>
> A day or so later, Nuri himself sent me a message summoning me to his home. In his salon, I found all the politicians who had paid me visits. Nuri had perhaps been informed of our meetings. 'Major Salim', he said, 'I have assembled for you all the ex-Premiers and ex-Foreign Ministers who are still alive in my country. I want you to hear our policy from them.' He then ordered them to speak and each repeated Nuri's arguments. I never saw any of them again. We flew back to Cairo, but Nuri's parting words to me were: 'I am not a soldier in 'Abd al-Nasir's army. Please tell him that I will never obey his orders.'[4]

The Arab Premiers' conference broke up on 6 February: no decision was reached or joint statement issued.

> The Arab world [Salah Salim declared at the time] is now standing at a crossroads: it will either form an independent and cohesive unit with its own structures and national character or else each country will pursue its own course. The latter would mean the beginning of the downfall of Arab nationhood. . . .[5]

On the following day, Faris al-Khuri's Government fell in Damascus. Egypt had won an early and decisive round.

SPLITTING THE NATIONAL PARTY

Of the many occasions cited as 'turning-points' in Arab politics, the fall of the Syrian Government on 7 February 1955 deserves to be counted as one. The neutralist 'left' seized the initiative and the

---

[4] Salah Salim to the author, 13 Apr. 1960.   [5] BBC, no. 542, 11 Feb. 1955.

pro-Iraqi 'right' faced defeat in the Chamber which had hitherto been its stronghold. Two contacts were made during the crisis: the Ba'th and Egypt were brought together by the similarity of their views on foreign policy, while at home the Ba'th edged towards the Communists in the face of common enemies. Much of Syria's subsequent history may be traced to this double link. The first meant that Syria had taken a step towards entering Egypt's sphere of influence, while the second, by rousing Soviet hopes and western fears, brought her squarely into the cold war.

Faris al-Khuri was overthrown because he was thought to have departed from the policy of hostility to foreign pacts to which he was pledged by his statement in the Chamber at his investiture. This policy had, moreover, been explicitly reaffirmed in a resolution adopted by the Chamber's Foreign Affairs Commission on the eve of Faris Bey's departure for the Cairo conference. (The Ba'th leader Salah al-Din Bitar was secretary of the Commission which also included Akram al-Hawrani and Khalid Baqdash.) The opposition's suspicions were aroused when press reports from Cairo during the conference suggested that the Syrian delegates had expressed sympathy for Iraq. Faris Bey had indeed returned briefly to Damascus during the conference's adjournment, declaring that 'if the Arab collective security pact had been fully effective, Iraq would not have been forced to seek other means of defence'.[6] His opponents considered this justification of Iraq's policy ground enough to engineer his downfall.

But Khalid al-'Azm and the Ba'th leaders knew that they could not by themselves alone secure a majority. They had been given a chance the previous autumn and failed. They needed to win further support in the Chamber and sought allies in the National Party, which was then in a promising state of decay. It had for some time shown signs of splitting into pro- and anti-Iraqi wings led respectively by Lutfi al-Haffar and Sabri al-'Asali.[7] The Baghdad Pact brought these differences into the open, giving 'Azm and Hawrani the opportunity to exploit them.

'Azm first approached 'Asali and Mikhail Ilyan with proposals for

[6] BBC, no. 541, 8 Feb. 1955.
[7] 'Asali had long vacillated between Baghdad and Cairo–Riyad before coming down on the anti-Iraqi side. His chief associates were Dr 'Abd al-Rahman Kayyali and, momentarily, Mikhail Ilyan, who later returned to the pro-Iraqi fold. Lutfi al-Haffar's faction included Suhayl al-Khuri (Faris Bey's son), Badawi al-Jabal, Najib al-Barazi, Salah Shaikh al-Ard, etc.

a coalition, playing down his prior agreement with Hawrani. But having secured their agreement to an alliance, he then urged on them the need to include Hawrani in it, 'to save him from the Communists'. But when the pact between 'Asali and Ilyan with 'Azm and the Ba'th became known, Lutfi al-Haffar and other prominent members resigned from the National Party, while two National Party ministers, Badawi al-Jabal and Fakhir al-Kayyali, withdrew from the Government. This destroyed Faris al-Khuri's coalition and he was forced to hand in the resignation of his cabinet.

It was then, on 10 February, that 'Azm, 'Asali, and Hawrani, claiming to represent a majority in the Chamber, went to President Atasi to ask that 'Asali be entrusted with forming a new Government. The People's Party and Munir al-'Ajlani's right-wing Independents cast around desperately for a way of checking the triumvirate; Faris al-Khuri was even approached to try his hand again at cabinet-making, but in vain. President Atasi was reluctantly forced to call on 'Asali, who formed his cabinet on 13 February.[8] As Foreign Minister and acting Defence Minister, Khalid al-'Azm was the dominant figure in the new Government. It was soon evident that Syria had changed course. 'Azm explained later:

> It was clear that after Shishakli's fall, Syria was in need of a political grouping which would be in a position to counter the influence of the pro-western parties. It seemed to me at the time that we could either continue with our basically pro-western policy which we had pursued since the war, or look elsewhere for help to defend our Arab interests. We felt we needed the support of a group of nations which had no preconceived notions on the Israeli issue and which could give us their backing at the United Nations.
>
> This was the reason we became pro-Russian, deriving great moral and material support from the eastern bloc. Our rapprochement with the East continued when I became Foreign Minister after Faris al-Khuri's downfall. It was to stand us in good stead at the time of Suez. But it must not be supposed that we became converts to Communist ideology. We distinguished between international affairs and internal social and political questions. It was only on the international level that we were prepared to go along with the Communists. Our independence from the French still

[8] Premier & Min. of the Interior, Sabri al-'Asali (NP); Foreign Affairs & acting Defence Minister, Khalid al-'Azm (Dem. Bloc); Public Works & Communications, 'Abd al-Baqi Nizam al-Din (Dem. Bloc); Education, Ra'if Mulki (Dem. Bloc); Agriculture, Hamid Khuja (Tribal Rep.); Nat. Economy, Fakhir al-Kayyali (NP); Finance, Leon Zamariya (NP); Justice, Ma'mum al-Kuzbari Ind., former Shishaklist); Min. of State, acting Health, Wahib Ghanim (Ba'th).

seemed precarious and we felt in need of powerful allies. Our approach to the Soviet Union was then strictly non-doctrinaire. We noted that although they might believe in socialism and in the common ownership of property, they were far from applying this principle on the international scale. Scratch a Bolshevik and you will find a nationalist.

But after my alignment with the East on international questions my natural allies at home became the Ba'th and the Communist Party. Both these groups were fighting over the same potential following of workers and peasants. They both wanted to dominate the trade unions and peasants' associations. I conceived it my task to try and mediate between them and bring them together.[9]

EGYPT'S ROLE

Egypt was very quick to realize Syria's importance in the battle of the Baghdad Pact, lending her support to 'Azm and his friends at every stage of their seizure of power. The task of winning over Syria was entrusted to Egypt's able Arab 'experts', Major Salah Salim and Brigadier Mahmud Riyad. Salim directed the propaganda side of the operation while Riyad was given the more delicate diplomatic role of Egyptian envoy in Damascus. Under Salah Salim's direction, the Egyptian press and radio campaigned tirelessly against the outgoing Syrian cabinet of Faris al-Khuri. The following is a sample broadcast from Cairo on 9 February, quoting *al-Ahram*:

> The vacillating and hesitant attitude of the Syrian Foreign Minister at the Cairo conference was one of the principal reasons for the conference's failure to publish its resolutions denouncing foreign alliances, including the Nuri–Menderes alliance.
>
> This regrettable attitude caused others also to hesitate and retract their earlier agreement to the resolutions. If the reports from Syria are true that the People's Party, to which the Foreign Minister belongs, has denounced his attitude and that the Foreign Affairs Commission has accused him of departing from Syria's agreed policy, and if the Syrian Premier is compelled to abandon the cautious policy which he followed during the conference, this transformation in Syria's attitude will have a powerful effect, and all the Arab Governments, except Iraq, will agree with Egypt on the frank and decisive policy declared at the Premiers' conference. Then it

[9] Khalid al-'Azm to the author, Damascus, 8 Nov. 1960. A member of 'Azm's Foreign Ministry staff who was present at his first briefing recalls him defending his pro-Soviet policy by saying 'Il faut tendre la main à qui nous tend la main'. His opponents argued that, finding it difficult to win support on the right, he had concluded a tactical alliance with the Communists before the 1954 elections. He was, as a result, elected with a handsome majority. The arrangement having worked so well, he persisted in it later, justifying his alignment in terms of national interest.

would be possible to point to signs of Egypt's victory in the first round of the battle which it entered on behalf of the Arab peoples.[10]

Major Salah Salim went further and, with characteristic ebullience, claimed direct responsibility for Faris al-Khuri's downfall:

When it was clear that the Premiers' conference would fail, I made a series of statements on the whole subject, revealing everything that had been said. All this was broadcast and aroused the hostility of the Syrian public against its Government.

Some Syrian members of parliament asked their Government whether what Salah Salim had written was true or false. Faydi al-Atasi categorically stated it was all lies. The same day we broadcast from Cairo a secret tape-recording of Faydi al-Atasi's speeches at the conference. Everyone in Syria then knew that Atasi was a liar. The Syrian Government resigned and a new Government under Sabri al-'Asali came to power.[11]

Mahmud Riyad arrived in Syria on 18 January 1955 with the express purpose of inviting Faris al-Khuri to the Premiers' conference. He stayed on as Egyptian ambassador until the formation of the Union three years later and, as one of its principal architects, must be counted an outstandingly successful envoy. He arrived at a time when Syria, recently freed from military dictatorship, did not look on the Egyptian junta with any sympathy. Moreover, 'Abd al-Nasir's trial of strength with the Muslim Brotherhood had created a great deal of bad feeling in Damascus. Mahmud Riyad set about reversing this trend by explaining to the Syrians that the Muslim Brethren in Egypt were terrorists, not believers. Copies of their trial were distributed by the thousand. Dozens of delegations, including 'Abd al-Nasir's enemies in the People's Party and the Islamic associations, were invited to Egypt to see for themselves what the regime was doing. Later in the year the Czech arms deal completed the process of winning over the Syrians.

But Mahmud Riyad's immediate task in January–February 1955 was, as he himself put it, to wean Syria away from the Baghdad Pact.

There was a clear and understandable tendency among the older Syrian politicians to sign the Baghdad Pact as well. It was not easy for a Syrian Government not to do so. In 1954 Egypt's policy was not yet absolutely clear and it was far from evident to what extent Egypt could support a Government or a country which chose to go against the current set by Iraq and the western Powers.

[10] BBC, no. 543, 15 Feb. 1955.   [11] Salah Salim to the author, 13 Apr. 1960.

Syria was surrounded by Governments all of whom were in favour of the Pact. Britain had bases in Jordan and Iraq, while Turkey and Lebanon were both committed to the West. The Syrian Government was also in a state of nerves due in part to the period of plotting and conspiracy which had preceded the fall of Shishakli and to the confusion which had followed it. It was still finding its feet and establishing its security.

Up to 1954–5 Egypt was still very much of an unknown quantity in the Arab world. The revolutionary Government had had very few contacts with other Arab Governments. In the early years of the Egyptian revolution a great many forces—including the Wafd, the Muslim Brethren, the Americans, and the British—had tried to seize the leadership of the movement and lead it by the nose to suit their interests. Those outside were puzzled. They did not know who was the real power behind the Egyptian regime, nor what 'Abd al-Nasir's policy was.

But by 1955 our policy was clear. We believed the Arab world should first secure its full independence before concluding any military agreements with foreign powers. We were very weak and we knew that in the event of our joining a foreign-sponsored pact, we should find ourselves at the tail.

My duty in Syria was to explain our policy of Arab solidarity and our dislike for the Baghdad Pact. I got in touch with all political parties, but it was natural that I should find myself on special terms with the Ba'th in view of the similarity of our views on foreign affairs . . .[12]

On 22 February, the new Syrian Premier, Sabri al-'Asali, made his statement of policy in the Chamber, condemning the conclusion of all foreign military pacts and wholeheartedly embracing Egypt's foreign policy themes. His statement was due to be debated on the 24th; but on the 23rd the Turkish Premier, Adnan Menderes, arrived in Baghdad. Cairo radio immediately charged that Turkey had sent two divisions to the Syrian frontier to exert pressure on the Syrian Chamber. Ankara vehemently denied the report (but not in Arabic until the next day when the Syrian debate was over) and, in the event, 'Asali obtained a vote of confidence on the night of 24 February by 66 votes to 53 with two abstentions.[13] That same evening Nuri al-Sa'id and Menderes signed their alliance in Baghdad, while Cairo's 'Voice of the Arabs' rose in a crescendo of denunciation:

We regret to announce that a communiqué has been issued in Baghdad stating that the Turkish-Iraqi alliance will be signed this evening and that the Iraqi Council of Ministers has consented to the final draft of this alliance. Thus Nuri al-Sa'id, rejecting the unanimous decision of the Arab

[12] Mahmud Riyad to the author, Cairo, Jan. 1961.
[13] See BBC, no. 547, 1 Mar. 1955.

peoples, concludes an alliance with the Turks, the enemies of Arabism, the friends of Zionism—an alliance which will destroy Iraq's aspirations to freedom, Palestine's hopes of independence, and the Arabs' hopes of unity, integrity, and glory. The 'Voice of the Arabs', which has resisted this alliance, declares to the entire world that the people of Iraq disown this alliance and that the chains imposed by it on the noble people of Iraq tie only Nuri al-Sa'id. The people of Iraq are not bound by this alliance; they have not signed it and will not sign it; they curse it and they will destroy this filthy piece of paper, the Nuri–Menderes alliance.[14]

Major Salah Salim arrived in Damascus on 26 February to consolidate Egyptian gains. He declared that now that Iraq had concluded her pact with Turkey, the Arab collective security pact no longer existed. Instead, he proposed an Arab 'federal union' providing for a joint military command and unified policies on foreign, cultural, and economic affairs. All the Arab states would be invited to join—except Iraq. Major Salim submitted a draft of these proposals to the Syrian Government but was met with some suspicion, particularly from the National Party members of the cabinet, for whom this seemed too great a step. This is how he relates subsequent events:

An event of great importance then took place: on 28 February Israel launched an attack on Gaza killing scores of Egyptians and damaging a great deal of property with tanks and aircraft. The Syrians who opposed our policy—and the pro-Iraqi People's Party in particular—attacked me vigorously, saying in effect: 'You have come to help Syria defend herself. Perhaps you had better see to your own defences first.' I answered simply that if we were both weak we would be stronger united.

I used every propaganda weapon to convince them and then, on 1 March, the Syrian army organized a big meeting in Damascus. The Chief of Staff Shawkat Shuqayr and his deputy, 'Adnan al-Malki, assembled a great many officers and politicians. It was then declared that Syria had agreed to a full alliance with Egypt and to a merger of their two armies. The next day Sabri al-'Asali and I signed the agreement. The first article declared the opposition of our two governments to the Turco-Iraqi alliance and to all other alliances. There followed provisions for a joint military command and for economic co-operation.

The key man in these negotiations was not 'Asali but Khalid al-'Azm. It was 'Azm, working together with Shuqayr and Malki, who pulled off the agreement.[15]

[14] Cairo Radio, 24 Feb. 1955 (BBC, 547, 1 Mar. 1955).
[15] Salah Salim to the author, 13 Apr. 1960.

Major Salah Salim and Khalid al-'Azm then visited Amman on 3 March, Riyad on the 4th and 5th, and Beirut on the 6th to secure the adherence of these Governments to their new pact. As was expected, the Jordanian and Lebanese Governments expressed great reserve and asked for more time to study the proposals, but Saudi Arabia added her signature. 'I returned to Cairo on 7 March', Major Salim said, 'thinking that the battle for Syria had been won and that we had succeeded in "freezing" the Baghdad Pact.'[16] Later that month he presided over a committee to draw up a text of the Egyptian-Syrian-Saudi agreement; but although he announced on 19 March that a draft was completed, none was published. It was submitted on the 30th to Syrian and Saudi delegations, but the conference broke up on 2 April deciding to continue negotiations through diplomatic channels. These continued in the wings of the Bandung Conference, but no final agreement was reached in spite of Egyptian press reports that it was imminent.

The Egyptian-Syrian-Saudi alliance of March 1955 was never either militarily effective or economically stimulating. These are not the criteria by which it should be judged. It was no more than a diplomatic coup, swiftly conceived and executed, to counter a challenge from Nuri al-Sa'id. King Faruq acted in much the same way to save Colonel Husni al-Za'im from the Hashimites in April 1949. For both Cairo and Riyad, the only *raison d'être* of the alliance was to prevent Syria from falling into Iraq's sphere of influence. But it also represented the junta's first major intervention outside the Nile Valley since the Egyptian revolution and the first success of its Arab policy.

'Abd al-Nasir had preached Arabism throughout 1954, meaning by it Arab solidarity in support of Egypt's policy of independence from Great Powers and her determination to make the Arabs a force to be reckoned with on the world stage. This policy struck a vein of indigenous neutralism in Syria; but it by no means exhausted the content of Arabism as conceived by Arab nationalists such as the Ba'th. When the Ba'thists spoke of Arab unity, they envisaged an organic link, a regenerative merger in which the whole Arab Nation would be born again. A united Arab front on foreign policy issues was only a small part of their ambitious, frontier-smashing hopes. While, therefore, the Baghdad Pact brought Egypt and the Ba'th together, it was also the beginning of a long misunderstanding be-

[16] Ibid.

12. Akram al-Hawrani, as President of the Syrian Chamber

13. The Communist Party leader, Khalid Baqdash

15. 'Abd al-Hamid Sarraj

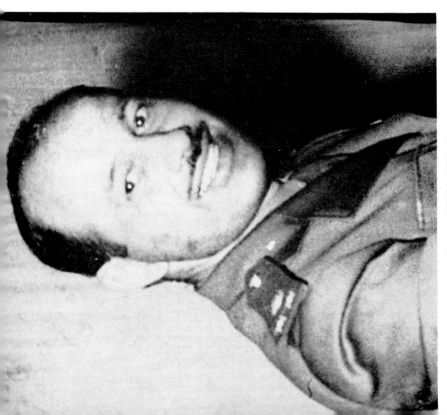

14. General 'Afif al-Bizri

tween them on what was meant by unity—a dialogue at cross-pur-
poses—which only the painful union experiment brought into the
open. The relationship was bound ultimately to disappoint the Syrians.
The simple truth was that Egypt was not ready for a relationship more
intimate than the co-ordination of foreign policies which it had been
her traditional Arab policy to seek. Her 'Arabism'—in the sense of
feeling at one with other Arabs—was as yet skin-deep.

A hint of these later difficulties is to be found in Michel 'Aflaq's
account of the Ba'th's first encounter with the Egyptians in February–
March 1955:

> We had a hand in preparing the draft of the Egyptian-Syrian-Saud
> pact, conceiving it as a first step towards a federation of the three countries.
> But the pact remained a dead-letter. It foundered in interminable discus-
> sions stretching over months on the question of a common defence budget
> and a common general staff. Egypt objected that she was poor and could
> not pay. Saudi Arabia was ready to pay but was reluctant to abandon any
> sovereignty. All parties were reticent when it came to discussing economic
> co-ordination.
>
> It seemed that only the Ba'th were keen. It was in these negotiations that
> we made our first contact with the Egyptians. It was not a very promising
> beginning. They were extremely reserved and were reluctant to step outside
> their familiar territory. But we were not easily discouraged. We considered
> the Egyptians novices in the Arab nationalist movement and, as a result,
> patiently encouraged them to merge themselves more completely with the
> rest of the Arab world.[17]

Egypt's view of Arab unity was both modest and level-headed. It
has often been outlined by 'Abd al-Nasir, but rarely so clearly as in
an interview with the *New York Times* some years later, when he
was wrestling with the problems of a 'merger' which the Ba'th,
among others, had finally persuaded him to accept:

> When the Arab countries united, they were always able to face and stop
> aggression. . . . When the Arab peoples gave up their unity, they were an
> easy target for foreign control. The meaning of this is clear—to safeguard
> the Arab countries, there has to be one Arab front. For further definition,
> all Arab countries have to be independent and have to be far from foreign
> influence which divides up these countries in order to divert their atten-
> tion. This, however, is one thing and constitutional considerations are
> another. As a matter of fact, we were surprised when we first had to deal
> with constitutional considerations, when unity took place between the two

[17] Michel 'Aflaq to the author, Beirut, 13 Jan. 1961.

regions of the UAR. . . . Once again, this does not necessarily mean that
Arab Unity means that all Arab countries should be combined in one
country. What I care for is the creation of Arab solidarity as well as a
unified Arab struggle because the Arab destiny and future are similar. . . .
The most important thing is that solidarity should prevail among Arab
countries under any circumstances.[18]

BRITAIN JOINS THE PACT

By the time Britain joined the Baghdad Pact in April 1955,[19]
little remained of Nuri al-Sa'id's grand design for harnessing the
Arab collective security pact to Turkey and the West. Egypt's
opposition had been uncompromising; the battle for Syria had been
lost and the centre of gravity of Arab politics had moved towards
Cairo. Hopes that the Pact would confer Arab leadership on Nuri
and overlordship on Britain could no longer be soberly entertained.
Why, then, did London persist in what was already a lost cause?
It is often said that had Britain then recognized 'Abd al-Nasir's
brand of nationalism as the most popular in the Arab world, she
might have averted that sharp decline in her local influence which
marked the four years from the Baghdad Pact to the Iraqi revolution
of 1958. But could Britain have done otherwise?

The first tentative outline of the Pact was drafted in London during
Nuri's visit in September 1954, and the decision to go ahead was taken
immediately after the signature of the Anglo-Egyptian agreement a
month later. Mr Anthony Nutting, who represented Britain in the
final stages of the negotiations, sounded out Colonel 'Abd al-Nasir
on his attitude towards the proposed alliance. The Egyptian leader
is believed to have replied that he would remain 'neutral', no doubt
indicating that he could not be induced to join. But he may have
been misunderstood to mean that he would not condemn a defence
system if attempts were made to set one up. Certainly, the British
Government appears later to have been taken aback by the violence
of Egypt's onslaught on the Baghdad Pact, and complaints were heard
in Whitehall that 'Abd al-Nasir had gone back on his word. The
confusion was not one-sided: 'Abd al-Nasir, in turn, complained
that Britain and the United States had violated a 'gentleman's agree-

---

[18] *Pres. Gamal Abdel-Nasser's Speeches and Press Interviews, 1959*, pp. 594–5.
[19] A Special Agreement between Iraq and Great Britain was signed on 4 April
1955. It replaced the previous agreement of 30 June 1930 between the two countries
and constituted Great Britain's accession to the Baghdad Pact, the formal date of
which is 5 April 1955 (Cmd. 9544).

ment' with Egypt which envisaged that she should take the lead in setting up a purely Arab defence alliance.[20]

These misunderstandings, together with the deceptive cordiality which followed the signature of the Anglo-Egyptian agreement, may have obscured for British officials the nature of the choice they were making in promoting the Baghdad Pact. There may have been a somewhat self-indulgent tendency to think that Britain could avoid taking sides in inter-Arab disputes—that backing Iraq would not necessarily mean opposing Egypt, and that Egypt might, in the end, be persuaded to come in. And once this policy was approved and its implementation set in motion, it was not easy to reverse it. Great Powers cannot change course overnight: too many conflicting interests have to be weighed and international partners considered.

Eden first met 'Abd al-Nasir in Cairo on 21 February 1955, three days before the Pact's signature. The Foreign Secretary, accompanied by Field Marshal Sir John Harding, the CIGS, spent a night in Cairo on his way to the SEATO Conference in Bangkok. Colonel 'Abd al-Nasir came to dinner at the Embassy. Eden writes:

> Sir John gave an excellent strategic appraisal with which Nasser entirely agreed. Nasser declared that his interest and sympathy were with the West, but he argued that the Turco-Iraqi pact, by its bad timing and unfortunate content, had seriously set back the development of effective collaboration with the West by the Arab States.
>
> I was familiar with this plea; it is never the right time for some. We used every argument we could to persuade Nasser at least to restrain his criticisms and, if the agreement were reasonable in terms, to cease his opposition. I do not think, however, that we made much impression. Colonel Nasser, whom I thought a fine man physically, was friendly throughout our talks. He referred repeatedly to the great improvement in Anglo-Egyptian relations, to the importance which his Government attached to this improvement and to his hopes for its continuance in the future. Nasser was not, however, open to conviction on the Turco-Iraqi enterprise. I commented on this in my report to London at the time, adding: 'No doubt jealousy plays a part in this and a frustrated desire to lead the Arab world.' Before our talks began we were photographed together. As the flashlights went off, he seized my hand and held it.[21]

This passage, with its undertones of distaste and irritation, may be set against Eden's account of his meetings in Baghdad where he stopped for an evening on his homeward journey.

[20] *New York Times*, 4 Apr. 1955.   [21] Eden, *Memoirs*, iii. 221.

I found from a talk with the Prime Minister [Nuri al-Sa'id] that plans
for a new defence agreement between us, together with our adherence to
the Baghdad Pact, had made good progress. My wife and I dined with
King Faisal that night, when the Crown Prince and the Prime Minister
were also present. It was a friendly evening and afterwards we had some
discussion of a tentative draft of the new agreement which the Prime
Minister had produced. I saw that we were only separated by points of
detail.

At dinner that evening there were some cornflowers on the table. I knew
that the King had enjoyed his years at Harrow and I asked him if they were
a reminder of these. Smilingly he gave me one and asked me if I would
carry it home to another old Harrovian, Sir Winston Churchill. I duly
discharged my responsibility.[22]

Trust, sentiment, mutual interest, and the familiarity of a long-
standing connexion bound Britain to Nuri al-Sa'id and the Iraqi
royal house. All this could not be set aside to please a young colonel
in Cairo. Indeed, Eden must also have felt under some obligation to
Nuri for having abandoned the American northern-tier alliance in
favour of a scheme designed specifically to protect British interests
in the Arab world. There could be no question of promoting 'neutral'
Egypt—which had, in any case, been nothing but an irritant since the
war—above the Iraqi 'ally'. Nor could a Conservative Government in
Britain even contemplate disengagement in Iraq when it was still
occupied in putting down a revolt against a policy of 'scuttle' in
Egypt in the ranks of its own supporters.

If these were some of the general considerations which inclined
Britain towards the Baghdad Pact, more immediate causes were the
military advantages to be derived from it and the growing importance
of Persian Gulf oil. The value of the Special Agreement with Iraq
of 4 April 1955, whereby Britain acceded to the Baghdad Pact, was
that it provided a substitute for the existing Anglo-Iraqi agreement
which was under fire in Iraq and was due to expire in 1957. Existing
facilities for over-flying, landing, and servicing British aircraft in Iraq
were maintained, although the airfields passed under Iraqi sovereignty.
'At a ceremony in Iraq, RAF jet planes evacuated the Habbaniyeh
base in accordance with the revised Anglo-Iraqi Treaty. The fighters
took off in the direction of Cyprus, turned in mid-air and landed again
at Habbaniyeh, as arranged under the Baghdad Pact.'[23] The effects
of the arrangements were therefore juridical rather than practical.[24]

[22] Ibid. p. 222.   [23] Arslan Humbaraci, *Middle East Indictment* (1958), p. 189.
[24] RIIA, *Survey, 1955–6*, p. 28.

It is very probable that military arguments were given undue weight in British policy-making at this time, to the neglect of Arab opinion, and that the British Government was insensitive to the force and attraction of the neutralist policy which Egypt had been preaching for over a year. Eden gives no hint in his account of his meeting with 'Abd al-Nasir that he was confronted with anything more than an irritating obstruction. There is no suggestion that the uncommitted Afro-Asians were then busily preparing for their first meeting at Bandung, or that both Tito and Nehru had conferred with 'Abd al-Nasir, publicly supporting his policies, only a few days before Eden's arrival in Cairo. But these portents may have seemed less compelling at the time than the need to maintain the British strong-point in Iraq.

The growing importance of Persian Gulf oil for western Europe lent weight to the military argument: no less than three-quarters of Europe's supplies came from this source. Its potential importance was even greater, in that it was then calculated that the Middle East contained two-thirds of the world's proven oil reserves. With the Iranian example in mind, there was considerable apprehension at the possible disruptive effects of nationalist and Communist influence. Indeed, Iraq and the whole Persian Gulf area as well as the oil lanes between the Persian Gulf and the Mediterranean had become a vital strategic area for the western alliance. So important was the economic interest in oil that there was a readiness to take political risks to defend it.

But by joining the Baghdad Pact, Britain found herself drawn into the inter-Arab tug-of-war over Syria; less than a year later, she had departed from her former neutrality towards the Fertile Crescent union project, becoming involved in Iraqi conspiracies to recover the initiative in Syria. The idea was not, of course, referred to in these terms: it was called strengthening the Baghdad Pact by securing Syrian membership, or saving Syria from Egyptian influence, or from Communist penetration. But in the mind of the Iraqi Crown Prince, for instance, it was no more than a fresh episode in a continuing endeavour. Britain fell in with these plans all the more easily as she had by this time less reason to nurse the susceptibilities of the principal opponents of Fertile Crescent union. A generation of friendship with Saudi Arabia had come to an end with King Sa'ud's accession and the dispute over the disputed Buraimi oasis on an undefined frontier in south-east Arabia. By her opposition to the

Baghdad Pact, France too had weakened her claim in British eyes to special privileges in Syria. Egyptian gains in that country were, in any case, rapidly making nonsense of such claims. Meanwhile, irritation with 'Abd al-Nasir had been fanned into hostility by the tireless clamour of Cairo radio, not only against the Baghdad Pact but against every remnant of British power in the Middle East and Africa.[25] But as important as all these factors in arousing western interest in Syria was the growing evidence of Soviet success there.

SOVIET GAINS

SEATO and the Baghdad Pact were less successful at containing the Communist Powers than at spurring them to a counter-offensive. Just as the establishment of SEATO confirmed China in her suspicion of the West, wiping out the small gains in confidence secured by the cease-fire in Indo-China, so western defence plans in the Middle East revived Soviet interest in the area. In the middle 1940s, between 1944 and 1947, the Soviet Union had made an aggressive bid to draw Greece, Turkey, Iran, and Afghanistan into her sphere of influence. But she had been held back from the Straits, from the Eastern Mediterranean, and from the Persian Gulf by the resolute action first of Great Britain, then of the United States.[26]

The Soviet campaign had been accompanied by the encouragement of local Communist parties and by a propaganda barrage directed not only against the British presence, but also against the Arab League and non-Marxist nationalist leaders throughout the area. Even religion was put to work in attempts to rally to the Russian cause the Greek Orthodox and Armenian communities in the Levant. But these policies were unsuccessful: their result was to bring the United States into the area in force, to arouse the hostility of Arab Governments and the fears of the Arab national bourgeoisie, and to draw upon the fledgeling Communist Parties the full repressive powers of the police, whether in Iraq, Iran, or Egypt.

It was clear that an adjustment in general Soviet thinking about the area was required but this had to await the early 1950s. The old Cold War divisions of the world into opposing 'Socialist' and 'Capitalist' camps were then breaking down. India and other Asian states had set out on their own third road between the two embattled blocs,

---

[25] More than any other single factor, Cairo radio transmissions in Swahili from July 1954 may be held to account for the early distrust of 'Abd al-Nasir in London.
[26] See François Laurent, 'L'URSS et le Moyen Orient', *Orient*, no. 2, Apr. 1957.

while the Soviet Union and its allies had themselves begun to move out of their international isolation and to consider making tentative overtures towards governments that had remained aloof from the Cold War.

Soviet theoreticians had prepared the way for this rapprochement by examining rather more generously the role of the national bourgeoisie in Asia, the Middle East, and Africa. In dating this readjustment, experts sometimes point to an early paper by Professor I. I. Potekhin as far back as 1949 in which he categorically states that 'in the majority of countries in tropical and southern Africa the leading role in the national liberation movement now belongs to the national bourgeoisie and the national intelligentsia.'[27] This line of thinking was carried an important stage further at the Nineteenth Soviet Party Congress in October 1952, when Malenkov proclaimed the right of peoples to choose their own ideology and made a direct appeal for the sympathy of governments that 'pursued an independent peace policy'.

Events were, in any case, playing into Russia's hand. The vigorous self-assertion of the newly independent states of Asia and the Middle East vis-à-vis their former western mentors was plain for all to see. It was essential for Moscow to come to terms with this new and vital, even if non-Communist, anti-colonialist sentiment.

In the Middle East, in particular, vast gains were to be had by a swift exploitation of western mistakes. Over the previous decade the West had gradually made itself ineligible as a partner for the Arabs—but like an importunate suitor it nevertheless insisted on being accepted as one in the face of what it took to be a Soviet military threat. But no accommodation was possible with the post-war generation of radical Arab nationalists: they charged the western Powers with the creation and continued support of Israel; with their impotence or unwillingness to impose a solution acceptable to the Arabs; with their continued military and political presence in many parts of the Arab world; and with their support for 'reactionary' regimes. To many Arabs, therefore, the West seemed the main obstacle to the independence, unity, and reform of their homeland. A defence pact directed against Russia, such as the West was insistently advocating, seemed both a distraction from their local quarrel with Israel and a new form of veiled colonialism. Under pressure to join, they retreated into neutralism.

[27] Quoted by David Morison, *The USSR and Africa* (London, 1964), p. 3.

But when the West denounced neutralism as 'immoral', Russia welcomed it as an ally. Soviet leaders saw clearly that Arab neutrality was enough to foil western defence plans since the West was aiming at active Arab participation. It was then only a small step for the Soviet Union to promote Arab national-bourgeois leaders to the position of valuable allies in the anti-imperialist struggle and, by 1954, to encourage local Arab Communists to collaborate with them in patriotic 'fronts'. Russia's welcome for the Bandung Conference of April 1955 reflected the importance she attributed to this alliance of Communists and nationalists in the common struggle against the West.

On both the Arab and the Russian side the ground was prepared for a rapprochement. It was precipitated by the Baghdad Pact and the long defence debate which preceded it. Russia was provoked into a counter-offensive by the military threat to her southern flank, while the Pact split the Arab ranks by forcing them to make a clear choice for or against the West, thereby providing Russia with natural allies among those who wished to remain uncommitted. These she proceeded to support with propaganda, arms, diplomatic backing, and economic aid.

Foremost among them was Egypt. The 'Czech' arms deal in the autumn of 1955 laid the foundations of a friendship which was to become a model for Russia's relations with many other Asian and African states. It was only after the arms deal that Moscow began once again to view with favour the movement for Arab unity which she had since 1947 dismissed as an instrument of imperialist policy. The Soviet writer L. Vatolina, who had previously treated the Arab League with reserve, rehabilitated it in a remarkable article in 1955 entitled 'The Growth of National Consciousness among the Arab Peoples'.[28] Arab nationalism was at last recognized as an authentic movement emanating from the people. These developments were given theoretical sanction at the Twentieth Soviet Party Congress in 1956, but, as David Morison puts it, the Congress 'at last gave party recognition to the reality that two years of Soviet diplomacy had recognized in fact'.[29] As evidence of the new line, the Syrian Communist Party issued a manifesto in 1956 in which it described Arab unity as a historical and progressive movement, the outcome of objective conditions and not the result of the activity of one party or person.[30]

[28] A. R. C. Bolton, *Soviet Middle East Studies* (RIIA memo. 1959), pt. 2, p. iii.
[29] Morison, p. 8.
[30] The Ba'th recognized this as a sly attack on their own claims but nevertheless admitted that it was a considerable advance on previous Communist positions.

Syria was singled out for special Soviet attention as early as Shishakli's overthrow in February 1954. The main purpose of Moscow's broadcasts at the time was evidently to impede any move towards a western-sponsored defence grouping.[31] Both Shishakli's fall and the results of the parliamentary elections were treated as evidence of a widespread, powerful, and increasing hostility towards any such alliance. The elections were said to have demonstrated the people's unconditional rejection of 'imperialist' treaties. Indeed, Moscow radio saw the internal situation in Syria as a conflict between the supporters and opponents of military collaboration with the West. Considerable publicity was given to the election of the Communist leader Khalid Baqdash to the Chamber of Deputies, while the gains of Khalid al-'Azm and Akram al-Hawrani were seen as part of the success of a 'wide national progressive front'.

Even before Egypt, Syria was the first to challenge the western monopoly of arms supplied to the Middle East by signing a small contract with the East in 1954. General Shawkat Shuqayr, Syrian Chief of Staff at the time, relates[32] that he was looking for supplies of German Mark IV tanks:

I had bought eleven Mark IVs from the French and wanted to make them up to forty. I had heard that some had been sent to Prague by the Germans for use there by their forces, but had never been unpacked. We opened negotiations with the Czechs and bought them for a song. An Italian ship was chartered and deliveries of the giant crates were made through Beirut. On the very last delivery, the Lebanese authorities, who suspected the contents of the crates, arranged to have one dropped on the quay side. The great shoulder of a tank appeared. When we subsequently bought Russian T 54s from the East in 1955 we arranged for deliveries to be made through our own northern port of Latakia and the armour rolled down through Syrian villages to the cheers of the peasants.[33]

But it was not until Khalid al-'Azm became Syrian Foreign Minister during the crisis over the Baghdad Pact in February 1955 that the Soviet Union scored what may be considered her first great diplomatic success in the Arab world by publicly taking Syria under her protection. Turkey and Iraq had reacted to the news of the Egyptian-

---

[31] See an analysis of Moscow broadcasts on Syria, BBC, no. 533, 11 Jan. 1955.
[32] Shawkat Shuqayr to the author, Beirut, 18 Dec. 1960.
[33] One of the reasons why the Syrians built the port of Latakia was to free their trade from dependence on Beirut and from surveillance by the Lebanese and by the many other interested parties. Syrian purchases of Mark IV tanks from the Czechs are mentioned in Humbaraci, p. 201, and in J. and S. Lacouture, *L'Egypte en mouvement* (1956), p. 213.

Syrian-Saudi alliance with threats and recriminatory notes addressed to Syria. They were reported on 20 March to have concentrated troops and armour on the Syrian frontier. The Syrian Government protested on 22 March against 'two harshly worded notes' from Turkey 'which give no consideration at all to Syria's natural right as an independent and sovereign state to follow the policy dictated by its national interest'. The Soviet Union then intervened. On 23 March the Soviet Foreign Minister, Molotov, informed the Syrian envoy in Moscow, Dr Farid al-Khani, that 'the USSR supports Syria's attitude and is willing to extend to it aid in any form whatsoever for the purpose of safeguarding Syria's independence and sovereignty'.[34] The Molotov guarantee was repeatedly headlined in the Arabic press and loudly proclaimed by the 'Voice of the Arabs'. At last the Arabs had found a protector.[35] 'If Turkey believes that force will settle the situation in Syria', Cairo radio declared on 29 March, 'then Turkey must remember that she too has a neighbour who is stronger than she is. . . .' On 31 March the Syrian Premier 'Asali received the Soviet Minister in Damascus, who repeated the Soviet assurances. These events demonstrated what was later to be brought home dramatically by Egypt's 'Czech' arms deal: that the western Powers were no longer the sole arbiters in the Middle East and that the Arab states had acquired a new freedom of action, hitherto unsuspected even to themselves.

Almost immediately Syria was driven to negotiate a more substantial arms deal with the Soviet Union. She was impelled in this direction by Israel's large-scale raids on Arab territory, by Turkish threats, by the reluctance of Britain and the United States to supply arms outside the framework of a defence pact, and by the disinclination of France—Syria's traditional supplier—to arm the Arabs after the start of the Algerian war. Preliminary contacts are believed to have been made at the United Nations in the summer of 1955 between Syrian and Soviet delegates; the agreement was signed in the autumn and was followed by others. Syria is estimated to have spent over £100 million on arms from the East between 1954 and 1957.

The same fear of Israel and a related desire to break out of the western straight-jacket imposed by the Tripartite Declaration of 1950 were the principal reasons for Egypt's first arms deal. Major Salah Salim recounts the sequence of events as follows:[36]

[34] BBC, no. 556, 1 Apr. 1955. [35] See Humbaraci, pp. 202–3.
[36] Salah Salim to the author, London, 13 Apr. 1960.

I was in Damascus when the Israelis launched their attack on Gaza on the night of 28 February 1955. You can imagine the tone of the talks on our military situation in Cairo where I returned early in March. I will be very frank with you: we were desperately weak. Our armed forces were short of everything. At the time of the Gaza raid, Egypt had six serviceable planes; about thirty others were grounded for lack of spare parts: Britain had stopped deliveries. We estimated that our tank ammunition would last for a one-hour battle. Nearly sixty per cent of our tanks were in need of major repairs. Our artillery was in the same deplorable state. We were even short of small arms. We had tried to buy arms from Britain and America—but in vain.

It was then that we went to Bandung where we met Chou En-lai. I was with 'Abd al-Nasir when we met him, and I remember him asking us about the situation in the Middle East. We explained the position as we saw it, mentioning the real threat from Israel and our desperate shortage of military equipment.

Our view was that the West was using Israel as a constant challenge to our leadership. The western Powers knew that if faced with the choice of defeat by Israel or yielding to the West, we should have to choose the latter. This was the blackmail to which we were subjected. We felt that the only way to restore our freedom of action and liberate ourselves from western subjection was to build up a real army able to face Israel on equal terms.

At Bandung, 'Abd al-Nasir asked Chou whether he was prepared to sell us arms. Chou replied that he would find it very difficult to let us have heavy equipment seeing he was still dependent on the Russians for such supplies. He promised to think it over.

I met him again a couple of days later when, after further discussion, he asked me whether we would agree to accept arms direct from the Soviet Union. I replied that, for my part, I would say yes, but that I had to discuss it with 'Abd al-Nasir. Chou then said that, in any event, a reply to our request would reach us through the Soviet Ambassador in Cairo. We then returned home.

On 6 May 1955 Mr Daniel Solod, the Soviet Ambassador, called on me at the Ministry of National Guidance. He informed me that he had received a reply from his Government to the request for arms which we had made to the Chinese. His reply was verbal and consisted of two points. First, that his Government was prepared to supply us with any quantity of arms, including tanks and planes of the latest design, against deferred payment in Egyptian cotton and rice. Secondly, that his Government was ready to help us with any industrial project, including the High Dam at Aswan.

This was the first time that the Soviet Government had expressed an interest in this project. I was naturally elated and hurried to tell 'Abd al-Nasir who immediately called a meeting of the Revolution Command Council. You will be interested to know that the Council, faced with this firm Russian offer, decided to make one last bid to secure arms from the West. In June 1955 'Abd al-Nasir summoned the British and American ambassadors and told them frankly that if they refused to supply him with arms he would try and get them from the Russians. But according to our information, the two Governments thought he was bluffing.

Two or three weeks later, 'Abd al-Nasir had a further meeting with Byroade, the American ambassador, at which he repeated his request, but once again with no results. It was then—and only then—that the Council agreed to begin negotiations with the Russians. We started talks with their Embassy people who were soon joined by Soviet technicians.

At about the end of June, Solod approached me with a special request. He asked me to invite Shepilov, then Editor in Chief of *Pravda*, to our independence celebrations in July. He told me frankly that Shepilov played a great role in shaping Soviet foreign policy and that he would shortly be appointed Foreign Minister. I accordingly sent Shepilov a personal invitation on behalf of my Government.

He flew in to Cairo on 22 July and rapidly completed with us the details of the arms deal. On 26 July the first Egyptian plane carrying Egyptian technicians left Cairo for Prague to check the first consignment of MIG 15s. Arms deliveries had begun although 'Abd al-Nasir did not announce the deal until September.

'Abd al-Nasir's policies were hailed throughout the Arab world. In Arab eyes, Bandung and the arms deal represented a victory for the forces of good over the forces of evil as seen in the Baghdad Pact, the Gaza raid, and in French arms deliveries to Israel. But at the same time, Egypt's neutralism had acquired, perhaps on contact with the Chinese, a new dimension: non-alignment was no longer merely conceived as a guarantee of sovereignty, as Nehru taught, but had become a positive instrument in the *continuing* struggle against imperialism. The fundamental basis of China's propaganda was—and still is—that the fight against imperialism is not yet over and that freedom from colonial rule is not the end of the struggle but only a small tactical gain. This became Egypt's cry.

In Syria the Czech arms deal was a turning-point in the Ba'th's relations with 'Abd al-Nasir. Both sides found themselves in full agreement in opposing the West which, in their view, supported Israel and imposed conditions on arms supplied to the Arabs. 'Positive neutralism' no longer meant putting relations with the two blocs on the same impartial basis. It meant seeking aid where one could, while continuing to fight western imperialism. Soviet aid without visible strings seemed exactly what was required.

Soviet arms deliveries also caused a rapprochement between the Ba'th and the Communists to flower. But the Ba'th were not easily won over: they were aware that Communist policy was dictated less by Syria's than by Russia's national interest, and that an alliance with the Communist Party would impede their own growth. So they compromised by discontinuing the political struggle with the Communists while making their ideological differences with them clear.[37] 'We may meet in the same trenches but we can't join up with them', was a current Ba'th slogan.

[37] These were outlined, for instance, in a booklet on Ba'th-Communist relations by Michel 'Aflaq and Dr Jamal al-Atasi published in January 1956.

18

The Army and the 'Malki Affair'

THE Baghdad Pact internationalized the struggle for power in the Middle East: it introduced fresh issues and slogans and cold war rivalries into the already turbulent scene of local Arab antagonisms. In this sense 1954–5, the year of the great defence debate which preceded the signature of the Baghdad Pact, was perhaps the most important in post-war Arab history. It brought about vast changes in the strength and strategy of the chief contestants. In crude terms, Britain's decision to evacuate the Suez land base, after seventy years' tenure, allowed Egypt to emerge as a major Middle East Power, staking her claim to Arab leadership on the basis of an independent foreign policy. Iraq, with British support, then made a counter-bid for dominance in the form of the Baghdad Pact, but was forced on to the defensive as Egypt rallied Syria to her side. This split in the Arab ranks provided Russia with a point of re-entry in the area, well to the rear of the Pact's defence line, which in turn aroused the active interest of the United States.

But although the area of conflict was thus enlarged, the local pattern of Arab inter-state relations was not supplanted but built upon, remaining the level at which matters of greater import were decided. And at the centre of things stood Syria, at once the evidence of Egypt's hard-won supremacy, the target of Iraq's frustrated hopes, the chosen field for Soviet penetration and western counteraction, and the ideological source of pan-Arabism as preached by the Ba'th. Syria remained, therefore, an arena in which rival Powers clashed, her own political convulsions sounding the end of one round and the beginning of the next. No truce followed the struggle over the Baghdad Pact. Instead the conflict entered a new phase with a political murder in Damascus which put the already nervous city into a state of agitation, and caused the Syrian delegation to hurry home from the excitements of Bandung.

THE MURDER

Lieutenant-Colonel 'Adnan al-Malki, aged 37, Deputy Chief of Staff of the Syrian army, was shot dead on a football field on 22 April 1955. His assailant, a military police sergeant called Yusuf 'Abd al-Rahim, immediately turned the gun on himself, and the match ended in turmoil. An analysis of the crime reveals a characteristic intermingling of motives, some personal and trivial, others drawn from the context of the international power struggle of which Syria was the focus.

In the political circumstances of the time, Malki was a considerable personage: the army was the most important single force in Syrian politics and he was perhaps its most powerful officer. General Shawkat Shuqayr, the Chief of Staff, was an able and soldierly figure, but he suffered from the disability of being a Druze of Lebanese origin, and was therefore considered something of a foreigner. Unlike Malki, he also failed to reflect the rather extravagant nationalism with which the younger Syrian officers were then fired. This heady conviction that the army had a mission to save the country and restore it to greatness was the source of Malki's strength. He was a leading representative of the post-war generation, for whom the disastrous war in Palestine and the collapse of civilian government had been symbols of their degenerate political society.

Malki was tall, clear-eyed, and strikingly European in appearance; he was young, exuberant, and popular with his brother officers; his voice and explosive laugh dominated any gathering. He was considered a natural leader, if somewhat intemperate and unstable. Dismissed from the army by Shishakli for heading an abortive revolt,[1] he was reinstated with great panache after the dictator's downfall, immediately becoming the chief military ally of the neutralist, pan-Arab, 'progressive' factions in the Chamber, opposed, as they were, to western defence plans, to union with Iraq, and to the receipt of foreign aid if assorted with any kind of condition. In the months which followed the September 1954 elections, Malki had gradually manoeuvred the army back into politics, lending his weight to the 'Azm–'Asali–Hawrani triumvirate in its attempts to overthrow Faris al-Khuri. He thus helped 'save' Syria from the Baghdad Pact and paved the way for the defence agreement with Egypt in March 1955, a month before his death. It was rumoured that had Faris Bey not given way, Malki would have attempted a *coup de force* with Ba'th support.

[1] See above, p. 127.

The Ba'th's attitude towards the army was ambiguous: it had no love for military regimes (Hawrani had seen some at very close range) and it did not encourage the army in its self-appointed role as the guardian of the nation's higher destinies. Indeed, the Ba'th leaders had no intention of taking orders from the military or of allowing the officer corps to become the leading political force in the country. But nor could they afford to let the army fall into the hands of their 'reactionary' enemies. They wanted to win it over to their ideas so as to put it to work as an instrument of social and political reform, and ensure that it was not used against themselves. Malki seemed to the Ba'th just the ally they needed: he dominated his brother officers, he was a keen patriot, and he stood for the army as a whole as an eloquent symbol of the Arab idea. Moreover his brother Riyad al-Malki was a leading Ba'th Party member. With such a man controlling the army, every reform seemed possible.[2]

Thus Malki's murder came as a great shock. The sergeant who killed him was soon identified as a member of the pan-Syrian, militantly anti-Communist and anti-Arab nationalist *Parti Populaire Syrien* (PPS), which, for months before the killing, had been competing with the Ba'th for influence in the army in the face of Malki's strenuous opposition. Malki was, in fact, reported to have set up, shortly before his death, a 'Revolutionary Council' on the Egyptian model to root out PPS sympathizers from the officer corps and break up their party cells. He had, in particular, been conducting a personal feud with the leading PPS officer in the army, Major Ghassan Jadid, as well as with the president of the party in Syria, Georges 'Abd al-Massih. Jadid had been dismissed from the army about a fortnight before the murder, while Massih had been threatened with extradition to Lebanon where he was under sentence of death. The motive of both men may have been revenge.[3]

But the crime should also be placed in a wider context. The PPS are thought to have believed that by eliminating Malki and replacing him with one of their own officers they could make a bid for power.[4]

[2] This at least was the view outside his immediate circle of friends. It was not generally known that his feelings for the Ba'th had cooled since his brother's defeat at the 1954 elections: he considered that the party had failed to give Riyad its full support. In retaliation, Malki had appointed two anti-Ba'thist officers to the general staff, Amin al-Nafuri and Ahmad 'Abd al-Karim.

[3] Both Major Jadid and the assassin, Sergeant Yusif, belonged to the Alawi sect and came from the same village near Latakia.

[4] The PPS later claimed that the decision to kill Malki was taken by Massih alone without consulting the party. (Abdallah Sa'ada, party president, to the author, Beirut, 1 Dec. 1960).

16. Officer cadets at the Homs Military Academy

17. A demonstration in the Merje Square, Damascus

18. General ʿAbd al-Hakim Amir, followed by ʿAbd al-Hamid Sarraj

19. Michel ʿAflaq, founder and leader
of the Baʿth Party

20. Salah al-Din Bitar, co-founder
of the Baʿth Party

Their strength in the army at the time was estimated at about 30 officers and 100 n.c.o.s.[5] Thus the broader background to Malki's murder was a struggle for control of the army—the deciding factor in Syrian politics. It may also be seen as an attempt to cripple the factions that stood for neutralism, militant Arabism, and freedom from foreign military pacts and so reverse the anti-western trend in Syria.

A bill of indictment against about 140 members of the party for alleged offences connected with Malki's murder was published on 29 June.[6] Thirty were charged with crimes carrying the death penalty, including murder, contacting a foreign Power, exposing Syria to hostile acts, prejudicing her relations with a foreign Power, and inciting military personnel to disobedience. Foremost among the accused were Georges 'Abd al-Massih, the party president, Juliette al-Mir, widow of Antun Sa'ada, 'Isam al-Mahaiyri, the secretary-general, Ghassan Jadid, and Dr Sami al-Khuri. The indictment named the PPS as a secret society violating the constitution and public order and alleged that the party's objective was to seize power by infiltration into the army. The party was accused of making several contacts with the Iraq Government and offering its services in carrying out Iraqi policy in Syria; of trying, through a Lebanese deputy and a Lebanese journalist, to contact the Egyptian authorities in order to offer the party's services to them (notwithstanding the contradictory policies of Egypt and Iraq); of being in touch with the American Government with the object of carrying out a coup d'état in Syria, and of endorsing a policy acceptable to the United States. In this connexion, the party's executive committee was alleged to have decided to send 'Isam al-Mahaiyri to America to make high-level contacts and to have been in touch with a United States embassy official in Damascus.

The indictment stated further that an espionage network had been uncovered among party members in the army, and that documents seized showed that the party had since the beginning of 1955 been supplying the American information office in Damascus with reports on the activities of the Muslim Brotherhood in Syria and of the Communist Party in Syria and Lebanon. A letter to the party executive from a party member in the United States, Hisham Sharabi, requesting co-operation with the United States was among the pieces of

---

[5] 'Abd al-Hamid Sarraj (chief of military intelligence at the time) to the author, Cairo, 27 Jan. 1961.
[6] BBC, no. 583, 5 July 1955.

evidence submitted at the trial.[7] But whatever the truth of these detailed allegations, there seems little doubt that the anti-Communism
of the PPS had attracted the favourable attention of the western
Powers.

CONSEQUENCES OF THE MURDER

Whatever the motives for the crime, its consequences were far-
reaching. It allowed the Communists, posing as nationalists, to call
for Malki's revenge. They thus had occasion to carry out the political
education of the Ba'th by pointing to the foreign hand behind the
PPS, planting in their minds the idea that western influence was
everywhere at work in Syria. This was perhaps the most striking
result of the affair. Indeed, the trial which followed Malki's murder
was a revelation to the Ba'th. Judicial inquiries into earlier political
assassinations in Syria, such as that of the nationalist leader, Dr
'Abd al-Rahman Shahbandar, in 1940, had been contained within
local bounds. Charges were only levelled against local enemies of the
victim, even if it were hinted out of court that these had been the
instruments of foreign interests. In the Malki trial, the crime was
from the start placed in a wider setting and the alleged role of the
western Powers, and notably of the Americans, was brought out in
open court. The murder seemed to demonstrate to Syrian opinion
how far the PPS, and their Iraqi and western allies, were prepared to
go to reverse the trend in Syria and restore their own position. The
Communists took great care that the lesson was well learned.

Both the Communists and the Ba'th decided, therefore, that quick
action against the PPS was required. For the Communists it was an
occasion to rid themselves of their ideological enemies, to weaken
the position of the West in Syria, and prepare the way for closer
relations with the USSR; for the Ba'th, the destruction of the PPS
meant a further step towards full neutralism; it also meant silencing
the voice of pan-Syrian nationalism which conflicted with their own
pan-Arab doctrines. Both parties believed that if justice were seen
to be hesitant or slow, 'democratic' elements in the army and among
civilians would be demoralized, while the PPS and their friends
might be encouraged to attempt a coup. It was with these thoughts
in mind that the Communists and the Ba'th clamoured for revenge:
the PPS was outlawed; large numbers of its members were arrested;
the party offices were put under seal; a mob burned down its printing

[7] BBC, no. 601, 6 Sept. 1955.

works; sympathizers were purged rom the army and administration, and provisional courts set up with special powers to try the accused. Fifty thousand mourners heard General Shawkat Shuqayr pledge, in a funeral oration at Malki's graveside, that his blood would be revenged. The press, the courts, the Premier himself, accused the PPS of plotting with a foreign Power to overthrow the Government.

Thus the PPS was eliminated from Syrian public life. Antun Sa'ada's widow was sentenced to twenty-two years' imprisonment, while sentences were passed *in absentia* on Georges 'Abd al-Massih and Ghassan Jadid, who had escaped to Lebanon (as well as on some lesser fry who failed to make their get-away). But the movement throve on martyrdom. Hounded in Syria, it regrouped in Lebanon—ex-officers, desperadoes, fanatical young men, dedicated cadres, bound by the rigid hierarchies of the party and the mumbo-jumbo of Sa'ada's ideas, all pledged themselves to overthrow the Damascus regime. Casting themselves for the role of victims of Communist conspiracy, they looked round for allies and found them in the western embassies. It was natural that they should overplay the threat of Communism in Syria, luridly colouring some western judgements of that country and helping to make of Beirut an unreliable vantage point from which to view the Syrian political scene. In this way western fears of Soviet penetration in Syria were artificially stimulated and this led eventually to counter-measures which in turn helped to create the very threat they were designed to ward off. Indeed, perhaps the greatest disservice the PPS rendered to the western cause was to cement the Ba'th–Communist alliance and so obscure the profound differences between the two.

In Damascus Malki at once became a martyr for the cause of Syrian independence and for the neutralist, 'progressive', pro-Egyptian sentiments he had expressed when alive. Although not a particularly remarkable young man, he had become in death a glorious symbol of embattled Arabism assailed on all sides by its enemies. His murder fanned the flames of intemperate, over-excited nationalism so that, from that moment, Syrian politics seemed largely to consist of a series of panic reactions to external and internal threats. Today his statue and giant mausoleum look out over the prosperous avenues of the new Damascus suburb of Abu Rummaneh, while his blood-stained uniform may be inspected in the room devoted to his memory at the military museum.

IMPACT ON THE ARMY

The young Syrian national army, formed after the departure of the French in 1946 and rapidly expanded by Za'im and Shishakli, could rely on no tradition of soldiering; no real 'military class' existed. More than in other Arab countries, Syrian officers fell under the influence of their non-military friends and families; they were not immune from civilian political currents. Malki's murder removed the one officer who could have imposed his views on the whole officer corps; after his death no single dominating personality remained. Instead of one chief, there were a score, each expecting to be consulted before any decision was taken. The unity of the army was destroyed as each political party and each neighbouring state scrambled for military allies; secret subsidies flowed in from Iraq, Egypt, Saudi Arabia, and Jordan, as well as from Great Powers farther afield. Young officers were sent abroad on arms purchasing missions; strict accounting was necessarily difficult in the proliferating security agencies; many officers found themselves handling enormous sums: money was diverted and embezzled; some officers were enriched. In this way money that might have been devoted to economic development was wasted. Thoroughly politicized, with its own budget and secret funds, the army became a jungle of intrigue, sometimes matching civilian factionalism, sometimes rent by its own indigenous rivalries.

From Malki's murder until the union with Egypt three years later, it was difficult to say with any certainty where power lay in Syria. As the self-appointed keepers of the nation's conscience, the officers enjoyed a certain moral ascendancy over the politicians; they also had the advantage of physical power: they could always threaten a *coup de force*. Yet the politicians were not mere puppets controlled by the army from behind a thin screen of parliamentary life, nor was the political scene a straight contest between civilians and military. The army became so fragmented and so much involved in the political process that civilian-army boundaries were lost in the vast, intricate struggle of the pre-Union years.

A dozen officers nevertheless gradually emerged as political figures in their own right and took up identifiable political positions. They were mostly younger men of the post-war generation who had graduated from the Homs military college in 1947–8 and for whom the Palestine War and the subsequent series of *putsches* had been the formative experience. They were the outstanding young men of their age-group in the army, but they had no experience of statecraft and few roots among the people. Like many of those who carry a gun at their side, they proposed short-cut solutions to most problems. Many of them had been among Shishakli's favourites and had been sent to France in the early 1950s for staff training.

The career of 'Abd al-Hamid Sarraj, a leading member of Shish-akli's entourage, followed this pattern. Born in Hama in 1925, he had known the socialist leader Akram al-Hawrani since childhood. He was a cool, taciturn, retiring young man with an early bent for police work. But on the departure of the French he left the *gendarm-erie* for the newly formed national army, won his commission and then almost immediately, in January 1948, deserted to join a battalion of Arab irregulars in Palestine in attacks on Jewish settlements. He returned to Syria nearly a year later, after the Palestine War, in time to witness the crumbling of Quwatli's regime and to take part in Za'im's coup d'état. In 1952 Shishakli sent him to France for further training before appointing him head of the army's *premier bureau* (personnel). But when the dictator was overthrown the new Government insisted on the removal of a number of officers who had been closely associated with him. Sarraj was accordingly posted to Paris for some months as assistant military attaché; however, he was soon back in Damascus. The Chief of Staff, General Shuqayr, had a high regard for him, appointing him head of the *deuxième bureau* (or military intelligence) in March 1955, a month before Malki's murder. His rise to prominence dates from his skilful and tenacious handling of the subsequent investigations. His major task in the next three years was to thwart the numerous Iraqi, PPS, and western-sponsored conspiracies against the Syrian regime. Sarraj was on friendly terms with the Ba'th, sharing its fierce nationalism and suspicion of foreign interference, but retaining a measure of detachment from it. He was an ally, not a dependant, of the party leaders. Indeed, his strength in the pre-Union years which mark his rise to supreme power lay in his care not to identify himself with any one faction or group. In short, as head of military intelligence, Sarraj enjoyed a position of considerable power and independence.

If Sarraj was something of a lone wolf, other officers were more closely identified with political factions. The Ba'th, in particular, had army sympathizers of whom Mustafa Hamdun, 'Abd al-Ghani Qannut, Bashir Sadiq, Hasan Hiddeh, and Jamal al-Sufi were perhaps the most prominent. It will be recalled that Hamdun was the first spokesman of the Aleppo revolt against Shishakli in February 1954. He too came from Hama, was related to Hawrani by marriage and was generally considered his disciple. As Minister of Land Reform after the Union in 1958, Hamdun was later responsible for putting into effect the somewhat vindictive land legislation which reflected Hawrani's long feud with landowners of the Hama area.

Opposed to the Ba'th faction was a group of 'independent' officers under the leadership of Amin al-Nafuri, another former associate of General Shishakli. Sometimes known as the *Tahrir*, or Liberation, group, in reference to Shishakli's Arab Liberation Movement, it included Jado 'Izzeddine, Ahmad 'Abd al-Karim, and Husayn Hiddeh (Hasan Hiddeh's brother). Without political conviction or party allegiance, these officers demanded their share of power in much the same way as did their civilian opposite numbers, the 'Independents' in the Chamber. They tended on the whole to lend their support to Khalid al-'Azm. Although springing from much the same background as Sarraj, they were inclined to be jealous of his superior abilities and discretion. To the Ba'th they seemed un-principled opportunists. Vacillating between the Ba'th and the Nafuri groups was another faction which included Tu'meh al-'Awdatallah and Ahmad al-Hunaydi, both later to hold ministerial posts in the Syrian executive under the first Syro-Egyptian union. Another of Sarraj's contemporaries at the Homs military college, Akram al-Dayri, headed yet another faction known as the 'Damascus group'. Finally, another 'lone wolf', 'Afif al-Bizri, was to emerge in 1957 as Chief of Staff and a Communist sympathizer. A clever officer with a good war record during the Palestine campaign, he had risen to command the map-making and survey division of the Syrian army. But he had no personal following and his later promin-ence was due mainly to his being a compromise candidate acceptable to the various rival factions. These, then, were the men who controlled the Syrian army in the years before the Union. Their alignments were shifting; their political vision was generally limited to the petty struggle for power which opposed one barracks or tank column to another. Their feuds brought the army to the verge of dismember-ment, until only 'Abd al-Nasir could compose their differences.

19

Syria's Road to Suez, I:
The Soviet-Egyptian Offensive

THE SETTING

BY nationalizing the Suez Canal Company in July 1956, 'Abd al-Nasir stung his enemies into taking direct action against him. The seizure of the Company was not the only or even the main cause of the Suez war. It brought to a head a number of long-smouldering conflicts, and the origins of the attack on Egypt must be traced farther back.

French official opinion believed that to overthrow 'Abd al-Nasir would decapitate the nationalist movement in North Africa, for

France is not blind to the direct help Cairo gives the Algerian rebels: arms, the training of future fellagha army chiefs on Egyptian soil, a refuge for the FLN leaders; and this in spite of Colonel Nasser's formal promises to M. Pineau when he visited Cairo in the spring.[1]

But the French overlooked the indigenous roots of the revolt against their rule in North Africa and overestimated 'Abd al-Nasir's connexion with it. Algerian nationalists did not always look to Cairo for leadership; nor was their movement modelled on or inspired by the Arab national movement in Arab Asia.

Israel identified Egypt as her main enemy as early as 1954 when 'Abd al-Nasir first made his bid for Arab leadership on the basis of an independent foreign policy free from Great Power control. He preached total Arab solidarity—a united Arab front under Egyptian direction—and demanded recognition as the foremost champion of Arab rights in Palestine. On both these counts he posed a serious threat to Israel. Israeli policy, therefore, sought to circumscribe his freedom of action by humbling him in war, thus exposing as empty his claims to leadership and independence. Any Egyptian diplomatic

[1] *L'Année politique, 1956*, p. 335.

success tended thereafter to be followed by an Israeli military riposte.

No sooner, for instance, had Egypt secured British agreement to evacuate the Suez base and stood out against the Baghdad Pact, than Israel launched the Gaza raid in February 1955 to demonstrate Egypt's weakness to Arab and world opinion. Similarly, the 1956 Sinai campaign was an attempt to deflate the vast gains in authority and prestige which 'Abd al-Nasir had scored throughout the Arab world by buying Russian arms. This must have been Israel's first goal even if her other war aims included a desire to put an end to the demoralizing incursions of *feda'yin* guerrillas into her border areas, to forstall a possible Egyptian attack and even, as has been suggested,[2] to annex the Sinai Peninsula, thus pushing back her western frontier to the Suez Canal.

But of the three parties to the attack on Egypt, Britain's motives were perhaps the most complex and deep-rooted. This is not the place to review the long history of Anglo-Egyptian relations or to discuss in any detail the origins and course of the Suez war: other writers have already done so. The aim here is to advance an argument which will connect the Suez crisis to the pattern of relations involving Syria which this book has so far examined—indeed, to show that the British attack on Egypt is inexplicable unless firmly related to the struggle for power which opposed Britain and Egypt in Arab Asia in the previous decade. Egypt had, in fact, been the one Arab state to stand up to Britain and challenge her hegemony in the Middle East since the end of the Second World War.

In the first phase of the Anglo-Egyptian contest, from 1945 to 1954, Egypt's role had been that of a passive resister: obstructive, non-co-operative, intransigent. The main vehicle for her influence was the Arab League, of which she secured the leadership in its earliest years. The League was the instrument which allowed her both to harness the other Arab states in support of her national struggle against the British and to contain Britain's client states, Iraq and Jordan, within their national boundaries, checking the expansion of Hashimite influence in Arab Asia

It was almost entirely thanks to Egyptian obstruction that the many western schemes for Middle East defence advanced in the early 1950s failed: the Wafd rejected the first formal defence proposals in 1950–1 and 'Abd al-Nasir all subsequent suggestions. Britain's decision to withdraw from the Canal Zone base in 1954

---

[2] Erskine B. Childers, *The Road to Suez* (1962), pp. 175 ff.

without securing Egyptian agreement to join in collective defence of the area ended this phase of the Anglo-Egyptian duel by confirming Egypt's independence and demonstrating for all to see the decline in British power.

Until then, Egypt's nuisance value, although great, had been explicable in terms of her own struggle for national liberation. It could not yet be said to constitute a threat to British economic and strategic interests in Iraq, Jordan, or the Persian Gulf. Indeed, after the signature of the Anglo-Egyptian agreement both parties were still able to speak of a new era of friendlier relations. But Egypt then passed to the offensive, opening the second more violent, 1954–6, phase in Anglo-Egyptian relations. Whether she opened the attack first or whether she was provoked by the Baghdad Pact is irrelevant to the present argument. A clash with Britain became inevitable as soon as Egypt evolved her new Arab policy of non-alignment early in 1954— a year before the Pact's signature. Egypt demanded Arab solidarity in support of a policy of complete independence from Great Powers at a time when Britain was still the reigning Great Power in the area.

It has been seen that Egypt won the first round in the battle over the Baghdad Pact by securing control of Syria's foreign policy following the overthrow of the Faris al-Khuri Government in February 1955. As a result, Britain's friends in the area—in Iraq, Jordan, and the Gulf—came under immediate Egyptian pressure and Britain was herself put on the defensive. These events illustrated a tacit principle in Arab politics: that control of Syria was the key to the struggle for local primacy.

The seeds of Suez lie, therefore, in the decade of Anglo-Egyptian rivalry which reached its climax over the Baghdad Pact. This was the turning-point which tilted the balance of power in Cairo's favour, causing 'Abd al-Nasir to be regarded in the eyes of Whitehall as an active threat to British interests. The need to oppose him emerged in the latter months of 1955 as he gradually consolidated his hold on Syria and turned his propaganda machine against every remnant of British power in the Arab world (and East Africa).[3] By early 1956, when Jordan—the 'outpost of Iraq'[4]—seemed in danger of falling to the Egyptians, a decision could no longer be delayed. 'Abd al-Nasir had to be stopped.

[3] See, for instance, BBC, nos. 570 of 20 May and 571 of 24 May 1955 for Cairo Radio support of Mau Mau as a 'nationalist movement for the liberation of Kenya from imperialism'.
[4] Eden, *Memoirs*, iii. 349.

This unfolding power struggle on the spot in Arab Asia provides the essential background to British action at Suez. Britain attacked Egypt not only because 'Abd al-Nasir had nationalized the Suez Canal Company—the Canal had in effect been under his sole control since the British evacuation of the Zone—but because the tide of his influence in Arab Asia threatened to engulf Jordan, Iraq, and the Gulf, together with British treaties, strongpoints, and oil interests. That is why, long before 'Abd al-Nasir's seizure of the Canal Company provided an occasion to strike at his home base, Britain and her Iraqi ally were scheming for a change of regime in Syria—the pivot of Egypt's power in Arab Asia. Indeed, events in and around Syria in 1955-6 provide a surer guide even than the tractations over the Canal to what was really at stake in the Anglo-Egyptian struggle.

But before examining in the next chapter the conspiracy against Syria—which the United States also joined, to counter growing Soviet influence there—some account must first be given of the trend of events inside that country which so alarmed these Powers.

THE SOVIET-EGYPTIAN OFFENSIVE

Both Egypt and the Soviet Union chose Syria as the main target for their parallel Middle East offensives in 1955. Egypt, as has been seen, challenged in February by the Baghdad Pact and threatened with isolation, riposted in Damascus, securing a change of Government there favourable to herself. A month later, in March, Russia made her first major intervention in Middle East affairs with a public guarantee to stand by Syria in the face of Turkish and Iraqi hostility. These two highly successful manoeuvres suggested that both Cairo and Moscow had made very similar appraisals of the situation: both appreciated the pivotal position of Syria in Arab politics; both also sought to harness the strong current of neutralism in Arab opinion which stemmed from the long history of western domination and from the West's role in the creation and continued support of Israel. Both wished to destroy the Baghdad Pact and overthrow the Governments associated with it.

Malki's murder in April 1955, by discrediting western positions still further, enabled Egypt and the Soviet Union to consolidate their gains. The crime gave the Syrian public an insight into the magnitude and the violence of the international contest in which Syria was a pawn and, by injecting an element of hysteria into Syrian public life, encouraged her to run for safety to the arms of her new protectors. Egypt's purchase of Russian arms in the summer of 1955 opened a phase of still more rapid penetration by the two Powers. Both benefited from the transaction, drawing closer together like successful business partners: Russia vastly strengthened her claim to Arab friendship, while Egypt demonstrated her freedom from western control, acquiring at the same time something of the aura of Soviet power.

Although British and French troops evacuated Syria in 1946, Syrian allegiance remained with the West for much of the subsequent decade; her military dictators, Za'im and Shishakli, retained close ties with France. The first real break with this tradition occurred at the time of the 1954-5 Middle East defence debate, when Syria stepped clear of western guiding strings to side officially with Egypt and neutralism. The fact that Syria's links had been with France rather than with Britain and that France herself opposed the Baghdad Pact made this choice easier. Indeed, it is possible that the French considered a Syrian-Egyptian entente less of an evil than a Syrian-Iraqi one. But the step was, nevertheless, a new departure for Syrian foreign policy, a complete change of stance in international politics, brought about by such men as Khalid al-'Azm and Akram al-Hawrani. The door was thrown open to the full flood of Soviet and Eastern European blandishments—arms, trade, credits, exchange visits of all sorts—and to the spectacular growth of Egyptian influence in Syrian and Arab affairs.

QUWATLI'S ELECTION

Seeing Syria drift away, Iraq sought to check this trend at the outset. In August 1955 she tried to induce the People's Party leader, Rushdi al-Kikhia, to stand against Khalid al-'Azm for the Presidency of the Republic. (The veteran Hashim al-Atasi, who had been invited to resume the Presidency when Shishakli was overthrown in February 1954, was due to retire in September.) But in spite of Iraqi support, Kikhia refused to stand. He was an elegant, cautious, old-world Aleppo notable, honest and widely respected but lacking political daring. The trend of events since the first coup d'état in 1949 had been increasingly distasteful to him. He had witnessed the decline of his party, its buffeting by the army, the triumph of political ideas and politicians whom he despised. And he lacked the heart to fight back. In consequence, the leadership of the pro-Iraqi, traditional, moderate elements in Syrian politics went by default at a critical moment. 'Azm was the candidate of the new trend, the man of the hour, the dominant figure in 'Asali's neutralist coalition and the architect of the Syrian-Egyptian alliance of March 1955.

In the search for a candidate to oppose him, the choice fell at last, *faute de mieux*, on the former President, Shukri al-Quwatli, whose previous term of office had been ignominiously interrupted by Husni al-Za'im. Quwatli was not a strong candidate: the record of his first term, 1943–8, was not brilliant; he had not given the country a sense of direction in the first years of its independence; he was unpopular with the army; corruption and nepotism had flourished under his regime. But his long years of nationalist agitation, first against the Turks then against the French, had earned him a certain uncritical affection from the masses, while to traditionalists and conservatives— and to the outgoing President Hashim al-Atasi himself—he seemed less dangerous than the opportunist 'Azm. Quwatli enjoyed one further temporary asset: the Americans were known to oppose 'Azm's candidature and the Chief of Staff, Shawkat Shuqayr, thought it best at this point not to alarm them further. He therefore braved the Ba'th and withheld army support from 'Azm. It is difficult to assess how much this influenced the outcome. The Chamber is the electoral body which chooses the President. But in the family circle of Syrian politics, the army's attitude undoubtedly weighed heavily with the deputies.

In the event, Quwatli was elected President on 18 August 1955 on a second ballot, having failed to secure the necessary two-thirds majority on the first vote.[5] He took office on 5 September but the result was unhappy: in the critical pre-union years, caught in the cross-fire of inter-Arab and East–West feuds, Syria needed more than a figurehead. From the start, Quwatli was weak and ineffective, unable to unite the nation, at odds with the Ba'th for whose support he bade in vain, and with the army who regarded him as in part responsible for the Palestine débacle. It was a mistake to have brought to the Presidency a man whose background, record, and temperament made him unable to come to terms with, let alone control, the most dynamic elements in Syrian affairs.

THE SYRIAN-EGYPTIAN DEFENCE PACT

Following 'Azm's defeat, the Ba'th withdrew from 'Asali's coalition, 'Azm himself had a heart attack, and 'Asali was forced to submit

[5] First vote: Quwatli 89; 'Azm 42; blank papers 6; invalid 2 (including one for 'Abd al-'Aziz ibn Zayd, Saudi Ambassador in Damascus).
   Second vote: Quwatli 91; 'Azm 41; blank papers 5; invalid 2 (including one for Nuri al-Sa'id, Premier of Iraq).

his Government's resignation on 6 September. The new President, appealing to all parliamentary factions to join forces in a 'national union', then called on Sa'id al-Ghazzi—the non-party lawyer whose stern impartiality had secured the freedom of the 1954 elections— to form a Government. The outcome was a mildly corrective swing of the pendulum in that Ghazzi's coalition,[6] formed on 13 September, was a good deal less radical in composition than 'Asali's. But even though the People's Party held four cabinet seats, including the Ministries of Defence and Economics, Ghazzi made no attempt to reverse the foreign policy of his predecessor. It would have required a superman to stem the neutralist, pro-Egyptian current. In his statement of policy to the Chamber on 20 September, Ghazzi declared that he saw no advantage in joining the Turco-Iraqi pact, but would instead pursue the negotiations begun by the previous Government for a tripartite pact with Egypt and Saudi Arabia. The explosion of joy which greeted the announcement of Egypt's 'Czech' arms deal swept Syria into a military alliance with Egypt a month later.[7]

The pact carried a stage further the process begun by Salah Salim in February: Syria was moving ineluctably into Egypt's sphere of influence. 'Abd al-Nasir declared at the ratification ceremony:

This agreement is the prelude to a new future. History shows that if Syria and Egypt unite they will protect the Eastern world from all dangers that may threaten it. That is what took place at the time of the Crusades. When Syria allied herself to Egypt, together they protected the Islamic world from the dangers that it feared. Today, Syria and Egypt will protect the Arab world against Zionism.[8]

The pact established a supreme council, a war council, and a joint command under the Egyptian general 'Abd al-Hakim Amir. But most of its provisions for military co-operation remained unapplied.

---

[6] Premier & Foreign Minister, Sa'id al-Ghazzi (Ind.); Interior, 'Abd al-Hasib al-Raslan (Ind.); Min. of State (Hijaz railway), Amir Hasan al-Atrash (Ind.); Min. of State (Waqf), As'ad Harun (Ind.); Education, Ma'mum al-Kuzbari (Ind.); Economy, 'Ali Buzo (PP); Defence, Rashad Barmada (PP); Finance, Rizq Allah Antaki (PP); Agriculture, 'Abd al-Wahhab Hawmad (PP); Min. of State (radio & information), Muhammad Sulayman al-Ahmad (Con. bloc); Public Works, 'Abd al-Baqi Nizam al-Din (Dem. bloc); Health, Badri 'Abbud (Dem. bloc). Reshuffle on 14 September: Raslan resigned; 'Ali Buzo moved to Interior; Antaki to Economy; Hawmad to Finance, and a newcomer, Mustafa Mirza (Con. bloc) to Agriculture.
[7] Signed in Damascus on 20 October 1955; instruments of ratification exchanged in Cairo on 8 November (text in *MEJ*, x (1956), p. 77).
[8] *al-Ahram*, 9 Nov. 1955.

'Abd al-Nasir, wary of Syrian factiousness, was reported to be reluctant even to agree to the minimum co-operation required to group operational forces on the Palestine front under a single command. But if militarily ineffective, the pact's political consequences were considerable: even rudimentary defence planning demands the co-ordination of foreign policies. And this was 'Abd al-Nasir's objective: he wanted control of Syria's foreign policy without assuming burdensome local responsibilities.

From then on the Egyptian ambassador, Brigadier Mahmud Riyad, 'Abd al-Nasir's chief instrument in Damascus, began to assume great importance in Syrian affairs. In the months before and after Suez, as the tide ran strongly in Egypt's favour, Riyad came to occupy a position at the centre of Syrian political life unrivalled by any other foreign envoy. He was on close terms with President Quwatli and in constant touch with political leaders. His influence with the rising junta of radical, nationalist officers was also great. Indeed, a friendship was then initiated between the Syrian and Egyptian armies which was later to develop. As Syrian Governments changed, Riyad played a decisive role in bringing Syria into line with Egyptian foreign policy. He became, in fact, much more than an ambassador of a foreign Power: to many levels of public opinion he was the symbol of the special ties which bound beleaguered, threatened Syria to her glorious 'elder sister', Egypt. His relationship with the Ba'th was especially intimate: they were the great pro-Egyptian force in Syrian politics and the spearhead of the union-with-Egypt movement; it was natural that Egypt should reward them with the full weight of its diplomatic support.

And to Egyptian political direction was added Saudi gold, both in official loans—a $10 million loan agreement was concluded in November 1955—and in a flood of bribe money directed at destroying Iraq's standing in Syria and at bolstering that of Egypt and Saudi Arabia.

Israel reacted to the Syrian-Egyptian defence agreement in characteristic style: it had to be shown to be militarily ineffective. In mid-December, therefore, Israeli troops launched a large-scale attack on Syrian positions at Lake Tiberias. 'We hope', the *Jerusalem Post* commented, 'that the Israeli raid has convinced many Syrians that the military pact with Egypt has increased the danger to Syria instead of guaranteeing Syria's defence.' But many more Syrians concluded that their future safety lay in still greater dependence on

Egypt and the Soviet Union. Queues formed in Damascus streets to contribute to 'Arms Week' funds; messages of solidarity were exchanged with Egypt; arms purchases from the Soviet Union were stepped up and a wave of hostility to the West— Israel's banker and armourer—swept the country.

Indeed, the Tiberias raid underlined the lesson of the Gaza raid ten months earlier: 'There happened what those who had followed closely the development of the [Palestine] problem had feared, that it became a universal problem intruding into every political relationship in the Middle East and making it more difficult.'[9] Not only did the direct Arab-Israeli confrontation become fiercer and more dangerous; the quarrel infected every other aspect of Middle East politics so that, even in their relations with the West, the Arab states found themselves once again face to face with Israel.

At the risk, therefore, of taking on both Israel and the West, Egypt prepared the ground for her undisputed ascendancy in Syria in the months before Suez. Syrian school children and university students volunteered by the thousand for military training. An Egyptian contingent joined Syrian troops in the traditional march-past in Damascus on Independence Day, 17 April 1956—the tenth anniversary of the withdrawal of foreign troops—while the Ba'th marked the occasion by calling on the Syrian and Egyptian Governments to proclaim a complete union of the two countries. Syria had become 'Abd al-Nasir's most fervent Arab ally.

SOVIET GAINS

The Soviet offensive in Syria was equally quick to gather pace. Soviet assurances of support for Syria in the spring of 1955 in the face of pressure from the Baghdad Pact were soon followed by offers of economic and technical aid and by visits to Moscow of Syrian parliamentarians and Peace Partisans. In August the Syrian Government approved the appointment of a Soviet military attaché in Damascus and in November diplomatic representation was raised to Embassy status, 'in order to reinforce and develop the friendly relations existing between the two countries'. Trade agreements with both Russia and China were signed in the same month. By the spring of 1956 Syrian contacts with the Communist bloc were so numerous as to make enumeration tedious: trade was under way with all the European satellites; invitations by the dozen flowed in from Moscow

[9] Hourani, *A Vision of History*, p. 137.

addressed to municipal councillors, trade unionists, lawyers, foot-ballers, students, *'ulemas;* Czechoslovakia offered to build an oil refinery and each day brought news of the visit of a Communist dance ensemble or of scholarship places for young Syrians in Eastern Europe. A Syrian shaikh, Muhammad al-Ashmar, was awarded a Stalin Peace Prize.

But it was deliveries of arms that cemented Syrian-Soviet friend-ship. During Sa'id al-Ghazzi's premiership, from September 1955 to June 1956, Soviet arms started reaching Syria in substantial quantities and teams of Syrian officers began going for training behind the iron curtain. The local Communists spared no efforts in these months. Although the party was technically illegal, four daily newspapers propagated Communist views, Communist publications were on every bookstall, and Khalid Baqdash was one of the most forceful and influential members of the Assembly.

By 1956 Ba'th resistance to the Communists' appeal for a popular front was weakening. Opposition to the Baghdad Pact and a sense of common danger had brought them together in 1955: they had found themselves fighting the same enemies and mobilizing public opinion in the same cause. The first instance of genuine co-operation took place at a by-election in Homs in 1955, when the Ba'th and the Communist Parties agreed to back a non-party candidate, Ahmad al-Hajj Yunes, against the People's Party nominee. Hajj Yunes was elected, providing the Communists with a further argument in favour of a common 'front'. Closer relations followed when Soviet and Syrian parliamentary delegations exchanged visits and when Soviet statesmen began publicly to recognize the legitimacy of the movement for Arab unity—a trend confirmed by the new Communist line on Arab nationalism adopted at the Twentieth Party Congress of the CPSU.

But the Ba'th were wary from the outset. As Michel 'Aflaq put it:

No positive aims brought us together. We were not, for instance, co-operating in a campaign for the betterment of the working class. The Communists had never really acquired rights of citizenship to enable such collaboration to take place. They had their men in the unions and else-where, but they were there as professionals, not to defend the rights of the workers but to make use of them for reasons of foreign policy. The Syrian Communist Party was an organization for manipulating the working class, the bourgeoisie, and the students to promote the objectives of Soviet foreign policy against pacts, alliances, and ties with the West. In Syria they never managed to voice popular aspirations, in contrast with the situation in Iraq where they did succeed in becoming a genuinely popular movement.[10]

Joseph Alsop, a shrewd American journalist who spent about a fortnight in Syria in May 1956, tipped a young army captain, 'Abd al-Hamid Sarraj, as 'Syria's next military dictator'. Real power, Alsop wrote, lay in 'the strangely assorted but highly effective combination of Egyptian political leadership, Saudi Arabian bribe money, and Communist organizational talent.'[11]

President Quwatli, unhappily aware of this ferment, expended himself in pleas to all factions to forget their differences and join in a 'national front'. An all-party committee was set up with the unlikely task of drafting a National Charter—a body of generally accepted principles to guide the policies of future governments. The right wanted a clause in the Charter naming Communism as the enemy on the home front. The left objected that Imperialism and Zionism were the only enemies of the Arabs. Both agreed, however, that Syria, like Egypt, should take advantage of the East–West conflict to obtain arms from both sides. Quwatli, weary of the debate, went to convalesce at Aswan in February 1956, expressing the hope that the Charter would be completed on his return.

In March agreement was reached on a draft Charter, so carefully worded as to be unobjectionable. All the major parties signed it, committing themselves to nothing bolder than 'democratic reforms' and a 'neutralist policy'. But no single faction felt strong enough to precipitate a crisis and the Ghazzi Government wobbled on until 3 June. Weakened by resignations,[12] it was suddenly overthrown when Syrian university students stormed and occupied the Ministry of National Economy in protest against the revision of a ban on wheat shipments to France and Algeria—withdrawing only after an emergency cabinet meeting had agreed to reimpose the ban. Ghazzi handed in his resignation a few hours later.

THE BA'TH ENTER THE GOVERNMENT

The moment had come for the convergence of Egyptian and Soviet currents in Syria. After a twelve-day interregnum, in which the

[10] Michel 'Aflaq to the author, Beirut, 7 Jan. 1961.
[11] *New York Herald Tribune*, 25 May 1956.
[12] Munir al-'Ajlani (Justice) and As'ad Harun (Min. of State) resigned on 24 May 1955.

right demonstrated its inability to assemble a majority,[13] the agile Sabri al-'Asali finally put together a Government of National Union on 14 June,[14] comprising the National and People's Parties, the Ba'th, Khalid al-'Azm's Democratic Bloc, and Munir al-'Ajlani's Constitutional Bloc—most of them not on speaking terms. The People's Party got the Ministery of the Interior, but the Ba'th secured the two key posts of Foreign Affairs and Economics. They had come a long way in the past fifteen months. Having only just squeezed into the previous 'Asali Government at the Ministry of Health in February 1955, they now held key posts in the cabinet.

As a result, union with Egypt became a live political issue. Indeed, the Ba'th had insisted, as a condition for their participation, on a government undertaking to begin union talks with Cairo. 'We shall embark', 'Asali accordingly declared in the Chamber on 27 June, 'on a consolidation of our ties with Egypt through immediate talks which we hope will lead to a common policy, to which the other liberated Arab countries will be invited to adhere, so that we may achieve a comprehensive Arab unity.'[15]

On the following day the cry for a Syro-Egyptian union was taken up in a petition signed by 3,000 Syrian university students and addressed to the Chamber of Deputies. On 5 July 1956, after talks with 'Abd al-Nasir in Cairo, Sabri al-'Asali announced the formation of a three-man ministerial committee to conduct the negotiations with Egypt: its members were himself, the Ba'th Foreign Minister, Bitar, and the People's Party Minister of the Interior, Ahmad Qanbar. On the same day the Chamber adopted a resolution to the effect that

The Syrian Chamber of Deputies, in pursuance of paragraph 3, Article 1 of the Constitution, which lays down that the Syrian people are part of the Arab Nation, supports the Government decision, announced by the Premier at this meeting, and wishes the Government success in following this holy

---

[13] On 4 June Rushdi al-Kikhia was asked to head a national Government but declined. On 6 June Quwatli called on Lutfi al-Haffar, but the Ba'th refused to serve under him and he was forced to withdraw three days later. Sabri al-'Asali, who in February 1955 had successfully bridged the gap between the Ba'th and the National Party (at the cost of splitting his own party), then came forward once more.
[14] Premier, Sabri al-'Asali (NP); Public Works, Majd al-Din al-Jabiri (NP); Interior, Ahmad Qanbar (PP); Education, 'Abd al-Wahhab Hawmad (PP); Agriculture, Rashad Jabri (PP); Foreign Affairs, Salah al-Din Bitar (Ba'th); Economy, Khalil Kallas (Ba'th); without portfolio, Muhammad Ayesh (Dem. Bloc); Health, 'Abd al-Baqi Nizam al-Din (Dem. Bloc); Justice, Mustafa Zarka (Con. bloc); Defence, 'Abd al-Hasib Raslan (Con. bloc).
[15] al-Ba'th (Damascus), 28 June 1956.

path bringing us in the near future to the goal awaited by the Arab peoples in all their countries.[16]

The Ba'th's joy at the passing of this resolution was tempered only by the thought that their success in the Chamber was perhaps because their opponents had not taken the vote seriously.

As Syria thus moved closer to Egypt, the Soviet Foreign Minister, Dmitri Shepilov, the architect of the Egyptian arms deal, was given a great popular welcome in Damascus where he arrived on 22 June, barely a week after 'Asali's investiture, bringing Soviet inroads into that country to a triumphant climax. Shepilov was at pains to convince the Syrians that the USSR was 'a sincere and honest friend without greed or private designs and with no desire to usurp the riches of others'. He offered long-term, low-interest development loans—paving the way for the major economic agreement of August 1957; he proposed wide-ranging cultural exchanges—which were embodied in an agreement signed two months after his visit; and he promised to supply Syria with all the arms she needed on easy terms—easier, it was reliably reported, than those the Egyptians had secured. Russian tanks, planes, and armoured cars were said to have arrived at Latakia during his visit. On 3 July, barely a week after his departure, Syria recognized Communist China. To many western observers, Syria seemed already in danger of becoming a Communist client state.

These fears were heightened by the sudden resignation in somewhat mysterious circumstances of the Chief of Staff, Shawkat Shuqayr, on 7 July. He had not been a docile instrument of either right or left, and both sides saw him therefore as a potential obstacle to their ambitions in the fierce period of feuding which was then beginning. So long as he was Chief of Staff, the Ba'th and the Communists could not be sure of army support in a crisis. The People's Party disliked him for much the same reasons. Although they professed to be hostile to military intervention in politics, they none the less wanted to secure the appointment of a general staff on which they could rely. Shuqayr was a nationalist of independent mind who had played an important role in the confused weeks following Shishakli's fall from power. He had then handed power back to Shishakli's civilian opponents, tending thereafter to behave, somewhat irritatingly, as if they were in his debt.

[16] BBC, no. 688, 10 July 1956.

But when 'Asali became Premier in June 1956, Shuqayr found himself cut off from policy-making: he was not included, for example, in the discussions on the question of a federal union with Egypt, and he was finally edged out of his job on the pretext that he was a Druze of Lebanese origin and therefore not wholly reliable. He was also said to have opposed the execution of PPS members implicated in 'Adnan al-Malki's murder. It was rumoured that his dismissal had been engineered, under left-wing pressure, by 'Abd al-Hamid Sarraj, chief of military intelligence and one of his former protégés. Shuqayr retired immediately to his native village of Karsun in Lebanon and was replaced as Chief of Staff by a colourless, politically unambitious soldier, Tawfiq Nizam al-Din, the brother of the Minister of Health in 'Asali's cabinet.

Shuqayr's departure brought into the open the fragmentation of the officer corps and its deep infiltration by rival political factions. Whereas he had been able to paper over the cracks, his withdrawal revealed a turbulent picture of the dozen or so young officers commanding the principal arms jockeying for position, openly taking up political attitudes, and seeking to influence day-to-day government. The politicians resented their interference but at the same time tried to recruit them against each other. Shishakli's long tenure of power had shown that Syria could be ruled through the army, and each politician sought therefore to deny its control to his rivals.

SUEZ

Three weeks after Shuqayr's downfall, 'Abd al-Nasir nationalized the Suez Canal Company. Although the two events are unconnected, the strength of pro-Egyptian sentiment in Syria must have encouraged his resolve to brave the Great Powers. It was largely because he had gained the initiative in Arab Asia by mid-1956 that he could afford to hit back after the cancellation of western offers to finance the High Dam. Indeed, it is significant that his nationalization speech in Alexandria on 26 July 1956 included a special appeal to the Syrians:

Today, compatriots, I turn towards the brethren, to you in Syria, dear Syria, sister Syria, who decided to unite with us—a union free, dignified, and grand—in order that we may together consolidate the principles of freedom, dignity, and prestige, and that we may build Arab nationalism and Arab unity together.

Today, I tell your brethren in Syria in your name—We welcome you
O brethren! As you said in your constitution, you are part of the Arab
nation, and as we said in our constitution, we are part of the Arab nation.
We shall proceed together, brethren, united as one man with one heart in
order to achieve the principles of true dignity and true grandeur, and in
order to establish throughout the Arab homeland and the Arab nation a
true political independence and a true economic independence.[17]

The Syrian Government immediately offered 'Abd al-Nasir its
'strong and absolute support' in the storm that followed the seizure
of the Canal Company. Mass meetings were held in the Damascus
municipal stadium and popular resistance forces were set on foot—
which the Communists considered joining *en bloc*. Cairo radio
declared early in August that in the event of western action against
Egypt, assistance from Syria would include the sabotage of pipelines
crossing the country: 'The Syrian people have found in Gamal 'Abd
al-Nasir the leader they have been awaiting and the commander they
have been hoping for. . . . The people in the streets worship Gamal
'Abd al-Nasir.'[18] In the event, when Egypt was attacked, Syria
behaved predictably: the President and three members of the cabinet
flew to Moscow on 30 October and the Iraq Petroleum Company
pipeline was blown up early in November.

Quwatli's mission to Moscow at the height of the Suez crisis was a
clear pointer to the road Syria had travelled in the previous eighteen
months. Russia had become the friend and protector to whom she
appealed in a moment of danger; conversely, Syria, of all the Arab
states, was the one on which the Soviet Government pinned its chief
hopes; the only one to tolerate overt Communist activity and to seem
promisingly 'progressive'. Quwatli's visit had been planned seveal
weeks earlier with the object, or so it was suggested, of concluding a
new arms deal. But when the time came to go, Syria faced the threat
of war and invasion. The cabinet had to decide whether the President
should ride out the storm at home or whether a personal high-level
intervention in Moscow might not be more useful. The latter course
was adopted. Quwatli accordingly went to Moscow to seek Soviet
military and political support in the event of an attack on Syria. He
was given blanket assurances: ties with the Soviet Union were thus
cemented and Russian arms flooded the country, giving teeth to
popular militias. Quwatli returned home believing, according to his

[17] BBC, no. 5, 28 July 1956 (for edited version see *Orient*, no. 1 (1957), p. 46).
[18] BBC, 7 Aug. 1956.

intimates, that the Soviet threat of a rocket attack on London was the result of his intervention.

As Israeli forces advanced into Sinai on 29 October, Syrian troops prepared to enter Israel at dawn on the following morning. But the Egyptian Commander-in-Chief, General 'Abd al-Hakim Amir, ordered them to hold fast. The Syrian cabinet met to consider these instructions which it found so extraordinary that it cabled back that everything was ready for an assault. A second message then arrived from Amir confirming the order not to attack. The next day the Syrians learned of the Egyptian withdrawal in the face of the Anglo-French intervention. Had Syrian and Jordanian troops entered Israel as prearranged—an Egyptian-Syrian-Jordanian military pact had been concluded on 23 October—they would have been the only forces fighting the Jews. According to Mahmud Riyad, 'Abd al-Nasir considered that if Syria attacked Israel, Britain and France would probably invade Syria. Many Syrian officers called on the Egyptian ambassador in Damascus imploring him to let them fight for Egypt. It was, he told the author, a very moving spectacle.

The sabotage of the oil pipeline and pumping station early in November was not carried out on the orders of the Syrian Government or of the chief of military intelligence, 'Abd al-Hamid Sarraj. It was the independent work of young nationalists in the army, in the Ba'th Party, and among oil workers. No specific instructions were necessary in the climate of nationalist fervour which then existed. Indeed, it was naïve of Britain and France to suppose that Syria would allow Iraqi oil to flow through her territory if Egypt came under attack.

In less than two years, between January 1955 and October 1956, Syrian suspicion of Egypt and distaste for her military junta had turned into passionate championship of 'Abd al-Nasir and everything he stood for. Syria's allegiance constituted the clearest proof of his international stature as an Arab leader; Syria was the base from which he could assault British and Iraqi positions in Arab Asia. To these two Powers, therefore, the immediate threat in 1956 was not so much Soviet as Egyptian satellization of Syria, and it was to counter this danger that they conspired to overthrow the Syrian regime.

20

Syria's Road to Suez, II: The Western-Iraqi Counter-Attack

THE triumphant march of the fellow-travelling, pro-Egyptian factions in Syria in the year before Suez was bitterly opposed at home and abroad. But the firmer their hold on the machinery of government and on the levers of power throughout the country, the more their enemies were driven to think that only an armed rebellion could dislodge them and set Syria on a different path. While the Soviet-Egyptian advance was the dominant theme of Syrian history in 1956, preparations for a counter-attack by opposition groups in Syria and exiles outside the country, in league with Iraq, Britain, and the United States, were steadily continuing.

This plot against Syria, although overshadowed by the parallel drama of Suez, was no less instructive about the shifting relationships between the Near East and the Great Powers. It brought to a violent climax tensions which had been building up over many years. The need to resort to such desperate methods marked the inability of the western Powers, in the mid-1950s, to establish a working relationship with the new generation of nationalist leaders. The Soviet re-appraisal of Arab nationalism in 1954–6 was matched by no comparable intellectual and imaginative effort in the West. In a sense, the Russians' task was easier in that their theoreticians were unburdened by the habits and traditions of an acquired position of local supremacy. They had few local interests to defend and much to gain. But they, too, had their difficulties. Stalin had failed to appreciate the political importance of the colonial liberation movement. To the end, he appears to have thought exclusively in terms of the 'two world camps' in which there was no room for a third force.[1] His successors had to break out of this mould and do much fresh thinking

[1] See Curt Gasteyger, 'The Soviet Union and the Tiers Monde', in *Survey*, no. 43, Aug. 1962, p. 12.

before coming to recognize in local nationalist movements useful allies in the struggle against entrenched western positions. At a time, then, when the Russians were actively readjusting to the changing political scene, British policy was still based on the premise that her Middle East interests could best be defended by retaining political and military supremacy in the area and by an unyielding attitude towards local nationalism. Great Britain thus set herself against the current of popular feeling, driving radical nationalists such as the Ba'th into alliance with the Communists.

On one level, the conspiracy against Syria may be seen as a defensive reaction to the collapse of the Nuri–Eden vision of an Arab world under Iraqi leadership, harnessed to Britain through the Baghdad Pact. The success of this grand design had hinged on the control of Syria and on the isolation of the centre of opposition in Egypt. But 'Abd al-Nasir had turned the tables on the Baghdad Pact and had himself secured Syria's allegiance, establishing a strong base there. The western-Iraqi objective in 1956 was to eject him from it and roll back Egyptian influence from Arab Asia. Britain and her Iraqi friends realized that they must regain the initiative in Syria if Nasir were to be checked and the old positions of strength in Iraq, Jordan, and the Gulf defended. This argument was given force when, following the dismissal of General Glubb from the Arab Legion, Jordan tilted towards the Syrian-Egyptian camp in the spring of 1956.

On yet another level, the conspiracy seemed like a last fling in the long unrequited Hashimite flirtation with Syria: a final bid to unite the Fertile Crescent under a common crown. Whereas these dynastic ambitions had been quietly discouraged by Nuri and the British in the late 1940s and early 1950s, they now seemed less objectionable in the light of the bitter power struggle with 'Abd al-Nasir. Whereas French, Saudi, and Egyptian hostility to Fertile Crescent unity in the first post-war decade had inhibited Britain from promoting it, by the middle-1950s these factors had ceased to carry weight. Anglo-Saudi relations had been soured by the Buraimi dispute, while France's insistence on 'special rights' in Syria lost all reality once Britain was no longer her only rival there. By the spring of 1956 Britain was therefore persuaded to lend Iraq her support in a bid to wrest Syria from Egyptian influence—and with it the initiative in Arab Asia.

As for American policy, it was concerned neither with Hashimite dreams nor British interests. Largely insensitive to local issues, its almost exclusive preoccupation was the global task of erecting a ring of strong-points and military alliances around Soviet-controlled territory. Communist gains in Syria, rather than Egyptian influence there, brought about the implication of the United States in the conspiracy.

IRAQI POLICY AND TACTICS

The 1956 assault on Syria was not planned as a neat overnight *bouleversement*, hatched in a barracks by a handful of officers and announced at dawn to an unsuspecting populace. It was instead an untidy, sprawling, ill-managed intrigue which took shape between March and October 1956, gathering accomplices and hangers-on, before ending ingloriously in a Damascus court room. The details of the plot as revealed in court were substantially confirmed by another set of political trials conducted by General Qasim's revolutionary Government in Baghdad eighteen months later. Both the Syrian and the Iraqi sides of the affair have thus been chronicled in considerable detail.[2]

Iraq's interventions in Syria, like those of her rivals, Saudi Arabia and Egypt, usually took the form of paying subsidies to Syrian newspapers and politicians and of contributing to the support of small groups of Syrian exiles in Lebanon and elsewhere. Such forms of patronage were normally channelled through the Iraqi military attaché in Damascus—Colonel 'Abd al-Mutallib al-Amin in the early 1950s—who thus became a focus for pro-Iraqi sentiment in much the same way as the Saudi ambassador became the centre of a rival group.

Interventions by foreign envoys were indeed a recognized feature of the Syrian political scene and a factor to be weighed in any

---

[2] On the Damascus trials see:
  (a) Document 239: the Bill of Indictment in the Conspiracy against the Security of the State, 22 Dec. 1956 (published as Document 239 by the Bureau de documentations arabes, Damascus);
  (b) Document 243: the report on the conspiracy by 'Abd al-Hamid Sarraj, then head of military intelligence, as well as the proceedings of the court, 8 Jan.–26 Feb. 1957 (Document 243, Bureau de documentations arabes);
  (c) BBC, nos. 185 and 186, 1 & 2 Mar. 1957, appendix D for the judgment of the military court.

On the Baghdad trials see Iraq, Min. of Defence, *Mahkamat al-Sha'b* (*The People's Court*; *The Official Proceedings of the Special Military Court*, 1958), vol. i (later referred to as *Official Proceedings*).

The author has checked the main findings of both these trials in interviews with some of the leading defendants.

political appraisal. Major-General Ghazi al-Daghistani, former Deputy Chief of Staff of the Iraqi army, was one of the prominent servants of the old regime who was tried in Baghdad by the revolutionary Government in August 1958 on charges of conspiring against Syria. He opened his defence with the following sweeping apologia: 'Mr President, members of the Supreme Military Court, most Iraqi Governments have made it a principle to interfere in the internal affairs of Syria from the time of Husni al-Za'im if not earlier. . . .'[3]

As the trend in Syria ran against Iraq, the broad objective of Iraqi policy from 1949 onwards was to help her friends in Damascus to seize power, in the expectation that they would then declare union with Iraq. Iraqi aid contributed, for instance, to the overthrow of Za'im in August 1949 and of Shishakli in February 1954; but these were only the highlights of a continuing endeavour. Indeed, many Syrian public figures remained in Iraqi pay for years. But it should be noted, first, that Iraq left the planning and execution of the various coups very much to the Syrians themselves, supplying only the finance and such tactical advice as the military attaché might himself offer; and secondly, that her success was never more than limited: no Syrian Government that Iraq helped to bring to power ever went so far as to take active steps to bring about a Syrian-Iraqi union. Once in power Syrian politicians appeared to lose all immediate taste for union, although their cupidity was unaffected.

Some of the reasons for the failure to bring about an Iraqi-Syrian union in the first post-war decade have already been considered. The French, the Saudis, and the Egyptians were all opposed to it; Britain understood their different susceptibilities and was, in any event, reluctant to disturb her own dominant position in Iraq. The United States did not encourage a merger between Iraq and Syria, first in deference to Ibn Sa'ud and then, after 1954, to 'Abd al-Nasir. Leading Iraqi politicians were divided on the issue: while such men as Fadil al-Jamali, Tawfiq al-Suwaydi, and Salih Jabr tended to favour union, Ahmad Mukhtar Baban was on the whole opposed to an adventure in Syria. Nuri al-Sa'id himself was felt to be lukewarm: he appreciated that Iraq and Syria were both difficult countries to govern; united, the task might have been insuperable. He knew, too, that in the event of union, Syrians would dominate the economic life of Iraq; they were more educated, skilled, and sophisticated.

[3] *Official Proceedings*, p. 271.

Moreover, apart from the dynastic ambitions of her ruling house, Iraq's real interests in Syria were not extensive: she had no surplus peasantry to settle, nor did she covet Syria's wealth. She wanted primarily to secure the safety of her oil pipeline across Syria and, secondarily, to gain access to the Mediterranean, thus freeing her commerce from exclusive dependence on Basra. She was also concerned to prevent Syria falling under the control of a hostile Power which might threaten her security and check her influence in the Fertile Crescent area. But as these interests could clearly be defended by something short of a political union of the two countries, Iraq pursued the union ideal with a certain half-heartedness.

Iraq's resources were, in fact, dispersed over a number of different and often rival schemes. There was little overall co-ordination of effort. Iraqi military attachés—'Abd al-Mutallib al-Amin and his successor in Damascus and then, in Beirut, Salih Mehdi al-Samarra'i —nursed their local protégés, while the Regent, 'Abd ul-Ilah, encouraged his own favourites among the Syrian notables. Iraq sent a host of emissaries of uneven calibre and often unsuitable background to take the pulse of Syrian opinion. Syrians relate with wry amusement that one Iraqi envoy, arriving in Damascus in tribal costume, established himself in the salons of the Orient Palace Hotel where he expected the Syrians, increasingly under the influence of the younger radicals, to come and converse with him about unity. Indeed, from 1955 onwards, the succession of Iraqi ambassadors in Damascus was no match for the astute Egyptian envoy, Mahmud Riyad, who remained at his post for four years, until after the formation of the Syrian-Egyptian union. In any event, the Syrians, republican, neutralist, and hostile in their large majority to the Hashimites, soon found in 'Abd al-Nasir a more attractive focus for their own union hopes.

Repeated disappointments led to growing Iraqi disillusionment with their 'client' politicians in Syria and to a certain amount of mutual recrimination. The Syrians criticized the Iraqis for not doing enough for them, while Baghdad hoped and waited in vain for Damascus to make a spontaneous movement in its favour.

Gradually, in the 1950s, 'Abd ul-Ilah, Nuri, and some Syrians themselves came to be persuaded that only an armed invasion of Syria from Iraq could guarantee success. A detailed plan was drawn up, probably as early as 1953, for a three-pronged Iraqi assault striking at Aleppo, Homs, and Damascus. At his trial, General

Daghistani admitted to having received such a plan—referred to in court as Operation X—from its author, 'Abd al-Mutallib al-Amin, in 1954; but there was never any real threat of its execution. Both Daghistani and the Chief of Staff, Rafiq 'Arif, were opposed to the use of force against Syria. They took the view that a clash between the Iraqi and Syrian armies would be catastrophic for both countries, serving no one but Israel. Any union which might result would be a weak attachment. When the politicians, therefore, demanded action, the generals stalled, pointing at times to the lack of desert transport and at others to the shortage of aircraft or to the need to train pilots and lay down airstrips. As a result, the idea of armed intervention was never given full priority, and the Iraq Government fell back on the old strategy of encouraging Syrians themselves to carry out a coup.

But by 1956 plans for a change of regime in Syria had acquired a fresh urgency. The Nuri–Nasir conflict, arising over the Baghdad Pact and tirelessly conducted on either side by clandestine radio stations, had become a war to the death. Syrian contacts with the Soviet bloc seemed daily more extensive, while the Ba'th's advocacy of a Syrian-Egyptian union was beginning to cause real alarm in Baghdad. It was clear that something more than the old tactics of petty subversion would be required if 'Abd al-Nasir's hold on Syria were to be loosed and Communist infiltration checked.

The Iraqi army was then inevitably brought into the conspiracy. In the first place, rumours reached Baghdad that the Russians were laying down airstrips east of Aleppo and in the Palmyra area. These reports were no doubt exaggerated by Syrian politicians eager to enlist Iraq's support, but they were true to the extent that Russian and Czechoslovak officers had reconnoitered the Syrian desert between Syria and Iraq, while access to large tracts of this area was denied to the public; agents sent in by Iraq to investigate had been turned away.

Another reason for the army's involvement was the fear that, in the event of a disturbance in Syria, Israel might seize the opportunity to attack. The Iraqi general staff argued that Israeli forces could reach Damascus in six hours. They would then present the Arabs with a *fait accompli*, withdrawing only when the Arabs had agreed to hold peace talks and recognize their state. There is no evidence that this appraisal bore any relation to Israeli plans at the time, but these were the lines on which the Iraqis were thinking. Yet another fear was that if Iraq did not lend her support to overthrow the Syrian regime, opposition factions might turn for aid to France. The former Syrian dictator, Adib al-Shishakli, who had settled in France and had long had close relations with that country, was thought to be scheming to return to power in Damascus with French help. By the spring of 1956, Iraq was therefore more than usually determined to recapture the initiative in Syria and instal in Damascus a Government of her choice. On whom could she count?

THE SYRIAN EXILES

So frequent were the purges in Syria which followed the political upheavals from 1949 to 1955 that there were sometimes said to be more officers outside the Syrian army than inside it. Each coup d'état swelled the ranks of exiles in Lebanon across the mountains. To many of them the 1956 conspiracy must have seemed a chance to settle old scores and return home in triumph. It mobilized in a common cause many pockets of rebellion, many different currents of disaffection, bringing into temporary alliance men who had often been rivals for power but who had at different times been edged out of public life by the emergence of the dominant, left-wing pro-Egyptian trend.

Of all these rancorous exiles, the PPS formed the most militant and cohesive group. Hounded from Syria after Malki's murder, many of its leaders, such as Colonel Ghassan Jadid, had fled to Beirut whence they watched the trial and decimation of their party in Damascus and planned their revenge. Their strict discipline, paramilitary traditions, and fidelity to party doctrine made them a serious threat to the Syrian regime. On the fringe of their movement was another exiled officer, Captain Salah al-Shishakli, influential primarily as an intermediary with his brother, the former Syrian dictator Adib al-Shishakli, but also because of his family attachments in Hama, where he could be counted upon to raise a number of armed men in an emergency. Another important exile was Colonel Muhammad Safa, who had formed a 'Free Syrian Government' in Iraq in 1953–4 in opposition to Shishakli, but who had not shared in the spoils after the dictator's downfall. An abortive coup had then led to his flight from Syria. Bitter and resentful, his main objective was to gain reinstatement in the Syrian army. Yet another ex-officer, Major Muhammad Ma'ruf, had served as Director of Military Police during Hinnawi's brief, pro-Iraqi regime in 1949. These four men, Ghassan

Jadid, Salah al-Shishakli, Muhammad Safa, and Muhammad Ma'ruf and their respective associates were the chief instruments available in Lebanon for a clandestine assault on Syria in 1956. All four were separately in touch with the Iraqi military attaché in Beirut, Colonel Mehdi al-Samarra'i.

The PPS were the first to take the initiative. Members held a series of meetings in Beirut in the winter of 1955–6 attended by their leaders, Ghassan Jadid, Georges 'Abd al-Massih, Iskandar Shawi, and Sa'id Taki al-Din—the first three under sentence of death at home—to draw up a statement of aims which would unite opposition forces in Syria. They drew into their talks Salah al-Shishakli, Muhammad Ma'ruf, and also, it would appear from the published evidence, a number of Syrian politicians sympathetic to their cause such as 'Adnan al-Atasi, son of the former President Hashim al-Atasi. The draft charter on which they finally agreed called for a popular revolution which would sweep away the Syrian constitution, dismiss the Chamber, and set up a strong presidential regime; a new Government would then be formed drawn from the charter's signatories; sentences passed at the Malki trial would be revoked and steps taken to bring about the unity of the Fertile Crescent. The charter also provided for the immediate formation of a military and a political committee to recruit soldiers and civilians into the movement and draw up detailed plans for the coup.

The PPS had enjoyed close relations with Adib al-Shishakli in the first years of his rule in Damascus. Casting around for allies, they now decided to try and interest him in their new bid for power. In April 1956 Salah al-Shishakli and Muhammad Ma'ruf were accordingly sent on a mission to the former dictator in Paris. Adib was encouraging, but advised them first to make overtures to Iraq. He suggested that the Iraq Government be requested to send a senior official to meet him in Geneva and discuss what part Iraq might wish to play in the conspiracy.

THE FIRST PHASE: APRIL–JULY 1956

An account of what then took place in Baghdad is given in General Daghistani's defence statement in court:

At about this time (spring 1956), as I believe, a meeting was held at the Palace to discuss the Syrian situation in general. It was attended by Faysal, 'Abd ul-Ilah, and the ministers, among whom I remember Nuri, Ahmad Mukhtar Baban, Burhan Bashayan, and 'Abdallah Baqr. I and my colleague 'Arif (the Chief of Staff) were asked to attend as representing the army.

We were informed in the course of this meeting that Adib al-Shishakli had asked for someone to be sent to meet him in Switzerland and it was at first the intention to send Bashayan (the Foreign Minister). But after further discussion it was decided to send an officer, as Shishakli himself was primarily a soldier and it would be easier for him to come to an understanding with an officer.

I was then ordered to go, which I did, meeting him once in Switzerland. He informed me that he intended to carry out a coup in Syria and wanted Iraq to acknowledge his Government. In return, he would change his former policy towards Iraq and adopt a friendly attitude. He also asked for financial help, explaining that he needed 30,000 dinars as a first instalment which should be handed to him in Beirut.

I then returned and informed the Government of what had taken place at another meeting at the Palace. . . . It was decided to comply with his demand and it was suggested that I should meet him in Beirut and hand over the amount. . . .[4]

Adib al-Shishakli arrived clandestinely in Beirut in July 1956. The PPS provided him with a car and a body-guard, arranging for him to spend the night at different addresses to avoid detection. Almost his first move was to summon two former associates from Damascus, Burhan Adham and Hamdi Salih, whom he cross-examined on the political situation in Syria and on the mood of the army. (His choice of advisers was unfortunate as both later became police informers and gave the plot away to the Syrian authorities.)

Shishakli presided over a number of meetings attended by the leading conspirators—his brother Salah, Muhammad Ma'ruf, the PPS leaders, and Burhan Adham—at which Ghassan Jadid outlined their plans for a coup. Jadid made it clear that the PPS did not believe success could be assured without the assassination of Akram al-Hawrani, Khalid Baqdash, 'Abd al-Hamid Sarraj, and a number of other young officers. Assassination squads were being prepared for the task.

But these plans were too sanguinary for Shishakli, who may have feared reprisals against his family in Hama. Moreover, he was sceptical of Jadid's confident assurances of massive support in the Syrian army. The odds seemed to him formidable and the resources of the conspirators derisory. He was too experienced and shrewd a *putschist* to commit himself to so foolhardy an enterprise. He therefore

---

[4] *Official Proceedings*, p. 272.

departed, waiting only long enough to collect from the Iraqis such funds as he could.

As Daghistani relates in his defence statement:

I went to Beirut, but after meeting Shishakli I did not turn over the whole amount to him but only 10,000 dinars on my own responsibility because I doubted his intentions. I deposited the rest of the money in the safe of the military attaché in Beirut where it was entered in the books. On the following day I heard that Shishakli had left Beirut and had disappeared. He had promised to meet me again and to let me know his plans and intentions. . . .

I returned and informed the Government of what had taken place at another meeting at the Palace, attended, so far as I remember, by the same ministers. . . . I hope they will remember, because it appears that most of them have forgotten or claim to have forgotten that they themselves approved my not giving him the whole sum in view of what happened later. . . .

With the disappearance of its leading figure, the first phase of the conspiracy fizzled out with no great loss except to Iraqi funds and to Salah al-Shishakli's authority: he had tried in vain to prevent his brother's precipitate departure.

THE SECOND PHASE: JULY–NOVEMBER 1956

Britain and the United States were by this time fully apprised of what was going on. The conspirators are believed to have approached British representatives in Beirut with requests for help as early as March 1956. General Glubb's dismissal in that month, following hard on the failure of the Templer mission to Jordan,[5] had brought to a head British hostility to 'Abd al-Nasir to whom these reverses were attributed. Both London and Washington had also become concerned at the quickening pace of Soviet penetration of Syria and Egypt since the announcement of Egypt's 'Czech' arms deal. To 'stop the rot', the battle for Syria would have to be engaged. The door was therefore not slammed in the conspirators' faces.

By midsummer an Anglo-American-Iraqi committee had been set up in Beirut to exchange intelligence, consider the international aspects of the plot, and examine plans and suggestions put up to it by the Syrians. But the Iraqis were eager that they alone should act

---

[5] As a result of Jordanian official inquiries about the Baghdad Pact, in December 1955 Gen. Sir Gerald Templer, CIGS, went to Jordan for discussions, but the visit gave rise to demonstrations against the Pact, which Jordan did not join.

as intermediaries between this controlling body and the Syrians. Daghistani explains in his defence that Britain and the United States were brought in to lend a hand in case the affair took on international proportions. Their chief role, he said, was to forestall Israeli, French, or Turkish intervention in Syria in the event of a pro-Iraqi coup, but he makes clear that they also contributed money and arms.

Shishakli's defection caused the conspirators only momentary dismay; they resolved to go ahead without him. Colonel Muhammad Safa, who had played little or no role in the first phase of the conspiracy largely because of his ancient feud with Shishakli, was now brought in although he was on scarcely better terms with the PPS leader, Ghassan Jadid. A go-between, Major Husayn Hakim, another exiled Syrian officer, enabled the two men to negotiate a working agreement and merge their respective factions in face of the common enemy.

On Shishakli's departure in July 1956, General Daghistani presided over a full meeting of the conspirators to take stock of the situation. All the leading figures were present: Jadid, Safa, Salah al-Shishakli, Muhammad Ma'ruf, Taki al-Din, and the Iraqi military attaché, Colonel Salih Mehdi al-Samarra'i. It was decided to push ahead with the para-military preparations and recruit politicians ready to assume power after the coup. Colonel Safa was charged with the task of drafting a fresh charter or statement of aims, to which all the chief conspirators put their signature, and they swore fidelity at another secret meeting in the Lebanese village of Shemlan on 11 August. The PPS were in the meantime busy training an assault force: some 300 young men were put through a combat course at Beit Meri in the Lebanese mountains.

There remained the crucial question of the scale of Iraq's contribution—a subject on which the exiles tended to hold inflated views. Daghistani relates in his defence statement that they requested no less than 20,000 weapons and one million dinars. They also asked for facilities to train Syrian volunteers at military camps in Iraq, and for a guarantee of Iraqi military support in the event of help reaching their opponents from neighbouring Arab states. Iraq, however, not only rejected their request for training facilities but also made it clear that her troops would not be used in support of the coup except in the event of Israeli attack or of a Communist intervention by sea from Albania or by air over Turkey. As for arms and finance, the exiles' demands were scaled down to a mere 2,000 weapons and

100,000 dinars.[6] Daghistani revealed that some weapons were supplied by the United States, while others were bought in Italy with allocations from the Iraqi Foreign Ministry budget.

Iraq's relative parsimony had several causes. In the first place, the Iraq Government had a budget—unlike its Saudi rival whose counter-expenditure on 'public relations' in Syria must have been several times greater. It would no doubt have been in Iraq's interest to spend up to £10 million to secure the safety of the oil pipeline and gain access to the Mediterranean, but the Government could not dispose of even half a million without facing awkward questions. Moreover, even though the Iraqis had good reason to be aware of the cupidity of Syrian politicians, they held somewhat ingenuously that they need not bribe the common man in Syria, so strong were the natural and brotherly ties between the two countries. A detail taken at random from the proceedings of the Damascus trials throws light on the scale of the operations: the conspirators sent £50 to a café proprietor in Hama so that he could offer free drinks and recruit likely young men into the movement.

But no brief account can properly describe the feverish, clandestine activity of the pre-Suez months in Beirut. Quarrels broke out between the various factions and were laboriously made up. Dates were fixed for the coup and then put back. More energy was expended on exchanging pledges, drafting charters, and jostling to step into the main stream of foreign bribe money than in cool planning to unseat the regime in Damascus. Colonels Safa and Jadid, their differences never quite papered over, competed for the private ear of the Iraqis, although both were members of the military committee which formed the fighting core of the conspiracy. There is also some evidence to suggest that Britain and the United States, while sitting together on the co-ordinating committee, never wholly concerted their efforts; each Power had its favourites both in Syria and among the Beirut exiles to whom it gave private support. The PPS was itself rent by internal feuds. A move by the party president, As'ad al-Ashqar, to arraign Georges 'Abd al-Masih before a party court for his alleged responsibility for Malki's murder, failed when Masih refused to

---

[6] *Official Proceedings*, pp. 273–4. The Syrian intelligence chief, 'Abd al-Hamid Sarraj, advances the figures of 5,000 weapons and 2,250,000 Lebanese pounds in his report (Document 243, p. 5); reliable sources estimate the Iraqi contribution to the funds of the conspiracy in Beirut at about 200,000 dinars. This does not include payments made by the Regent to his Syrian friends. The exact figures will no doubt never be known.

appear. He was, as a result, 'isolated' from party activity and subsequently expelled, taking with him about a hundred members. But whereas the core of 'activists' was divided, the outer fringe of disgruntled, talkative politicians privy to the conspiracy was still less of an effective force. Consumed with impatience, these men waited for their enemies to be destroyed and power to be handed to them. The political committee in which they were loosely gathered was less a planning body or a shadow cabinet than a list of men who, it was hoped, would help secure a pro-Iraqi vote in the Syrian Chamber once the coup had paved the way for new elections.

Of all these, perhaps the most considerable personality was the Aleppo notable and National Party leader Mikhail Ilyan who, in previous years, had spent a good part of his personal fortune in promoting the cause of union with Iraq. (His rivals were quick to point out that he had been largely reimbursed later by Iraqi subsidies.) He was a close personal friend of Prince 'Abd ul-Ilah, so that his association with the conspiracy took place at the highest level, bypassing the petty squabbles of Beirut. Indeed, Iraq would have liked to see him Prime Minister of Syria. But although courageous and energetic, Ilyan suffered from the crippling disability that he was a Christian: in his own native city he could command no more than minority support. It was, therefore, at the very least unrealistic to have cast him in the role of a Syrian national leader.

Other prominent political figures to be drawn into the movement included 'Adnan al-Atasi, a former ambassador in Paris and a leading member of the People's Party, and his cousin Faydi al-Atasi, a former Foreign Minister; Munir al-'Ajlani, a professor of law at Damascus university well known for his Hashimite sympathies; Sami Kabbara, a former Minister of Justice during Hinnawi's regime and publisher of the newspaper *al-Nidal*; Shaikh Hail al-Surur, a tribal leader,[7] and the Druze notable, Amir Hasan al-Atrash. As was the case with the military committee, these politicians expended more energy in reaching agreement among themselves than in planning the enemy's defeat. The PPS were known, for instance, to have plans to exploit the situation created by the coup to form a Government on their own and proceed with their pan-Syrian plans; it was only with the greatest difficulty that they were persuaded to accept a more modest share of the projected fruits of victory. It was agreed that if the coup were successful they would be allowed to

---

[7] From the village of Umm al-Jimal on the Jordanian-Syrian border.

function legally once again as a political party; but they were refused seats in the future cabinet on the ground that their inclusion might give the Government a bad name.

The shape of this new regime was necessarily left rather vague. The Iraqis and their Great Power allies knew that the conspiracy as a whole was split by group, party, and personal conflicts. Their only hope was to keep the alliance together until the moment of the coup, fully expecting that it would then disintegrate—by which time, it was hoped, Syria's left-wing pro-Egyptian Government would have been otherthrown. In so far as they looked beyond this point, they envisaged the formation of a transitional Government drawn from the ranks of the political committee; the purging of socialists and Communists from the ranks of the army and security forces; the holding of elections from which members of these parties would be excluded and, finally, a vote by the new Chamber for union with Iraq.

Meanwhile the conspirators in Beirut redoubled their activity in the late summer of 1956, recruiting fresh members into the military and political committees,[8] making contact with the Druzes, the Alawis, and the tribes and generally spending money on propaganda in a bid to win popular support for their cause. Arms and ammunition were flown from Iraq to swell the PPS armouries, and then smuggled into Syria.

The conspirators were agreed that the PPS should provide the shock-troops. Their para-military force of young men was to infiltrate across the border into Syria, seize key centres in Damascus disguised as military police, and carry out the assassinations as planned. At the same time Ghassan Jadid was to occupy Homs at the head of another PPS force while Salah al-Shishakli was to seize Hama with the help of his men there. The Druzes in the south and the Alawis in the west were then to rise so as to draw off government troops.

In October 1956 Iraq concentrated troops on the Jordanian frontier in support of the projected Syrian coup and to forestall a possible Israeli intervention in Jordan. But these concentrations were only of brigade strength. No preparations were made for a full-scale Iraqi invasion of Syria. The Iraqi general staff wanted at all costs to avoid a clash between the Syrian and Iraqi armies. But, in any event, General Daghistani did not rate high the chances of success.

[8] Membership of the political committee was finally established as follows: Mikhail Ilyan, 'Adnan al-Atasi, Munir al-'Ajlani, Jalal al-Sayyid, Hasan al-Atrash, Sa'id Taki al-Din, Muhammad Fadil (see Document 243, p. 86).

After looking at the situation in Beirut [he told the Baghdad court] and seeing the half-heartedness and the doubts of the various groups which took part in the work; knowing also of the connexion between some of them and the [Syrian] *deuxième bureau*, I was sure that the plot would fail.[9]

Daghistani was right. Throughout the late summer and early autumn of 1956, the Syrian intelligence chief, Colonel 'Abd al-Hamid Sarraj, patiently pieced together the jigsaw puzzle as reports from his agents reached him in Damascus. The conspiracy was so far-flung, so labyrinthine, that he could not be sure of uncovering the whole of it. He knew an assault was being planned but when and where it would be launched was uncertain. Were the intrigues of the exiles in Beirut merely part of a plan which would include a western armed intervention in Syria? As the arms build-up proceeded against Egypt in the immediate pre-Suez weeks it seemed clear that Syria, 'Abd al-Nasir's closest ally, was threatened also. And when Egypt was finally attacked, Syria prepared for invasion.

It was at that moment, in the last days of October 1956, that the Syrian authorities learned that several hundred rifles had been smuggled in from Iraq and distributed among the Druzes and the Beduin of south Syria. The Druzes, traditionally hostile to rule from Damascus, have played so prominent a role in Syria's many upheavals that all would-be revolutionaries seek their aid. The Beirut exiles were no exception. They knew that to give substance to their demands for arms from Iraq, they must be able to claim the support of the Druzes. The PPS therefore made persistent efforts to win them over to the conspiracy.

The Druze leader, Hasan al-Atrash, had been active in the political wing of the movement. He and his friends had sought to harass and overthrow the Syrian Government by organizing a parliamentary front, backed by friendly newspapers.[10] But Hasan claims to have had no direct knowledge of the arms smuggling or of the more violent aspects of the plot. Indeed, he was at odds with the PPS because of their support of Adib al-Shishakli in 1953–4 and so had no direct relations with them. The PPS strategy, then, was to implicate Hasan by drawing into their net such Druze protégés of the Atrash family as the ex-officers Shakib Wahab and Fadlallah Abu Mansur (whose

[9] *Official Proceedings*, p. 279.
[10] Hasan al-Atrash's secretary and right-hand man, Salman Hamzeh, bought the Damascus newspaper *Alif Ba'* in mid-1956 and ran it until January 1957.

role in the 1949 coups will be recalled), an aged Druze deputy, Fadlallah Jarbu, who owed his seat largely to Hasan's influence, and other retainers.

Hasan al-Atrash gives the following account of the arms smuggling incident:

> Shakib Wahab advised the PPS to ask Iraq for arms in my name, as this might seem to offer some chance of success. An agreement was eventually reached to take delivery at the Iraqi frontier of 800 rifles, 500 for the Druzes and 300 for the Masa'id beduin led by Hail al-Surur.
>
> Shakib then hired an ex-officer, Faris Duei'er, to lead the arms convoy across the desert. Faris, accompanied by some beduin, collected the arms at the frontier and headed back for the Jabal Druze. But his truck broke down and the arms were pillaged by some 300 beduin and local Druze villagers who rapidly dispersed with the loot. Faris Duei'er, instead of going into hiding, quietly returned to his village as if nothing had happened.
>
> The authorities very soon got to know of the distribution of such a large number of weapons. They rounded up some villagers who at once gave Faris Duei'er's name. He was arrested and, under interrogation, gave the names of all my friends and associates who were connected with the conspiracy. It was only when the arms were already on their way to the Jabal that Hail al-Surur came to tell me about them.
>
> By this time, the Anglo-French attack on Egypt had begun and I was furious at being implicated in so ill-managed a plot. Did the conspirators in Beirut think that I could take on the whole Syrian army with 500 rifles?[11]

Thus by early November 1956 the Jabal was disarmed and the Syrian Government felt safe from attack from this quarter. In the meantime the tripartite attack on Egypt had run into difficulties and Syria viewed with less anxiety the possibility of invasion. On 23 November Sarraj felt confident enough to announce the uncovering of the plot over Damascus radio:[12]

> At a time when the Anglo-French-Israeli forces of iniquity and aggression were invading Egypt, our courageous brother country, with a ferocity unexampled in history; at a time when all units of the Syrian army were mobilized, proud to play their part, side by side with the Egyptian and Jordanian units, in the battle for national honour, according to the dictates of brotherhood and the common cause; at this solemn and critical moment the Syrian military authorities discovered large quantities of military weapons which were being smuggled into Syria from a neighbouring

---

[11] Hasan al-Atrash to the author, Beirut, 24 Oct. 1960.
[12] *Orient*, no. 2, Apr. 1957, p. 170.

country. An inquiry held as the result of this discovery was successful in arresting the culprits who were preparing to stab their nation, their country, their army in the back.

Preliminary investigations brought to light the group with whom the culprits were dealing. It is with a heavy heart that we reveal that this was a Government we hoped to see at our side on the day of battle, even though it had taken the wrong political road of imperialist pacts.

We undertake . . . to arrest all these accomplices and bring them to trial . . . so that they may be judged and their shameful treachery . . . may be justly punished.

As for that Government, the Government of Nuri al-Saʻid in Iraq, which instigated these wretches to plot against us for the benefit of the enemy and of Israel, we are certain that the wronged and gallant Arab people will settle their account. For this nation has never been wanting in forcefulness; from the time of Khalid ibn Walid and al-Rashid to the day of the decisive national battle, it has always been heroic. The hour of revenge has come.

A Bill of Indictment published on 22 December 1956 listed 47 accused, including the former dictator Adib al-Shishakli; the 'activist' leaders of the conspiracy, Muhammad Safa, Ghassan Jadid, Muhammad Maʻruf, Salah al-Shishakli, and Saʻid Taki al-Din; the Druze notable Hasan al-Atrash; the tribal chief Hail al-Surur; prominent members of the political committee such as Mikhail Ilyan, ʻAdnan al-Atasi, Munir al-ʻAjlani, Sami Kabbara, and a host of smaller fry. The trial opened on 8 January 1957 in the amphi-theatre of Damascus university with Colonel ʻAfif al-Bizri as president of the military court. The hearings ended five weeks later and the sentences were pronounced on 27 February. But nineteen of the accused, including many of the principal figures, were abroad and were sentenced, many of them to death, in their absence. A week or so earlier, Ghassan Jadid was murdered in a Beirut street.[13]

Was the conspiracy against Syria timed to coincide with the attack on Egypt? Were both operations part of a master-plan to overthrow ʻAbd al-Nasir and his Syrian allies and set up a new order in the Middle East? Some of the conspirators came to hold this opinion. Thus Dr ʻAbdallah Saʻada (a future president of the PPS, implicated in an abortive coup in Lebanon on 31 December 1961) said later:

---

[13] He was shot dead in a main street on 19 February by a Syrian named ʻIzzat Shath who was himself killed after an exchange of fire with the police. The shot which actually killed the murderer is said to have been fired by another Syrian, ʻAziz Zayyub, who was wounded and arrested.

After the collapse of the movement it became clear that our Great Power backers, and Britain in particular, had timed the conspiracy to coincide with Suez. Ghassan Jadid received instructions from the Iraqis to carry out the coup on a particular day at the end of October 1956. But he felt that as he was the military commander on the spot it was up to him to fix the day most suitable for the deployment of his forces. He refused to be tied to the date requested by the Iraqis. They insisted but he stood firm. It was then that the attack on Egypt was launched on the very day the Iraqis had been pressing for. In my view, the Iraqis were as much in the dark as we were. They were merely transmitting instructions given them by the British.[14]

Evidence submitted at the trials does not wholly support or disprove this hypothesis. One witness said that 28 October had been fixed as the day of the coup;[15] other sources reported that at the last moment the date had been deferred to 3 November. It is not clear whether these dates were chosen to match the timetable of the Suez operation or whether they were determined by purely local Syrian factors. Thus the conspirators may first have planned to carry out the coup before President Quwatli left for Moscow on 30 October, but then have thought it preferable to act in his absence. 'Abd al-Hamid Sarraj inclines to a broader strategy: 'The 1956 plot against Syria', he said later, 'seemed specifically aimed at preventing us intervening in the Suez war and at swinging Syria into the orbit of the Baghdad Pact in the confusion which would follow the attack on Egypt.'[16]

On balance, it seems unlikely that the assaults on Syria and on Egypt were carefully co-ordinated. The Americans were partners in the first but reproved the second; the Iraqis, also partners in the assault on Syria, were aghast at evidence of Anglo-French collusion with Israel; the French were associated in the assault on Egypt but took no part in the conspiracy against Syria.[17] Britain alone had a hand in both operations, but much of the official British hierarchy, in the Foreign Office and other government departments, was itself kept in ignorance of what was being planned. The two operations, then, may not have been master-minded, but they shared a common

[14] Dr 'Abdallah Sa'ada to the author, Beirut, 1 Dec. 1960.
[15] An Egyptian journalist, Mahmud Sa'di of al-Gumhuriya, appearing as a witness, said that he had been given this date by the PPS leader Sa'id Taki al-Din at an interview on 11 January 1957 (see Document 243, p. 38).
[16] 'Abd al-Hamid Sarraj to the author, Cairo, 27 Jan. 1961.
[17] In fact, the conspirators in Beirut were spurred to action in October 1956 by reports that the French were independently arming the Alawis. The Iraqis and their allies did not want a pro-French group to seize power.

objective: to unseat 'Abd al-Nasir and check the expansion of Egyptian and Soviet influence in Arab Asia. To this extent at least they were part of the same strategy. Indeed, the Suez operation and the fierce emotions which it reflected can best be understood if linked to the struggle against Nasirism on the hinterland of Arab Asia, of which the abortive conspiracy against Syria is perhaps the best example.

But just as 'Abd al-Nasir emerged strengthened from the trial of Suez, so the failure of the conspiracy powerfully reinforced the radical, pro-Egyptian factions in Syria by eliminating from the scene their most dangerous opponents. The triumvirate of Akram al-Hawrani, Khalid al-'Azm, and Khalid Baqdash ruled supreme, backed by 'Abd al-Hamid Sarraj, the taciturn, coldly competent chief of the *deuxième bureau*. Sarraj was indeed the real victor of the contest. His handling of the inquiry into 'Adnan al-Malki's murder in 1955 had first brought him to the attention of the public. Now, the uncovering of the 'Iraqi plot' confirmed him as a tireless guardian of the nation's security. This sullen young man with the square jaw and the perpetually puckered brow had become the eyes and ears of beleaguered Syria. Not an ant moves but Sarraj knows about it, the people said.

His accusations cut ruthlessly into the tangle of family patronage and local loyalties which make up much of the substructure of Syrian politics. Many of the men he put on trial bore respected names: Atasi, Ilyan, 'Ajlani, Atrash. They were also members of parliament, their immunity set aside by the state of emergency. They had in common their pro-Iraqi sympathies, their leanings towards the West, their traditionalism, their distaste for the extremes of nationalism. To Sarraj, they were all traitors.

The trial [he told an Egyptian journalist][18] perfectly illustrates President Nasir's lucid views on the feudalists and career politicians. Before taking action against the chief enemies of Egypt, your President managed to liquidate these agents of imperialism. . . . He was thus able to turn with full confidence against those who had colonized his country, without running the risk of suffering the unhappy fate of Musaddiq and being stabbed in the back by his fellow countrymen.

Michel 'Aflaq too, writing in his party newspaper, placed full responsibility for the conspiracy on 'a social class driven to treachery

[18] Quoted in *Le Monde*, 2 Mar. 1957.

in defence of its interests'.[19] But by the time these statements were made, the purge of the 'traitors' was already well under way.

Within a few days of the uncovering of the plot, the Ba'th clamoured for a 'national parliamentary front' to defeat imperialist machinations and a new Government better suited to defend the nation's integrity. The Communists, glad to let the Ba'th set the pace, gave their eager assent. On 31 December 1956 Sabri al-'Asali reshuffled his cabinet,[20] excluding the People's Party and Munir al-'Ajlani's Constitutional Front, both implicated in the conspiracy. The Ba'th retained their commanding posts at the Ministries of Economy and Foreign Affairs, while Khalid al-'Azm entered the cabinet as Minister of Defence.

All the currents and emotions which had racked Syrian opinion in the two years since the signature of the Baghdad Pact were now brought to a violent climax: solidarity with Egypt, hatred of Nuri al-Sa'id, suspicion of Britain, fear of Turkey, gratitude towards the Soviet Union. 'Asali undertook to begin immediate negotiations with Egypt for a federal union of the two countries; attempts were made to prize Jordan away from the British alliance by substituting Arab funds for the British subsidy;[21] Nuri became the butt of ever more strident attacks: he was an 'ally of the Jews', a 'valet of colonialism', a 'traitor and tyrant such as the East had never known'. Meanwhile the Communists in Syria became daily more high-handed. Thus, the collapse of the western-Iraqi counter-attack decisively altered the balance of forces inside the country leaving Syria still more exposed to the violent gusts of 1957, and inviting the disturbing attention of the greatest Powers of all.

---

[19] al-Ba'th (Damascus), 18 Jan. 1957.
[20] Premier & Min. of Interior, Sabri al-'Asali (NP); Foreign Affairs, Salah al-Bitar (Ba'th); Economy, Khalil Kallas (Ba'th); Defence, Khalid al-'Azm (Dem. Bloc); Agriculture, Hamid al-Khuja (Dem. Bloc); Min. of State, Salih 'Akil (Dem. Bloc); Public Works, Fakhir al-Kayyali (NP); Public Health, As'ad Harun (NP); Education, Hani al-Siba'i (Ind.); Finance, As'ad Mahasin (Ind.); Justice, Ma'mun al-Kuzbari (Arab Lib. Movt).
[21] A convention of Arab solidarity was signed in Cairo on 18 January 1957 whereby Saudi Arabia, Egypt, and Syria undertook to pay the Jordanian Government an annual sum of £E12 million.

21

America Single-Handed

THE SETTING

THE British action against Egypt, whether those who were responsible were aware of it or not, was an attempt to reassert British strength as the final decisive factor in Near Eastern politics: to say, in effect, that when interests or ideas of policy clashed, it was British interests or British conceptions of policy which should be supreme. It was an action which could succeed only if the other Powers were willing to allow the Near East to be, in the last resort, a British preserve; if they were willing not to use their strength, or to use it only in support of England. Quite apart from the moral repugnance aroused by the manner of the action, it was a challenge to the essential interests of Russia and also of the United States; for it implied that, on issues which were bound to affect the whole network of American relations with all parts of the world, the final decisions should be made not by the United States but by England. It therefore led inevitably to the intervention of the two greatest Powers.[1]

After Suez, then, Russia and the United States found themselves face to face in the Middle East. America was there as Britain's heir: called in a decade earlier to shore up Greece and Turkey against Soviet pressure, she found herself by 1957 in the unnerving role of sole champion of western interests in much of the Arab world. Russia had elbowed her way into the area over the previous two years by recognizing and enlisting Arab nationalism as an ally against the West, by arms deals, trade, and aid. Both Powers now sought, in characteristic style, to consolidate and legitimize their new positions of strength.

Soviet strategy was to make direct contact with the Arab public, to demand the full reward in Arab gratitude and admiration for Russia's role at Suez, to redouble offers of aid, friendship, and arms, and to seek recognition, meanwhile, of her right to a voice in Middle East affairs by calling repeatedly for a Great Power declaration renouncing the use of force in the area.

[1] Hourani, *A Vision of History*, p. 140.

The American retort was the Eisenhower Doctrine, which gave notice to the world that the United States had assumed new Middle East responsibilities. But if the Doctrine branded International Communism (always spelled with ominous capitals by Mr Dulles) as the sole enemy, United States diplomacy was sometimes hard put in practice to identify this animal in the jungle of Arab politics. Some of the shots went wild. Indeed, the Soviet-American confrontation did not long remain on a two-Power basis for it was soon enmeshed in a tangle of local issues which largely determined the terrain on which it was fought. Of all these local factors, Egypt's bid for Arab hegemony was perhaps the most important.

Since 1954, as has been seen, 'Abd al-Nasir had struggled to impose his conceptions of policy on the other Arab states. He had called on the Arabs to unite under his leadership, to adopt a common foreign policy, to free the area from all trace of Great Power tutelage, and to undertake its defence by their own unaided efforts. In support of his claim to leadership, he had tried to channel the two most powerful currents of political sentiment then at work in Arab opinion: the desire for Arab union and the fear and hatred of Israel. These emotions were widespread, but Nasir's attempts to use them for his own political ends were contested. He had to face, in particular, a challenge from Iraq as well as from Britain—Egypt's main Middle East rival in the whole post-war period. Yet he had been successful in the early encounters and his reward had been to see his influence unfurl over Arab Asia. The keystone of this success was his alliance with Syria, forged during the battle over the Baghdad Pact and strengthened by each succeeding crisis. With Syria at his side, he need fear no local alliance against him. He could also, from this central base in Arab Asia, threaten his Arab rivals on their home ground and bring pressure to bear on Britain's remaining strongpoints and centres of influence in the region.

Having turned defeat into triumph at Suez, 'Abd al-Nasir was eager, as was the Soviet Union, to exploit these further important gains in popular sentiment throughout the Arab world. He could not agree to the conscription of the Arab states against a Power which had been his chief support since the 1955 arms deal. He could not tamely acquiesce in an American overlordship such as was implicit in the Eisenhower Doctrine; in particular, he could not tolerate American pressure on Syria, which might weaken his own hold on that country and shift the balance of power against him in the area.

Had Syria then slipped from 'Abd al-Nasir's grasp, Suez would indeed have meant defeat.

In 1957 Syria was thus once more the focal point for rivalries between the Great Powers and at the same time the nub of Egypt's struggle for local primacy. But before examining the Syrian crisis of 1957—which by midsummer was taking up a very large part of Mr Dulles's time[2]—it is necessary to look briefly at the preoccupations concerning Soviet intentions which shaped American policy at this time.

THE EISENHOWER DOCTRINE

The Eisenhower Doctrine was devised to meet what was thought to be an imminent Soviet threat to the Middle East in the disturbed aftermath of Suez. Mr Dulles believed that the Russians might seize the opportunity created by the embarrassment in which Britain and France then found themselves to make an overt bid for control of the area, either by armed attack or internal subversion. Soviet ground, naval, and air forces were stationed in force on the frontiers of the Middle East: in Bulgaria, in the Black Sea area, in the Ukraine, the Caucasus, and Central Asia. Moreover the Anglo-French fiasco at Suez had created a vacuum of influence, removing a serious deterrent to Communist penetration. Finally, the Soviet Union had demonstrated in Hungary her willingness to use brute force. What she had done in Europe, she might attempt in the Arab world. Mr Dulles argued, then, that three things were clear: the Soviet capacity, the temptation, and the lack of any moral restraints.[3]

To this external military threat was added the fear of internal subversion: the ground had been prepared by Communist infiltration and propaganda and by the dangers of a financial crisis in countries deprived of oil revenues by the closure of the Suez Canal and of the trans-Syrian pipeline from Iraq. 'I can assure you', Mr Dulles warned, 'that the leaders of International Communism will take every risk that they dare in order to win the Middle East'.[4]

---

[2] *New York Times*, 21 Aug. 1957.
[3] See a statement by Secretary of State Dulles before a Joint Session of the Foreign Relations and Armed Services Commissions of the Senate, 14 January 1957, in U.S. Dept of State, *United States Policy in the Middle East, September 1956–June 1957* (1957), p. 31. This volume assembles many of the key American documents of the period including statements by President Eisenhower at his News Conference on 14 November 1956; his Message to Congress on 5 January 1957; the Joint Resolution introduced in the Congress on the same day, as well as statements by Dulles in the following weeks.
[4] Ibid. p. 38.

These dangers seemed very real to the American Administration and urgent measures were thought necessary to counter them. On 5 January 1957 President Eisenhower sought Congressional authority to use the armed forces of the United States to protect any Middle East state requesting assistance 'against overt armed aggression from any nation controlled by International Communism'; and to offer aid to a total of $200 million to strengthen internal security and promote orderly government; the money was to be drawn from funds already available under the Mutual Security Act for use in the remaining months of the 1957 fiscal year ending on 30 June.[5]

These measures were approved by Congress in a Joint Resolution of the Senate and House on 9 March 1957. Three days later, on 12 March, President Eisenhower sent James P. Richards, his newly-appointed Special Assistant for Middle East affairs and former chairman of the House Foreign Affairs Committee, on a tour of the Middle East to explain the purposes of the resolution and report on the most effective ways of carrying it out.[6] Ten days later, on 23 March, the United States joined the Military Committee of the Baghdad Pact.

This activity reflected American's alarm at finding herself alone in the field against the forces of 'International Communism' in as vital an area of the 'free world' as the Middle East. The danger had to be clearly demonstrated and American will mobilized to meet it. This was the ultimate rationale of a Doctrine which seemed better designed to stiffen America's resolve than to reassure the countries whose protection she thus unilaterally assumed. The Doctrine was an expression of how America saw the world and, in particular, of how the Eisenhower Administration viewed the implacable struggle with the Communist camp. There was no room for compromise or middle ground. No allowance was made for the extent to which cold war labels had been put to work in local inter-Arab disputes, blurring issues which to Americans might seem crystal clear. By endorsing the Doctrine, for example, an Arab state would be forced to make a public stand not only against Russia but also against an Arab neighbour. Moreover, by demanding alignment against the East, the Doctrine closed the door to the possibility of Arab dealings with the West without political strings. These were some of the weaknesses of the policy, as indeed of the absolutist conception of international

[5] Ibid. p. 20.
[6] The choice of Mr Richards, a Democrat, was no doubt also intended to increase support for the President in Congress.

affairs associated with the name of Mr Dulles. But were the Secretary's fears of an imminent Communist take-over justified?

It was obvious that Russia's vociferous support for Egypt at Suez had made a great impact on the Arab mind: the current of pro-Soviet sentiment set in motion by the 'Czech' arms deal of 1955 now swelled into something like a tidal wave. Evidence of the regard and fervour with which Russia was held was everywhere to be seen: in newspapers, broadcasts, and statements of all kinds, in demonstrations and at public meetings, in the jubilance and bold demeanour of the local Communists in Syria. But the clamour reflected little profound ideological conviction. In Egypt and Syria, where such sentiments could then be freely expressed, men hailed the Soviet Union not because they were Communists but because they were nationalists. For the first time since the birth of their national movement, the Arabs were no longer at the mercy of the western Powers; they had found a powerful protector.

This alliance between nationalists and Communists was cemented by the western failure clearly to distinguish between them. Faced with the Ba'th–Communist Party front in Syria and with evidence of 'Abd al-Nasir's growing dependence on the Soviet Union, western diplomats tended to overlook the fierce anti-Communist record of the Ba'th Party and Nasir's treatment of his local Communists. The truth is that Communists and nationalists were exceedingly wary of each other and were united only in opposing western pressures: it had been a gross tactical error to push them into each other's arms. But then both the Ba'th and 'Abd al-Nasir were dedicated to the destruction of all trace of western influence in the Arab world and there was, therefore, some sense in considering them at least as dangerous as the Communists. There could, in fact, be no accommodation with the nationalists so long as western policy was to hang on to acquired positions in the area on anything like the old terms.

Another cause for western concern was the rout of their friends in Syria following the collapse of the 'Iraqi' conspiracy in November 1956. This appeared to destroy the political balance and open the way for a Communist take-over. These fears were reinforced by reports of the growing strength and lawlessness of the People's Resistance Forces—a para-military citizen body equipped with small arms from the eastern bloc—and by rumours of Soviet 'volunteers' poised to spring to the defence of the beleaguered Arabs. President Quwatli had himself declared on his return from the Soviet Union in November 1956 that 'thousands of Soviet Muslims had announced their readiness to come to the Middle East to rid the Holy Land of imperialist aggressors'.

Quwatli's visit to Moscow at the height of the Suez crisis started the scare in the western press of the Soviet satellization of Syria. It came as the climax to a long tradition of alarmist reporting of Syrian affairs fed by the repeated changes of regime, by Syria's reputation for xenophobia, and by the vigour and purposefulness of Soviet attempts to woo her. Another factor, to which reference was made in a previous chapter, was the impact on Arab opinion in neighbouring countries—and on foreign correspondents in Beirut—of the views of such Syrian exiles as the PPS.

Newspapers in a great many countries—but particularly in Britain, France, the United States, Turkey, and Israel—now published lurid reports of massive deliveries of Soviet aircraft and tanks to Syria, of the arrival there in force of Soviet officers and technicians, and of the establishment of secret desert bases. Evidence for these reports was remarkably scant, but they helped form the climate of opinion which produced the Eisenhower Doctrine. Dissenting views were not heeded, such as a dispatch from a *New York Times* correspondent in Damascus on 9 December reporting that he could find no confirmation whatsoever of the arrival of large quantities of Soviet arms. Repeated assurances by the Syrian President, the Premier, and other leaders that Syria was not 'going Communist' were equally ignored. 'There is not the slightest indication of Communist infiltration in Syria', said the Ba'th leader Akram al-Hawrani in February 1957; but he added that 'what does exist is the Syrian people's will to fight imperialism to the end'.[7] The point was simply that Arab nationalists, tired of western tutelage, saw in America's heavy-handed solicitude a greater threat to their freedom than the attentions of the Soviet Union. To acknowledge the existence of a 'power vacuum' in the Middle East on American terms was to abandon their claim to run their own affairs and to admit a new mentor on the local scene more formidable even than Britain had been.[8] But the longer Damascus

---

[7] *al-Sha'b* (Damascus), 10 Feb. 1957.

[8] The 'vacuum' theory made the Arabs not only indignant but amused, as is illustrated by an incident in a novel by the young Lebanese woman writer, Leila Baalbaki. The heroine is sitting in a café watching a young man reading a political newspaper. She wonders to herself whether the party fills the vacuum in his life. Then she laughs: the word 'vacuum' was enough to suggest 'the current American plan which arouses savage comment everywhere' (Leila Baalbaki, *Ana Ahya* (1958). See *Je Vis*, French trans. by Michel Barbot (1961), p. 65).

held out, the more Mr Dulles became convinced that he could discern there the workings of a Soviet master-mind. As 1957 wore on, the crusade against International Communism led the Secretary of State into an unbecoming tussle with the Syrians which was an important contributory factor to their eventual leap into union with Egypt.

THE SUMMER CRISIS OF 1957

The Syrian-American quarrel came to a head in midsummer 1957, but the opening shots were exchanged several months earlier. Syria was, in fact, the first Middle East state to attack the premises on which American policy was founded. On 10 January, less than a week after President Eisenhower's message to Congress, the Syrian Government issued a statement rejecting the theory of the 'vacuum', disputing the view that economic interests gave any Power a right to intervene in the area, and denying that Communism presented any immediate threat to the Arab world. Imperialism and Zionism were the main dangers to which Arabs remained exposed.

It was clear to both Egypt and her Syrian ally that American interference in Arab affairs in the name of anti-Communism threatened to rob them of that local initiative for which they had fought since 1955. Their resentment at American tutelage grew into open hostility in the spring of 1957 when it became clear that Mr Richards's tour was resulting in a redrafting of Middle East alliances hostile to them. When the United States sprang to the support of King Husayn during the April crisis in Jordan, Syrian and Egyptian indignation knew no bounds. With American aid, Husayn succeeded in ousting from power the political leaders ideologically akin to the radical and revolutionary elements which were the mainstay of the Egyptian and Syrian regimes. In their place, he established his own firm authoritarian rule, based on the more traditional props of his army and the old tribal organizations east of the Jordan. In retrospect, this upheaval was the first major set-back for Nasirism in Arab Asia.

King Saud firmly backed Husayn in this resolute action, splitting the four-Power alliance of Egypt, Syria, Saudi Arabia, and Jordan which had been symbolized by a meeting of heads of state in Cairo in February. Husayn, meanwhile, followed up his coup by demanding the withdrawal from Jordan of Syrian troops stationed there since the Suez crisis—a request which the Syrians received with 'distress and bitterness', seeing in it another link in the long chain of anti-Arab conspiracies.[9]

But if Richards was cold-shouldered by the Syrians, he received a warm welcome in Lebanon where President Sham'un and his Foreign Minister, Charles Malik, were committed to a policy of close relations with the western Powers. Malik had taken over the Foreign Ministry in November 1956 on the understanding that Lebanon had no future if she severed her links with the West; relations had accordingly been maintained with Britain and France throughout the Suez episode. This brought the Lebanese leaders under very sharp attack from Cairo and the Soviet bloc so that, by 1957, they were casting around anxiously for means of fortifying themselves in advance of the day of reckoning which they knew must come. Sham'un and Malik saw themselves threatened by the twin forces of Nasirism and Communism. Hence their policy of intimate friendship with the United States and, more specifically, their acceptance of the Eisenhower Doctrine on 16 March. By early summer, then, Cairo radio was in full blast not only against the Governments of Jordan (diplomatic relations were severed on 9 June), Lebanon, Iraq, and Saudi Arabia, but also against the United States on the charge that 'U.S. colonialism' was now waging open war against the Arabs.

Events inside Syria were meanwhile adding to American apprehensions. In mid-March an important contract for Syria's first oil refinery was awarded to the Czechoslovak Techno-Export Company after a fierce debate between left- and right-wing factions. Later that month, attempts by President Quwatli and the moderate Commander-in-Chief, Nizam al-Din, to replace the radical 'Abd al-Hamid Sarraj as military intelligence chief failed owing to strong opposition from the Ba'th and Khalid al-'Azm. At by-elections in May the Government and its left-wing supporters emerged triumphant, further strengthening their internal position.[10]

[9] See Foreign Minister Bitar's press conference, 31 May 1957 (BBC, no. 262, 3 June 1957).
[10] The by-elections were held in Damascus, Homs, Suwayda, and the Jabal al-'Arab following the trial and conviction of four deputies, Munir al-'Ajlani, 'Adnan al-Atasi, Fadlallah Jarbu, and Hail al-Surur for complicity in the 1956 'Iraqi' conspiracy against the state. Left-wing candidates were returned in the first three constituencies while the fourth was a tribal area where party affiliations played no part. Over half the electorate abstained. The main trial of strength was in Damascus where the Ba'thist Riyad al-Malki opposed the leader of the Muslim Brotherhood, Shaikh Mustafa al-Siba'i, and won by a short head. Sib'ai however, polled 47 per cent of the votes cast—demonstrating that Islam was far from being a spent force in Syrian politics—in spite of the fact that his opponent was backed by the Ba'th,

In a stormy debate in the Chamber on 1 June the People's Party leader, Rushdi al-Kikhia, was driven to threaten the mass resignation of his supporters in the House. In a particularly provocative speech, Khalid Baqdash had delivered a long apologia for the Soviet Union and had attacked the People's Party as 'lackeys and agents of imperialism'. Kikhia rose immediately and accused Baqdash of aiming at shaking public confidence and at spreading chaos and corruption throughout the homeland. He accused the Government of condoning Baqdash's statement by its silence. In the ensuing tumult, he collected his papers and left the Chamber. This prompted another People's Party leader, Ahmad Qanbar, to accuse Baqdash of using the rostrum to disseminate Communist propaganda. He then charged the parliamentary majority with becoming arrogant and despotic: 'A great reign of terror prevails in this Chamber. I stand opposed to this terror and to the Government and I challenge it.'

Some observers in Damascus saw this move as an unsuccessful attempt to bring about the downfall of the 'Asali Government: the opposition was particularly anxious to deny the cabinet four months of undisturbed tenure during the approaching summer recess. Strong at home but ringed by hostile apprehensive neighbours, it was feared that the left in Syria might now attempt an outright bid for power. These, then, were some of the preliminary rumblings which heralded the approach of the crisis.

Three events in quick succession were then to precipitate it. On 6 August the Syrian Defence Minister, Khalid al-'Azm, signed a wide-ranging economic and technical agreement with the Soviet Union in Moscow; a week later, on 13 August, Syria expelled three American diplomats, who were accused of plotting to overthrow the regime; this was in turn closely followed by the retirement of the Commander-in-Chief, Nizam al-Din, and his replacement on 17 August by 'Afif al-Bizri, an officer of suspected Soviet sympathies. A dozen other officers were purged at the same time.

The news of these happenings caused consternation in Washington. Nerves were somewhat frayed by the months of vigilance and by the spectre, constantly evoked, of a Communist assault on the Middle

the Communists, and all the 'progressives', as well as by factions of the National and People's Parties—and benefited from the prestige of being 'Adnan al-Malki's brother. The Soviet Embassy is said to have intervened vigorously to secure the withdrawal of the Communist candidate in both Damascus and Homs in favour of a more generally acceptable left-wing candidate. (For this last point see H. A. R. Philby, *Observer Foreign News Service*, no. 12238, 30 Apr. 1957.)

East. It was a situation in which the United States could be said to have been mesmerized by a monster of its own creation. The danger of a Soviet take-over had been so explicitly heralded, a battle-drill of such precision had been prepared, resources of such magnitude had been deployed to guard against a surprise attack that, now that the enemy appeared to have struck, action could no longer be avoided.

The great question Mr Dulles and other leaders of Western diplomacy will face this week [the *New York Times* declared on 18 August] will be whether the United States and Syria's pro-Western neighbors can tolerate a Soviet satellite, or something very much like one, in the heart of the Middle East.

But were these internal Syrian developments really of a nature to warrant American intervention under the terms of the Eisenhower Doctrine? In what sense could Syria be said to be the victim of aggression 'from a country controlled by International Communism'? Was not the Doctrine, with its carefully restrictive definition of the conditions for American action, more of a straight-jacket than a deterrent? As Mr Dulles (under Democrat prodding in the Senate) wrestled with these problems, it was perhaps permissible to conclude that by reducing Syrian and Arab conflicts to a straight contest between the West and Communism the United States had robbed its diplomacy of much flexibility.

Looking a little more closely at the events of early August beginning with Khalid al-'Azm's mission to Moscow, it will be seen that there were many good reasons—political, economic, and personal—why he should have gone at this time. In the first place, the agreement which he negotiated was a natural climax to the growth of Syrian-Soviet relations over the previous two years. The Russians had been extremely helpful: their warm and continuous solicitude had helped the Syrians to stand up to equally persistent western pressure. The Russians had been unstinting in arms deliveries and in public assurances of support. At times of great anxiety, for instance during the battle over the Baghdad Pact in 1955 or the Suez war of 1956, they had given the Syrian public a new confidence that in the event of an armed attack on their country they would not stand alone. Khalid al-'Azm had been one of the principal architects of this rapprochement. He now, no doubt, felt justified in believing that it had paid handsome dividends in securing both Syria's continued independence and his own personal ascendancy. But by mid-1957 a further consolidation of relations with Russia was thought necessary to counter America's rather importunate attentions and to strengthen 'Azm's hand in the internal political struggle which he knew lay immediately ahead. Hence his triumphant Moscow visit. There was also important business to transact. Arrangements had to be made for paying for the arms which the Russians had so liberally provided; Syria had a large grain surplus which she was keen to dispose of; most important of all, large-scale foreign credits and technical aid were required for the next stage of economic growth after the private enterprise heyday of the 1940s and 1950s. Just as Khalid al-'Azm had been one of the first Syrian statesmen to appreciate Syria's need to end the customs union with Lebanon and build a Mediterranean port of her own, so he also understood the need for dams and irrigation works to free her essentially agricultural economy from the vagaries of seasonal rains; for a modern transport system to move export crops to the sea from the new lands of the north-east; for domestically produced fertilizers to improve yields; for more systematic prospection for oil and other minerals. All this was provided for, on generous terms, in the agreement concluded with the Soviet Union. It was, then, a treaty fully justified on national grounds even if, in western eyes, it might seem to indicate the long-term subordination of Syria's economy to Soviet control.

But more immediately alarming was the announcement by the Syrian Government on 12 August of the discovery of an American plot to overthrow the regime. The following day three American diplomats—Lieut-Colonel Robert W. Malloy, the military attaché, Howard E. Stone, a second secretary, and the vice-consul, Francis Jetton—were declared *personae non gratae*. They were the first United States diplomats since the Second World War to be officially accused of plotting to overthrow an Arab Government. Washington riposted by expelling the Syrian ambassador, Farid Zayn al-Din, and a member of his staff.

Were the Syrian charges well founded? On examining the evidence —confused and untidy though it is—it is hard to dismiss them as fabrications.[11] Convinced that Syria was 'going Communist', the

[11] See (a) Statement by the Syrian Foreign Ministry on the discovery of an American conspiracy against the security of the State, 19 Aug. 1957 (Document 284 issued by the Bureau de documentations arabes, Damascus);

(b) Syrian Indictment in the American conspiracy case: statement by the military examining magistrate, 28 Sept. 1957 (Document 311);

(c) Proceedings of the Military Court, 11 Dec. 1957–12 Feb. 1958 (Document 318).

United States had been exploring ways of reversing the trend. Its officials had had clandestine contacts with members of the Syrian armed forces with a view to organizing the overthrow of the Government. This, at least, is what emerges from the evidence. Like the 1956 'Iraqi' conspiracy—the abortive course of which was traced in the last chapter—this further attempt to counter Soviet penetration was a meandering tale of secret assignations, double agents, and furtive contacts with PPS militants in Lebanon. Half a dozen Syrian officers approached by American officials immediately reported back to the authorities so that the plot was doomed from the start.

In the course of this intrigue, two familiar figures make a brief appearance under heavy disguise: the former dictator, Adib al-Shishakli, and his chief of police, Colonel Ibrahim al-Husayni, who had been living in Rome as Syrian military attaché since Shishakli's overthrow in 1954. Both men paid clandestine visits to Damascus in the summer of 1957, under American auspices, to give heart to the conspirators and take over the leadership of the movement. But it soon became clear that their prime target was not the spectre of International Communism, or even such civilian politicians as Baqdash and Hawrani, but the small group of officers who at that time formed the backbone of the Syrian regime: Sarraj, Hamdun, Bizri, 'Awdatallah, Nafuri, and their colleagues. Like Husayni himself, most of these men owed their first important commands to Shishakli; they had been rival members of the team of young men around the dictator in the early 1950s. But whereas some of them, like Sarraj, had survived his downfall to rise to new commanding positions, others, such as Husayni, had had to face obscurity and exile.

The Arab side, then, of the so-called American plot was much more a contest between rival groups of officers than a struggle between Communists and their opponents. One would, indeed, have been hard put to find a single Communist sympathizer in the Syrian general staff at that time, with the exception of Colonel Bizri who was far from being the most influential member of the group. United States backing for Husayni undoubtedly bred in his rival Sarraj a fierce anti-Americanism which remained with him throughout his later years of supreme power. But this did not make him a Communist. The recurrent American mistake—and the root cause of much unnecessary alarm—was to see what was essentially a local power struggle in cold war terms. In any event, the conspiracy never got beyond the stage of exploratory attempts at recruitment; it was nipped in the bud and the offending Americans—of whom Stone appears in the commanding role—were expelled.

A day later General Nizam al-Din resigned as Syrian Chief of Staff and was replaced by 'Afif al-Bizri, whom the *New York Times* described on 17 August as a 'ranking Communist' and an 'openly pro-Soviet officer'. The change was thus inevitably interpreted as a Communist capture of the Syrian high command. But was this alarmist view correct? Colonel Sarraj, perhaps the most influential officer at the time, advanced a different explanation:

> Bizri's appointment had nothing to do with his supposed Communist leanings (which in any case only emerged later) nor with Khalid al-'Azm's visit to Moscow. It was simply that we had demanded from Nizam al-Din the dismissal of a number of senior officers implicated in Ibrahim al-Husayni's attempted coup. Nizam al-Din refused. We then engineered his dismissal and his replacement by Bizri who seemed a non-controversial figure; he had no personal following in the army and was connected with none of the major factions then feuding inside the general staff. His appointment was therefore acceptable to everyone.[12]

These details are given here in order to show how ill advised, if not grotesque, was the panic with which the situation was viewed in Washington. Mr Dulles was reported on 19 August to have held crisis talks with President Eisenhower and the British ambassador, Sir Harold Caccia. It was thought that a new Soviet satellite had emerged in the Middle East. But it soon became evident that even if Syria had fallen under Soviet control there was little, short of an armed attack, that the United States could do on its own about the supposed change. The doctrine was then evolved that it was up to Syria's neighbours to assess the situation and determine policy. In the meantime the direction of thinking among American Middle East specialists was towards the idea of putting Syria into 'quarantine'—of isolating the virus. 'It is legitimate diplomacy for the United States', the *New York Times* said in a leading article on 22 August, 'to encourage all the anti-Communist countries in the Middle East to use what pressure they can to restrain Syria.'

This hue and cry caused some understandable bitterness but little loss of nerve in Damascus. Khalid al-'Azm declared that Syria's policy, in spite of American provocations, would still be based on 'positive neutrality'. But, he went on, 'We are at the outer edge of that

---

[12] Col. 'Abd al-Hamid Sarraj to the author, Cairo, 27 Jan. 1961.

policy; do not force us to go beyond it'. Undeterred by this warning, Washington pressed ahead with its efforts to mobilize Syria's neighbours against the menace in their midst.

LOY HENDERSON'S MISSION

The means chosen—the dispatch of a high-level American envoy on a brisk Middle East tour—seemed guaranteed to cause the maximum hostile fuss, to sacrifice the possible advantages of secret diplomacy and to yield no hard, unbiased information on the situation inside Syria. On 24 August Mr Loy W. Henderson, Deputy Under-Secretary of State for Administration and one of the State Department's leading Middle East experts, left Washington for Turkey. (He had been active in the formulation of the 1947 Truman Doctrine shielding Greece and Turkey and in the settlement of the Persian oil dispute in 1953.) In Ankara he conferred with the Prime Minister, Menderes, and with the Kings of Jordan and Iraq who had journeyed there to meet him; he then flew to Lebanon to see President Sham'un before returning to Turkey for further talks with Menderes, Crown Prince 'Abd ul-Ilah of Iraq, and the Iraqi Chief of Staff. He did not go to Syria or make contact with the Syrian authorities.

His movements aroused a great storm of indignant comment. Moscow charged that the United States was preparing the ground for direct intervention. Cairo accused Henderson—an 'expert in coups d'état'—of planning the isolation and siege of Syria (which was no more than the American press expected of him). Having despaired of subverting Syria from the inside, America was now inciting Syria's neighbours against her. The plan, Cairo alleged, was to provoke a clash which would justify the application of the Eisenhower Doctrine.

According to an official statement read to press correspondents on 5 September, Mr Henderson reported that the situation was extremely serious. His initial report to Mr Dulles, the State Department announced, told of 'deep concern' in the area lest Syria should become 'a victim of international communism and, as such, become a base for further threatening the independence and integrity of the region'.[13] Once again contrary evidence was swept under the carpet, such as a dispatch from Damascus on 31 August by a *New York Times* correspondent, Osgood Caruthers:

There is no sign [he wrote] either in Egypt or in Syria that the Soviet bloc, with its technical, economic, military and cultural missions, is trying

[13] U.S. Dept of State, *American Foreign Policy: Current Documents, 1957*, p. 1037.

to sovietize these two Arab countries or to stir up a classic Marxist revolution. What the Soviet Union has found are two friendly Arab countries who are willing to help block Western efforts. . . . So far as it is known, there are no card-carrying Communists among the officers of the Syrian armed forces.

This was not Mr Henderson's view. His return led to an immediate stiffening in American attitudes. Prompt action was thought to be required both to serve notice on Syria against adventuring outside her frontiers and to strengthening the defences of her pro-western neighbours. Plans were accordingly announced on 5 September for an immediate airlift of American arms to Jordan and for the reinforcement of Iraq and Lebanon. Reaction from Damascus was angry and bewildered. Washington, an official spokesman said, had been 'seriously misinformed' about the real situation. Syria did not intend attacking anyone; her armaments policy had been purely defensive. But she would not tolerate any threat to her security.

The presence at Henderson's talks in Ankara of King Faysal of Iraq, Crown Prince 'Abd ul-Ilah, and the Iraqi Chief of Staff, Rafiq 'Arif, was a reminder of Iraq's continuing preoccupation with Syria in spite of the collapse of her major effort to overthrow the Syrian Government in 1956. For some months after this set-back Nuri al-Sa'id and 'Abd ul-Ilah nursed their disappointed hopes but took no active steps to promote their cause in Syria. This was a period of bitter stock-taking. Nuri was busy saving Faysal's throne from the wash of the Suez tidal wave and parrying as best he could charges of collusion with Britain and Israel. It was not until after the Eisenhower Doctrine was launched that Iraq's active interest in Syria revived.

For detailed evidence we must turn once more to the trial of Major-General Ghazi al-Daghistani, the Iraqi Deputy Chief of Staff, before the Special Military Court set up in Baghdad after the July 1958 revolution to try servants of the old regime. General Daghistani reveals in his defence[14] that Nuri summoned him to the Defence Ministry some five months after Suez—that is in the spring of 1957—and showed him a plan for staging a coup in Syria backed by a three-pronged attack by the Iraqi army on Aleppo, Homs, and Damascus. 'He told me', Daghistani said, 'that the General Army Command should take the necessary steps to prepare the army for action.'

The internal coup in Syria was given the code name of *Operation*

[14] *Official Proceedings*, i. 217 ff.

Nasr (victory) while the military intervention was called *Operation Sayf al-Arab* (Sword of the Arabs). *Operation Nasr* gave a prominent role to the Aleppo leader Mikhail Ilyan, who was to set up a National Organization of Refugee Syrians which, if the revolt were successful, would be recognized by Iraq as the legal Government of Syria. Daghistani relates that he copied out the plan and promised to proceed with it as soon as possible; but he then 'put the papers away and took no action'.

The cabinet of Nuri al-Sa'id later resigned and the matter remained secret [Daghistani continued]. I took the file with me when I was appointed to command the 3rd Brigade and kept it in my safe there. . . . But the study of Nuri al-Sa'id's plan shows that it was no more than a narrative purporting to forecast certain happenings and making certain suggestions. To turn this into a military plan which could have been carried out in practice— to make an appreciation of the situation, to draft orders for troop movements and administration—would have required considerable efforts by the whole General Command. But the headquarters and administrative personnel did nothing of this kind when I was Deputy Chief of Staff. . . .

Nothing really serious was planned by the Iraqis at this time. Contacts were maintained with a number of Syrian politicians— generally through the Iraqi military attaché in Beirut—and some of their proposals were examined. But nothing much was done about it. The Iraqis had lost their nerve in 1956. So far as I have been able to establish there was no link between Iraq and the so-called 'American conspiracy' of August 1957.

What precisely passed between Loy Henderson and the Turkish, Iraqi, and Jordanian leaders at Ankara must remain a matter for conjecture. At the trial of Ahmad Mukhtar Baban, a minister in Nuri's cabinet, the President of the Military Court ordered the reading of notes said to have been made (in Arabic) by the Chief of Staff, Rafiq 'Arif, when Henderson was addressing the meeting. The following extracts from these notes were broadcast live from the Court Room. Henderson is alleged to have said:

I have talked with Dulles and Eisenhower and they both regard the situation as a serious one. . . . Early this week, the White House and the State Department received a number of cables all expressing concern over developments in Syria. . . .

We have analysed the situation and it is our belief that the present state of affairs in Syria tends towards gradually handing Syria over to Russia in the name of Arab patriotism, progress and neutrality.

We believe that within a few months of this (supposed?) neutrality many arms and experts will come from Russia and that Syria will gradually become a (word indistinct) Russian camp. This will be followed by treaties between Syria and Russia stipulating that interference with Syria will involve Russia in war. We feel that Syria will become a (radio transmitter?) for political influence in the Middle East. . . .

My coming here to discuss the subject with you direct is the best way to face up to these questions. I did not come to insist on Turkey or any other country adopting a certain attitude or plan, but to convey to you our views and to assist you in action. It is for you to decide and, if you plan to act, let us know (words indistinct) . . .

If armed action is taken, reasons should be devised beforehand to make it possible to defend such action at the United Nations and to dispose of the matter. The case should also be put in such a way as to reassure the other Arab states that this is not a war against Syria but action against a (treacherous?) state of affairs, and that Communism is opposed to Islam as well as to Christianity.

Saudi Arabia suspects Iraq's intentions in Syria, but the situation has now improved. An Iraqi-Syrian union should not be sought at present. This does not mean that it should not take place at some future date; but it should be made clear that it is not an immediate objective . . .

I emphasize that action must be one hundred per cent successful when you decide on it. It is our belief that if there is to be action it must be efficient. If necessary, Turkey may be called upon if anything should happen to defer success. . . .[15]

In answer to a question about the possibility of Egyptian interference, Henderson is alleged to have replied: 'The fleet is now steaming in the Eastern Mediterranean. We believe that this will make Egypt hesitate.'

Henderson's visit to Turkey served to underline the extent to which that country had become an instrument of American policy in the Middle East. The United States had long hoped that Turkey would provide an element of cohesion in organizing the area for defence. In American eyes, Turkey's role was to bridge the gap between the major NATO system and a subordinate Middle East regional defence arrangement. But these plans never fully matured owing to systematic Arab obstruction; with the sole exception of Iraq, the Arab response was wholly negative. Turkish pique was reflected in bellicose 'manoeuvres' on Syria's northern frontier which, it was evident, did nothing to soften her hostility to western defence

[15] See BBC, no. 682, 17 Oct. 1958.

plans but rather, by unsettling and demoralizing her, eased the way for other 'protectors'.

Syria's anger at these Turkish activities stemmed as much from the immediate military threat as from the long history of Arab-Turkish antagonism. The Arab national movement had, after all, sprung from a revolt against Turkish rule, while a series of more recent grievances such as the loss of Alexandretta, Turkey's suspected designs on Mosul, her recognition of Israel, and her integration into the western defence system served to keep Arab and Turk apart. To both Arab neutralists and Soviet publicists, Turkey had become a 'Trojan horse' or, in another popular phrase, a *'gendarme* of American imperialism' in the Middle East.

Since the middle 1950s Turkish 'manoeuvres' had, in fact, become a standard method of putting pressure on Damascus. On several occasions Turkey had hinted that she might move into Syria if a Communist or Soviet-controlled Government took over. These scarcely veiled hints were dropped through the Turkish press at the time of Suez when Syria seemed the likeliest target for the 'volunteers' the Russians were then talking of sending to the Middle East. The hints were repeated in April and May 1957, when it seemed possible that the Syrian army might move to support the opposition to King Husayn in Jordan. On each occasion Turkey backed up her words with unacknowledged but well-publicized movements of two or three divisions on the frontier. This was once more the case in the autumn of 1957.

So provocative, indeed, was the Turkish attitude that from about mid-September, what had been a direct Syrian-American contest took on the form of a more localized Syrian-Turkish one, with Russia and the United States each backing one of the contestants. On 13 September the Soviet Premier, Bulganin, accused Turkey of poising troops on Syria's borders for what he called a United States-planned attack. Armed conflict over Syria, he gave warning, 'would not be limited to that area alone'.[16] Mr Dulles retorted in the United Nations General Assembly on 19 September with the charge that it was Turkey who was in danger—threatened in the north by Soviet military power and in the south by the 'major build-up of Soviet arms in Syria'.[17] He was answered the following day by General Bizri in Damascus (who called his speech a 'vicious call to war')

---

[16] *New York Times*, 14 Sept. 1957.
[17] *General Assembly Official Records*, 12th sess., 680th mtg, p. 21.

and by Mr Gromyko in the General Assembly. Russia, the Soviet Foreign Minister said, 'cannot remain indifferent and observe from afar the attempts that are being made to turn the Near and Middle East into a permanent hotbed of armed conflict'.[18] Next day, 21 September, as the Syrian Foreign Minister, Salah al-Din Bitar, arrived in New York to put his country's case against Turkey before the General Assembly, two Soviet warships—the cruiser *Zhdanov* and an escorting destroyer—steamed into Latakia harbour to the plaudits of the Syrian press.

At this point it is useful to consider Washington's handling of the crisis. There had been, it must be remembered, no direct approach to the Syrians to learn their real position at first-hand or to explore whether their anti-western sentiments could in any way be moderated. Mr Henderson had seemed to have less than an open mind: he had sought confirmation of Syria's Communism rather than facts. American policy had, in the event, succeeded in achieving the precise opposite of what had been intended. Putting pressure on Syria, arming her neighbours, branding her as threatening the peace, had strengthened rather than weakened the position of the men in power; it had made it far more difficult for pro-western voices to be raised in Syria; it had barred the Syrian Government from peaceable communication with the West without risking loss of face and defeat at home; and it had driven the Syrians to seek comfort and aid in the Soviet camp.

American belligerency had given the Russians great opportunities to leap to Syria's defence, to reiterate their claim to a voice in Middle Eastern affairs, and to denounce the 'interventionist fever' of 'American imperialism'. On 3 September—the eve of Henderson's return to Washington—the Soviet Union proposed for the third time, in a note to the United States, Britain, and France, a four-Power declaration renouncing the use of force in the area. Similar proposals had been made in notes on 11 February and 19 April. They had, of course, been indignantly rejected.

Typical of Soviet comment at this time was an article in the Soviet army newspaper *Red Star* of 10 September which claimed to unveil a 'diabolical American plot' to invade Syria. It was, the paper affirmed, a five-stage operation whereby the Americans prepared to re-enact the Anglo-French aggression against Egypt:

(1) Israel would make provocative troop movements on her frontier with Syria; (2) Turkey would then concentrate forces on Syria's northern

---

[18] Ibid. 20 Sept., p. 36.

border evoking the possibility of a Syrian-Israeli clash; (3) Iraq would in turn concentrate troops on the pretext of coming to Syria's aid; (4) Iraqi and Turkish aircraft would raid Syrian frontier posts claiming that Syria had violated their frontiers; (5) these two Powers would then march in on Syria, appealing at the same time for American help to repel Syrian aggression.

But, the Soviet journal concluded—and it was an inevitable appendage to the many Soviet commentaries of the period—,Syria had powerful allies and enjoyed the support of 'all freedom-loving peoples'. This argument was given some force by the announcement on 26 August of the first successful testing of a Soviet intercontinental ballistic missile.

KING SA'UD'S MEDIATION

Overshadowed by this Great Power contest and its Syrian-Turkish extension, another wholly Arab struggle was taking place at this time, largely ignored by foreign chanceries. By the late summer of 1957 those Arab Governments which had publicly rallied to the Eisenhower Doctrine—Lebanon, Jordan, Iraq, and Saudi Arabia—were finding it increasingly embarrassing to be identified with American policy. In the giddy aftermath of Suez, they were well aware of their vulnerability to nationalist slogans. King Husayn had nearly lost his throne in April; Faysal had only survived the Suez crisis thanks to Nuri's *sang froid*; Sa'ud was unwilling to risk a public break with 'Abd al-Nasir, while in Lebanon Sham'un and Malik could feel beneath their feet the ominous rumblings of Nasirist agitation.

To placate public opinion, the first instinct of these leaders had been to try and present the Doctrine as a weapon directed not only against International Communism but also against colonialism in its various local and reviled forms: French 'colonialism' in Algeria, British in South Africa, and Israeli in Palestine. But these efforts carried little conviction and presented the United States with unpleasant dilemmas in her relations with Israel, as well as further antogonizing Britain and France, who had never viewed the Doctrine (which consecrated their exclusion from the Arab scene) with any enthusiasm.

The uncovering of the American 'plot' against Syria in August added to the embarrassment of America's Arab allies. It was a little 'Suez' all over again: they could not allow themselves to be found in the camp of Syria's enemies. The State Department's public anxiety on their behalf was extremely irksome as it merely damaged them further in the eyes of an inflamed public. The spectacular American airlift of arms to Amman, for instance, only served to label Husayn as a traitor to the Arabs who had allowed his country to be used as a base for operations against sister Syria. Washington, its gaze fixed on the Russian adversary, had tended once more to underrate the stresses and strains of the local background against which its greater contest was conducted.

King Sa'ud was perhaps the first Arab leader to seek to extricate himself from this uncomfortable situation. He saw clearly that pressure on Syria served neither American interests nor his own. He therefore directed his diplomatic efforts at getting those Arab Governments most hostile to Syria to edge away from Washington and moderate their views. He began his campaign with a visit to Beirut on 7 September in a reported bid to heal the breach between Syria and Lebanon. Jordan soon rallied to this way of thinking: her Foreign Minister, Samir al-Rifa'i, gave assurances on 10 September that his country had no intention of interfering in Syria; Syria, he declared, 'is independent and entitled to do what she likes in her own interests'. On the 12th King Sa'ud was reported to have sent a message to President Eisenhower urging moderation towards Syria.

The Saudis seized every occasion to proceed with their strategy. On the 21st, the Saudi Under-Secretary for Foreign Affairs said in Cairo that his Government did not believe Syria represented a threat to any of her Arab neighbours or to Turkey. This view was firmly repeated in Washington on the 23rd by Crown Prince Faysal after a meeting with President Eisenhower and Secretary Dulles. On the 25th King Sa'ud himself arrived in Damascus where he denounced any attempt at aggression against Syria and underlined the solidarity of the Arab peoples. He was joined the following day by the Iraqi Premier, 'Ali Jawdat al-Ayubi, who, after amicable talks with President Quwatli, declared that Syria and Iraq had arrived at 'complete understanding'.

The summit of Sa'ud's endeavours was a public pledge on leaving Syria on 27 September:

I wish to declare [the King said] without ambiguity or doubt and with the sincerity for which I am known to my Syrian brothers and to the Arabs in general that I deplore every aggression on Syria and on any other Arab country from whatever source it comes, and that I will oppose with my

Syrian brothers and with the other Arabs any aggression against them and against their independence irrespective of its source.[19]

These views were elaborated to an international audience by Ahmad Shukayri, Saudi Arabia's United Nations delegate, on 2 October:

> Who is in power and who is not in power in Syria is the concern of Syria alone. . . . We are not here to deal with . . . the change of Governments. This domestic realm of internal affairs must remain immune, for it has been declared immune in the Charter. As for the arms deal [with Russia], we see no valid justification to interfere. . . . Saudi Arabia shall stand by Syria in the defence of its sovereignty and independence.[20]

By early October King Sa'ud had emerged as the leader of a movement to hold the Arabs together against all outside attractions. He was reported to be trying, in his role of impartial negotiator, to convene a meeting of Arab heads of state to examine Arab differences and dissipate misunderstandings with the United States. Washington was itself beginning to question the wisdom of its earlier panic and there was talk of a meeting in New York between the Syrian Foreign Minister and the Secretary of State. President Eisenhower admitted on 3 October that the Syrian situation 'seems to be solidifying to some extent'. He added that the 'original alarm of countries like Lebanon, Jordan and Iraq and, to some extent, Saudi Arabia, seems to have been quietened by what they have learned'.[21]

The launching of the first Russian Sputnik on 4 October—barely a month after the first ICBM—was greeted with delirious enthusiasm in the Arab press; nowhere, perhaps, were the cries of triumph louder: the missile would 'destroy the legend of U.S. military strength'; it would 'if necessary, annihilate the Sixth Fleet in a few days'. But even though excitement still ran high in embattled Syria, the crisis seemed past its peak. King Sa'ud, arriving in Lebanon on a state visit on 10 October, was hailed by the Beirut press as the 'lion of the Peninsula' and the 'embodiment of Arab nationalism'.

The success of his diplomacy seemed complete. By rallying behind Syria and edging away from Washington—he had even gone so far as to deny having adhered to the Eisenhower Doctrine—his aims had been twofold: to rehabilitate his and other pro-western

---

[19] al-Sha'b (Damascus), 28 Sept. 1957.
[20] General Assembly Official Records, 12th sess., 697th mtg, p. 231.
[21] New York Times, 4 Oct. 1957.

Arab Governments in the eyes of nationalist opinion and to silence Cairo's attacks. His manoeuvres had, in fact, been designed to seize the initiative from 'Abd al-Nasir and isolate him. In his weeks of mediation between Syria, Lebanon, Jordan, Iraq, and Washington, Egypt had not been consulted and had had no part.

This was not a situation which 'Abd al-Nasir could easily tolerate. His claim to Arab leadership demanded that every challenge to his position, whether from a Great Power or an Arab rival, must be immediately contested and put down. His sense of timing did not desert him. On 13 October, while Sa'ud was still enjoying the fulsome tributes of the Lebanese press, Egyptian troops landed unannounced at Latakia to take up battle positions in northern Syria side by side with their Syrian brothers. Another crisis had arisen. By this spectacular move 'Abd al-Nasir had broken out of the isolation with which Sa'ud had threatened him and had demonstrated that no settlement could be reached in the Middle East without him. He was once again the unrivalled champion of Arab rights. Sa'ud's efforts at mediation seemed overnight timid and irresolute in contrast with 'Abd al-Nasir's wholehearted commitment to the Syrian cause. The fragility of Sa'ud's earlier successes was now evident. High and dry in Beirut, he was angry and perturbed by Egypt's surprise intervention. His miscalculation was to have hoped to wean Syria in a month from an Egyptian alliance which had been painstakingly forged over the previous two and a half years.

The Syrian-Egyptian rapprochement had in fact been progressing steadily. Leaders of both countries had repeatedly stressed the need for a political union—a 'desired national aim' which President Nasir had himself warmly welcomed in a speech to the inaugural meeting of the Egyptian National Assembly on 22 July. President Quwatli visited Cairo in April, June, and August, declaring after the last occasion that 'Syria's dearest wish was to achieve a union with Egypt which would serve as the nucleus for universal Arab unity'. There was talk at this time of setting up a committee to study a federal project while, early in September, a commission was formed to prepare the ground for an economic merger.

But speech-making by politicians lagged far behind the example of close co-operation which the Syrian and Egyptian high commands already provided, keenly fostered by the Egyptian ambassador in Damascus, Brigadier Mahmud Riyad. An event which passed virtually unnoticed during King Sa'ud's mediation efforts was a visit to Cairo by General Bizri and Colonel Sarraj on 11 September. The two Syrian officers had talks with the Egyptian Commander-in-Chief, 'Abd al-Hakim Amir, and with Brigadier Hafiz Isma'il, the Chief of Staff of the joint Egyptian-Syrian command. Later they dined with President 'Abd al-Nasir. It was then, as was later revealed, that plans were made for Egypt's decisive military intervention in Syria in October.

The Syrian crisis petered out shortly after the Egyptian landings. A few more shots were exchanged; Russia issued fresh warnings which the United States threw back in accustomed style, but much of the heat had gone out of the dispute. On 18 October the General Assembly decided to debate a complaint by Syria that Turkey was endangering world peace. King Sa'ud then made a fresh attempt to mediate between the two parties, while the United States reminded Syria that Turkey had denied any aggressive intentions and that there was no reason not to believe her. On 22 October the United Nations debate was adjourned until the 23rd, pending the outcome of Sa'ud's efforts, and then again until the 25th after the Syrians had rejected his mediation; it was then continued until 1 November.

Two rival draft resolutions emerged: one, sponsored by Syria and supported by the Soviet Union, proposed the setting up of a fact-finding commission to investigate the situation on the Syrian-Turkish border and report back within two weeks; the other, sponsored by seven nations[22] and supported by the United States, left it to the Secretary-General 'to undertake discussions with representatives of Syria and Turkey' and seek a solution in this way. But both resolutions were eventually withdrawn before being put to the vote.

In short, the net effect of America's brusque intervention in Arab affairs in 1957 was to confirm the Soviet Union and Egypt as Syria's twin protectors in the face of western hostility. This had been their role since the battle over the Baghdad Pact in 1955, but in the year following the Suez war they secured something like official status in Syrian public life. How Syria, *in extremis*, then came to choose Egypt rather than the Soviet Union as her ally is the subject of the next chapter.

[22] Canada, Denmark, Japan, Norway, Paraguay, Peru, and Spain.

22

Headlong into Union

*L'État est perdu pour peu qu'on permît
à l'anarchie de se discipliner.*

THIERS.

BY the late summer of 1957 Syria was on the verge of disintegration
as an organized political community. Not only was there no general
agreement on the rules governing political behaviour but, worse still,
many Syrians had lost confidence in the future of their country as an
independent entity. A fault had developed in that safety mechanism
which, in most societies, ensures that internal dissensions are not
carried to the point of destroying the state itself, so that there are no
spoils left to fight over.

There were complex reasons why the conventions of politics should
have broken down. Syria had been the scene of genuine conflicts of
interest between social groups in a revolutionary period. She had also
been the focus of inter-Arab feuds of increasing savagery, aggravated
by Great Power rivalries, which had given her no peace in the decade
since the Palestine War. The Hashimites' obsessive interest in Syria
and their efforts to bring about an Iraqi-Syrian union had, in the
1950s, been overtaken by the great debate on the defence of the
Middle East against Russia, culminating in the crisis over the
Baghdad Pact and the Malki affair. This had been closely followed
by Egyptian and Soviet penetration, by the excitements of the Suez
war, by the 'Iraqi' conspiracy of 1956, and, finally, by the American
interventions of 1957. Bribe money and external pressures of all sorts
had for years been undermining whatever moral basis there might
once have been for Syrian political life, while the public was assailed
by rival radio stations and propaganda campaigns and driven to near
hysteria by plots, coups d'état, and threats of invasion. These were not
ideal conditions for the flowering of civic virtues or the proper func-
tioning of elective democratic institutions.

Feuding within the Syrian officer corps was another more specific factor leading to the breakdown of orderly government. The moral justification for the army's first coup in 1949 had been the poverty of civilian preparations for the Palestine War and the graft and incompetence which this trial of strength had uncovered. But, by 1957, nearly a decade later, the army's claim to represent the conscience of the people was wearing thin. The years of indifferent military rule had shown that the officers had lost their taste for reform but not their appetite for power. Repeated military intervention in government—or indeed only the threat of it—had been a grave disruptive factor; whether openly in power or temporarily back in barracks, the army was, in effect, the most powerful single force in Syrian politics if only because no Government or line of policy could long survive its hostility. When the army was united under a single chief, its intervention had at least served to give the country's external policy a certain coherence: it was, in the last analysis, due to sustained army pressure that Syria had resisted Iraqi blandishments over the years and turned decisively towards Egypt in the mid-1950s. But when, as in the last year or two before the Syro-Egyptian union, no one officer could establish his supremacy over the whole general staff, army dissensions contributed an element of unpredictable violence to the political scene, aggravating the already deep cleavages of civilian politics. This was especially the case in the autumn of 1957.

Another threat to Syria's liberal republican regime came from the radical change in the content and direction of nationalist thinking which had taken place since the Second World War. This may be illustrated by the difference in membership, organization, political objectives, and modes of action between, say, the inter-war National Bloc and the post-war Ba'th Party. A loose association of conservative minded notables concerned primarily with securing Syria's internal unity and independence by treaty negotiations with the Mandatory Power had given way to a revolutionary party of middle-class intellectuals, bound by ideas rather than petty alliances, dedicated to the unity and social reform of the whole Arab world, and demanding *total* freedom from European tutelage. The sights had been raised. Political boundaries, forms of government, and a continued western 'presence', to which the earlier nationalists, in their long dialogue with the Mandatory, had grown accustomed, seemed to their successors like so many obstacles to be swept away in the realization of their wider ambitions. Loyalty to Syria as a territorial unit and faith in her political survival could not easily take root in the face of the appeal of a greater Arab homeland.

Syrians have always been expecially vulnerable to this appeal: in no other Arab country is the drive for unity so powerful, and none lays claim so insistently to being the home of Arabism. This impulse to burst out of the frontiers of the Syrian Republic feeds on historical memories, sentiment, and economic aspirations. Damascus, the seat of the first caliphate, was for centuries a centre of Muslim territorial power. It was Syria that, towards the end of the last century, was the birthplace of the idea of a concerted Arab national opposition to the Turks. Syria, too, suffered more than other Arab provinces from the chauvinistic policies of the Young Turks. The dream of Arab independence which grew up with the Arab Revolt was of a great Arab rectangle, open to the Mediterranean, including both 'natural' Syria and Iraq. But the peace settlement carved up this area, cutting off Damascus from its outlet to the south and severing Aleppo from its Mesopotamian and southern Turkish hinterland. Permanent dissatisfaction with the frontiers of Syria, considered unnatural and restrictive, thus contributed to the feeling that the Syrian Republic was an artificial political unit that could not long survive.

The rise of 'Abd al-Nasir as an Arab leader in the mid-1950s, coinciding with that of the Ba'th as a pan-Arab movement, dealt a further blow to the harmonious working of Syrian institutions. As a broader stratum of Arab public opinion was awakened to political consciousness, and as direct appeal was made to these new masses over the heads of established Governments, the tone of political discourse became more strident, slogans and catch-phrases tended to replace any attempt at reasoned argument, propaganda invaded the Arab press and radio. Leadership such as 'Abd al-Nasir provided did a great deal to promote first Egyptian and then Arab national dynamism and corporate self-consciousness, but the reverse of the coin was an abdication of individual responsibility and the sterility of hero-worship. Seeing that Nasir was about to unite the Arabs single-handed, defeat their enemies, and lead them to a glorious future, there was little incentive among the rising generation in each Arab country to give thought and effort to the humdrum, unglamorous problems of local, piecemeal reform and constitutional organization. Everything could safely be left to the *ra'is*.

'ABD AL-NASIR AND THE BA'TH

By 1957 the Ba'th and 'Abd al-Nasir had become the two most dynamic forces in Syrian politics. They knew what they wanted, which is not to say that they wanted the same thing. Indeed, differences imperfectly grasped at this time were to cause much subsequent bitterness and mutual disenchantment. The Ba'th were devoted to the pursuit of Arab unity: they envisaged the creation of a unitary Arab state. This vision was more than an ideological goal; it was defended on grounds of utility. In their thinking, unity was functionally linked with the other aims of the establishment of a progressive social system and the liberation from foreign influence of all parts of the Arab world. They believed that unity, socialism, and freedom were interdependent and would together lead to the regeneration of the Arabs.

But how was this programme to be realized? It was soon clear that even in Syria, their home base, they could not hope to win power at the polls. At the height of their electoral success in 1955 they controlled barely twenty of the 142 seats in the Chamber. They were no more than an élite pressure group which would, in any free contest, be swamped by more traditional forces. It was therefore not surprising that they had no special attachment for the existing political institutions and saw in 'Abd al-Nasir a more promising instrument for the realization of their plans. In their view, Arab unity would not be achieved if events were allowed to take their peaceable course. Strenuous action was necessary against established interests, against all defenders of the *status quo*, against the strongly entrenched particularist sentiment in each Arab country. Nasir's foreign policy was a major claim to their favour as the struggle against imperialism loomed larger in their programme than internal social and political problems. They found that they agreed with him on all important issues. Indeed, they thought he had become a Ba'thist, so faithful did he seem to their principles in his dealings with Great Powers and in his uncompromising view of national independence.

But as precious to the Ba'th as 'Abd al-Nasir's policies and personal gifts was the fact that he was ruler of Egypt. Their experience had taught them that Arab union must start with Egypt. As Michel 'Aflaq explained:

We had the conviction that there could be no Arab unity without Egypt. This was not because we believed she was destined to be the Prussia of the

Arab world, uniting it by force; nor because we thought that no other country could serve as rallying centre. It was more because we had seen at work Egypt's powers of obstruction: she could and would successfully oppose any movement towards Arab unity which excluded her—as the dismal story of the Fertile Crescent project surely proves.[1]

It was by this lucidity that 'Aflaq stood out from his political rivals. He had been preaching his unionist doctines for a decade before the Egyptian revolution and had played his part in the 1940s and 1950s in rejecting all plans for a Syrian-Iraqi union on the view that they amounted to extending British influence to Syria and to gratifying the ambitions of the Iraqi Crown Prince, 'Abd ul-Ilah. Now he drew the principal lesson of the post-war years which this book has surveyed. Egypt had to be drawn firmly into the community of Arab states. This, then, was the basis for the Ba'th's alliance with Cairo. It became the first political group outside Egypt to give 'Abd al-Nasir its confidence and to overcome that suspicion of the Egyptian junta which was widespread in the Arab world in 1954–5. Patiently, it coaxed the wary, isolationist Egyptians into accepting ties and commitments in Arab Asia dictated not only by Egyptian self-interest but by common Arab nationalist sentiment. As Salah al-Din Bitar put it:

'Abd al-Nasir's mind was awakened to Arabism in 1953 or 1954. It was the first time an Egyptian ruler started to think about the Arab world in terms other than the mere desire to dominate. But the Arab idea never went very deep in Egypt; the ordinary Egyptian does not yet *feel* Arab. We, in the Ba'th, always hoped that a union would foster in Egypt the same nationalist sentiments that fired us.[2]

A 'special relationship' grew up between 'Abd al-Nasir and the party so that by 1956 the Ba'th were his warmest propagandists, enjoying in return the full weight of Egyptian political support. By early 1957 the party's campaign for a Syro-Egyptian union had been so successful that the project was inscribed in the programme of the National Front Government which Sabri al-'Asali formed in the immediate aftermath of the Suez war.

But the fervour with which the Ba'th dreamed and worked for union was not matched by the Egyptians. Egypt's Arab policy, as it had evolved since the early 1940s and as it had been reshaped by 'Abd al-Nasir and his colleagues during the battle over the Baghdad

[1] Michel 'Aflaq to the author, Beirut, 13 Jan. 1961.
[2] Salah al-Din Bitar to the author, Damascus, 23 Sept. 1960.

Pact, made no provision for a unitary Arab state. Quite the contrary: the roots of this policy lay in the Arab League charter of 1945 whereby Egypt lent her weight to the defence of the existing divisive frontiers in Arab Asia against any unionist initiative. The guarantee of her leadership and security was thought to lie in maintaining the existing pattern of Arab nation-states, in promoting a grouping of them under her aegis but never a fusion of small Asian Arab units into larger ones. These were the principles on which the Arab League was built; they were also the grounds for saying that the League was a victory for Egyptian diplomacy against rival Hashimite plans for 'Greater Syria' or 'Fertile Crescent' union. The League, in fact, laid down a postwar pattern of inter-Arab relations weighted heavily in Egypt's favour, which was further reinforced by the Arab collective security pact of 1950. For a decade, from 1948 to 1958, the League often seemed little more than a propaganda section of the Egyptian Foreign Ministry, while the security pact, throughout the whole of its abortive life, was used by Egypt, under the slogan of Arab unity, as a device to contain Iraq and assert Egyptian supremacy. The League and the pact, therefore, with their provision for Egyptian primacy over a family of smaller, less powerful, and less advanced Arab states, remained valuable props of Egypt's Arab policy right up to the union with Syria.

But they were instruments into which 'Abd al-Nasir breathed new life. The Palestine War, the tussle with Britain over the Canal Zone, the Baghdad Pact, and the Suez engagement caused him to reinterpret the notion of Arab solidarity with greater urgency. Arab unity meant, above all to him, the unification of the Arab struggle; it meant 'to stand in one rank in face of imperialism'. When he preached Arab unity before the union with Syria, he meant Arab solidarity on foreign policy issues under Egyptian direction and not unity in any territorial or constitutional sense. He wished to control the foreign policy of his Arab neighbours—if necessary by unseating a hostile Government—but not to annex them or merge with them. An authoritative statement of Egypt's Arab policy at this time may be found in Anwar al-Sadat's *Story of Arab Unity*,[3] published in December 1957, less than two months before the union with Syria. The Arab collective security pact—with its built-in prohibition of divergence in foreign policy—is mentioned on the second and on most subsequent pages of the opening chapter. The recurrent theme

---

[3] Anwar al-Sadat, *Qussat al-wahda al-'arabiyya* (1957).

is a vigorous rallying cry to all Arabs to fall in behind Egypt, to put teeth into the pact—'sole hope of the Arabs'—and to throw off all foreign domination. There is no hint in the book of the aspirations for territorial and political union which have traditionally fired nationalists in Syria and Iraq and which the Ba'th was then voicing.

But the control of Syria was necessary if Egypt's conceptions of foreign policy were to triumph throughout the area. Just as the overthrow of Faris al-Khuri's Government in Damascus in February 1955 and its replacement by a pro-Egyptian regime marked the turning-point in Egypt's struggle against the Baghdad Pact, so the landing of Egyptian troops in Syria in October 1957 doomed King Sa'ud's attempts to wrest the initiative from 'Abd al-Nasir under the umbrella of the Doctrine. Thus Egypt's policy of Arab solidarity came to have a very special significance with regard to Syria. Syria's allegiance had to be secured, as it was there that the decisive engagements were fought. Egypt therefore embraced Arabism in a cool and practical spirit. It was a policy dictated not by any deep-rooted belief in political unity, as in Syria, but by the dangers of the continuing confrontation with Israel and by the recognition of the essential unity of the struggle of the Arab states in the cause of total independence from their Great Power mentors. The special relationship with Syria was, in turn, dictated by the exigencies of the inter-Arab power struggle: only by controlling Syria could Egypt be certain of local leadership.

The Suez war injected some warmth into this level-headedness. Egypt was astonished and moved by the great wave of popular sympathy in her favour which then swept the Arab world from Tangiers to the Gulf. Effective joint action by Arab trade unions dates from 1956.[4] It was also at this time that Egyptian journalists and official publicists—all those concerned with exploring and defining the intellectual and historical bases of Egypt's new Arab policy— avidly discovered the works of Arab nationalist writers, including those of Michel 'Aflaq and the Ba'th. Reports from Damascus by the Egyptian ambassador, Mahmud Riyad, of his growing intimacy with the party found an echo in the Cairo editorial offices of such newspapers as *Rose al-Yusuf*, *Sabah al-Khair*, and *al-Gumhuriya*, which were then expounding to their readers the relevance to Egypt of these Arab ideas.

But the Arab world was not the only area with which Egypt was

[4] See Anouar Abdel-Malek, *Égypte: société militaire* (1962), pp. 249–50.

becoming increasingly identified: her feeling of kinship with Afro-Asia exerted as strong a pull. While the Baghdad Pact early in 1955 caused Egypt to define her Arab policy, Bandung introduced her at much the same moment to a wider fraternity, seeking like herself escape from poverty and from the tentacles of the Great Powers. Fellow-feeling for the Afro-Asian underdog is at least as important an element in 'Abd al-Nasir's emotional make-up as any sentiment of identification with his Arab brothers. 'Abd al-Nasir felt Egypt's field of action could not be restricted to the Arab circle; but for these wider ambitions to be realized, the Arab home base had first to be secured. Hence, once again, the added importance of the control of Syria.

This was the background to Mahmud Riyad's embassy in Damascus from the early spring of 1955 to the Syro-Egyptian union three years later. 'Abd al-Nasir and other Egyptian leaders have since repeatedly asserted that they did not seek this union; that it was, in a sense, forced upon them by the pressure of events in Syria. As Mahmud Riyad himself put it:

We never asked for union with Syria. We always argued that it was premature. We told each pressure group in favour of unity that we would always refuse a union brought about by force. We believed that it would never last if brought about by the army.

All Syrian party leaders claimed to be in favour of union, but the Ba'th were alone in actively planning it, in seeking and demanding practical steps to bring it about.

Our policy was in fact to avoid union. We knew it would arouse all the Powers against us, and that we would be accused of annexing Syria—which is in fact what happened.[5]

All this was true: union was not a logical outcome of Egypt's Arab policy; it shattered the territorial *status quo* which she had been at such pains to defend; Egyptian opinion was unready for an organic link with another Arab state; 'Abd al-Nasir himself had not yet fully recovered from the Suez war. But these disclaimers must be immediately qualified by the reminder that if Mahmud Riyad did not seek union, much of his activity was open to this interpretation. His job was to align Syria on Egypt's policy: to win over the Syrian Government, army, and public to Egypt's side. He was a very successful envoy. Indeed, he sought and secured such great influence in

[5] Mahmud Riyad to the author, Cairo, Jan. 1961.

Syrian affairs that Egypt's local allies, and principally the Ba'th, may be forgiven for having assumed that a merger was the obvious sequel.

FORCES OF THE LEFT

In much the same way as Egypt never thought seriously of union before 1957, so it is extremely doubtful whether the Soviet Union ever really hoped at this time to set up a 'people's democracy' in Syria. From 1955 onwards the Russians had assumed certain responsibilities in Syria: they had supplied arms and had offered public guarantees of support in the face of western threats. But they must soon have come to realize that Syria would be difficult to defend as a 'progressive' enclave in a hostile and anti-Communist Middle East. They must also have considered that full-blooded Soviet support for a Communist take-over in Damascus would alarm and antagonize 'Abd al-Nasir and other bourgeois nationalist leaders to whom Soviet political strategists had assigned an important role in the struggle against the West. Soviet policy, therefore, seemed to be aiming not at a popular revolution but at the more modest target of setting up a 'bourgeois' regime friendly to the Soviet Union, manipulated from behind the scenes by the Communist Party. This was Khalid al-'Azm's role. Perhaps the key to his success in Syrian politics at this time lay in the fact that his ambitions accorded with Soviet policy objectives. As has been seen, 'Azm could rely on little support from the right. He had no nationalist past and had taken no part in the struggle against the French—the central experience on which the political reputation of most Syrian politicians of the older generation had been built. He had moreover no personal party organization on which to lean. It may have been for these reasons that he looked to the left for support.

'Azm's chief prop was the Communist Party boss, Khalid Baqdash, who, although holding no government post, was one of the most powerful men in the country. His strength lay in the very substantial aid which the Soviet Union was then giving Syria. Baqdash was also in a position to give directives to the Chief of Staff, 'Afif al-Bizri, although this was not as decisive as it may sound because Bizri's own power was circumscribed by the rivalry between the two most important groups of officers—'independents' and 'Ba'thists'—who were only nominally under his command. One of these groups, Amin al-Nafuri's 'independents', was in loose liaison with 'Azm.

Behind the façade of cabinet Government, Syria had been ruled since 1956 by a 'progressive front' whose leading members were on the one hand Khalid al-ʿAzm and his Communist associate Khalid Baqdash, and on the other the Baʿth leaders, Akram al-Hawrani and Salah al-Din Bitar, with poised between them, the 'Independent' Premier, Sabri al-ʿAsali, whose position was based on the skilful exploitation of the others' differences. These five men used to meet frequently in ʿAzm's residence to discuss and co-ordinate policy. They in turn shared power with their respective military allies: ʿAbd al-Hamid Sarraj, the military intelligence chief, had thrown his weight on the side of Egypt and the Baʿth; Bizri was associated with Baqdash, Nafuri with ʿAzm, while Hawrani had numerous army disciples, of whom perhaps the most prominent were the Colonels Hamdun and Qannut.

This 'front' had served the Communists well by pressing for closer relations with the Soviet Union in the wake of the Suez war and of the parallel western conspiracy against Syria. But by mid-1957 the Communists came to believe that still further political advantage could be drawn from their great popularity with the public. Men were then flocking to the party less out of ideological conviction than because it was thought to represent, with Soviet support, the trend of the future. At the same time the confident bearing of the party leaders and the activities of the popular resistance forces led by Salah al-Bizri, the Chief of Staff's brother, seemed to suggest that the ground was being prepared for a classic bid for power.

It had been a summer disturbed by the 'American conspiracy' and by fears of a Turkish invasion. But October brought some comfort: the launching of the first Soviet Sputnik was followed rapidly by the Egyptian troop landings in north Syria and by the election of Akram al-Hawrani to the Presidency of the Chamber—perhaps the last joint effort of the 'progressive front'. When National Fortification Week opened on 1 November, President Quwatli himself helped dig the first trench on the northern outskirts of Damascus. The informed public was divided between those who lived in dread of a Communist take-over and those who thought the main danger still lay in an armed attack on Syria from Turkey and the West. To the Baʿth, both possibilities were equally distasteful. The Communists were becoming aggressive partners and the Baʿth viewed their growing strength with concern. It was not so much that the Baʿthists ever really believed that ʿAzm and Baqdash could make a successful bid for power on their own. Their fear was that they might try. They understood that a Communist-led coup, even if abortive, would justify vigorous right-wing counter-measures and western intervention. This was the nature of the dilemma they now faced.

The Ba'th's exposed position became plain when it was proposed to hold municipal elections on 15 November. 'Azm and his allies, anticipating a landslide victory, were eager for the elections to take place as planned. But the Ba'th was unwilling to campaign with 'Azm in a subordinate role. Nor could it seek support from the conservative People's Party and its friends in Baghdad and the West. It knew that the results would be closely studied abroad, particularly in Europe, where local elections were often considered a pointer to trends on the national level. Threatened from both left and right, it was too much of a minority group to stand alone. It therefore decided to boycott the elections as the only way of stopping them.

It was, therefore, the Ba'th's weakness as much as its unionist doctrines which caused it to press with special urgency for a formal link with Egypt in the late autumn of 1957. We have seen that the party's alliance with Egypt was forged during the battle over the Baghdad Pact. Its relations with the Egyptian ambassador, Mahmud Riyad, had become extremely intimate and there is some evidence to suggest that 'Abd al-Nasir had come to believe it was the only political force that counted in Syria. A union with Egypt seemed to the party the means whereby it could triumph over its local rivals and propagate its doctrine to the whole Arab world. This was the objective which seemed threatened by the fragmentation of the Syrian political scene. The parliamentary mandate was running out. If elections were announced for the New Year, attention would be diverted from the quest for union to the preparation of the campaign. Moreover, the split between Communists and Ba'thists would allow the 'reactionary' parties to gain ground. An election campaign would also destroy the existing, if superficial, unanimity on the union issue without which, as the Ba'th knew, 'Abd al-Nasir would not agree to act.

Another consideration was the state of inter-Arab relations: although the immediate threat of aggression against Syria had receded, Iraq, Lebanon, Jordan, and Saudi Arabia remained variously committed to the West. Syria and Egypt were the only two Arab states sharing the same policy and basic beliefs: the moment seemed right for them to unite. The triumphant visit of an Egyptian parliamentary delegation to Damascus in late November helped to crystallize this feeling.

It was with this in mind that the Ba'th drafted in December a project for a federal union. As Michel 'Aflaq later explained:

We wanted two things which may seem contradictory. On the one hand we wanted a federal state strong enough and centralized enough to stand firm against the manoeuvres of opponents at home and foreign Governments abroad. The federal institutions would have to be more than a façade; they would have to be more serious and effective than the Arab League. In brief, we believed that the federal apparatus would have to be much stronger than the local provincial administrations.

But our wish for a strong central Government was tempered by a second consideration. We wanted a federation to make allowances for the different political histories of the two countries. We believed that a sensitivity to local traditions was not only in the interests of the proposed union itself, but was also essential to make it attractive to other Arab countries. In our project we provided, for instance, for effective local parliaments and Governments in each province.

But events moved too fast for our project to be given serious consideration.[6]

From the Suez crisis onwards, when the notion of a Syro-Egyptian union had become practical politics, the Communists too had expressed support for a federation, believing that a loose federal formula would both prevent the union from becoming effective and allow them to continue their party activities in Syria. But towards the close of 1957 their quarrel with the Ba'th led them to revise their tactics. In a bid to snatch the initiative from their rivals, they went one step beyond federation, demanding instead a total merger with Egypt. Their confident expectation was that 'Abd al-Nasir, who was already balking at the federal project, would surely refuse. The Communists hoped in this way to frustrate the union plans altogether, damage Nasir's prestige, and earn for themselves a popular reputation for nationalism of the most ardent, self-sacrificial sort. But the Ba'th, unwilling to see the leadership of the union movement escape it, was forced in turn to abandon its federal project and demand a merger with Egypt. All the cards were therefore in 'Abd al-Nasir's hands as the Syrian principals outbid each other in their apparent eagerness to hand over their country to him.

THE ARMY INTERVENES

If the Ba'th-Communist rivalry was a factor which precipitated the union, another was the feuds and ambitions of the Syrian officer

[6] Michel 'Aflaq to the author, 13 Jan. 1961.

corps. Many of the officers had been deeply influenced by the preval-
ent anti-Iraqi sentiment of the 1949–56 period. Opposed to 'reaction'
and 'imperialism' in Iraq, they could only approve the revolutionary
fervour of Egypt and of her chief. They therefore developed good
relations with Egypt as a matter of course, both officially within the
framework of the joint command set up in 1955, and unofficially
through the intermediary of the Egyptian embassy in Damascus, one
of whose principal tasks it was to encourage and strengthen such ties.
A visitor to the office of Colonel Sarraj in 1957 would have noticed
wall portraits of Gamal 'Abd al-Nasir and of Colonel 'Adnan al-
Malki, killed by the PPS in 1955, but none of the Syrian President
Quwatli. But not all the officers were high-minded devotees of the
cause of unity. To the dozen or so senior men who held the key posts
in the Syrian army, a union with Egypt, where the army had tri-
umphed over all rivals, seemed the best guarantee of their own rule
at home. Many officers came to believe that a union would rid them
for ever of the civilian politicians and that Nasir would encourage
them to set up a *Majlis al-Thawra* or Council of the Revolution on
the Egyptian model. Union, when it came about, was therefore in
part an outcome of the long contest between the army and the politicians with which much of Syrian politics had been concerned since
1949.

But the officers were also driven to look to Cairo by their own failure
to agree among themselves. Since Shishakli's overthrow in 1954, the
army had been without a chief able to impose himself on the whole
officer corps. By late 1957 petty rivalries and political enmities had
reduced the Syrian army to a number of competing factions, each
fearing the other more than any outside force. The official hierarchy
of the army had been undermined so that each unit operated like a
private army. Early in January 1958 an incident occurred which had
a sobering effect: two senior officers came to blows and drew guns
on each other. No shot was fired and no one was hurt, but the leading
commanders then decided to go to Egypt in a body to seek the
arbitration of the Egyptian Commander-in-Chief, 'Abd al-Hakim
Amir—their nominal chief in the joint Syrian-Egyptian command.

The Ba'thist leader Salah al-Din Bitar also had a hand in encouraging the officers to go to Cairo.[7] The Ba'th had cause to doubt
the sincerity of many Syrian politicians who claimed to approve the
union scheme but secretly opposed it. It felt, therefore, that vigorous

[7] Ibid.

action by the officers was necessary if the project were not to founder. The Ba'th also knew that 'Abd al-Nasir would not take on responsibility for Syria unless he were reassured about the notorious factiousness of the Syrian army. He had repeatedly made known to the Ba'th his concern on this score. The Ba'th came then to believe that nothing would be more likely to still these fears than a comprehensive delegation of Syrian army chiefs testifying their loyalty and putting themselves unreservedly in Nasir's hands. On 12 January 1958 fourteen officers led by the Chief of Staff, 'Afif al-Bizri, boarded a plane for Cairo,[8] leaving behind them the Deputy Chief of Staff, Amin al-Nafuri, and the intelligence chief, 'Abd al-Hamid Sarraj, whose task it was to deliver a note to the Government explaining the officers' precipitate departure. This note was, in effect, an ultimatum. It reminded the cabinet of its pledge, made when it took office, to take steps to bring about a union with Egypt; it declared that the country was on the verge of collapse; that Communism was gaining ground and that the officers had gone to Egypt to seek a remedy.

Shortly before this sudden move by the officers, the Communists thought fit to change their tactics once more. When it became apparent to them that some sort of union was inevitable and that their attempts to outbid the Ba'th and so bring the talks to nothing had only driven their opponents into a closer embrace with Egypt, they urgently sought to patch up their quarrel with the Ba'th. The Damascus daily al-Ra'i al-'Amm of 2 January quoted a Communist Party statement on the 'necessity of an understanding between Communists and Ba'thists who together form the corner-stone of the National Front'. At the same time the Communists reverted to advocating a loose federal tie which, in the words of a Communist Party pamphlet issued on 13 January, would give due consideration to the 'peculiar conditions prevailing in each of the two countries'. This form of union, it argued, would 'provide opportunities for the further promotion of freedom and democracy'. These statements betrayed a certain nervousness about the future.

But the Chief of Staff did not follow the Communists in this change of line. Almost from the moment of his arrival in Cairo, flanked by

[8] The delegation is believed to have included 'Afif al-Bizri, Chief of Staff; Mustafa Hamdun, head of *Premier bureau* (personnel); Ahmad 'Abd al-Karim, head of *Troisième bureau* (operations); Ahmad al-Hinaydi, Tu'meh al-'Awdatallah, Husayn Hiddeh, 'Abd al-Ghani Qannut, Muhammad al-Nisr, Yasin Farjani, and 'Abdallah Jassuma, commanders of armoured units; Jado 'Izzedine and Mustafa Ram Hamdani, infantry brigade commanders; Akram al-Dayri, commander of the Palestine front; Jamal al-Sufi, naval commander.

the army chiefs, it became obvious that he had been won over to the Egyptians, throwing his weight in favour of unconditional union on Egypt's terms. Bizri's real motives have not been made plain. Some believe it was opportunism and personal ambition; he may also have been reluctant to oppose a trend of which the army as a whole approved. Perhaps the most plausible explanation is that he was acting on Communist instructions: unable to stop the union taking place, the Communists may have preferred to have their man at the centre of power than to see him eliminated by openly adopting their line.

THE DÉNOUEMENT

The officers' unheralded departure threw the cabinet into alarm: it was far from clear what the officers intended to do save that their move was some desperate gesture of self-immolation. 'Do with us what you will', they said in effect to 'Abd al-Nasir, 'only save us from the politicians and from ourselves.' On 15 January, the Cairo daily *al-Gumhuriya* quoted Bizri as saying that henceforth the Syrian and Egyptian armies were one. Faced with this perplexing situation, the cabinet decided to send the Foreign Minister, Bitar, to Cairo to see how far the officers had gone. Union was evidently the great under-lying issue of the crisis, but it was one on which the Government, because of the divisions in its ranks, had not framed a concerted policy. When, therefore, Bitar asked for specific instructions from the cabinet as to the negotiations he was to conduct with 'Abd al-Nasir, President Quwatli, Khalid al-'Azm, and other members of the Government refused to commit themselves. As a result, Bitar went to Egypt on 16 January with little authority; his bargaining power was further undermined by the Ba'thists rivalry with the Communists and by the officers' impulsive move. He could do little more than join the officers as a petitioner, listening to 'Abd al-Nasir's conditions but advancing none of his own.

'Abd al-Nasir's aim since 1955 had been to control Syria's foreign policy—but not to assume responsibility for her Government. Arab solidarity rather than political union was his declared objective. It was only when the first was threatened that he was persuaded to contemplate the second. Indeed, only when his alliance with Syria was endangered by anarchy in the Syrian army, and by the vulner-ability of his Ba'th friends to attack from both left and right, was he driven to intervene. But once this decision was taken, it was soon clear that he had no interest in a union which gave him less than full control. He could not agree to throw himself into an adventure such as this until he had neutralized the two effective centres of power in Syria: the army and the political parties. His conditions were simply that the first should withdraw from politics and that the second should be dissolved. He insisted that the forms of political life in Syria should be brought into line with those in Egypt: there was to be no glaring asymmetry. Syria, for example, could not keep her parliament so long as Egypt had none. He demanded complete confidence and a completely free hand and, by the nature of things, he was granted them.

Reluctant 'Abd al-Nasir may well have been. But he must soon have realized what powerful backing Syria's immolation would give to his own claims to Arab leadership. He would become overnight the heir to all the dreams, hopes, and patriotic fantasies for which Syria had so long been the focus. After marriage to this most Arab bride of all, there would be no doubting Egypt's Arab destiny. On 20 January the Cairo daily *al-Ahram* reported that a 'historic decision' had been taken at a four-hour meeting between 'Abd al-Nasir, Salah al-Din Bitar, and 'Afif al-Bizri. Union, it declared, had entered its 'practical and concrete phase'. On boarding the plane for Damascus the following day, Bitar announced that 'full agreement has now been reached on the shape and content of the organic union between Egypt and Syria'.

But on arriving home, his most delicate task was not so much to inform the Government of the sweeping measures proposed as to explain to his party militants that, in so far as they were concerned, the immediate result of union would be the suspension of all party activity. These men had been ready to die for Arab unity, but not to commit party political suicide. The party leadership was forced into theoretical explanations: unity with Egypt, it told the cadres, had been forged in battle; the party was engaged in a revolutionary war; in these exceptional circumstances, a leader was needed who must be given full authority. Certain adjustments were therefore called for in the nature of party activity. But if the Ba'th were to be dissolved, it would soon be reborn in the form of the National Union —the new organization which 'Abd al-Nasir proposed should replace the political parties.

'Abd al-Nasir gave the Ba'th verbal reassurances at this time that elections for the National Union would be held immediately, allowing it to think, not unreasonably, that as the chief architect of the union, it could expect to emerge triumphant. It envisaged the National Union as a novel political instrument embracing all those who wished to build an Arab socialist society. The new state would become a 'progressive' stronghold and a base for spreading the nationalist gospel throughout the Arab world. The Ba'th would provide the ideas and Nasir the leadership: it would be the ideological fount and he the secular arm. This was the Ba'th's heady dream at the moment of union.

Not unnaturally, this view of things was very distasteful to Khalid al-'Azm and his allies. They opposed both the concept of a total merger and the dissolution of political parties. On 21 January the Damascus press reported 'Azm as questioning the need for a National Union seeing that Syria already had a national parliamentary coalition. Meanwhile, with time running heavily against him, he set about trying to organize his supporters and friends into a political party more effectively to challenge the union plans. It was largely on his initiative, but with the support of President Quwatli and the Prime Minister, 'Asali, that the cabinet drafted the broad lines of a federal project, allowing each member country a larger measure of autonomy, and charged Bitar to take the draft to Cairo on 25 January. But he was back in Damascus two days later: Nasir had rejected the federal proposals. It was to be total union on his terms or nothing at all.

To break the deadlock, the Egyptian ambassador and his military attaché held a meeting in Damascus with the Syrian army chiefs in the last days of January. Bizri came out strongly in favour of a full merger and carried the officers with him. The Government had no alternative but to bow to this decision. Bizri ordered a plane to stand by, assembled the cabinet, and embarked on it for Cairo. To the more recalcitrant members he is rumoured to have said: 'There are two roads open to you: one leads to Mezze (with its famous dungeon outside Damascus); the other to Cairo.' On the following day, 1 February 1958, at a session between the Syrian and Egyptian Governments, union between Syria and Egypt was proclaimed.[9]

The union was in the first place a monument to 'Abd al-Nasir, a symbol of his personal ascendancy. Unification came as the climax of four years of successful defiance of the Great Powers, in which he had demonstrated time and again that there could be no settlement in the

[9] See 'Charter of the United Arab Republic', in Arab Information Center, N.Y., *Basic Documents of the Arab Unifications* (1958), p. 21.

Arab world to which he was not a party. It was he, and not Britain, France, Russia, or America, who was now shaping the new political order. It was to him, as the foremost Arab leader of his day, that the Syrians appealed in their troubles. Egypt, under his direction, had moved from the periphery to the very centre of the Arab stage. The agreement was also a triumph for the dogged persistence and manoeuvring skill of the Ba'th: the party had prepared the ground by its teaching, befriended Nasir before any other group outside Egypt, stood by him stalwartly in every crisis, helped to convince him of his Arab destiny and, in the last stages, played a decisive role in delivering the goods: without the Ba'th Syria would not have accepted union on 'Abd al-Nasir's terms.

But the union was also, in a sense, a monument of self-deception. The Ba'th had been naïve to imagine that 'Abd al-Nasir could be harnessed for the propagation of its philosophy or that it could retain its influence and its special relationship with him when he no longer needed its support in the internal power struggle; to have thought, indeed, that any dialogue with him would again be possible once all power was his. By focusing on the man, it had artlessly ignored the nature of his regime.

And again, both those politicians who had thought that union would discipline the officers and those officers who had thought to rule alone without the politicians found they had miscalculated; power passed into more resolute hands. The union negotiations—if such they may be called—had taken place at a time of great public excitement. Arab unity had been a dream for years; the Syrian public was inflamed and wanted action. But if the young boisterously applauded the union, to many older Syrian nationalists the manner in which it was effected represented the destruction of the independence for which they had struggled all their lives. 'It was done in a minute, in a foolish minute', the liberal Syrian statesman Faris al-Khuri whispered on his death-bed to the author. 'If you report this', he added, 'you will be telling the truth but you will also be showing me up as a hypocrite. For although I did not approve of the union, I did not openly oppose it. I thought at the time it was the only way to check the progress of Communism in the country.'[10] The Communists had, in effect, lost a decisive round. More clear-sighted than most, they drew the immediate consequences: on 4 February three days after the union proclamation, Khalid Baqdash left for Eastern Europe while the party returned

[10] Faris al-Khuri to the author, Damascus, 6 Nov. 1960.

to clandestinity. No Communist Party, Baqdash declared, had ever been known to dissolve itself.

But how aware was the principal figure in the drama? 'Abd al-Nasir agreed to bind Egypt to a country he had never seen: this was a measure of his leap in the dark. 'On s'engage', Napoleon said, 'et puis on voit.' He knew it would be hazardous, but he was seduced by the boldness and the magnitude of the enterprise. He was also trapped by his role of champion of Arab rights and arbiter of Arab destinies: he had so often urged the Arabs to unite behind him that now that a full-blooded political union was offered he could not retreat; it was too late to explain that by unity he had meant solidarity alone. In any event, the virtual collapse of the Syrian state demanded more direct intervention.

Did 'Abd al-Nasir grasp at this stage the extent to which he was departing from Egypt's traditional Arab policy? He proposed to attack the territorial *status quo* which Egypt had been at such pains to defend against the Hashimites and to destroy the Arab League formula of a family of sovereign states which had served her so well. Consciously or not, in creating the United Arab Republic he embraced overnight a unionist, frontier-smashing philosophy which had grown up in the rectangle of Arab Asia but which was virtually unknown in Egypt, where it struck no cord. He thus engaged his compatriots in an adventure which, at bottom, aroused their suspicion rather than their enthusiasm. This was perhaps the gravest handicap the union had to bear, the result of Egypt's geographical self-sufficiency and of the half-century in which she had marched out of step with the Arab national movement in Asia.

But the union was also a challenge to 'Abd al-Nasir's powers of statecraft. For the UAR to grow and have life—for it to serve, as some had dreamed, as a nucleus for a wider Arab union—a new constitutional formula was required. Egypt and Syria together could not be governed like Egypt alone. The magic of 'Abd al-Nasir's person and Egypt's state apparatus had, in this wider context, to be allied to new institutions, to new forms of political organization. But progress in this direction was disappointing. Throughout the union's brief life, government in Syria bore the marks of improvisation and impermanence. As Michel 'Aflaq once put it, "Abd al-Nasir n'a pas su s'ouvrir à ce nouvel espace.' Syria was ruled, in the event, on strict authoritarian lines. Severed from her neighbours by Egyptian power, she played no role in inter-Arab politics; for three and a half years she was taken out of play. As a result the Arab Near East was frozen into impotence: no combination of Arab states could challenge Nasir's primacy. The minimum requirements of Egypt's traditional Arab policy were thus satisfied, but the new state never became the magnet to which others were drawn.

Arabs often argue that the *form* union takes is of no importance. 'Let there only be union', they cry, 'and the form will take care of itself.' But it was precisely for lack of a convincing constitutional structure, for lack of institutions in which the diverse interests and wishes of the member states might be reflected, that the union foundered. And it was for just such a formula that, at the time of writing, the Arabs were still searching.

Select Bibliography

I. WORKS IN ARABIC

'Abd al-Nasir, Jamal. *Falsafat al-thawra*. Cairo, n.d. (Eng. trs.: Abdel-Nasser, Gamal. *The Philosophy of the Revolution*. Cairo, n.d.).

'Abd Allah, King. *Mudhakkirat* (Memoirs). Amman, 1947.

Abu Mansur, Fadlallah. *A'asir Dimashq* (Damascus storms). Beirut, 1959.

'Aflaq, Michel. *Ma'rakat al-masir al-wahid* (Battle for the one destiny). Beirut, 1958.

—— *Fi sabil al-ba'th* (In the cause of the Ba'th). Beirut, 1959.

al-'Ajlani, Munir. *Difa' al-doctor Munir al-'Ajlani amam al-mahkama al-askariyya fi Dimashq* (The defence of Dr Munir al-'Ajlani before the military court in Damascus). Damascus, 1957.

al-'Alami, Musa. *'Ibrat Filastin*. Beirut, 1949. (Eng. trs.: 'The Lesson of Palestine', *MEJ*, no 3 (1949), pp. 373–405.)

'Allush, Naji. *al-Thawra wa'l-jamahir* (Revolution and the masses). Beirut, 1962.

Arab League. *Jam'iyat al-duwal al-'arabiyya; mithaquha wa nubdha tarikhiyya 'anha* (The League of Arab States; its Charter together with a short historical account). Cairo, 1947.

al-Arsuzi, Zaki. *al-Umma al-'arabiyya* (The Arab nation). Damascus, 1958.

—— *Mashakiluna al-qawmiyya* (Our nationalist problems). Damascus, 1958.

Ayyub, S. *al-Hizb al-shuyu'i fi suriyya wa lubnan, 1922–58* (The Communist Party in Syria and Lebanon, 1922–58). Beirut, 1959.

Ba'lbaki, Leila. *Ana ahya* (I live). Beirut, 1958. (Fr. trs.: *Je vis*, by Michel Barbot. Paris, 1961.)

Baqdash, Khalid. *Fi sabil huriyyat al-sha'b al-wataniyya wa'l-demokratiyya* (For the sake of the national and democratic freedoms of the people).
Speech delivered in Aleppo, 22 Jan. 1937.

—— *Fi sabil najah al-hukm al-watani fi sabil tatawwur biladina al-zira'i wa'l-sina'i nadhdhifu suriyya wa lubnan min al-'anasir al-fashistiyya al-ifransiyya* (For the sake of the success of the national government, for the sake of the agricultural and industrial development of our country, purge Syria and Lebanon from the French fascists).
Speech delivered in Damascus, 25 Apr. 1937.

328   SELECT BIBLIOGRAPHY

Baqdash, *cont.*

—— *al-'Arab wa'l-harb al-ahliyya fi ispania* (The Arabs and the civil war in Spain). Damascus, 1937.

—— *al-Shuyu'iyyun wa tarikh al-'arab.* (The communists and the history of the Arabs). Damascus-Beirut, 1938.

—— *al-Hizb al-shuyu'i fi suriyya wa lubnan siyasatuhu al-wataniyya wa barnamijuhu al-watani* (The Communist Party in Syria and Lebanon: its national policy and national programme).
Speech delivered in Beirut, 1 May 1942.

—— *al-'Arab wa'l-thawra al-faransiyya* (The Arabs and the French Revolution). Baghdad, 1942.
Lecture delivered in July 1942 on the anniversary of the French Revolution.

—— 'Shu'un al-tanzim' (Questions of organization). MS., 1942.
The organizational part of the report delivered by Khalid Baqdash at the plenary meeting of the Communist Party of Syria and Lebanon in Sept. 1942.

—— *Ba'd masa'iluna al-wataniyya* (Some of our national questions). Damascus, 1943.
Contains the text of three speeches.

—— *'Umar Fakhuri, hamil liwa'l-ruh al-jadida fi lubnan* ('Umar Fakhuri, standard-bearer of the new spirit in Lebanon).
Speech delivered in Beirut, 18 Aug. 1943.

—— *al-Hizb al-shuyu'i fi'-l nidal li ajl al-istiqlal wa'l-siyada al-wataniyya* (The Communist Party in its struggle for independence and national sovereignty). Beirut, 1944.
Text of report delivered by Baqdash before the national congress of the C.P. of Syria and Lebanon, 31 Dec. 1943 and 1, 2 Jan. 1944.

—— *al-Ittihad al-watani fi sabil al-taharrur al-watani* (The national union for the sake of national independence). Beirut, 1944.
Final speech delivered at C.P. national congress, 2 Jan. 1944.

—— *al-Shuyu'ia wa'l-qawmiyya* (Communism and nationalism). Beirut 1944.

—— *Nidaluna al-watani wa akhtar al-fashistiyya al-kharijiyya wa'l-dakhilliyya* (Our national struggle and the internal and external dangers of fascism).
Report delivered at meeting of Central Committee, 23 July 1944.

—— *al-Sha'b al-suri yatlub al-istiqlal wa'l-hurriyya wa hukman demo-kratiyyan sahihan* (The Syrian people demands independence, freedom, and genuine democratic government). Beirut, 1945.

—— *Tariqan amam suriyya wa lubnan* (Two roads facing Syria and Lebanon). Damascus, 1945.

—— *Suriyya ba'd al-jala'* (Syria after the evacuation). Damascus, 1946.

—— *al-Shuyu'ia fi Suriyya* (Communism in Syria). Damascus, 1946.

—— *Mumayyizat al-wad' al-siyasi fi suriyya* (The characteristics of the political situation in Syria). 1946.

Baqdash, *cont.*

—— *Intifad al-sha'b al-'iraqi wa atharuha fi tatawwur al-qadiyya al-'arabiyya* (The uprising of the Iraqi people and its impact on the development of the Arab cause). 1948.

—— 'Mawqif al-hizb al-shuyu'i al-suri hawl al-inqilab al-suri al-akhir' (The attitude of the Syrian Communist Party towards the latest Syrian coup d'état). MS. End May–early June 1949.

—— *Li-ajl al-nidal bi najah fi sabil al-silm wa'l-istiqlal al-watani wa'l-demokratiyya yajib al-ittijah bi hazm nahwa'l-'ummal wa'l-fallahin* (For the sake of the successful struggle for peace, national independence, and democracy, it is necessary to turn determinedly towards the workers and peasants). Damascus-Beirut, 1951.

A 2nd ed. of the same work was published in Beirut in 1955 under the title *Hizb al-'ummal wa'l-fellahin* (The Party of the Workers and Peasants); but omitting key passages containing disparaging remarks on the Ba'th and other nationalist groups.

—— *al-Nidal fi sabil al-jabha'l-wataniyya wa fi sabil hukuma wataniyya demokratiyya fi suriyya* (The struggle for the national front and for a national democratic government in Syria). Damascus-Beirut, 1954.

—— *Hawl al-wad' al-iqtisadi fi suriyya* (On the economic situation in Syria). Damascus, 1955.

—— *Dawr suriyya'l-tarikhi fi'l-'alam al-'arabi* (The role of Syrian history in the Arab world). Damascus, 1955.

—— *Sanatun kamila fi khidmat al-sha'b taht qubba al-parlaman* (A full year in the service of the people under the dome of Parliament). Damascus, 1955.

Text of a speech delivered by Comrade Baqdash at a mass meeting attended by 52,000 Syrian citizens of Damascus concerning his parliamentary activity during the past year.

Bitar, Salah al-Din. *al-Siyasa al-'arabiyya bayn al-mabda' wa'l-tatbiq* (Arab politics between principle and practice). Beirut, 1960.

—— and Michel 'Aflaq. *al-Qawmiyya al-'arabiyya wa mauqafuha min al-shuyu'iyya* (Arab nationalism and its attitude towards communism). Damascus, 1944.

—— *al-Ba'th wa'l-hizb al-shuyu'i* (The Ba'th and the Communist Party). Damascus, 1944.

Darwaza, al-Hakam. *al-Shuyu'iyya al-mahalliyya fi ma'rakat al-'arab al-qawmiyya* (Local communism in the national struggle of the Arabs). Beirut, 1961.

Fawzi, Gen. Muhammad and Mahmud Hafiz. *Dirasat fi'l-qawmiyya al-'arabiyya* (Studies in Arab nationalism). Cairo, n.d. [*c.* 1959.]

al-Haffar, Lutfi. *Dhikriyat* (Reminiscences). Damascus, 1954. 2 vols

al-Haffar, Wajih. *al-Dustur wa'l-hukm* (The constitution and rule). Damascus, 1948.

Hadhihi hiya Suriyya al-kubra (This is Greater Syria). Damascus, n.d.
A collection of documents.

al-Hasani, 'Abd al-Razzak. *Tarikh al-wizarat al-'Iraqiyya* (History of the Iraqi cabinets). Vol. viii. Sidon, 1955.

al-Hizb al-Suri al-Qawmi al-Ijtima'i [usually referred to as the Parti Populaire Syrien]. *Ila al-nayu-raj'iyyin al-'urubiyyin* (To the Arabizing neo-reactionaries). Beirut, 1949.

al-Husri, Sati'. *Ara' wa ahadith fi'l-qawmiyya al-'arabiyya* (Views and addresses on Arab nationalism). Cairo, 1951.

—— *Ara' wa ahadith fi'l-wataniyya wa'l-qawmiyya* (Views and addresses on patriotism and nationalism). Cairo, 1954.

—— *Difa' 'an al-'uruba* (Defence of Arabism). Beirut, 1956.

Iraq. *Majra al-hawadith al-muta'tiya min al-inqilab fi Dimashq bima yata'allaq bi'l-hukuma al-'iraqiyya.* (The course of events resulting from the Damascus coup d'état which relate to the Iraq Government). Baghdad, 1949.

—— Min. of Defence. *Mahkamat al-Sha'b* (The People's Court). Baghdad, 1958.

'Isa al-Fil, Ahmad. *Suriya al-jadida fi'l-inqilabayn al-awwal wa'l-thani* (New Syria in the first and second coups d'état). Damascus, 1949.

Kahaleh, Habib. *Dhikriyat na'ib* (Memoirs of a Deputy). Damascus, n.d.

al-Kayyali, 'Abd al-Rahman. *Marahil fi'l-intidab al-faransi wa nidalina al-watani* (Stages in the French Mandate and in our national struggle). Vols. i–iv. Aleppo, 1958–60.

al-Khuri, Sami. *Radd 'ala Sati' al-Husri* (Reply to Sati' al-Husri). Beirut, n.d.

Kurd 'Ali, Muhammad. *al-Mudhakkarat* (Memoirs). Vol. ii. Damascus, 1948.

Maqsud, Clovis. *Nahu ishtirakiyya 'arabiyya* (Towards Arab socialism). Beirut, 1957.

—— *Azamat al-yasar al-'arabi* (The crises of the Arab left). Beirut, 1960.

'Mafhumina li'l-tadamun al-'arabi' (Our understanding of Arab co-operation), *in Ittihad al-Sha'b* (Baghdad), 20–24 Aug. 1960.

Nassur, Dr Adib. *Qabla fawat al-awan* (Before it is too late). Beirut, n.d.

Nidal al-ba'th fi sabil al-wahda al-huriyya al-ishtirakiyya (The Struggle of the Ba'th for Unity, Freedom and Socialism). Beirut, 1963–4.
Five volumes of collected documents have so far appeared covering the period from 1943 to the present day.

al-Qal'aji, Qadri. *Tajribat 'arabi fi'l-hizb al-shuyu'i* (The experience of an Arab in the Communist Party). Beirut, n.d.

al-Quwatli, Shukri. *Majmu'at khutab.* (Collected speeches). Damascus, 1957.

al-Rumi, Shamil. *al-Fatayir* (Cream Cakes). Damascus, 1960.

Sa'ada, Antun. *Nushu' al-umam* (The rise of nations). Vol. i. Beirut, 1938.

Sa'ada, Antun, *cont.*

—— *al-Ta'lim al-suriyya al-qawmiyya al-ijtima'iyya* (Syrian national social teaching). 4th ed. Beirut, 1947.

Shuruh fi'l-aqidah (Explanations on ideology). Beirut, 1958.

al-Sadat, Anwar. *Qussat al-wahda al-'arabiyya* (The story of Arab unity). Cairo, 1957.

Sayigh, Anis. *al-Fiqra al-'arabiyya fi Misr* (The Arab idea in Egypt). Beirut, 1959.

al-Shahbandar, Dr 'Abd al-Rahman. *al-Qadaya al-ijtima'iyya al-kubra fi'l-'alam al-'arabi* (The great social issues in the Arab world). Cairo, 1936.

Shmays, 'Abd al-Na'im. *al-Qawmiyyun al-suriyyun* (The Syrian nationalists). Cairo, 1958.

Zuraik, Dr Qustantin. *Ma'na al-nakba* (The meaning of the disaster). Beirut, 1948.

II. WORKS IN OTHER LANGUAGES

Abdel-Malek, Anouar. *Égypte; société militaire*. Paris, 1962.

Abdullah ibn Hussein. *The Memoirs of King Abdullah of Transjordan*, ed. P. P. Graves. London, 1950.

Abouchdid, Eugénie Élie. *Thirty Years of Lebanon and Syria. 1917–47*. Beirut, 1948.

Abul-Fath, Ahmed. *L'Affaire Nasser*. Paris, 1962.

Ahmed, Jamal Mohammed. *The Intellectual Origins of Egyptian Nationalism*. London, 1960.

Bekdash, K. (tr. H. Glidden). Report of the Central Command of the Communist Party in Syria and Lebanon in January 1951. *MEJ*, vii. (1953).

—— *La Charte national du Parti Communiste en Syrie et au Liban*. Beirut, 1944.

Berger, Morroe. *The Arab World Today*. New York, 1962.

Berque, Jacques. L'Univers politique des arabes. *Encyclopédie française*, xi. Paris, 1957.

—— *Les Arabes d'hier à demain*, Paris, 1960.

Binder, Leonard. Radical Reform Nationalism in Syria and Egypt. *Muslim World*, xlix/2–3 (1959).

Birdwood, Lord. *Nuri as-Said: a study in Arab leadership*. London, 1959.

Campbell, John C. *Defense of the Middle East*. Rev. ed. New York, 1960.

Carleton, Alford. The Syrian Coups d'Etat of 1949. *MEJ*, iv/i. (1950).

Childers, Erskine B. *The Road to Suez*. London, 1962.

Colombe, Marcel. *L'Évolution de l'Égypte, 1924–50*. Paris, 1951.

—— L'Égypte et les origines du nationalisme arabe. *L'Afrique et l'Asie*, no 14 (1951).

Crow, R. 'A Study of Political Forces in Syria based on a Survey of the 1954 Elections'. Unpubl., May 1955.

Dawn, C. Ernest. The Rise of Arabism in Syria. *MEJ*, xvi/2 (1962).

Documents sur les origines de la ligue des états arabes. *Orient* no 14 (1960).

Eden, Anthony. *The Memoirs of the Rt Hon. Sir Anthony Eden, KG, PC, MC*, iii: *Full Circle*. London, 1960.

Egypt, Min. of Foreign Affairs. *Records of conversations, notes and papers exchanged between the Royal Egyptian Government and the United Kingdom Government, March 1950–November 1951*. Cairo, 1951.

Faris, N. A. and M. T. Husayn. *The Crescent in Crisis: an interpretative study of the modern Arab world*. Univ. of Kansas Press, 1955.

Fisher, Sydney N., ed. *Social Forces in the Middle East*. Cornell, N.Y., 1955.

Frye, R. N., ed. *The Near East and the Great Powers*. Cambridge, Mass., 1951.

Gabby, Rony E. *A Political Study of the Arab-Jewish Conflict*, Geneva, 1959.

Gibb, Sir Alexander & Partners. *The Economic Development of Syria*. London, 1947.

Haim, Silvia. *Arab Nationalism: an Anthology*. Los Angeles & London, 1962.

Halpern, Manfred. *The Politics of Social Change in the Middle East and North Africa*. Princeton, N.J., 1963.

Hamide, Abdul-Rahman. *La Région d'Alep: étude de géographie rurale*. Paris, 1959.

—— *La Ville d'Alep: étude de géographie urbaine*. Paris, 1959.

Helbaoui, Youssef. *La Syrie: Mise en valeur d'un pays sous-developpé*. Paris, 1956.

Heyworth-Dunne, J. *Religious and Political Trends in Modern Egypt*. Washington, 1950.

Hitti, Philip K. *History of Syria, including Lebanon and Palestine*. New York, 1951.

Hourani, Albert H. *Syria and Lebanon*. London, 1946.

—— The Decline of the West in the Middle East. *International Affairs*, Jan.–Apr. 1953.

—— *A Vision of History*. Beirut, 1961.

—— *Arabic Thought in the Liberal Age, 1798–1939*. London, 1962.

Hourani, Cecil. The Arab League in Perspective. *MEJ*, i/2 (1947).

Humbaraci, Arslan. *Middle East Indictment*. London, 1958.

Hurewitz, J. C. *Middle East Dilemmas: the Background of United States Policy*. New York, 1953.

—— *Diplomacy in the Near and Middle East; a documentary record*, ii: *1914–56*. Princeton, N.J., 1956.

Husaini, Ishak Musa. *The Moslem Brethren*. Beirut, 1956.

International Bank for Reconstruction and Development. *The Economic Development of Syria*. Baltimore, Johns Hopkins Press, 1955.

Ionides, Michael. *Divide and Lose: the Arab revolt 1955–8*. London, 1960.

Jargy, Simon. Déclin d'un parti. *Orient*, no 2 (1959).

—— *Syrie*, Paris, 1962.

Karanjia, R. K. *Arab Dawn*. Bombay, 1958.

Kerblay, B. La Pénétration économique des pays du bloc soviétique au Moyen-Orient. *Orient*, no 13 (1960).

Khadduri, Majid. Constitutional Developments in Syria. *MEJ* (1951).

—— *Independent Iraq, 1932–58*. 2nd ed. London, 1960.

Khalidi, Walid. 'Political Trends in the Fertile Crescent', in W. Z. Laqueur, ed., *The Middle East in Transition* (1958).

Kirk, George E. Cross Currents within the Arab League: the Greater Syria Plan. *World Today*, Jan. 1948.

—— *A Short History of the Middle East*. London, 1948.

—— *The Middle East in the War, 1939–46*. London, 1952.

—— *The Middle East, 1945–50*. London, 1954.

—— *Contemporary Arab Politics*. New York, 1961.

Kirkbride, Sir A. *A Crackle of Thorns*. London, 1956.

Lacouture, J. and S. *L'Égypte en mouvement*. Paris, 1956.

Laissy, Michel. *Du Panarabisme à la Ligue Arabe*. Paris, 1948.

Lammens, H. *La Syrie et sa mission historique*. Cairo, 1915.

—— *La Syrie: précis historique*. Beirut, 1921. 2 vols.

Laqueur, Walter Z. *Communism and Nationalism in the Middle East*. London, 1956.

—— *The Middle East in Transition*. London, 1958.

—— *The Soviet Union and the Middle East*. New York, 1959.

Laurent, F. L'URSS et le Moyen-Orient. *Orient*, no 2 (1957).

Lewis, Norman. The Frontier of Settlement in Syria, 1800–1950. *International Affairs*, Jan. 1955.

Little, Tom. *Egypt*. London, 1958.

Longrigg, S. H. *Iraq, 1900 to 1950: A political, social and economic history*. London, 1953.

—— *Syria and Lebanon under French Mandate*. London, 1958.

Majdalani, Gebran. 'The Arab Socialist Movement', in W. Z. Laqueur, *The Middle East in Transition* (1958).

Marlowe, John. *Arab Nationalism and British Imperialism*. London, 1961.

Monroe, Elizabeth. *Britain's Moment in the Middle East, 1914–56*. London, 1963.

Nasser. See 'Abd al-Nasir, Jamal *in list of Works in Arabic above*.

Nuseibeh, Hazem Zaki. *The Ideas of Arab Nationalism*. Ithaca, N.Y., 1956.

Nuri Pasha as-Said. *Arab Independence and Unity*. Baghdad, 1943.

Oron Yitzhak. History and Ideas of the Arab Socialist Renaissance Party. *New East*, ix (1959).

Polk, W. R. America in the Middle East: 1947–58. *St Antony's Papers* no 11. London, 1961.

Rabbath, Edmond. *Les États-Unis de Syrie*. Aleppo, 1925.

—— *Unité syrienne et devenir arabe*. Paris, 1937.

Rastier, J. À la Recherche du socialism syrien. *Orient*, no 4 (1957).

Rondot, Pierre. Les États-Unis devant l'Orient d'aujourd'hui. *Orient*, no 2 (1957).

—— Tendances particularistes et tendances unitaires en Syrie. *Orient*, no 5 (1958).

—— *Le Destin du Proche-Orient*. Paris, 1959.

Royal Institute of International Affairs (RIIA). *Survey of International Affairs, 1951, 1952, 1953, 1954, 1955–6*, and *1957–8*.

—— *The Middle East: a political and economic survey*. 3rd ed. London, 1958.

—— *British Interests in the Middle East; a report by a Chatham House study group*. London, 1958.

Safran, Nadav. *Egypt in Search of Political Community*. Harvard, 1961.

Sayegh, Fayez A. *Arab Unity: Hope and Fulfilment*. New York, 1956.

Stirling, Col. W. F. *Safety Last*. London, 1953.

Tarazi, Salah al-Din. *Les Services publics libano-syriens*. Beirut, 1946.

U.S. Dept. of State. *United States Policy in the Middle East: September 1956–June 1957: Documents*. Washington, 1957.

Vatikiotis, P. J. *The Egyptian Army in Politics*. Indiana, 1961.

Vaucher, George. *Gamal Abdel-Nasser et son équipe*. Paris, 1959–60. 2 vols.

Warriner, Doreen. *Land Reform and Development in the Middle East*. London, 1957.

Weulersse, Jacques. *Paysans de Syrie et du Proche Orient*. Paris, 1946.

Wheelock, Keith. *Nasser's New Egypt*. New York & London, 1957.

Wint, Guy and Peter Calvocoressi. *Middle East Crisis*. London, 1957.

Wynn, Wilton. *Nasser of Egypt; the Search for Dignity*. Cambridge, Mass., 1959.

Zeine, Zeine N. *Arab-Turkish Relations and the Emergence of Arab Nationalism*. Beirut, 1958.

—— *The Struggle for Arab Independence*. Beirut, 1960.

Ziyadeh, N. A. *Syria and Lebanon*. London, 1957.

Index

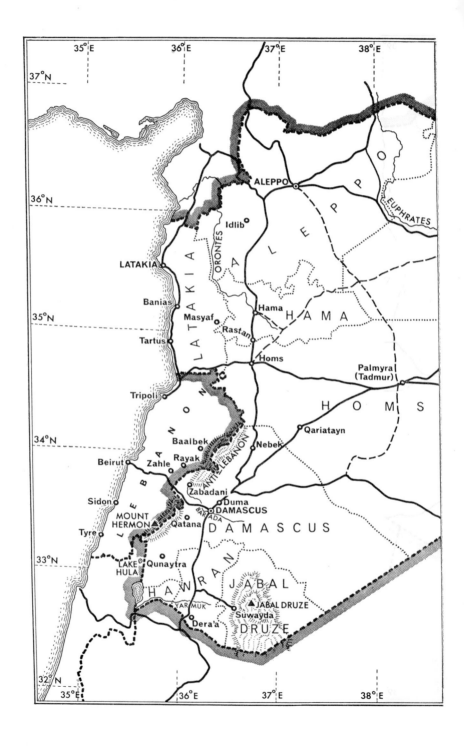

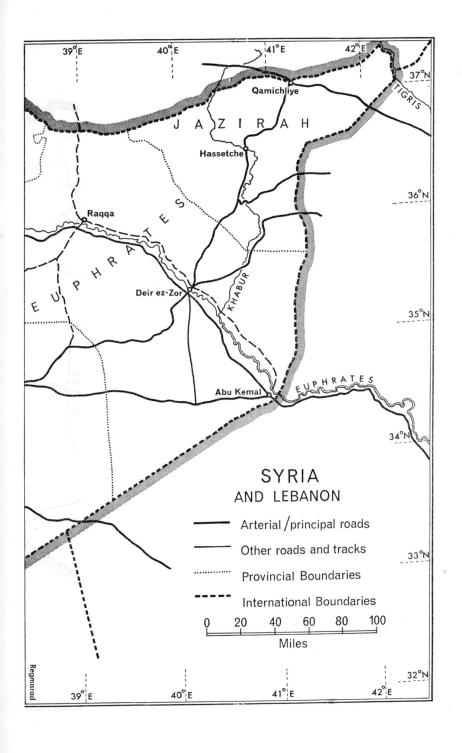

SYRIA
AND LEBANON

Arterial /principal roads

Other roads and tracks

Provincial Boundaries

International Boundaries

0   20   40   60   80   100

Miles

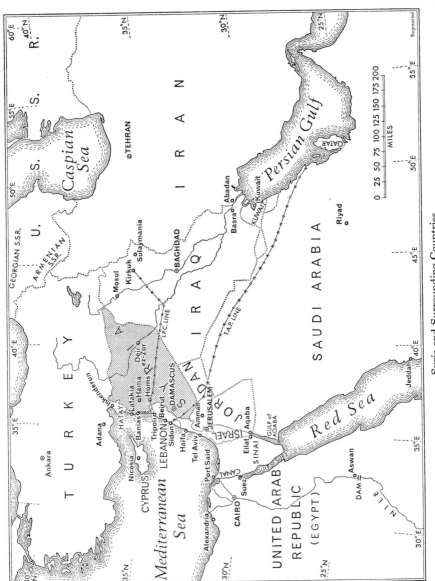

Syria and Surrounding Countries